Jürgen Beyerer, Alexey Pak and Miro Taphanel (Eds.)

Proceedings of the 2017 Joint Workshop of Fraunhofer IOSB and Institute for Anthropomatics, Vision and Fusion Laboratory

Karlsruher Schriften zur Anthropomatik
Band 34
Herausgeber: Prof. Dr.-Ing. habil. Jürgen Beyerer

Eine Übersicht aller bisher in dieser Schriftenreihe erschienenen Bände finden Sie am Ende des Buchs.

Proceedings of the 2017 Joint Workshop of Fraunhofer IOSB and Institute for Anthropomatics, Vision and Fusion Laboratory

Edited by
Jürgen Beyerer, Alexey Pak and Miro Taphanel

KIT Scientific Publishing

Impressum

KIT Scientific Publishing

Karlsruher Institut für Technologie (KIT)
KIT Scientific Publishing
Straße am Forum 2
D-76131 Karlsruhe

KIT Scientific Publishing is a registered trademark
of Karlsruhe Institute of Technology.
Reprint using the book cover is not allowed.

www.ksp.kit.edu

Print on Demand 2018 – Gedruckt auf FSC-zertifiziertem Papier

ISSN 1863-6489
ISBN 978-3-7315-0779-6
DOI 10.5445/KSP/1000081314

Preface

In 2017, the annual joint workshop of the Fraunhofer Institute of Optronics, System Technologies and Image Exploitation (IOSB) and the Vision and Fusion Laboratory (IES) of the Institute for Anthropomatics, Karlsruhe Institute of Technology (KIT) has again been hosted by the town of Triberg-Nussbach in Germany.

For a week from July, 30 to August, 5 the PhD students of the both institutions delivered extended reports on the status of their research and participated in thorough discussions on topics ranging from computer vision and optical metrology to network security and neural networks. Most results and ideas presented at the workshop are collected in this book in the form of detailed technical reports. This volume provides a comprehensive and up-to-date overview of the research program of the IES Laboratory and the Fraunhofer IOSB.

The editors thank Lars Sommer, Matthias Richter, and other organizers for their efforts resulting in a pleasant and inspiring atmosphere throughout the week. We would also like to thank the doctoral students for writing and reviewing the technical reports as well as for responding to the comments and the suggestions of their colleagues.

Prof. Dr.-Ing. habil. Jürgen Beyerer
Alexey Pak, PhD
Dr.-Ing. Miro Taphanel

Contents

Automatic Inspection Planning for Optimizing the Surface Coverage in Industrial Inspection 1
Mahsa Mohammadikaji

Wavelet Based Feature Extraction in Near Infrared Spectra for Compositional Analysis of Food 15
Julius Krause

Adaptive Measurement Method for Area Chromatic Confocal Microscopy 31
Ding Luo

Deterministic Industrial Network Communication: Fundamentals 45
Ankush Meshram

Phase Detection in Medical Context: Overview and Outlook 63
Patrick Philipp

Deep Learning based Vehicle Detection in Aerial Imagery 83
Lars Sommer

Automatic Inspection Planning for Optimizing the Surface Coverage in Industrial Inspection

Mahsa Mohammadikaji

Vision and Fusion Laboratory
Institute for Anthropomatics
Karlsruhe Institute of Technology (KIT), Germany
mahsa.mohammadikaji@kit.edu

Technical Report IES-2017-01

Abstract: Optical product inspection plays an important role in today's industrial manufacturing. Therefore, design of optimized solutions corresponding to the industrial requirements are essential for efficient product quality assurance. To configure an inspection setup one requires to determine the position and orientation of the cameras and illuminations as well as the optical configurations. This problem is commonly known as inspection planning. Today's optical inspection setups are mostly being designed based on trial and error requiring a lot of engineering experience and experimental work. As the design space is high dimensional, the empirical designs typically lead to suboptimal solutions and compromise between contrary requirements. In today's industry we are missing a generic automatic method to translate the inspection requirements into optimized inspection solutions. In this report we propose an optimization framework to automatically propose optimized setup solutions, by minimizing the number of acquisitions which fulfil the inspection requirements. As an example, we consider maximizing the surface coverage for the inspection of a cylinder head in a laser triangulation setup. We characterize the design space and propose different approaches to solve the problem. We finally demonstrate the planning results which successfully cover hard to reach areas on the object.

1 Introduction

A fast, automated, and precise quality inspection process is of high importance in today's industrial production. Automated inspection first made its way into industry with Coordinate Measuring Machines (CMMs) [WPH06], the tactile probes which scan the product in a number of key points. Although CMMs deliver precise measurements, they are being more and more replaced by optical inspection techniques due to two main reasons: the very low inspection rate and their requirement to touch the object [NJ95]. The optical inspection techniques, on the other hand, offer fast touchless scans even with lower hardware costs.

The very benefits that optical methods offer are however not without an extra cost: the inspection planning. If the configuration of CMMs needed a preselection of the target key points on the surface, designing an optical inspection setup which would deliver the same measurement quality is not a trivial task [CBL02]. Apart from choosing among the existing inspection techniques such as fringe projection, laser triangulation, deflectometry, interferometry, and etc. (see [BLF15]), one requires to determine the position and orientation of the cameras and illuminations as well as their optical configurations. This problem is commonly referred to as inspection planning in the literature [SRR03, TTA^{+}95]. As the design space is high dimensional, today's optical inspection setups are mostly being designed based on a trial and error process requiring a lot of engineering experience and experimental work. In addition to the high design costs, the empirical designs typically lead to suboptimal solutions and a compromise between contrary requirements. In today's industry we are missing a generic automatic method to translate the inspection requirements for a given industrial product into optimized inspection solutions. Especially for precise inspection of geometrically complex products, such as an engine block in figure 1.1, the need for an automatic inspection planning is more evident.

In this report we try to address this question by proposing an optimization method for planning the inspection of a cylinder head in a laser triangulation setup. The

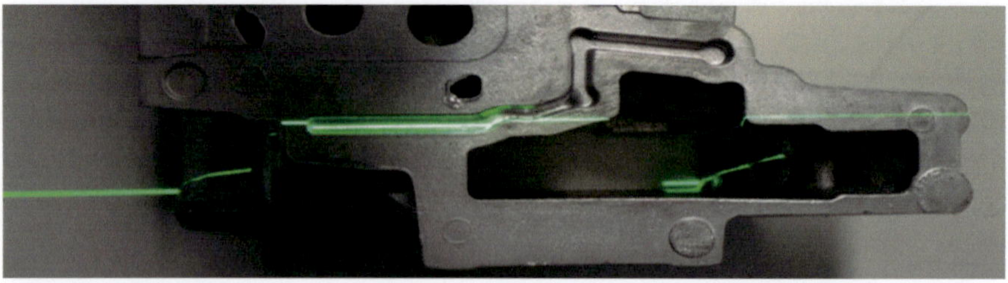

Figure 1.1: Cylinder head illuminated with a laser line

input to this optimization framework is the CAD model of the product with the desired region of interest and the inspection requirements for each region. For the automatic setup planning, we associate each design configuration to a fitness value which enables us to optimize the designed cost function to come up with optimal solutions according to the industry requirements.

The content of this report is organized as follows. In section 2 we formally define the problem of inspection planning as an optimization problem. Section 3 discusses the parameter space of a typical laser triangulation setup. In section 4, we further search for the solution of the optimization problem using two different approaches, the greedy and the combinational approach, with each of them using the Particle Swarm Optimization [BK07] method for the global optimization. In section 5 the achieved planning results will be discussed.

2 Inspection Planning Problem

Let us assume the parameter vector $\mathbf{c}$ determines all the parameters to specify a particular measurement constellation. This means parameter $\mathbf{c}$ includes all the information regarding the positioning and optical configuration of the setup. Similarly, we can define a sequence of k measurements $\{\mathbf{c}_1, ..., \mathbf{c}_k\}$. Let's further assume there is a cost function $f(\mathbf{c}_1, ..., \mathbf{c}_j) \in \mathbb{R}$ which associates each sequence of measurements to a fitness value corresponding to the quality of the measurement with a maximum value of f_{opt}. In a real measurement setup there are of course always constraints. Therefore, not every sequence of measurement can be realizable. Let's quantify all the constraints as a function $r(\mathbf{c}_1, ..., \mathbf{c}_j)$ which takes positive values if the constraints are met.

With the above definitions, the planning problem can be defined as finding the minimum number of N measurements $\{\mathbf{c}_1^*, ..., \mathbf{c}_N^*\}$ which optimize the cost function and at the same time meet the constraints. Therefore

$$\begin{aligned} f(\mathbf{c}_1^*, ..., \mathbf{c}_N^*) &= f_{opt}, \\ \text{s.t.} \quad r(\mathbf{c}_1^*, ..., \mathbf{c}_N^*) &> 0. \end{aligned}$$

For dimensional inspection, the cost function f usually encompasses either of the surface coverage, the scan resolution, or the measurement uncertainty. In our previous works [MBI$^+$17, MBI$^+$16] we have studied different useful cost functions for this problem.

One can easily verify that the optimization problem defined above is at least as hard as the "Set Cover" problem which is known to be NP-hard [Cor07]. The planning problem would be exactly equivalent to the set cover problem when we only consider a discrete set of constellations C for possible solutions, and the surface coverage as the cost function with no further constraints. In this scenario each constellation can cover a subset of the surface. Let us assume the union of all measurable areas by any of the constellations in C is the total area A. In the planning problem, we look for the minimum number of constellations which cover A. In the general case however, the problem is more complex. Often the number of valid constellations are not finite and the cost function is based on complex quantities such as the measurement uncertainty. The optimum value f_{opt} is also often unknown.

For large and complex object surfaces, one is often not able to search the whole parameter space and therefore, needs to resort to approximations. For the set cover problem there is a simple greedy approximation which is actually shown to be the best possible polynomial approximation to the problem [LY94]. In the context of inspection planning, the idea of the greedy approximation is to choose a constellation which covers the most of the surface (or achieves the best fitness values) and continue choosing next best constellations in the same manner. Later in section 5 we discuss the results of the greedy and non-greedy approach.

2.1 Simulations

Typical optimizations require evaluation of many different constellations which are of course not possible to be evaluated in a real setup. Therefore inspection planning always relies on simulations. The planning cost function is consequently based on evaluating the simulation results which is in general a multi-modal non-derivable function.

Evaluation of different cost functions may require different levels of realism in the simulations. The coverage of the surface can be, for instance, estimated by means of fast rasterization-based [AMHH08] simulations (milliseconds per frame), whereas evaluation of the resulting measurement uncertainty requires physically correct image formation simulations using advanced techniques [DBB16]. In such simulations, the emitted photons from the light sources are traced as they get differently scattered by the objects in the scene, all the way to reaching the camera sensor and being converted to intensity values. In our previous work [IBM+17] we have discussed and compared the results of different simulation techniques for simulation of the images of a laser triangulation setup.

3 Design Space

In this section we discuss the degrees of freedom for the planning of a laser triangulation inspection. In such an inspection setup, we have at least one camera and one laser line projector which illuminates a profile on the object (see figure 1.1). The camera captures images of the illuminated profile which are further processed for obtaining the 3D information [MBI+16]. To scan the whole surface, the laser and camera can follow an arbitrary trajectory around the object and capture image frames all along the trajectories. Figure 3.1 depicts the cylinder head CAD model in an arbitrary constellation. For now we assume that the optical parameters of the laser and the camera (e.g. laser power, shutter time, objective f-number, etc.) are already set and are not supposed to be optimized. We solely consider the determination of the geometrical degrees of freedom of the setup. Positioning the camera and the laser as two rigid bodies has a total of 12 degrees of freedom, which can arbitrarily change along the trajectories for each single image frame. To cover a typical product with an average area comparable with the cylinder head, one needs thousands of frames. Obviously this general parametrization leads to an enormous optimization complexity.

One can however make meaningful simplifications to reduce the complexity. For instance, we can assume the scan trajectory to be a linear motion along a particular axis but allow the object instead to freely position under the sensor. The effect of laser distance to the surface can be neglected as lasers can be later focused to any particular distance. We may also parametrize the space in a way that the laser and camera both look towards a common point so that the laser always remains in the camera field of view.

Figure 3.2 illustrates the proposed 9-dimensional degrees of freedom for parametrization of one acquisition. Each acquisition is defined as completely scanning the object along the predefined scan direction. Therefore, instead of planning for each single frame we plan for a number of N acquisitions. In the proposed design space, we dedicate four parameters to sensor placement

(ϕ, θ, τ, d) and five to the object $(\alpha, \beta, \gamma, \Delta x, \Delta z)$. Similar to spherical coordinates, camera placement is determined using polar angle θ, azimuthal angle ϕ, and distance d. The laser holds a triangulation angle τ to the camera, with positive values corresponding to bright field illumination and negative values for dark field illumination. The distance of the laser to the origin is set to a predefined value and does not change during the optimization. The rotation angle ϕ rotates both the camera and the laser to always keep the laser line aligned with the image rows. The object can be freely positioned under the sensor by a 3D rotation using rotation angles α, β, γ, as well as a translational vector. The translation has however only two degrees of freedom because during the acquisition the object is completely scanned in one direction and the translational components parallel to the scan direction do not introduce any new constellations. In the proposed parametrization we consider the y-axis as the scan direction and consider it invariable. Due to rotational degrees of freedom of the sensor and the object, variations of the scan direction within the xy plane will be redundant and do not count as an extra degree of freedom.

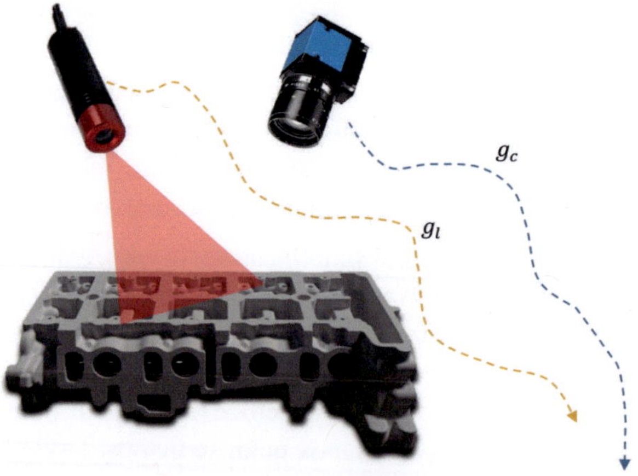

Figure 3.1: Camera and laser can move along arbitrary trajectories g_c and g_l to scan the whole surface.

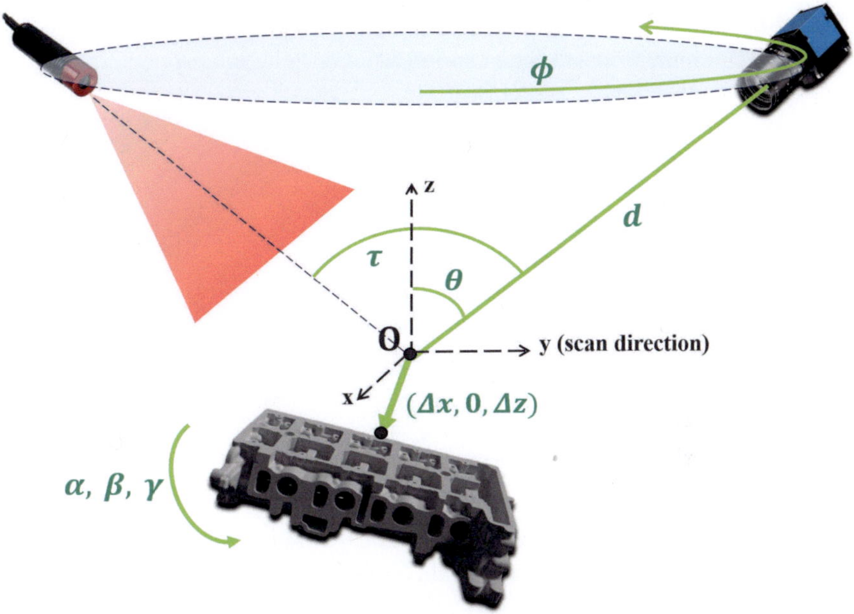

Figure 3.2: Proposed 9D design space for one acquisition

4 Optimization

After definition of the degrees of freedom, in this section we go back to the main optimization problem in equation 2. The main difficulty with the optimization is that we not only want to optimize the constellation parameters but also minimize the number of acquisitions. For a fixed number of M acquisitions, one has an optimization problem with 9M parameters for which we can use standard optimization algorithms. To find the optimal value for M one needs another optimization on possible values of M. The psudo-code in algorithm 4.1 can be a potential solution to the problem.

Algorithm 4.1 Inspection planning algorithm - combinational

Result: Minimum number of acquisition M^*, constellation parameters $\mathbf{p}^*$

$\mathrm{M} = 0, \mathbf{p} = [\,]$

$\mathrm{lastFitness} = 0, \mathrm{nextFitness} = 0$

repeat

```
/* try the solution to M+1 acquisitions */
```

$\mathrm{M} = \mathrm{M} + 1$

$\mathrm{lastFitness} = \mathrm{nextFitness}$

$[\mathrm{nextFitness}, \mathbf{p}] = optimizeMultipleAcquisitions(\mathrm{M})$

until $(\mathrm{nextFitness} - \mathrm{lastFitness} \leq \mathrm{T}$ or surfaceIsCovered);

$\mathrm{M}^* = \mathrm{M}, \mathbf{p}^* = \mathbf{p}$

In the above algorithm, one goes through a $9(\mathrm{M}+1)$-dimensional optimization in each iteration to obtain the optimized fitness value and the corresponding parameter vector $\mathbf{p}$, and compares the gain of having $\mathrm{M}+1$ optimized acquisitions compared to M optimized acquisitions. If the gain of allowing one more acquisition is zero or insignificant we stop the optimization and return the result of the previous step. Of course one can modify the linear search in this algorithm into a binary search to significantly increase the performance; however, even for moderate values of M like 20, the high-dimensional optimization ($9 \times 21 = 189$ free parameters) imposes a great overhead. This is not only a problem from the performance point of view (the algorithm is in the complexity class NP), but it makes it significantly less probable for a heuristic optimization algorithm to find the global optimum of a non-convex non-derivable high-dimensional cost function.

As mentioned earlier, the best polynomial approximation to the set cover problem is the greedy approach. In this algorithm, one already uses the previously optimized constellations and adds only a single constellation to the previous ones. This keeps the optimization overhead constant with the increase of the acquisitions; however, this may result in more acquisitions than the theoretical optimal value. For the set cover problem, the approximation factor is shown to be bounded by a logarithmic upper-bound [LY94]. Algorithm 4.2 contains the pseudo-code of the greedy approximation to the inspection planning algorithm.

Algorithm 4.2 Inspection planning algorithm - greedy approximation

Result: Minimum number of scans M^* with parameters $\mathbf{p}^*$

$\mathrm{M} = 0$, $\mathbf{p} = [\,]$

$\mathrm{lastFitness} = 0$, $\mathrm{nextFitness} = 0$

repeat

```
    lastFitness = nextFitness
    /* 9-dimensional optimization                        */
    [nextFitness, c] = findNextBestScan(p)
    /* append to previous scans                          */
    append(p, c)
    M = M + 1
```

until $(\mathrm{nextFitness} - \mathrm{lastFitness} \leq \mathrm{T}$ or $\mathrm{surfaceIsCovered})$;

$\mathrm{M}^* = \mathrm{M}$, $\mathbf{p}^* = \mathbf{p}$

4.1 Particle Swarm Optimization

Using either of the algorithms for solving the inspection planning problem, we need a global optimizer. As mentioned earlier, the cost function is based on evaluating simulations, taking any complex form with multiple local optimums. Therefore, derivative-free randomized heuristic search algorithms seem to be the right choice for the global optimization problem.

Among the many existing global optimizaters in the literature (see [Wei09] for a good review), the Particle Swarm Optimization (PSO) has been widely applied in many fields. PSO is a variant of swarm-based intelligent methods [BDT99] whose main idea is to imitate the behavior of biological species which live in colonies such as birds, ants, and bees. We observe that these species exhibit a high intelligence in their social activities such as searching for food, although they exhibit simple individual acts. The PSO algorithm is especially inspired by the way birds communicate when searching a field for food [Wei09]. The approach of PSO is very intuitive. For optimizing a cost function $f(\mathbf{x})$, one initiates a number of K random particles in the parameter space (the swarm size). The particles are not only individual searchers in the paramter space (similar to many parallel simulated-annealing [Wei09] optimizers), but they also communicate with each other and share the results of their local searches which guides them for the rest of the search.

Every particle in this algorithm is composed of three vectors: its current position in the search space $\mathbf{x}_i$, its best individually found position so far $\mathbf{b}_i$, and its velocity $\mathbf{v}_i$. The particles are also aware of the best position $\mathbf{g}_i$ found by the rest of the particles so far. This might be actually the globally best found position, or the best position that the particle has so far heard from those who have communicated with it. The algorithm updates the particles at each iteration by updating their velocities and positions according to

$$\begin{aligned}\mathbf{v_i}^{t+1} &= \mathbf{v_i}^t + \epsilon_1(\mathbf{b}_i^t - \mathbf{x}_i^t) + \epsilon_2(\mathbf{g}_i^t - \mathbf{x}_i^t),\\ \mathbf{x}_i^{t+1} &= \mathbf{x}_i^t + \mathbf{v_i}^t.\end{aligned}$$

The random factors ϵ_1 and ϵ_2 weight tendencies of the particle to search further towards the local and global optimum. A particle also has a tendency to keep its previous direction, therefore we also add the $\mathbf{v_i}^t$ term to the velocity update rule. The position is simply computed as moving from the previous position along the updated velocity.

Since the introduction of PSO, there have been a few standardizations proposed which give recommendations on choosing the parameters of the algorithm like the swarm size, the communication structure, and weightings. In this work, we have orientated the PSO implementation based on the standardization given in 2007 [BK].

5 Coverage Planning Results

The cylinder head object contains hard to reach areas such as deep intake and exhaust manifolds. Therefore, maximizing the surface coverage with minimized number of scans is a non-trivial problem which is of high interest for the industry. In this section, we present the inspection planning results with the goal of maximizing the surface coverage. For evaluating the surface coverage, we use a fine mesh model of the object as shown in figure 5.1. The granularity of the mesh elements must correspond to the required inspection resolution. The surface coverage can be then evaluated as the area of all the patches which have been measured with at least one point.

For the optimization, we have used the proposed parameter space in figure 3.2 with a simplification of setting the camera distance d to a constant value of 0.5 meter. This choice can be justified by the fact that the object translation component along the z-axis introduces very similar effects to changing the camera distance. However, in the future we intend to get the results with the full degrees of freedom. As optimization constraints, we assume valid ranges for each of the parameters, based on the degrees of freedom of the real physical setup. For the current results we have bounded the parameters to

$$\phi \in [0°, 360°), \qquad \theta \in [0°, 80°], \qquad \tau \in [-80°, -10] \cup [10°, 80],$$
$$\alpha, \beta, \gamma \in [0°, 360°), \quad \Delta x \in [-0.4, 0.4]\, m, \quad \Delta z \in [-0.5, 0.5]\, m.$$

Many parameters can already take their full range, such as ϕ. Others such as the triangulation angle τ must be constrained to deliver meaningful measurements.

Figure 5.2 compares the results of the greedy vs. the combinational approach. This chart displays the optimized measurable area for each number of acquisitions. The orange line determines the full area of the object, which is however not fully measurable because some areas are either completely unreachable or require constellations which violate the optimization constraints. The blue dotted graph displays the improvements of the greedy surface coverage planning vs. the number of acquisitions. One can see that the algorithm makes rather big improvements at the beginning; however, the contribution of the next acquisitions gradually reduces until it falls below the threshold for the 30th acquisition. For comparison, we have also applied the combinational planning algorithm for

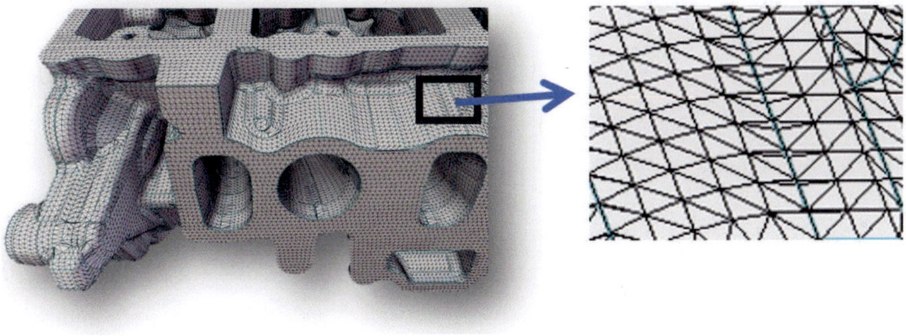

Figure 5.1: Cylinder head fine mesh model for evaluating surface coverage

5, 10, 15, and 20 acquisitions, where we allow the optimizer to combinationally optimize all the acquisitions together. In theory the combinational approach is able to find the global optimum as it looks for every possible combination of constellations. The greedy approach however, might be trapped in local optimum solutions as the constellations are optimized in a non-reversible approach. In practice, however, we see that the results of the combinational approach can even underperform the greedy method. This is due to the fact that it is less probable for a heuristic random optimizer to find the optimum of a high dimensional problem, compared to a problem with significantly less degrees of freedom.

Figure 5.3 illustrates the resulting point cloud of the object after applying the 30 optimized acquisitions obtained by the greedy planning. As it can be seen, the deep cavities corresponding to the intake and exhaust manifolds have been covered.

6 Summary and Future work

In this report we proposed and implemented an optimization framework for automatic optimization of industrial inspection setups. We went through the

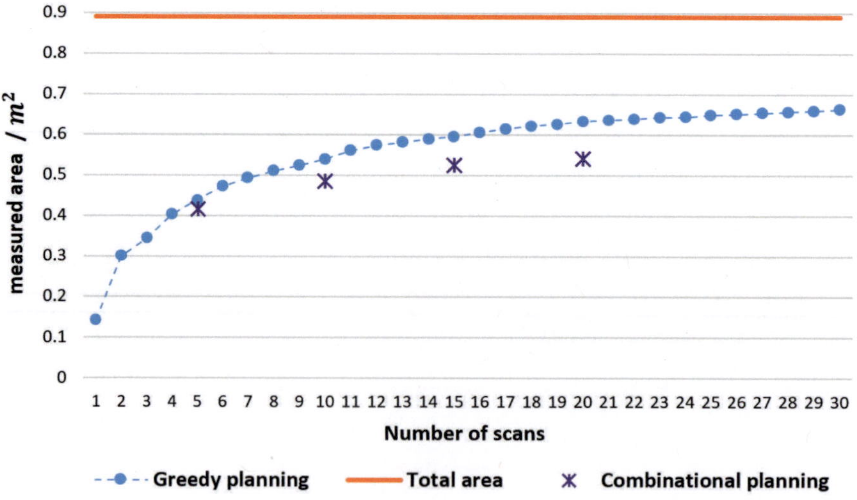

Figure 5.2: Optimized surface coverage vs. number of acquisitions

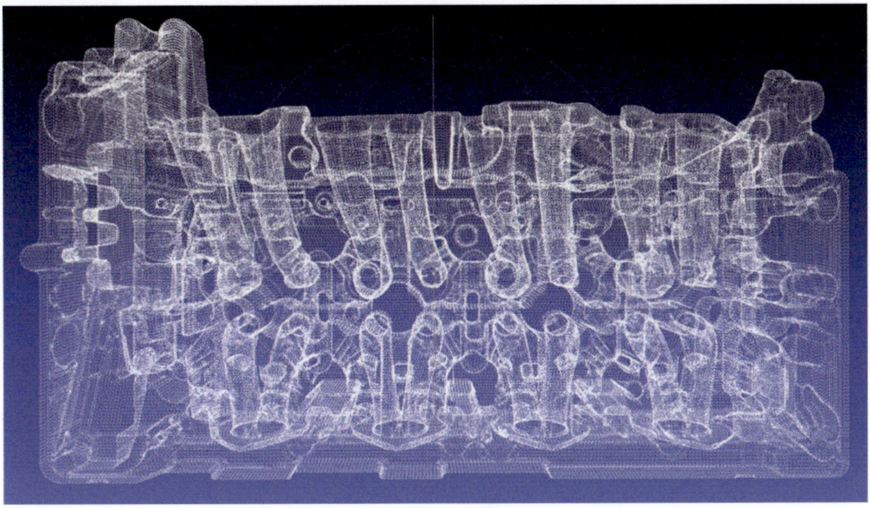

Figure 5.3: Point cloud of the resulting measurement after applying 30 optimized acquisitions obtained by the greedy planning.

parametrization of the design space for inspecting a cylinder head in a laser triangulation setup and compared different approaches for finding the minimized number of acquisitions which maximize the surface coverage.

It is very insightful to calculate the actual measurable area on the cylinder head to better evaluate the achieved coverage results. As a future work, we plan to apply methods for calculating ambient occlusion [Mil94] to calculate the area measurable for a given set of inspection constraints. In addition, there is also potentials to combine the greedy and the combinational optimization approaches to benefit from both. In a hybrid approach, one can use the greedy approach to come up with good starting points with less optimization overhead and further apply the combinational approach on the achieved suboptimal results to globally improve the results.

Bibliography

[AMHH08] Tomas Akenine-Möller, Eric Haines, and Naty Hoffman. *Real-Time Rendering*. A. K. Peters, Ltd, Natick, MA, USA, 3 edition, 2008.

[BDT99] Eric Bonabeau, Marco Dorigo, and Guy Theraulaz. *Swarm intelligence: from natural to artificial systems*. Oxford University Press, 1999.

[BK07] Daniel Bratton and James Kennedy. Defining a standard for particle swarm optimization. In *Proc. 2007 IEEE Swarm Intelligence Symposium*, pages 120–127, 2007.

[BLF15] Jürgen Beyerer, Fernando Puente León, and Christian Frese. *Machine Vision: Automated Visual Inspection: Theory, Practice and Applications*. Springer, 2015.

[CBL02] A. Contri, P. Bourdet, and C. Lartigue. Quality of 3D digitised points obtained with non-contact optical sensors. *CIRP Annals - Manufacturing Technology*, 51(1):443–446, 2002.

[Cor07] Thomas H. Cormen. *Introduction to algorithms*. MIT Press, Cambridge, Mass., 2 edition, 2007.

[DBB16] Philip Dutre, Philippe Bekaert, and Kavita Bala. *Advanced global illumination*. CRC Press, 2016.

[IBM+17] S. Irgenfried, S. Bergmann, M. Mohammadikaji, J. Beyerer, C. Dachsbacher, and H. Wörn. Image formation simulation for computer-aided inspection planning of machine vision systems. In Jürgen Beyerer and Fernando Puente León, editors, *Proc. SPIE Optical Metrology*, SPIE Proceedings, page 1033406. SPIE, 2017.

[LY94] Carsten Lund and Mihalis Yannakakis. On the hardness of approximating minimization problems. *Journal of the ACM*, 41(5):960–981, 1994.

[MBI+16] M. Mohammadikaji, S. Bergmann, S. Irgenfried, J. Beyerer, C. Dachsbacher, and H. Wörn. A framework for uncertainty propagation in 3D shape measurement using laser triangulation. In *IEEE International Instrumentation and Measurement Technology Conference (I2MTC)*, pages 6–11, 2016.

[MBI+17] M. Mohammadikaji, S. Bergmann, S. Irgenfried, J. Beyerer, C. Dachsbacher, and H. Wörn. Probabilistic surface inference for industrial inspection planning. In *Proc. 2017 IEEE Winter Conference on Applications of Computer Vision (WACV)*, pages 1008–1016, 2017.

[Mil94] Gavin Miller. Efficient algorithms for local and global accessibility shading. In Dino Schweitzer, Andrew Glassner, and Mike Keeler, editors, *Proc. SIGGRAPH 1994*, pages 319–326, 1994.

[NJ95] Timothy S. Newman and Anil K. Jain. A survey of automated visual inspection. *Computer Vision and Image Understanding*, 61(2):231–262, 1995.

[SRR03] William R. Scott, Gerhard Roth, and Jean-François Rivest. View planning for automated three-dimensional object reconstruction and inspection. *ACM Computing Surveys*, 35(1):64–96, 2003.

[TTA+95] Konstantinos Tarabanis, Roger Y Tsai, Peter K Allen, et al. The MVP sensor planning system for robotic vision tasks. *IEEE Transactions on Robotics and Automation*, 11(1):72–85, 1995.

[Wei09] Thomas Weise. Global optimization algorithms – theory and application. *Self-Published*, 2009.

[WPH06] A Weckenmann, G Peggs, and J Hoffmann. Probing systems for dimensional micro-and nano-metrology. *Measurement Science and Technology*, 17(3):1–504, 2006.

Wavelet Based Feature Extraction in Near Infrared Spectra for Compositional Analysis of Food

Julius Krause

Vision and Fusion Laboratory
Institute for Anthropomatics
Karlsruhe Institute of Technology (KIT), Germany
julius.krause@kit.edu

Technical Report IES-2017-02

Abstract: Near infrared spectroscopy is a common method for analysis of food, soil and pharmaceutical products. New developments in sensor technology, like hyperspectral camera systems and mobile spectrometers, allow broad applications of spectroscopy with devices out of specialized laboratories. Therefore, it is necessary to develop robust algorithms for classification and regression, regardless of the device. The key to robust analysis lies in data preparation to get standardized spectral information from each device. Wavelet based feature extraction could be a possible method to compress spectral data to its material specific absorption information. A method for wavelet based feature extraction, which also reduces the influence from elastic scattering effects is proposed in this report.

1 Introduction

In order to ensure the high standards of food quality, monitoring measurements are required throughout the entire production process right up to the customer. Optical spectroscopy in the visible and near-infrared spectrum can be used as a non-destructive and non-contact measuring method on foods for quality determination. Compared to laboratory tests, the result of an optical measurement is immediately available [LGGFR17].

In the future, the development of compact and cost-effective sensor technology will facilitate the dissemination of spectroscopy. Due to advancing developments in microsystems technology, it has been possible to integrate different measurement methods like tunable Fabry-Perot filter, fourier-transform or scanning grating systems into miniaturized sensors. A series production at prices of a few US dollars has already been announced. A "food scanner" is just one possible application. The integration of these sensors in the Internet of Things (IoT) or a smartphone is also possible and opens up a variety of other applications in the field of quality and process control [RDC17, DWKR16].

The comparability of spectroscopic data across different devices is one of the great challenges in spectroscopy. It is gaining in importance as networking of spectral sensors grows. In the history of spectroscopy, many approaches to spectral preprocessing [RvdBE09] and transfer of models [FWT+02] have been developed. Wavelet transformation has also been used for pre-processing [MNHG96].

The approach presented below attempts to extract physical features from spectral data, which only represent the absorption by molecule vibrations or electron excitations. Therefore, a wavelet transformation of the spectral data with an approximation function like Gaussian or Lorentzian shape is used to get these features in connection with derivative pre-processing.

2 Physical model of the interaction between light and matter

The method presented in this article is based on the idea of describing the measurement signal by a physically motivated model. The analysis, based on physical model parameters, provides a level of abstraction in which specific disturbing influences can be specifically suppressed. At the same time, sensor-independent chemometric modeling is possible. The following section summarizes the physical factors that the author considers relevant to the theoretical signal model.

Interaction with matter leads to an extinction Q of light intensity. The extinction process depends on the wavelength and contains an overlay of different signals from different origin. In the following, the name spectral signature is used as an umbrella term for the raw signal, which is an overlay signal of chemical and

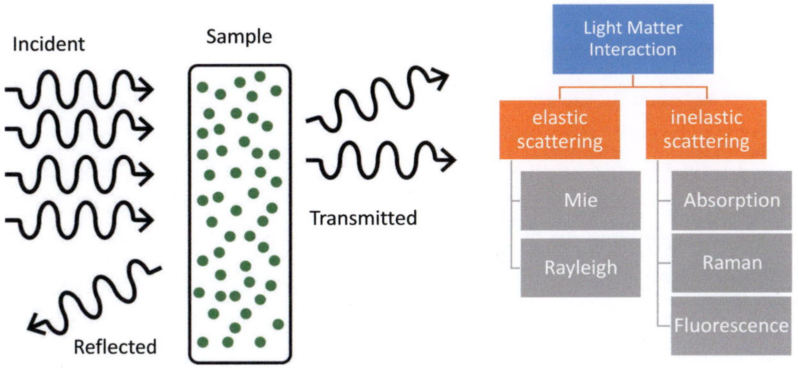

Figure 2.1: The incident light interacts with a sample. By elastic scattering within the sample, the photons are deflected by an angle θ. The most common interaction processes of the photons with the sample are shown in a block diagram.

physical properties as well as the environment. In the following, influencing variables are exemplified and summarized in three categories.

- **Chemical properties** of the sample, which are determined by absorption and fluorescence effects, which are related to specific excitations of electron states and molecular vibrations and thus produce a material-specific spectral signature.
- **Physical properties**, which depend, for example, on the shape of the sample, a surface condition of the sample or, in the case of a sample in powder form, on a degree of grinding of the powder and other properties. There is also an influence of the geometry between the measurement object and the sensor or the light sources and the sensor. This influence changes the measured spectral signature and thus also makes the comparability of different measuring devices more difficult.
- **Sensor properties**, which are caused for example by different sensitivity or different spectral measuring ranges, complicate the comparability of measurement results of different measuring devices.

It is reasonable to assume that the three categories are independent. The scattering theory will be used, to describe these processes in detail.

The occurrence of fluorescence effects should not initially be considered in the following model. However, the analysis model shown below can be extended at any time by fluorescence effects. Inelastic scattering signals from Stokes and Antistokes processes, also known as the Raman effect, are neglected due to the signal strength from 10^{-6} to 10^{-9} compared to the output signal.

The following model summarizes the influencing variables of the measurement signal: An optical sensor detects the light emitted by a sample. The measured reflection or transmission signal is considered with respect to the light emitted from the light source. Only a part of the light emitted by the sample can be detected in the solid angle $\Delta\Omega_{\text{sensor}}$ of the detector. This extinction Q_{ext} is composed of the scattering of the incident light Q_{sca} into the solid angle Ω not detected by the sensor (Fig. 2.1). The absorption process by the electrons and the molecular states is considered independent of the scatter and added as an additional term Q_{abs}:

$$Q_{\text{ext}}(\lambda, \theta, r) := Q_{\text{sca}}\left(\frac{r}{\lambda}, \theta\right) + Q_{\text{abs}}(\lambda)\,.$$

The model includes the particle size or micro structure with a radius r, the angle θ between the light source and sensor, and the wavelength λ dependency. The two terms of the equation are described in detail below.

2.1 Elastic Scattering Theory

Many optical systems can be well described by geometric optics. In cases where the object radius r is in or below wavelength ranges, the phenomena occurring can be well described by the scattering theory of Rayleigh and Mie [CDL02].

The Rayleigh theory can be applied to describe the light scattering by particles with radius $r < 1/10\lambda$. In this regime, the particle act as an oscillating dipole driven by the electromagnetic field. A microscopic dipole absorbs a photon in a virutal state, and the subsequent emission has the characteristic of a dipole antenna. The intensity distribution

$$I(\theta, \lambda) \propto 1/\lambda^4(1 + \cos^2\theta)$$

of the scattered light results from the probability of the individual scattering angles.

In particles and structures whose dimension correspond to the wavelength λ, plasmon resonances can be excited. A complete analytic solution of the Maxwell equations exists only for spherical objects and is described in detail in the Mie theory [Mie08]. The Mie theory can also be used for particle size determination by laser diffraction and, in particular for small objects, provides a better result than Fraunhofer diffraction. For the following analysis, however, it is sufficient to know that the solution of the Mie theory is given by the so-called Bessel functions, which are smooth and differentiable.

In summary, the elastic scattering gives a smooth and differentiable low-frequency signal contribution in the detected spectral signature.

2.2 Absorption

The model of a harmonic oscillator (Lorentz oscillator) can approximately describe the absorption by molecular vibrations. Wherein the solution for determining refractive indices and absorption coefficients is reproduced substantially correctly. The dependence of wavelength of the absorption is given by the so-called dielectric function which be approximated by a Lorentz profile. In addition, the Lorentz profile corresponds to the so-called natural linewidth, which e.g. can be derived from the Fourier transform of a damped harmonic oscillator.

Regardless of which model is used, the exact absorption spectrum can not be calculated as long as the individual coefficients of the electric field distribution in the solid state, the anharmonicity of the molecular vibration, and the interaction with neighboring molecules are unknown. However, the course of the dependence of wavelength of a single absorbance (or emission by fluorescence) is represented approximately correctly by a bell shaped curve such as Lorentz profile or Gaussian function [Dem10].

Following the preceding qualitative analysis of the dependence of wavelength of the absorption, the relationship between an amount of substance and its absorption is now to be determined in a simple model. From the exponential attenuation of a light beam after entering a medium, the Beer-Lambert law can be derived:

$$\ln\left(\frac{I_1}{I_0}\right) = -c\eta\delta\,.$$

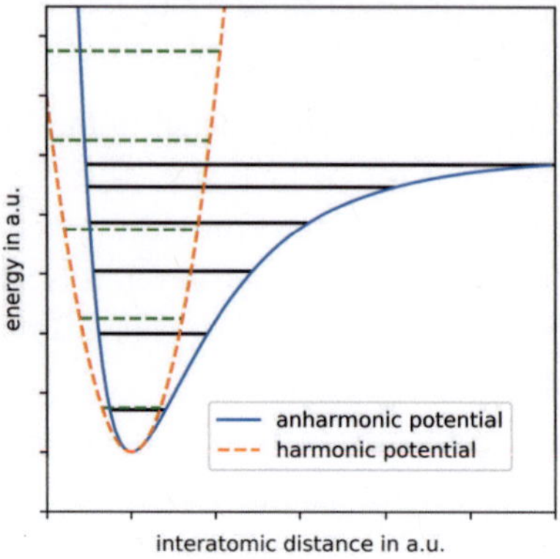

(a) The Lennard-Jones potential describes the interaction potential of a diatomic molecule and can be described in quadratic approximation by a harmonic oscillator. With increasing energy above the ground state, anharmonic corrections must be considered.

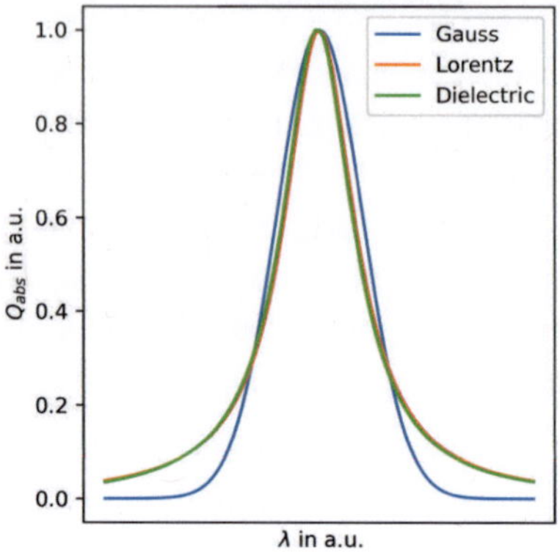

(b) Clearly recognizable is the good approximation of the dielectric function ϵ by a Lorentz profile. A Gaussian profile differs more, but this is justifiable because absorption lines are usually extended by disturbing effects.

Figure 2.2: Absorption on the model of diatomic molecular vibrations.

The extinction $Q_{\text{abs}} = I_1/I_0$ causes the scaling of the bell shaped absorption curve. A quantitative content determination appears possible due to the connection to the substance-dependent attenuation factor η, the concentration c, and the optical path length δ.

In summary, a single absorption can be described approximately by three parameters of a bell curve like a Gaussian.

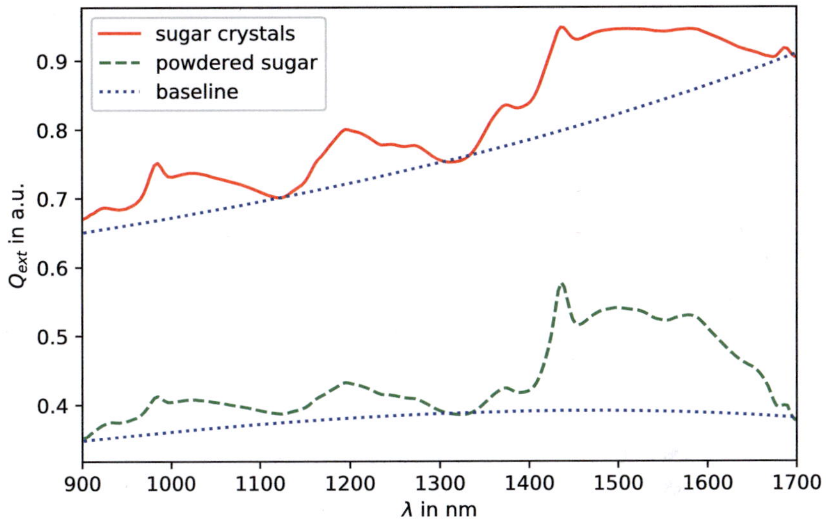

Figure 2.3: The extinction Q_{ext} of the chemically identical substances differs in scale and in the baseline due to different scattering properties and due to different particle size.

3 Wavelet Based Feature Extraction

The extinction Q_{ext} of the measurement signal in Figure 2.3 is compared to a white reflection standard. Both spectra describe the identical substance which is sugar and only the particle size differs. It can clearly be seen that the figure shows differences in the baseline of the two spectra and the signal strength. Therefore, pre-processing is needed for chemical component analysis.

The most common methods for spectral pre-treatment like scatter correction, normalization, and dimensional reduction are based on the spectral signature of a single measurement system as a whole, e.g. by inclusion of the mean signal. In addition, linear operators are destroying the connection to Beer-Lambert law. Therefore, analysis models based on these methods can not readily be used in another measurement environment.

Another established possibility for the correction of multiplicative influences is the gradient formation over the spectrum. However, the noise is amplified and human interpretation is difficult. The wavelet analysis based on the derived spectrum is intended to counteract these two disadvantages.

The wavelet analysis includes the neighbourhood information in the spectrum which counteracts the noise. The easily interpretable parameters of the approximated bell curve can be taken from the wavelet scalogram afterwards. In addition, the mean value of the wavelet transformation corrects another term of the baseline. Moreover, a later normalization based only on the absorption bands used in the model is more robust to changes in the spectral signature.

The algorithm is based on two assumptions that were explained previously:

- The baseline of the spectrum is due to the anisotropy of the elastic scattering and can be approximated by a smooth polynomial function.
- The absorption can be approximated by a bell-shaped absorption function with three parameters.

For the mathematical description, the spectrum is referred to as a function $g(\lambda)$ and the continuously differentiable bell-shaped approximation function is referred to as $\psi_{\lambda_0,s}(\lambda)$. Where λ_0 is the center and s is the width of the approximation function.

Step 1: Baseline Correction and Peak Deconvolution

The n-fold derivative of the spectrum reduces the polynomial order of the baseline, at the same time superposed peaks are unfolded [NW84]. Noise is greatly amplified by the derivative, which is why smoothing according to Savitzky-Golay is used in many cases [SG64].

In the following the fact is used that the derivative operator can also be applied to the function ψ. In the case of the second derivative, one obtains the *Mexican Hat* function, which is widely used in signal processing.

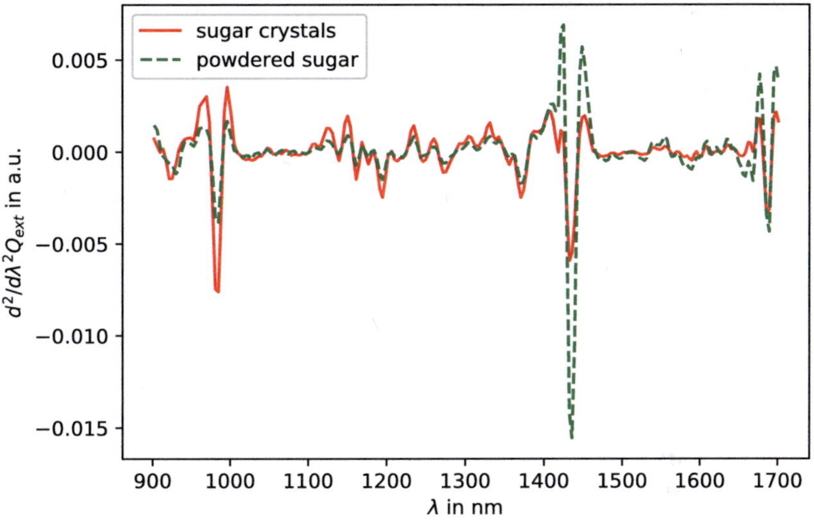

Figure 3.1: By applying the second derivative, the baseline of the spectrum was eliminated. Characteristic features are clearly shown in the shape of an inverted Mexican Hat with identical width and position in both spectra.

Step 2: Wavelet Transformation

The wavelet transformation has the character of a correlation analysis [Mal89, Mor83]. The description of the wavelet transformation as

$$\Gamma_{\psi}(\lambda_0, s) := \langle \psi_{\lambda_0, S}(\lambda), g(\lambda) \rangle$$

shows this fact.

The scalar product is performed for different values of λ_0 and s, the resulting wavelet coefficients from the example of sugar is shown in a scalogram (Fig. 3.2).

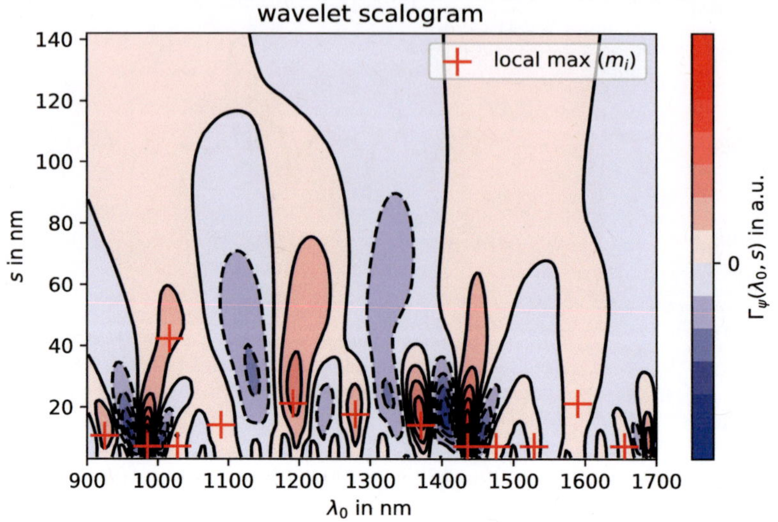

Figure 3.2: For the example of sugar, the wavelet coefficient is plotted for a selected region of s_i and λ_i. Where of the red (blue) color indicates positive (negative) energy of the wavelet coefficient. Local maxima are highlighted by red crosses.

Step 3: Feature Extraction

Local maxima of the wavelet coefficient show the location of the best match between the correlation function and the spectrum. From the coordinates of the local maxima, the parameters of each feature

$$m_i = (\lambda_i, s_i, \Gamma_\psi(\lambda_i, s_i))$$

can be found. Wherein the wavelet coefficient also indicates the height or the strength of the peak, which is linked via the Beer-Lambert law with the amount of existing ingredients. Although the amount $i \in \mathbb{N}^+$ of found features is initially not limited.

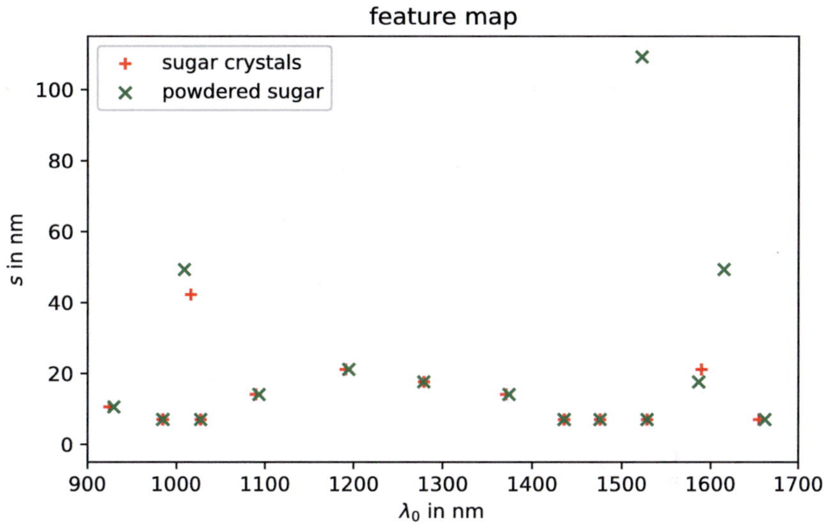

Figure 4.1: In many cases, the algorithm has extracted the identical values even for superimposed peaks.

4 Experimental Results

Using different sugar granules as an example, it could be shown that, despite different scattering properties, nearly identical features are found for the individual features (Fig. 4.1). This confirms the invariance of the found features against changes in the scattering properties.

Another example is to show that the features contain additional information of individual ingredients. For this purpose, the data set of a competition for the determination of protein in cereals by NIR spectroscopy was selected. The training dataset comprises 1488 spectra from 248 different samples, measured with 6 spectrometers, three spectrometers of the same model from two different manufacturers.

Figure 4.2 shows an example of two spectra from different Instruments. For comparison, a virtual absorption spectrum was formed from the previously extracted features m_i. The relevant feature for the protein concentration also determined in the competition literature is the small peak at 1016 nm. The information about the protein content is thus in a small hidden peak [IAB+17].

The determined features m_i of all 6 spectrometers for all 248 samples are shown in a three-dimensional feature map in a section around the relevant protein peak (Fig. 4.3). The wavelet coefficient is normalised by referencing to a protein independent peak. The presented method found the relevant peak in all 1488 spectra. The figure also clearly shows, that the width s_i and wavelet coefficient $\Gamma_\psi(\lambda_i, s_i)$ of the protein peak increases with the protein content.

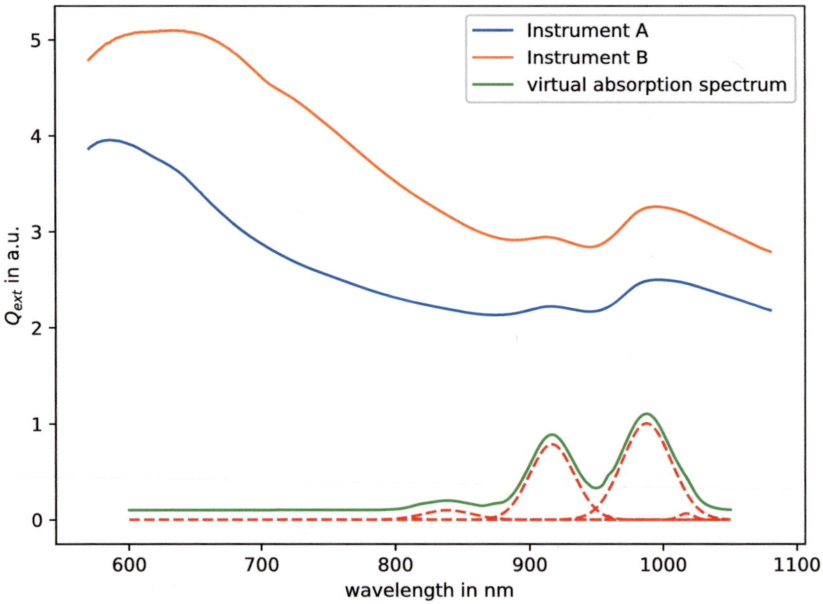

Figure 4.2: The spectra of an identical sample recorded by two spectrometers models from different manufacturers A and B. In the lower part is shown as an example a virtual absorption spectrum, which was determined from the previously extracted features m_i

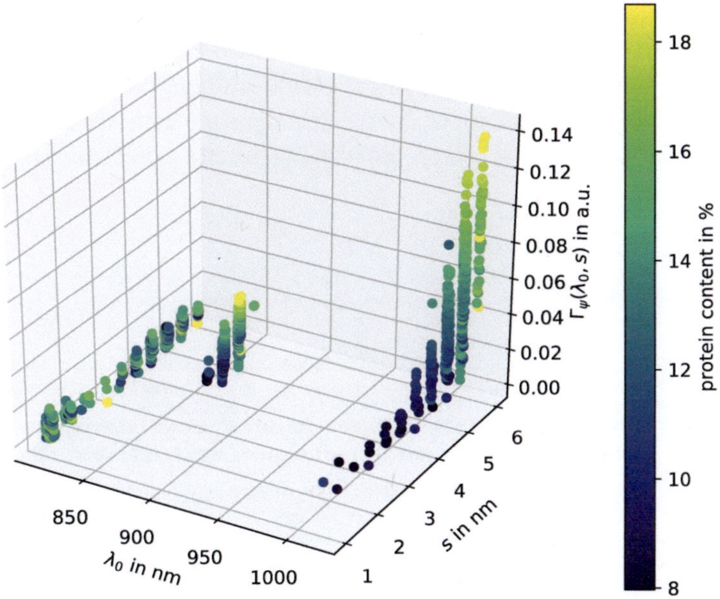

Figure 4.3: The three-dimensional feature map shows the parameters of the features extracted from the training set. The protein content of the sample is shown in color. For better visibility of the protein content, the presentation is limited to three small features.

5 Summary

The presented method is suitable for the feature extraction of superimposed absorption signals. The position and width of a peak are independent of the scaling of the signal strength and are therefore suitable for a robust material identification, regardless of the sample geometry and the measuring device used. The information of the signal intensity is included in the wavelet coefficient and offers the possibility to quantify an ingredient. The representation of the spectral features m_i as a list of triplets $(\lambda_i, s_i, \Gamma_\psi(\lambda_i, s_i)$ can be created for measurements of sensors of different types. Classification and regression models based on evaluation of the triplets are thus invariant with respect to the sensor used.

The knowledge of the position and width of the absorption features also allows further evaluations. Optical filters can be selected based on the individual features. In addition, components of the elastic scattering parameters can be determined from the residuum of the spectral signature after deduction of the absorption properties. In hyperspectral imaging, feature extraction can be used for compression.

Bibliography

[CDL02] A. J. Cox, Alan J. DeWeerd, and Jennifer Linden. An experiment to measure Mie and Rayleigh total scattering cross sections. *Am. J. Phys.*, 70(6):620–625, 2002.

[Dem10] Wolfgang Demtröder. *Expirmentalphysik 3, Atome, Moleküle und Festkörper*. Springer-Lehrbuch. Springer Berlin Heidelberg, Berlin, Heidelberg, 2010.

[DWKR16] Anshuman J. Das, Akshat Wahi, Ishan Kothari, and Ramesh Raskar. Ultra-portable, wireless smartphone spectrometer for rapid, non-destructive testing of fruit ripeness. *Sci. Rep.*, 6(September):1–8, 2016.

[FWT+02] Robert N. Feudale, Nathaniel A. Woody, Huwei Tan, Anthony J. Myles, Steven D. Brown, Joan Ferre, and Joan Ferré. Transfer of multivariate calibration models: a review. *Chemom. Intell. Lab. Syst.*, 64(2):181–12, 2002.

[IAB+17] Benoit Igne, Md Anik Alam, Dongsheng Bu, Pierre Dardenne, Hanzhou Feng, Ali Gahkani, David W Hopkins, Shikhar Mohan, Charles R Hurburgh, and Cathleen Brenner. Summary of the 2016 IDRC software shoot-out. *NIR news*, 28(4):16–22, 2017.

[LGGFR17] Mercedes G. López, Ana Sarahí García-González, and Elena Franco-Robles. Carbohydrate analysis by NIRS-chemometrics. In *Dev. Near-Infrared Spectrosc.* InTech, mar 2017.

[Mal89] Stephane G. Mallat. A theory for multiresolution signal decomposition: The wavelet representation. *IEEE Transactions on Pattern Analysis and Machine Intelligence*, 11(7):674–693, 1989.

[Mie08] Gustav Mie. Beiträge zur Optik trüber Medien, speziell kolloidaler Metallösungen. *Ann. Phys.*, 330(3):377–445, jan 1908.

[MNHG96] C. R. Mittermayr, S. G. Nikolov, H. Hutter, and M. Grasserbauer. Wavelet denoising of Gaussian peaks: A comparative study. *Chemom. Intell. Lab. Syst.*, 34(2):187–202, 1996.

[Mor83] J. Morlet. Sampling theory and wave propagation. In C. H. Chen, editor, *Issues in Acoustic Signal — Image Processing and Recognition*, pages 233–261, Berlin, Heidelberg, 1983. Springer Berlin Heidelberg.

[NW84] KH Norris and PC Williams. Optimization of mathematical treatments of raw near-infrared signal in the measurement of protein in hard red spring wheat. I. Influence of particle size., 1984.

[RDC17] Giovanni Rateni, Paolo Dario, and Filippo Cavallo. Smartphone-based food diagnostic technologies: A review. *Sensors (Switzerland)*, 17(6), 2017.

[RvdBE09] Asmund Rinnan, Frans van den Berg, and Soren Balling Engelsen. Review of the most common pre-processing techniques for near-infrared spectra. *TrAC Trends in Analytical Chemistry*, 28(10):1201 – 1222, 2009.

[SG64] Abraham Savitzky and Marcel J.E. Golay. Smoothing and differentiation of data by simplified least squares procedures. *Anal. Chem.*, 36(8):1627–1639, 1964.

Adaptive Measurement Method for Area Chromatic Confocal Microscopy

Ding Luo

Vision and Fusion Laboratory
Institute for Anthropomatics
Karlsruhe Institute of Technology (KIT), Germany
ding.luo@kit.edu

Technical Report IES-2017-03

Abstract: Although well known for its depth discerning capability, conventional confocal microscopy has limited application due to its slow scanning speed. From Nipkow disk to various programmable spatial light modulator, various research has been conducted with the aim of improving the speed of confocal microscopy. Nevertheless, the fundamental conflict between axial sensitivity and lateral density remains unsolved. In this report, a novel adaptive measurement method is proposed based on iterative refinement of the axial measurement as well as condensation of the lateral measurement grid. Initial experimental investigation has shown overall good measurement result with a specific type of artifacts due to inaccurate estimation in earlier measurement stages. Despite of this problem, the proposed system and the accompanying algorithms have shown great potential in improving the measurement speed of area chromatic confocal microscopy.

1 Introduction

Conventional scanning confocal microscopy suffers from a relatively slow measurement speed due to its requirement for mechanical scanning, which largely limits its application in various fields. To tackle this problem, Egger et al. first proposed to utilize the Nipkow disk to generate a moving array of measurement locations in order to accelerate the scanning process [EP67]. Recently, more advanced disk pattern has been designed to be coupled with structured illumination technology, in order to achieve superresolution imaging [HO15].

With the development of new optical components and computer technology, this idea of using an array of measurement locations has transformed into an important field of research, i.e. programmable array microscopy (PAM). Programmable array microscope refers to a family of imaging systems where a spatial light modulator (SLM) is applied to dynamically change the patterns of illumination and/or detection. With the target of eliminating lateral mechanical scanning, different SLMs have been applied, including digital mirror device (DMD) [HVG+99, CRS15], liquid crystal on silicon (LCoS) [HCT+07, KDP+14], and polymer-dispersed liquid crystal (PDLC) [CS17].

Despite the improvement achieved through these developments, one fundamental problem remains unsolved. The unique depth discerning capability of the confocal technology originates from the fact that the light which is not focused on the object is distributed to the adjacent area, thus dramatically reducing the reflected light collectable to the confocal pinhole. Such a principle intrinsically demands larger numerical aperture (NA) to generate highly focused spot, in order to achieve better axial sensitivity and lateral resolution, which has not been a problem for conventional scanning confocal microscopy. Nevertheless, for array scanning microscopy, realized through whether mechanically scanned disk or spatial light modulator, the blurred illumination spot of one measurement location quickly generates crosstalk over its adjacent measurement locations. This leads to an inverse relationship between the minimum allowable pitch of the measurement array and the NA of the system as well as the axial measurement range.

This report aims to provide a potential solution for this problem through an adaptive measurement strategy based on a particularly dynamic hardware setup, which will be discussed in details in the following sections.

2 System Setup and Calibration

The proposed system is composed of two components, i.e. a programmable light source and a DMD-based programmable array chromatic confocal microscope. Due to its nature of adaptability, the system is denoted as AdaScope.

2.1 Programmable Light Source

The programmable light source is based on two-dimensional dispersion of a white light laser. As illustrated in Fig. 2.1, the laser is firstly dispersed horizontally by a prism and then dispersed vertically by the echelle grating to achieve very high overall dispersion. A digital mirror device is used to select the desired wavelengths, which is collected by the output liquid light guide. The system is capable of generating light spectrum in the range of 480 nm to 680 nm. More details regarding the programmable light source can be found in the corresponding paper [LTLB17].

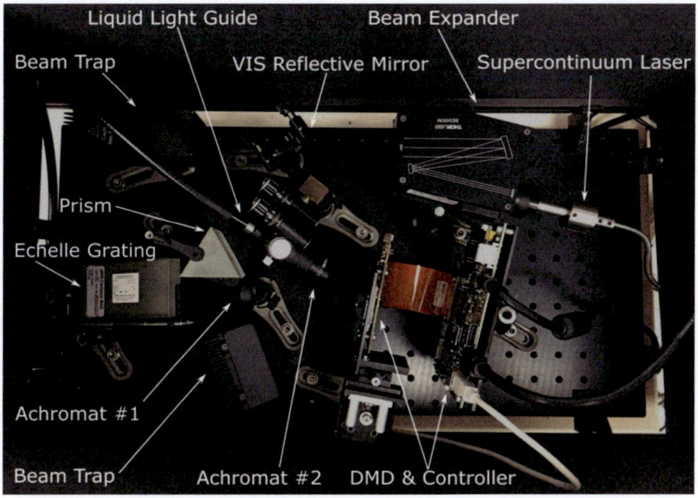

Figure 2.1: Setup of programmable light source.

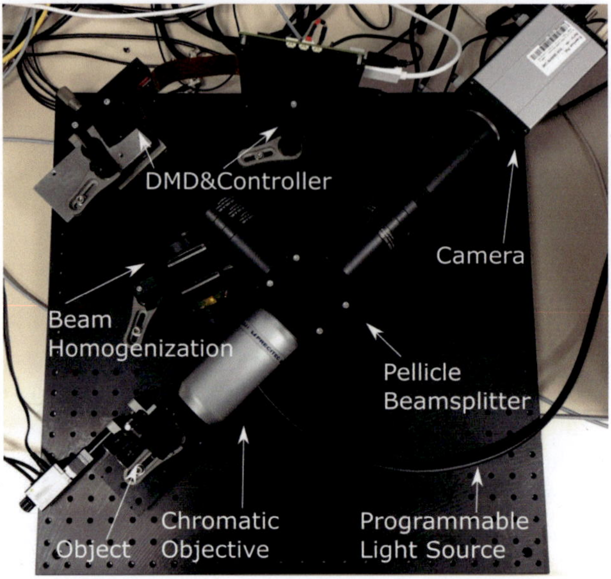

Figure 2.2: Setup of programmable array microscope.

2.2 DMD-based Programmable Array Microscope

In the microscope setup, light coming from the programmable light source is first homogenized and projected onto the DMD, which acts as an array of secondary sources. Illumination light is projected onto the object using an objective (Precitec CLS4) with designed chromatic separation along the optical axis. The reflected light travels through the same objective and is collected by the camera. The sCMOS camera (Andor Zyla 5.5) in the system has very good signal to noise ratio and color depth (dynamic range) but not a very fast speed. As will be later discussed, since the speed of the programmable light and the DMD in the microscope are both very fast, the frame rate of the camera will be a major limiting factor that has to be considered when designing the measurement algorithm. The measurement area is $5.4\,\mathrm{mm}$ by $3.0\,\mathrm{mm}$ laterally and the depth measurement range is $4.6\,\mathrm{mm}$ for a wavelength range of $200\,\mathrm{nm}$.

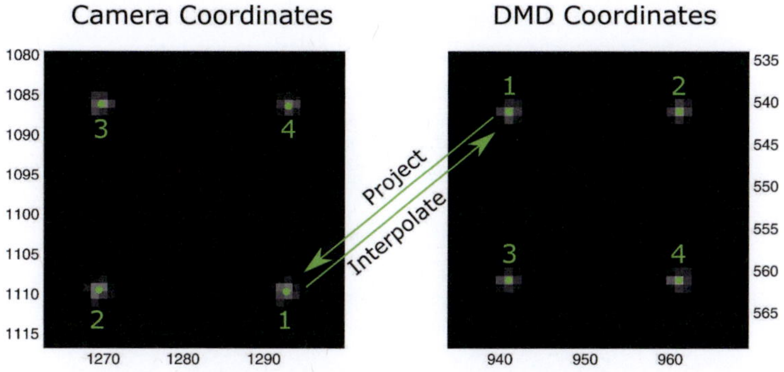

Figure 2.3: Camera calibration for AdaScope.

2.3 Camera Calibration

As a microscope system, the illumination homogenization and projection system, the DMD and the camera arm all have to be aligned very accurately for the confocal principle to work. After the alignment, camera calibration is implemented. Since the system is designed to be telecentric, the camera is only calibrated for one wavelength ($555\,\mathrm{nm}$) where a registration is made between the camera coordinates and the DMD coordinates. The registration toward the object / world coordinate system is not considered at the moment. All measurements with AdaScope shown in this report are in the DMD coordinate system by first projecting the DMD coordinate to the camera coordinate system and then making an interpolation, as shown in Fig. 2.3.

As demonstrated in Fig. 2.4, due to the large NA of the microscopic objective, when a flat mirror serves as the target object, the blurred spot due to defocus covers a large area even at a small distance. The image demonstrates the burred spot when the mirror is located at a distance of $95.25\,\mu\mathrm{m}$ from the focal plane. This corresponds roughly to a wavelength shift of $4\,\mathrm{nm}$ in the chromatic confocal scan. It can be seen that the crosstalk reaches more than a distance of 10 pixels already. To fully suppress the effect of crosstalk, a minimum pitch of 20 pixels is required. To scan through 200 wavelength steps, 80000 frames have to be taken, which costs roughly $0.75\,\mathrm{h}$ of acquisition time. If certain levels of crosstalk can be tolerated, a pitch of 10 pixels can be taken, which leads to an acquisition time of 11 minutes. Even in this case, the speed of measurement still cannot be considered to be practical for real industrial applications.

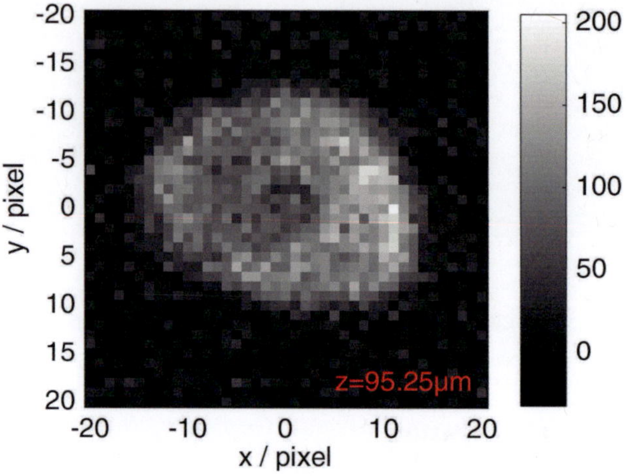

Figure 2.4: Defocus blurring.

3 Adaptive Measurement Method

To further accelerate the speed of area chromatic confocal measurement, an adaptive grid resizing algorithm has been developed. The idea originates from the observation that the uncertainty of the chromatic confocal measurement is in fact coupled with the lateral density of measurement locations, as shown in Fig. 3.1. When little information of the measurement locations is gathered, the crosstalk could potentially be very large and therefore a larger distance between adjacent points is required. As the measurements at each point become more and more accurate, the possibly generated crosstalk also gets smaller which allows for a denser measurement array.

Based on this observation, the measurement is conducted in several iterations. In each iteration, measurements with limited accuracy are made for all positions through array scanning with a fixed pitch distance. Based on the result from one iteration, more refined measurements are made with a denser grid in the next iteration.

3.1 Axial Measurement Refinement

In this iteration, a two-channel linear measurement system is applied to each measurement location. The two measurement functions are two ramp-shaped functions in opposite directions. To measure the axial location of the corresponding chromatic confocal peak, illuminations with spectra in the shape of the measurement functions are applied and the corresponding images are captured. As 1st order Bernstein polynomials, these functions have the nice property that the corresponding linear transformation maintains the centroid of the original signal. Therefore, the centroid of the chromatic confocal peak can be estimated with very fast computation:

$$\mathbf{m} = \begin{bmatrix} m_1 \\ m_2 \end{bmatrix} = \begin{bmatrix} \mathbf{f_1}^T \\ \mathbf{f_2}^T \end{bmatrix} \mathbf{g}$$

$$centroid(\mathbf{g}) = centroid(\mathbf{m}) = \frac{m_2}{m_1 + m_2}$$

where $\mathbf{g}$ represents the original confocal signal, $\mathbf{m}$ denotes the measurement, $\mathbf{f_1}$ and $\mathbf{f_1}$ represent the illumination spectra.

There are several reasons for using such a linear measurement system. Firstly, since more than one iterations are performed, each iteration must be very efficient in terms of the number of frames taken. Secondly, the crosstalk at a fixed distance should be proportional to the measurement range. This means that as the location of the object becomes more certain, the crosstalk should become smaller. Lastly, the uncertainty should be inversely proportional to the measurement range. This means that for a smaller measurement range, the sensitivity should be higher.

All these properties are achieved by iteratively reducing the wavelength range of the illumination according to the previous estimation, such as illustrated by

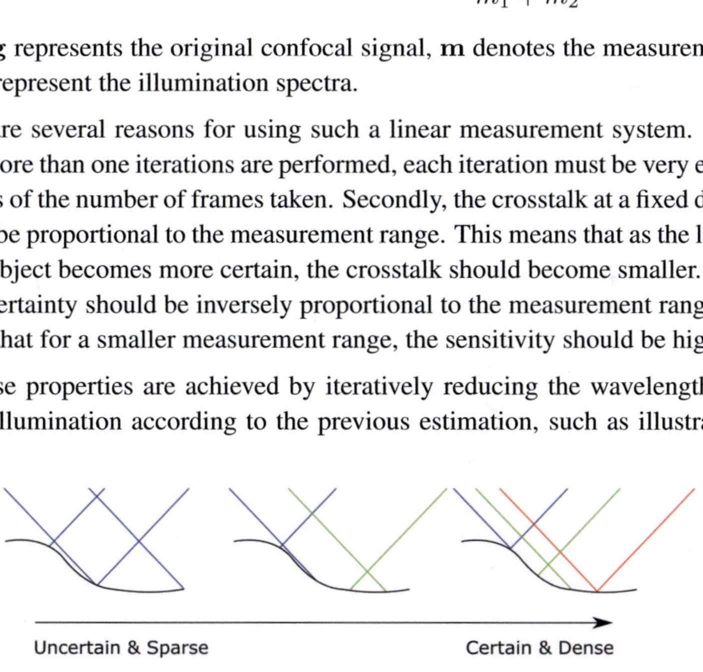

Figure 3.1: Coupling of axial measurement uncertainty and lateral measurement density.

Fig. 3.2. Suppose the position of the object is represented by the arrow. In the first iteration, the camera takes two frames with the two illumination spectra covering the complete wavelength range. Based on estimation result from the first iteration, which is not extremely accurate, the object is determined to be in the top half of the measurement range. In the second iteration, the AdaScope makes measurement in the new measurement range with two similar illumination spectra. This appears to be like a binary search, but if the measurement in each iteration is accurate enough, the search process can be much faster. For example, a direct jump from iteration #1 to iteration #3 will also be possible.

Apparently this method is not very sensitive and is not robust against the noise due to the limited number of linear measurement channels, but it should be sufficient to bound the measurement range to a certain level for the next iteration.

3.2 Lateral Grid Condensation

As mentioned previously, in each iteration, the measurement density is also increased accordingly. As shown by the example in Fig, 3.3, in iteration #1 with a pitch of 20 pixels, grid has to be scanned 20 by 20 times, and in each time, the system makes two measurements using the corresponding illumination spectra. In the next iteration, the density of the grid can be increased depending on how much the new measurement range is bounded.

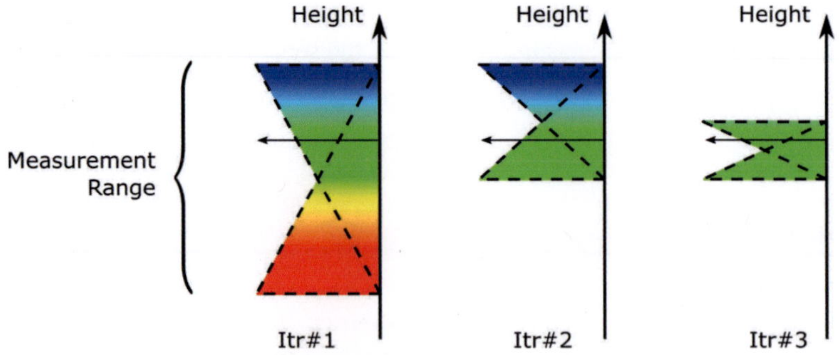

Figure 3.2: Iterative refinement of axial measurement.

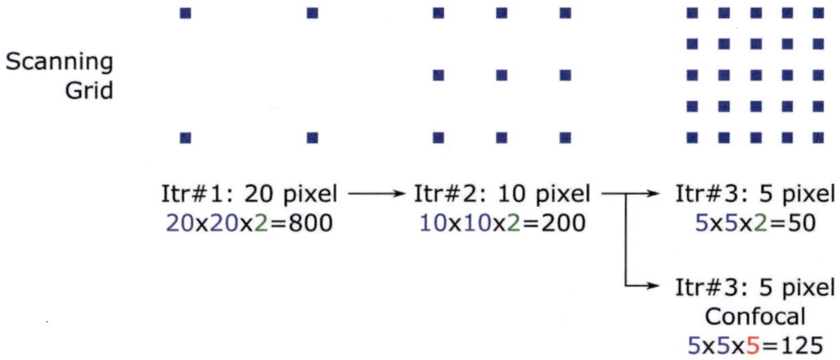

Figure 3.3: Iterative condensation of lateral grid.

At a certain iteration, based on the estimation uncertainty from previous iteration, the measurement process can be switched to a localized chromatic confocal measurement centered around the previous estimation result, in order to get more accurate measurement result.

3.3 Hardware Triggering

As an example, the triggering diagram for the second iteration as well as the corresponding illumination spectra are illustrated in Fig. 3.4. Since the camera is the slowest component, it serves as the master which triggers the spectral DMD in the programmable light source. This DMD displays several patterns corresponding to several illumination spectra. Each spectral DMD patterns triggers its corresponding spatial DMD pattern in the microscope. Based on estimation from the first iteration, all points are already bounded to either the top half or the bottom half of the complete measurement range. For each measurement grid, two frames are captured. Within each frame, two spectra are projected to two different spatial patterns. In the second frame, the spatial patterns are repeated but the spectra are different. This process is then repeated pitch^2 times for complete measurement of this iteration.

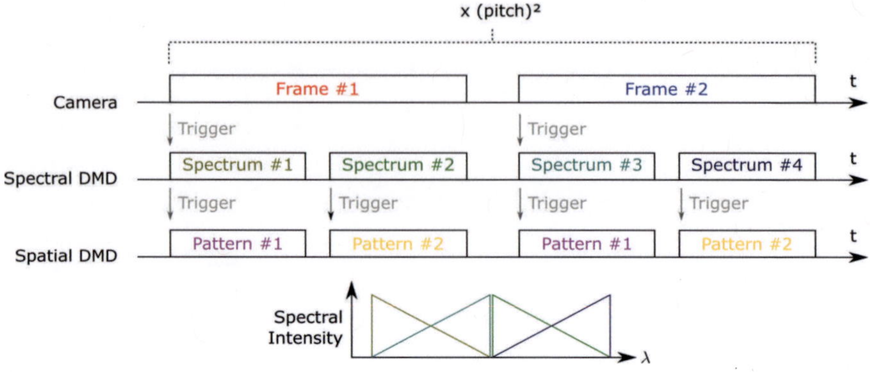

Figure 3.4: Exemplary triggering diagram of iteration #2.

4 Experiment and Analysis

To investigate the feasibility of this adaptive measurement method, a test measurement is conducted with a one euro coin serving as the target. For proof of concept, the wavelength range is limited to $530\,\mathrm{nm}$ to $580\,\mathrm{nm}$, which corresponds to a measurement range of $1.15\,\mathrm{mm}$.

For the adaptive scan, in each iteration, two images are captured with different illumination spectra and spatial patterns. Fig. 4.1 shows the raw measurement data from the first iteration with their corresponding illumination spectra. It can be seen that the image with first illumination spectrum is much brighter than the second one. This indicates that the centroid of the chromatic confocal peak is closer to the focus position of $530\,\mathrm{nm}$.

After the first iteration, a rough estimation of the height can be performed based on the two-channel linear measurement principle, which is then binarized into two levels. As can be seen in Fig. 4.2, for most of the area, the height lies in the upper half of the current measurement range.

After the second iteration with a denser grid, more accurate estimation is performed, which generate four measurement range divisions (Fig. 4.3).

After iteration #2, the system directly makes localized chromatic confocal measurement with five wavelength steps with a step size of $1\,\mathrm{nm}$. These five steps are centered around the estimation result from iteration #2. In this iteration, the pitch is further reduced to 5 pixels. As shown in Fig. 4.4, estimation of the height and the intensity (texture) is performed through Gaussian fitting on the localized measurements.

Although the overall estimation is correct, there are apparent artifacts all across the measurement area. The major reason for this kind of artifact is the inaccurate estimation result before the localized chromatic scanning. Since the iteration of the localized scan is initialized based on previous estimation, when the starting point is already too far away from the actual chromatic peak, two adverse effects could happen. On one hand, the five wavelength scanning steps are not enough to cover the peak position of the chromatic confocal signal. On the other hand, when the scanning wavelength steps are too far from the peak, the generated crosstalk for the adjacent locations will no longer be tolerable for the selected pitch distance of the measurement grid. To avoid such artifacts, more accurate estimation from the linear measurement stage must be achieved in order to correctly initialize the localized chromatic scanning, which will be the key part in future research.

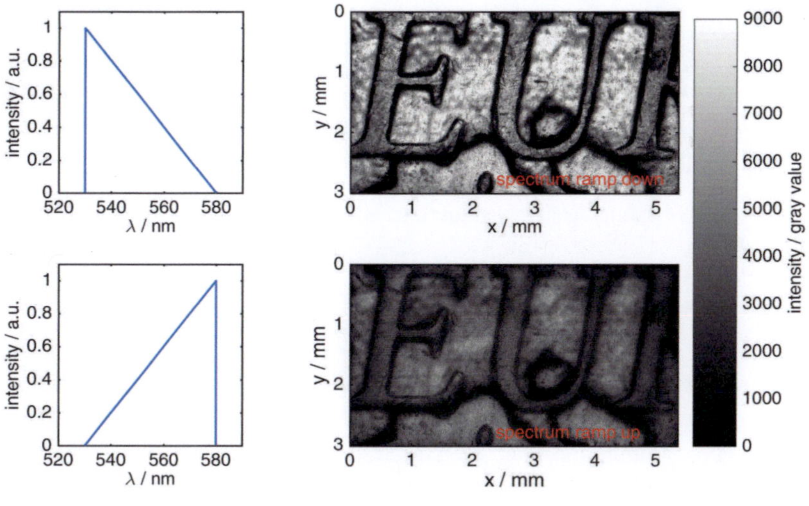

Figure 4.1: Illumination spectra (left) and raw measurements (right) from iteration #1.

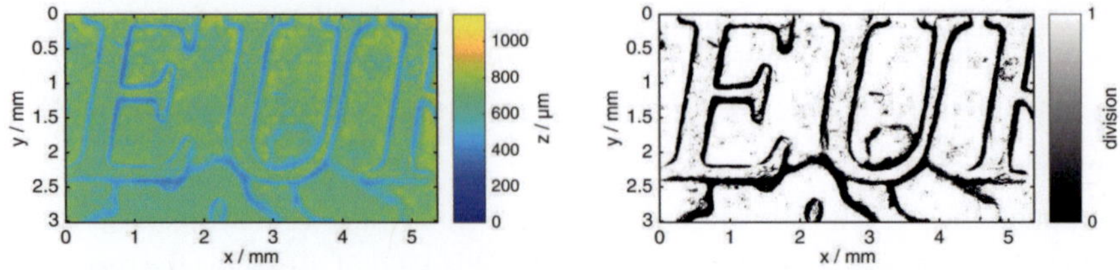

Figure 4.2: Estimation (left) and binarized levels (right) from iteration #1.

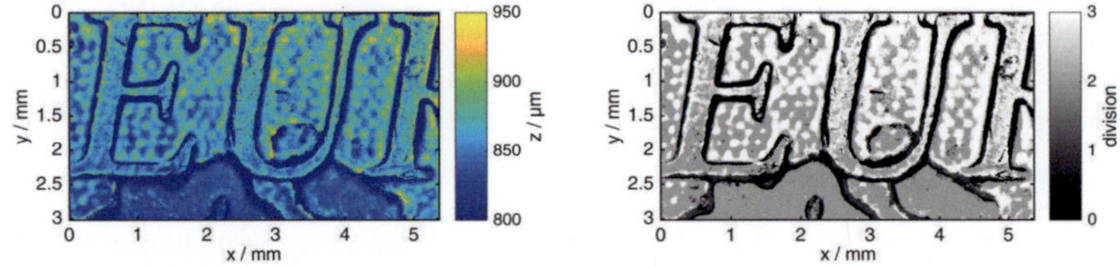

Figure 4.3: Estimation (left) and binarized levels (right) from iteration #2.

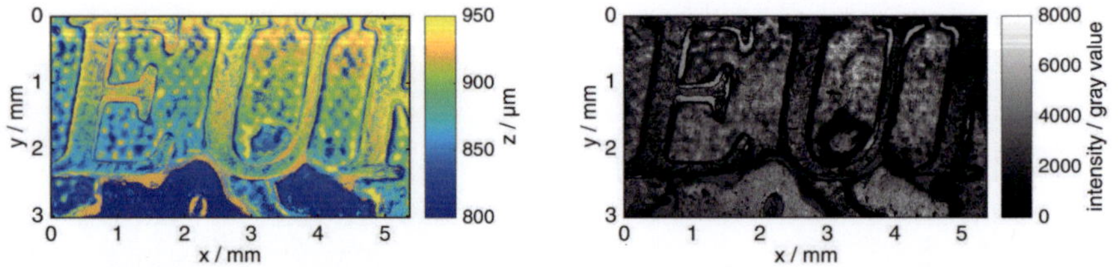

Figure 4.4: Height estimation (left) and intensity (right) from iteration #3.

5 Conclusion

This report presents a novel approach to the problem of area chromatic confocal microscopy. The hardware setup consists of two fundamental components. One part is a programmable light source based on a white light laser. The other part is a DMD-based programmable array chromatic confocal microscope. The combination of both, namely the AdaScope, provides an adaptive platform which can be utilized for 3D measurement of reflective/defusing samples. An adaptive measurement method is developed based on this system setup, which iteratively improves the axial measurement uncertainty and lateral measurement density. Although initial experimental investigation has revealed certain artifacts in the measurement result mainly due to inaccuracy in the linear measurement iterations, it is believed that such approach has great potential in increasing the measurement speed compared to a naive fixed grid scanning. This could lead to applications of the area chromatic confocal measurement technology in real industrial settings.

Acknowledgement Research conducted in this report is financed by the Baden-Württemberg Stiftung gGmbH.

Bibliography

[CRS15] Nadya Chakrova, Bernd Rieger, and Sjoerd Stallinga. Development of a DMD-based fluorescence microscope. *Proc. SPIE*, 9330:9330–9330–11, 2015.

[CS17] Ting-Jui Chang and Guo-Dung J. Su. A confocal microscope with programmable aperture arrays by polymer-dispersed liquid crystal. *Proc. SPIE*, 10376:10376–10376–7, 2017.

[EP67] M. David Egger and Mojmir Petran. New reflected-light microscope for viewing unstained brain and ganglion cells. *Science*, 157(3786):305–307, 1967.

[HCT+07] Guy M. Hagen, Wouter Caarls, Martin Thomas, Andrew Hill, Keith A. Lidke, Bernd Rieger, Cornelia Fritsch, Bert van Geest, Thomas M. Jovin, and Donna J. Arndt-Jovin. Biological applications of an LCoS-based programmable array microscope (PAM). *Proc. SPIE*, 6441:6441–6441–12, 2007.

[HO15] Shinichi Hayashi and Yasushi Okada. Ultrafast superresolution fluorescence imaging with spinning disk confocal microscope optics. *Molecular Biology of the Cell*, 26(9):1743–1751, 2015.

[HVG+99] Q. S. Hanley, P. J. Verveer, M. J. Gemkow, D. Arndt-Jovin, and T. M. Jovin. An optical sectioning programmable array microscope implemented with a digital micromirror device. *Journal of Microscopy*, 196(3):317–331, 1999.

[KDP+14] Sharon V. King, Ana Doblas, Nurmohammed Patwary, Genaro Saavedra, Manuel Martínez-Corral, and Chrysanthe Preza. Implementation of PSF engineering in high-resolution 3D microscopy imaging with a LCoS (reflective) SLM. *Proc. SPIE*, 8949:8949–8949–7, 2014.

[LTLB17] Ding Luo, Miro Taphanel, Thomas Längle, and Jürgen Beyerer. Programmable light source based on an echellogram of a supercontinuum laser. *Applied Optics*, 56(8):2359–2367, 2017.

Deterministic Industrial Network Communication: Fundamentals

Ankush Meshram

Vision and Fusion Laboratory
Institute for Anthropomatics
Karlsruhe Institute of Technology (KIT), Germany
ankush.meshram@kit.edu

Technical Report IES-2017-04

Abstract: Industrial networks came into existence with the third industrial revolution to support manufacturing and automation. Over the years, there has been technical advancement in different aspects of networking technologies in order to make production and governing automation efficient and intelligent. This also brought along advancing threats leading to the need of advancements in counterattacking or prevention methods. However, to contribute in challenging the Advanced Persistent Threats (APTs) the understanding of the fundamentals of industrial communication is needed. Determinism is at the core of automation, hence this report comprehends various literature sources on the industrial network communication strategies to achieve deterministic industrial network communication.

1 Introduction

Networks have become an integral part of manufacturing over the years replacing point-to-point communications at all levels. At lower levels in factory infrastructure, networks provide higher reliability, visibility and diagnosability and enable capabilities such as distributed control, diagnostics, safety and device interoperability. At higher levels, networks can leverage Internet services to enable factory-wide automated scheduling, control, and improve data storage and visibility. Industrial networks were introduced considering varying requirements of factory automation, distributed process control, home automation, and of critical

Infrastructures such as energy distribution as well as transportation. Appropriate networking technology evolved simultaneously within the application field. The three major influences identified for industrial network evolution [Zur14] are:

- Communication engineering for data transmission over large telephone networks in telecommunication sector.
- Instrumentation and measurements systems with parallel buses to account for limited data processing speed and real-time requirements for synchronization.
- Computer science with high-level communication protocol designs, such as WANs and LANs, leading to gradual change of analog to digital systems in telecommunication sector.

Fieldbus systems were the landmark in industrial networks evolution for automation, which replaced traditional expensive point-to-point cabling of devices to central control room. It brought concepts of decentralization, modularity to extend installations, and communication between intelligent devices, capable of data preprocessing, for transferring process data, and parameterization and configuration purposes. The idea of computer-integrated manufacturing (CIM) comprehended the structure of information flow required for automation in a hierarchical model — to create a transparent, multilevel network — called automation pyramid [SSKD11]. It comprised of 5 or more levels, in order of lowest level at the bottom to highest level at top: Field level (sensor/actuator), Process level (Programmable Logical Controller (PLC), Human Machine Interface (HMI), Cell level (Operator station), Factory level (Manufacturing execution systems (MES)), Company level (Enterprise resource planning (ERP)). Fieldbuses populated the field, process and cell levels while bridging the gap between lower levels which traditionally consisted of point-to-point connections to higher level networks. The distinction between lower level and higher level networks of the automation pyramid is maintained by fieldbus systems. The popularity of Ethernet as the LAN technology in automation and its penetration of all levels of this pyramid to process level is likely to replace mid-level fieldbus systems. Industrial Ethernet is resulted in reduction of the levels in the automation hierarchy, and ultimately to flattening out of pyramid to at most three or two levels.

In further sections, first we will build on communication fundamentals to understand industrial communication paradigms. This is followed by section 3 on relation between industrial communication and determinism. In section 4, we elaborate on the foundations of deterministic industrial protocols and ending the report with short summary.

2 Fundamentals of Industrial Communication

2.1 Communication Layers

Introduction of the ISO/open system interconnection (OSI) seven-layers reference model for data communication has been the foundation for development of complex communication protocols [Zim80, DZ83] (Figure 2.1). There are three important concepts to understand before dwelling into layers:

1. *Protocol*, is a set of rules and convention that communication layer N of open system must confer to communicate with layer N of another open system. Rule sets of each layer define the respective layer protocol.
2. *Service*, defines the functionality of services offered by one layer (service provider) to layer above it (service user). The OSI model doesn't enforce the way services are implemented.
3. *Interface*, specifies interface between layers with services offered by the lower layer to the upper layer. It also defines access methods with parameters and what results to expect.

An application system sends information to another system through packaging data at top layer and requesting services of layer below to transmit data, repeating until lowest layer. On the way down the layers, the data of the application process are augmented by layer-specific data needed to execute the respective protocols. These data are typically address and control information that is mostly combined in a protocol header. In addition, the data may be segmented into individual packets to match the allowed maximum packet size for a given layer. This way, the number of bits being actually transmitted can be significantly larger than the pure user data provided by the application process,and the communication overhead can be substantial. The receiving system strips additional information of the peer layer to recover data for the application process. The layers of the OSI model, bottom-up, are briefly described next.

- Layer 1, or Physical Layer, presents all mechanical, physical, optical, electrical, and logical properties of the communication system to upper layers necessary for transferring data frames.
- Layer 2, or Data Link Layer, is responsible for data frame formation from bits with frame's coding and checking for transmission errors (via Cyclic Redundancy Check). It is subdivided into the logical link control (LLC) and medium access control (MAC). LLC takes care of error detection mechanism and sets up the connection to layer 3. MAC links to layer 1 and controls who is able to transmit when.
- Layer 3, or Network Layer, establishes routing paths between origin and destination nodes of end-to-end connections while assigning special target addresses. The transmission paths are optimized to reduce congestion in the presence of multiple physical transmission mediums with varying transmission speeds and not exceed maximum allowed delay.
- Layer 4, or Transport Layer, sets up the end-to-end connection and splits up the data in small numbered packets whenever either the data size is too big or transmission times are long. The peer layer on the receiving system takes care of recombining the individual packets in the right order.
- Layer 5, or Session Layer, synchronizes the communication between participating systems while handling the authentication and identification of devices. To perform its synchronization task effectively it introduces any synchronization markers to resume after communication breakdown.
- Layer 6, or Presentation Layer, codes the transmitting data and its interpretation on the receiving system. It interprets the syntactic bit sequence of data into a character and its semantic meaning, such as currency or physical units.
- Layer 7, or Application Layer, provides the interface between the application and the communication unit for transparent representation of communication. It defines the procedures or protocol processes of various application functions for calling up data, file transfer, etc. It is designed in such a way that a system accesses information through its communication unit without the need to know the functions of underlying layers.

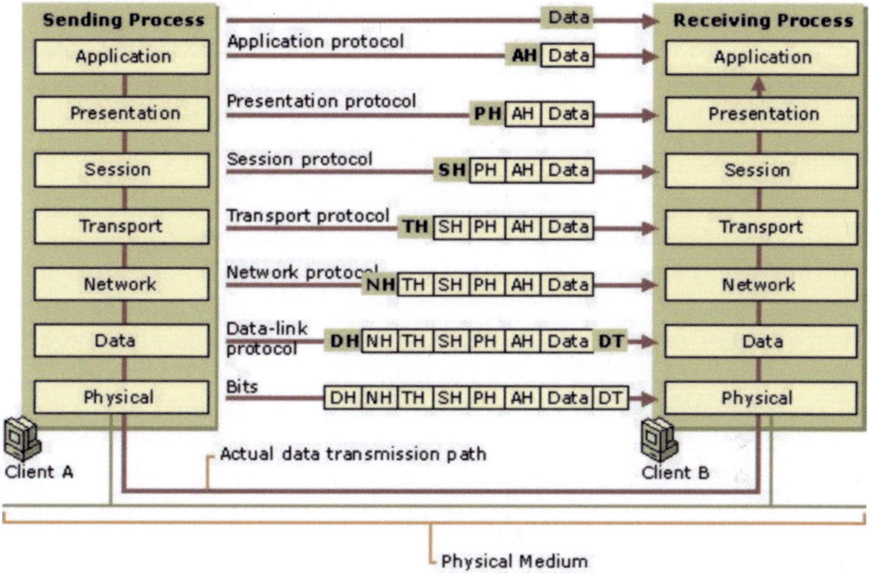

Figure 2.1: ISO/OSI stack with frame headers [Shi12].

Following the hierarchical OSI model, it is possible to set up complex communication system between heterogeneous systems on different layers. Through the use of repeaters, one can overcome the limitations of a given physical layer. The interconnecting devices share a common data link layer. Bridges interconnect different networks by translating data and protocols on layer 3. Routers link networks on layer 4, whereas gateways (especially, application layer gateways) interconnect entirely different communication systems on the application layer.

2.2 Communication Types and Services

Two distinct techniques are used in data communications to transfer data – connection-oriented and connection-less [Zim80]. A connection-oriented method (virtual circuit service) requires a session connection be established before any data can be sent. This method guarantees that data will arrive in the same order. Connection-less method (datagram service) doesn't require a session connection between sender and receiver. There is no guaranteed data arrival however it is useful for periodic burst transfers. TCP (Transmission Control Protocol) is a connection-oriented transport protocol, while UDP (User Datagram Protocol) is a connectionless network protocol, both operating over IP at the Transport Layer.

The interface between neighboring service provider and service user layers is called service access point (SAP). The user data of layer N to be sent across the network for its peer layer is encoded as service data unit (SDU) and passed on to lower layers in the hierarchy for further processing. The communication between two peer layers is governed by the rule sets (protocol) that can only be understood by them. This information is added to SDU with interface control information (ICI) and protocol control information (PCI) to form a cohesive protocol data unit (PDU).

There are four primitive operations through which interaction between layers occur – Request, req, Indication, ind; Confirmation, con; and Response, res. Service user layer invokes request and response while resulting confirmation and indication originate from corresponding service provider. The combination of these primitive operations can be categorized into 3 major service categories – unconfirmed service, confirmed service, and acknowledged service. The unconfirmed and confirmed service comprise of a request, an indication and a confirmation, whereas acknowledged service comprise all the operations.

2.3 Communication Mechanisms

The multitude of application domains of automation systems have different timing and consistency requirements which varies too within the application areas such as manufacturing, process automation, etc [Tho05].

The timing behavior of a technical process can be conceptualized as either state-based or event-based. In the state-based approach, the status of internal state variables (temperature, pressure) of the process are continuously sampled and transmitted in discrete-time for continuous process control and monitoring. The event-based approach transmits data only when the process state changes and are well-suited for discrete processes or subprocesses which can be modeled as a state machine.

The traffic in industrial networks could be periodic or aperiodic based on how often process data is accessed. Periodic, or cyclic, traffic follows time-slot-communication strategy where each state variable is assigned a dedicated slot in the available bandwidth based on the a priori information of its data generation rate or sampling time. The update rate in a periodic traffic is usually dynamic adapting to the sampling rate demand of current process state information and the data exchange is connection-less. The periodic data is handled through buffers following the FIFO (first-in-first-out) structure where older values are overwritten by latest data. Aperiodic, or acyclic, traffic is generated on demand in an event-based manner and transmitted when free communication bandwidth is available or idle time is reserved between time slots of periodic traffic. Aperiodic data is connection-oriented where acknowledgment is used to allow for re-transmission of lost configuration data. Queues handle aperiodic data where messages are not overwritten and no new data is accepted when the queue is full.

Based on the consistency of accessing information in automation systems, the traffic data can be classified as continuously updated process data and on-demand parameterization data. The process data are real-time data and could be periodic or aperiodic requiring strict delivery timing to be meaningful for process control. The process data in the events of transmission errors could be reconstructed from historical data via interpolation. However, aperiodic process data additionally requires that no data lass occurs or atleast detected in due time through appropriate mechanisms. The parameterization, or configuration, data are non-real-time and usually aperiodic though session information, authentication information or updated communication parameters are transmitted periodically or quasi-periodically. The configuration data contains necessary information to set up or adjust the operation of automation system and needs guaranteed consistent delivery across the system.

2.4 Network Topologies

The star topology was the default wiring structure in automation before fieldbus was introduced. The PLC is at the center connected to I/O elements individually. The line, or bus, topology evolved as most efficient replacement to star-like point-to-point cabling and was quickly adapted network topology. The nodes are all connected in one single line. In the ring topology, nodes are arranged one after another in the form of a chain where each nodes has two independent interfaces for input and output. It is very fast and deterministic method to exchange data with low jitter (variance of time delay) as nodes don't need explicit addressing. A variant of the ring topology is daisy-chain structure where nodes are cascaded like a string of pearls. In the tree topology, nodes are arranged in hierarchical composite network structure where each node could be a root for a lower-level segment. The root nodes usually have routing capabilities, so that the data traffic can at least partly be confined to individual areas of the network. In the mesh networks, there exists multiple paths between nodes through the network. It requires appropriate routing strategies to keep messages from circling in the network and causing congestion.

2.5 Medium Access Control

The topology being used by the networking technology influences the selection of the medium access control (MAC) method, or vice versa [Zur14].

The data transfer mechanism can be classified into two – single-master (or master-slave) and multimaster. In the single-master approach follows centralized communication architecture where the master either retrieves data from its slaves following request-response communication or synchronizes time slots with slaves to send their data. Such networks are usually single-segment structures with limited size and found at lowest levels of automation pyramid. Within the multimaster approach, participating nodes have equal rights over the communication medium and share it in a democratic way. These networks are found on the middle level of automation pyramid.

Time division multiple access (TDMA) is the actual MAC strategy used over multiplexing methods such as frequency division multiple access (FDMA), code division multiple access (CDMA), or space division multiple access (SDMA) for industrial communication. In TDMA, the network nodes shares the bandwidth and communicate sequentially. The basic methods of multiple access follows either centralized approach by polling or time-slot-based techniques, or in decentralized way by token passing or random access methods.

Polling is a master-slave mechanism where a slave node sends information only when explicitly called upon by the master node. In the network, alternate poll messages from master to each of its slave and responses from them is observed. Polling is strictly cyclic where the master polls all the slaves sequentially and restarts the cycle. It's cyclic behavior suits well for periodic traffic where process variables are polled equidistantly. Polling polls data data either by explicit node addressing or process variable identifier irrespective of device generating the values. The later variant is also called as central polling. Strict polling doesn't offer functionality for aperiodic traffic and slaves cannot become active themselves to send event of an alarm condition. However, there exist alternate mechanisms to rectify these disadvantages.

Time-slot-based method divides available transmission time on the medium into distinct slots where slaves access the medium at its assigned time slot. The cyclic polling in its essence too partitions the polling cycle into time windows, however in time-slot-based method slaves can send the data themselves without a request from central master. Time-slot-based methods are mostly referred as TDMA. Synchronous TDMA equally distributes time slots whereas asynchronous TDMA dynamically distributes time slot according to amount of data to be sent. Aperiodic traffic is accommodated between the cyclic time slots. Based on the mechanism incorporated to synchronize slots there are two variants of TDMA – centralized and decentralized. In the centralized approach, a dedicated master sends some sort of synchronization message at the start of the cycle followed by nodes exchanging data in their pre-assigned time slots. On the contrary, in the decentralized approach all the nodes synchronizes themselves without explicit node to initiate cycle. Either explicit clock synchronization mechanisms or set of timers that set operation to a stable state state are used by the nodes.

Token Passing (TP) method of medium access is based on a special piece of information, called token, passed on between peer network nodes and only the node possessing it can initiate the data transfer. A set of rules ensure its fairness and its detection when lost or duplicated. Compared to time-slot mechanisms, when a node possessing the token doesn't have any data to send it passes the token on to the next node thus saving time. TP can be implemented either explicitly through a dedicated short message or implicitly through distributed, synchronized access counters (ACs) included in all nodes. The explicit form of TP uses target token rotation time (T_{tr}) to enforce the maximum time duration to posses the token. The implicit TP uses two counters, ACs and Idle Bus Bit Period Counter (IC), included in every master to simulate the token.

Another peer-to-peer communication based medium access method is random access where a network node tries to access the communication medium whenever it wants to without any imposition. This is also called carrier sense multiple access (CSMA). However, the major drawback of this approach is collisions when several nodes try to send data at same time, even if they noticed idle communication line before sending. The variants of CSMA deals with collisions in different ways to avoid bandwidth wastage and communication delays. In CSMA-CD (collision detection), collisions are detected by sending nodes which aborts the data transfer and wait for a random time before trying to send again. In p-persistent CSMA variant , the waiting time depends on the value of probability (p) that the node will try again in a certain time interval after collision. The probability of each node is adaptable to the estimation on its backlog and the monitored network load. The widely used CSMA-CA (collision avoidance) variant uses asymmetric symbols for coding the bits on the communication line, so that when two different bits are sent at a time, the dominant one wins over the recessive one. It is also called CSMA-BA (bitwise arbitration).

2.6 Communication Paradigms

There are 2 basic communication paradigms governing the information exchange between two or more network entities [Zur14]. The first approach is built upon the cooperation of actions or functions into which more complex process can be decomposed. This paradigm is called client-server, where the responsibility to interpret information lies with the sender. The service or data providing entity is called server, and the service requesting entity is called client. The server becomes active only when its services are requested by the client, hence this paradigm suits well for state-based traffic handled in some scheduled manner.

The other approach concentrates on exchanged data rather than actions and the responsibility of its interpretation lies with the receiver. The publisher-subscriber and producer-consumer paradigms follows the data-oriented approach. In the publisher-subscriber paradigm, the information is produced by the publisher and mulicasts on the network to be listened by the subscribers. The producer-consumer model is similar to the publisher-subscriber and only differs in broadcast communication of information. There are two variants of publisher-subscriber models based on how the information exchange is initiated – pull-type, the publishing action is triggered by a centralized publishing manager,

	Client-Server	Producer-Consumer	Publisher-Subscriber
Communication relation	*Peer-to-peer*	*Broadcast*	*Multicast*
Communication type	*Connection-oriented*	*Connection-less*	*Connection-less*
Communication service	*Confirmed,unconfirmed, acknowledged*	*Unconfirmed, acknowledged*	*Unconfirmed, acknowledged*
MAC type	*Mono-master(polling, centralized TDMA), multimaster (CSMA, TDMA or Token Passing)*	*Multimaster (TDMA, centralized polling or random access)*	*Multimaster (TDMA, centralized polling or random access)*
Application class	*Parameter transfer, cyclic communication*	*Event notification, alarms, error, synchronization*	*State changes, event-oriented signal sources (eg. switches)*

Table 2.1: Properties of Communication Paradigms

and push-type, publishers become active themselves without centralized manager triggered by a timer or an event. Interestingly, in order for the subscription of the subscribers to correct communication group or multicast group the client-server-type communication is used.

The properties of these three communication paradigms are summarized in Table 2.1 [TMV95].

3 Industrial Networks and Determinism

The technical selection of networks for a particular application revolves around evaluating and balancing quality of service (QoS) parameters. Two parameters which are evaluated to find the balance between network components competing for limited bandwidth and time to deliver information between end components are network average speed and determinism. Network speed is a function of network access time and bit transfer rate. On the other hand, determinism is a measure of the ability to communicate data consistently from end to end within a guaranteed time. The MAC component of network protocols defines the mechanism for delegating network bandwidth for optimized communication (eg. large packets with low determinism vs small packets with high determinism).

The basic QoS measures of industrial networks incorporates the speed and bandwidth of a network (i.e. how much data can be transmitted in a time interval), the delay and jitter associated with data transmission (time for a message to reach its destination and repeatability of this time), and the reliability and security of the network infrastructure.

The bandwidth of an industrial network is the number of bits that can be transmitted per second. The Ethernet-based industrial networks support data rates of 100 Mb/s or 1 Gb/s. The speed is the inverse of the data rate, thus the time to transmit 1 bit of data over the network, T_{bit} = 10 ns for 100 Mb/s Ethernet. The transmission time for a message on the network can be computed from the network's data rate, the message size and the distance between two nodes. It is considered a deterministic time in a network system. The transmission time (T_{tx}) can be written as the sum of the frame time and the propagation time:

$$T_{tx} = T_{frame} + T_{prop}.$$

Where, T_{frame} is the time required to send the packet across the network, and T_{prop} is the time for a message to propagate between any two devices.

The typical transmission speed in a communication medium is 2 x 10^8 m/s which means the propagation time T_{prop} is negligible, for example, T_{prop} = 67.2 μs for 2500 m Ethernet. The frame time (T_{frame}) depends on the size (in bytes) of data/message (N_{data}), the overhead (N_{ovhd}), padding used to meet minimum frame size requirement (N_{pad}), and the bit time (T_{bit}). Some protocols need extra bytes based on the bit-stuffing mechanism they use (N_{stuff}). The frame time can be expressed as:

$$T_{frame} = [N_{data} + N_{ovhd} + N_{pad} + N_{stuff}] \times 8 \times T_{bit}.$$

A network's time delay is defined as the total time between the sampled or computed data being available at source node and it being received and decoded at the destination node. The jitter is the variability in the delay. Many techniques have been developed to handle constant time delays however large variability in time delays is difficult to compensate for. The total time delay (T_{delay}) depends on the preprocessing time taken at the source node for data encapsulation and encoding (T_{pre}), waiting time of the node when network is busy (T_{wait}), transmission time to send data across the network (T_{tx}) and the postprocessing time of the received data at the destination node for data decoding and postprocessing (T_{post}). T_{wait} is a function of the MAC mechanism of the protocol and can be computed based on network traffic, how many nodes are there, the relative priority of these nodes and the messages they are sending, and how much data they send. T_{pre} and T_{post} depend on the device and can be major sources of delay and jitter in a network. In an equation form, the total time delay is:

$$T_{delay} = T_{pre} + T_{wait} + T_{tx} + T_{post}.$$

The reliability of data transmission medium in a network gets affected by electromagnetic interference resulting in data corruption. To increase the reliability handshaking mechanism can be used. Acknowledgment messages (ACK) are sent between the devices to confirm the data delivery. If no ACK is received, the data is resent. However, the handshaking techniques increases the required overhead and thus decreasing the overall effective bandwidth.

Security of networked systems is another concern as the networks and operating systems are vulnerable to Internet-based attacks and viruses. Most industrial fieldbuses were not designed to be highly secure and relied on the principle of “security by obscurity” instead of authentication or encryption techniques. The intent of incorporating security in the network is usually to prevent misuse of process data than counteracting network attacks. Firewalls are installed to prevent unknown traffic from entering the network and for secure encrypted transmission virtual private network (VPN) is used. In the recent years, there has been vast progress in development of intrusion detection/prevention systems (IDS/IPS) to handle increasingly complex attacks [DNVHC05, ZJS11, McM17, BG16].

4 Industrial Communication Protocols

The first implementation of the full ISO/OSI seven-layer stack was manufacturing automation protocol (MAP) developed as a framework for the comprehensive control of industrial processes covering all automation levels. However, its complexity made implementations costly and unjustifiable for general-purpose.

Learned from the failure of MAP, further automation protocols stack was reduced and layers were combined based on the domain requirements for simplicity [GH+13] (Figure 4.1). The Internet is governed by protocols based on fully functional TCP/IP stack consisting only physical, network, transport and application layers. The IEC 61158 fieldbus standard reduced model (EPA) consists of only three layers — physical, data-link and application. Many fieldbuses are single-segment networks with limited where routing functionality and end-to-end control is not necessary. Thus, network and transport layer are removed. Also, fieldbuses were not designed for sophisticated tasks hence session and presentation layers are also not needed. However, when the layer 3 and layer 4 functions are needed they can be placed either in layer 2 or layer 7. Furthermore, layer 7 always covers layer 5 and 6 functionality.

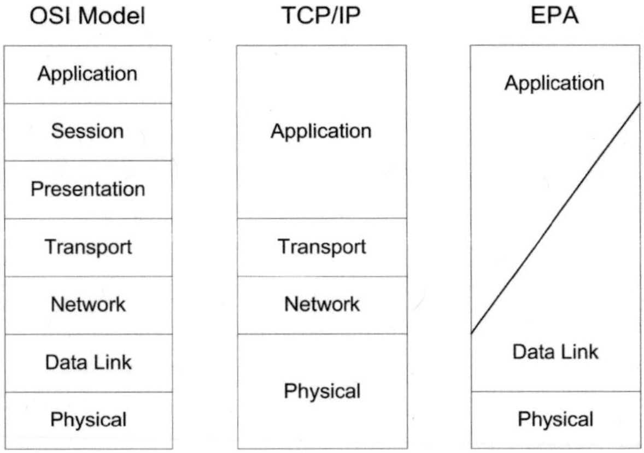

Figure 4.1: Reduced ISO/OSI stack comparison [GH+13].

As discussed earlier, Ethernet has penetrated the automation network. However, the office Ethernet didn't support deterministic capabilities hence couldn't be used for lower levels of automation pyramid. Collisions can occur on the network, and messages must be retransmitted after random amounts of time. To address this inherent nondeterminism, many different flavors of Ethernet were proposed for use in industrial automation. An effective solution in recent years has been the utilization of switches to manage the Ethernet bandwidth utilizing TDMA approach among time-critical nodes giving rise to switched Ethernet.

Switching technology does eliminate collisions, but delays inside the switches and lost packets under heavy load conditions are unavoidable also with switches. The hard real-time requirements of drive controls can't be made through these industrial Ethernet solutions. This led to development of Real Time Ethernet (RTE) standard IEC 61784.

For different application domains there are different RT performance requirements which require different implementations to achieve determinism. RTE implementations are all based on the TCP/IP model (Figure 4.2) and can be classified based on transmission time [Dec05] as follows:

- A low-speed class for human control with transmission time around 100 ms. This timing requirement is typical for the case of humans involved in the system observation, for engineering and for process monitoring. This requirement may be fulfilled with the use of Ethernet cabling and TCP and UDP for non-RT communications. This approach is called 'on top of IP' where the application layer is responsible for scheduling communication to meet the requirements. It is possible to communicate over network boundaries transparently. However, such communication introduce non-deterministic delays and the scheduling device must be equipped with adequate resources. The industrial protocols Modbus/TCP and EtherNet/IP are based on this RTE implementation.

- In the second class, for process control, the transmission time requirement is below 10 ms. This is a requirement for most tooling machine control system like PLCs. To reach this timing behavior, modification of the TCP/IP stack may be done only at the application level to use standard data packets and the transport level may be modified to use custom ethertypes for real-time communications. This approach is 'on top of Ethernet' where custom ethertypes are defined in the Ethernet frame alongside standard types such as IP. The network components and connected devices must have the knowledge of the custom protocols. Often the custom ethertypes will be given dedicated bandwidth or priority within the network. Ethernet Powerlink is the widely popular protocol within this approach-based protocols.

- The last and most demanding class is imposed by motion controls requiring a cycle time less than 1 ms with jitter not more than 1 μs. This can

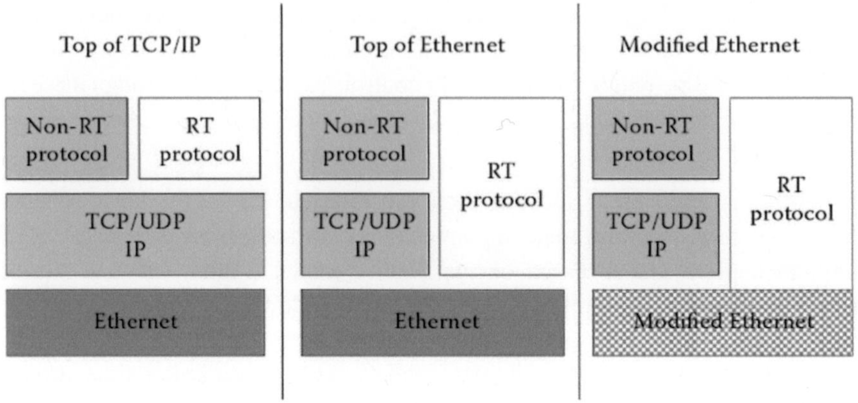

Figure 4.2: RTE implementations.

only be reached when the Ethernet data-link layer is may be modified to apply mechanisms and infrastructure that allow for real-time communication. This approach is called 'modified Ethernet' which enables non-standard topologies such as rings or buses to be implemented. To enable these topologies, the switching functionality is integrated inside the field device. The modifications are mandatory for all devices inside the RT segment but allow non-RTE traffic to be transmitted without modifications. Certain variants of PROFINET (Ethertype 0x8892), EtherCAT (Ethertype 0x88A4) and SERCOS (Ethertype 0x88CD) protocol types follow this approach to provide 1 ms transmission time requiring customized hardware.

5 Summary

This report outlined how industrial communication paradigms differ w.r.t. various communication fundamentals. The important aspect of Quality of Service (QoS) and related parameters were discussed in brief. At the end, we looked at why and how OSI/ISO model is reduced for automation system requirements, and the approaches based on the TCP/IP model for Real Time Ethernet implementations.

Bibliography

[BG16] Anna L Buczak and Erhan Guven. A survey of data mining and machine learning methods for cyber security intrusion detection. *IEEE Communications Surveys & Tutorials*, 18(2):1153–1176, 2016.

[Dec05] J-D Decotignie. Ethernet-based real-time and industrial communications. *Proceedings of the IEEE*, 93(6):1102–1117, 2005.

[DNVHC05] Dacfey Dzung, Martin Naedele, Thomas P Von Hoff, and Mario Crevatin. Security for industrial communication systems. *Proceedings of the IEEE*, 93(6):1152–1177, 2005.

[DZ83] John D Day and Hubert Zimmermann. The OSI reference model. *Proceedings of the IEEE*, 71(12):1334–1340, 1983.

[GH+13] Brendan Galloway, Gerhard P Hancke, et al. Introduction to industrial control networks. *IEEE Communications Surveys and Tutorials*, 15(2):860–880, 2013.

[McM17] David McMillen. Security attacks on industrial control systems. Technical report, Technical Report. IBM, 2017.

[Shi12] Aaron Shi. OSI model data flow. `http://aaronshi.blogspot.de/2012/11/data-link-layer-add-both-header-and.html`, 2012. [Online; accessed 01-March-2018].

[SSKD11] Thilo Sauter, Stefan Soucek, Wolfgang Kastner, and Dietmar Dietrich. The evolution of factory and building automation. *IEEE Industrial Electronics Magazine*, 5(3):35–48, 2011.

[Tho05] J-P Thomesse. Fieldbus technology in industrial automation. *Proceedings of the IEEE*, 93(6):1073–1101, 2005.

[TMV95] J-P Thomesse, Zoubir Mammeri, and L Vega. Time in distributed systems cooperation and communication models. In *Distributed Computing Systems, 1995., Proceedings of the Fifth IEEE Computer Society Workshop on Future Trends of*, pages 41–49. IEEE, 1995.

[Zim80] Hubert Zimmermann. OSI reference model – the ISO model of architecture for open systems interconnection. *IEEE Transactions on communications*, 28(4):425–432, 1980.

[ZJS11] Bonnie Zhu, Anthony Joseph, and Shankar Sastry. A taxonomy of cyber attacks on SCADA systems. In *Internet of things (iThings/CPSCom), 2011 international conference on and 4th international conference on cyber, physical and social computing*, pages 380–388. IEEE, 2011.

[Zur14] Richard Zurawski. *Industrial communication technology handbook*. CRC Press, 2014.

Phase Detection in Medical Context: Overview and Outlook

Patrick Philipp

Vision and Fusion Laboratory
Institute for Anthropomatics
Karlsruhe Institute of Technology (KIT), Germany
p.philipp@kit.edu

Technical Report IES-2017-05

Abstract: To provide assistance functions, e.g. in context of surgical interventions, the use of a phase detection plays an important role. For instance, by assessing the progress of an on-going surgery, a tailored (i.e. context sensitive) decision support for medical practitioners can be carried out. The optimization of a workflow, e.g. by comparing recorded data with a predefined target model, is another application example. Subsequently, a phase detection provides opportunities to prevent errors, injuries, negligence or malpractices in the medical context. In this work, an overview of notable model approaches for a phase detection in medical context is presented. Based on this, further suggestions for future models are proposed.

1 Introduction

In contemporary medicine, the use of advanced computer-based assistance (including both: hardware and software) becomes increasingly important [PFHB16]. E.g. the global market for medical robotics and computer-assisted surgical equipment is projected to grow to 6.8 billion dollars by 2021 (using a five-year compound annual growth rate of 11.3%) [McW17].

As part of a computer assisted surgery (CAS), assistance functions can be realized to enable a decision support for medical practitioners [KWN$^+$15]. Thereby, a decision support opens up a field of optimization, e.g., concerning the prevention of errors, negligence, injuries or (as a result) malpractices.

In this context, a surgical phase detection plays an important role. Namely, because by assessing the progress of an on-going surgery, a tailored (i.e., context sensitive) and interactive decision support during an intervention can be enabled. In doing so, there is not only a passive dissemination (e.g. distribution via print media) of support (e.g. medical guidelines) – which has only little effect on the actual practitioners behavior [FL92, SGM+11]. Moreover, a tailored decision support allows for filtering physically available information in order to be operationally effective by preventing an informational overload of medical practitioners [JL83, KSF+13, LDC+13].

The optimization of a workflow, e.g. by comparing recorded data with a predefined target model, is another application example of a phase detection. This is especially relevant as surgeries have been identified as an important source of improvement to the hospital efficiency [Her03].

In this work, an overview of notable model approaches for a phase detection in medical context are presented. Based on this, further suggestions for elaborating future models are proposed. This contribution is structured as follows: first in Section 2, the constituents of the phase detection problem are elaborated. In Section 3 notable modeling approaches are presented and summarized in Section 4. Section 5 focuses on future implications for models concerning a phase detection and, finally, a conclusion is drawn in Section 6 on page 78.

2 Constituents of the Problem

Figure 2.1 depicts a workflow of a surgery using an UML activity diagram [OMG11]. This formalism is also used in previous research concerning the modeling of medical workflows [PFHB15a, PFHB15b, Phi16, PFHB16, PFB17].

The start of the activity "Surgery" is symbolized by a solid circle (inital node), whereas the end of the activity is given by a double circle (activity final). Performed actions are shown as rounded rectangles, while the control flow is represented by arrows (directed edges). In this example, the actions are performed sequentially – i.e. one after another.

The notation elements "...", the red rectangle as well as the red arrows are added as visual aids – they are not part of the UML specification [OMG11]. Thereby

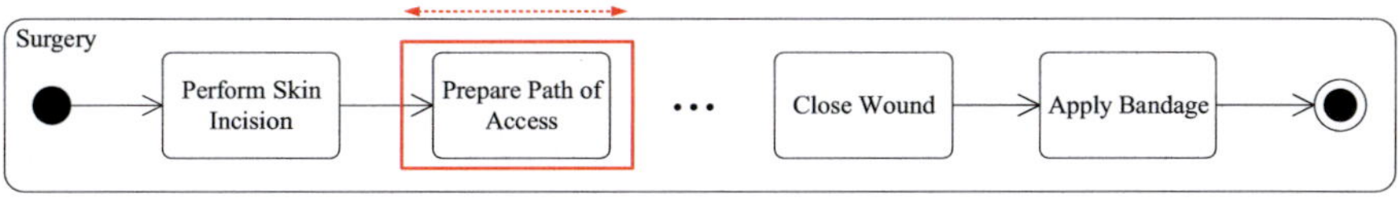

Figure 2.1: Figure shows a pre-modeled workflow of a surgery. Goal of a phase detection is to match a pre-modeled workflow with the current conditions in the operating room.

"..." symbolize a sequences of arbitrary actions which are not shown in the Figure for simplification. The red rectangle highlights the current predicted action, which changes over time.

Goal of a phase detection is to match online a pre-modeled workflow with the current situation in the operating room. It means in effect (cf. Figure 2.1) that we want to know, e.g., is the surgeon currently performing the skin incision or is he already preparing the path of access.

To reach this goal, feature values x are made available by sensors in the operating room. Such values are e.g. "number of persons at the table", "number of used instruments" and so forth. These values are bundled by a feature vector $\boldsymbol{x}$ which is defined as a column vector whose elements are these feature values x – i.e.

$$\boldsymbol{x} = (x^1, \ldots, x^D)^T \,.$$

Whereby D represents the number of features, i.e. the dimension of the resulting feature space as well as of the corresponding feature vector. To save space, vector $\boldsymbol{x}$ is shown horizontal (i.e. transposed, indicated by T).

In each time step a new feature vector $\boldsymbol{x}$ with index t is observed by the technical system in the operating room:

$$\boldsymbol{x}_t = (x_t^1, \ldots, x_t^D)^T \,.$$

As a consequence, there is an observation sequence of feature vectors

$$\boldsymbol{x}_{1:t} = \boldsymbol{x}_1, \ldots, \boldsymbol{x}_t \,.$$

The observation sequence $\boldsymbol{x}_{1:t}$ is available to the technical system, whereas the current phase is not. I.e. there is a gap between the observation sequence $\boldsymbol{x}_{1:t}$

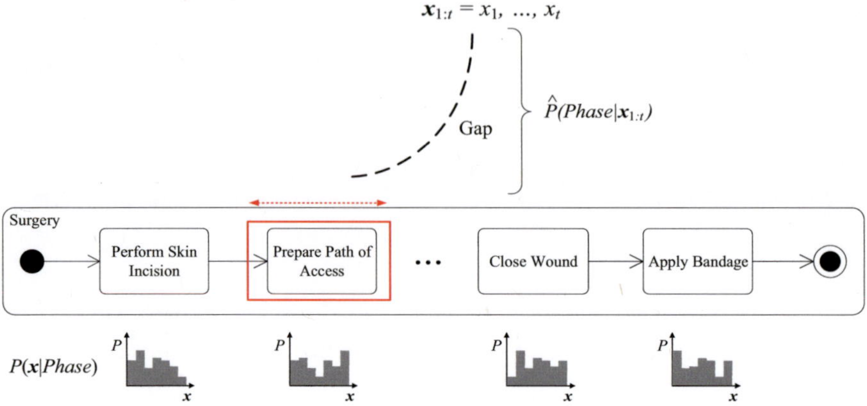

Figure 2.2: Figures depicts the gap between a sequence of feature vectors and the surgical phase. The latter is hidden to the technical system (w.l.o.g.). To bridge the gap between them, a probability distribution P can be used to specify how likely it is to emit a certain feature vector being at a specific phase (i.e. $P(\boldsymbol{x}|Phase)$). A Hidden Markov Model (HMM) can be used to infer the probability of being in a phase given the observation sequence.

and the surgical phase which is not directly visible (i.e. hidden) to the technical system (w.l.o.g. cf. Figure 2.2).

In traditional approaches like Hidden Markov Models (HMM), a probability distribution P is used to specify how likely it is to emit a certain feature vector being at a specific phase (cf. Figure 2.2 bottom row).

Using further parameters of the HMM (cf. Section 3.3), vice versa, the probability of being in a Phase given the observation sequence can be inferred. As a consequence the gap between the observation sequences and a specific phase is bridged. Further model characteristic details are elaborated in the following sections.

3 Modeling Approaches

In the following section notable modeling approaches for a medical phase detection are elaborated. Thereby, the different characteristics of the models are illustrated.

3.1 Random Forest (RF)

A RF is a model which derives its decision from a set of classifiers and therefore belongs to the so called ensemble methods [Rok10, Zho12]. A RF predicts the class of a feature vector $f(\boldsymbol{x})$ by a weighted sum [Bre01]

$$f(\boldsymbol{x}) = \sum_{n=1}^{N} \alpha_n t_n(\boldsymbol{x}) \,.$$

Thereby a set of decision trees (i.e. a forest) is used:

$$\{t_n(\boldsymbol{x}) : n = 1, \ldots, N\} \,.$$

These classifications results are equally weighted, i.e. $\alpha_n = (N)^{-1}$. Conceptually, a RF utilizes randomization in two ways:

Firstly, the decision trees $t_n(\boldsymbol{x})$ are trained by randomly sampling the training set $\mathcal{D} = \{\boldsymbol{x}_1, \ldots, \boldsymbol{x}_M\}$ with known class memberships $\omega(\boldsymbol{x}_i)$ for $i = 1, \ldots, M$. The idea behind this is, to lower the variance by averaging over a large number of trees which are highly uncorrelated (bootstrap aggregation aka bagging).

Secondly, during the training of a decision tree, for each node only a random subset of feature values are considered for splitting the tree. I.e. the size of the considered feature vector $\boldsymbol{x}$ in each split is $d < D$. Based on a quality metric (e.g. entropy or genie) and under consideration of d feature values, the split with the highest quality is calculated. Stopping criteria of the training algorithm of a tree is, e.g., that a minimum size of a leaf is reached. I.e. the split of a set of feature vectors would result in subsets that are too small.

For classification, each decision tree $t_n(\boldsymbol{x})$ of the RF receives the same feature vector $\boldsymbol{x}$ and maps it to a class $\omega \in \Omega$. The corresponding a-posteriori probability is given by:

$$\hat{P}(\omega|\boldsymbol{x}) = \frac{1}{N} \sum_{n=1}^{N} [t_n(\boldsymbol{x}) = \omega] \,. \tag{3.1}$$

Please note that $[\cdot]$ represents a predicate mapping, i.e. $[\cdot]$ has a value of 1 iff the corresponding expression evaluates to true.

The predicted class $\hat{\omega}$ is then given by [Bre01]:

$$\hat{w} = \arg\max_{\omega\in\Omega} \hat{P}(\omega|\boldsymbol{x})\,. \tag{3.2}$$

The use of the RF model for a medical phase detection by the application example of a cholecystectomy (removal of the gallbladder) is elaborated in [SOP+14]. 7 phases are considered in context of this surgery. The training set comprises 9 surgical interventions. Nominal features are the use of eight specific instruments (yes/no), the state of the surgical light (on/off) as well as the state of the room lights (on/off). The authors claim that an RF is suitable, because it is highly applicable for multi-class problems and it is able to predict phases in a-typical order. The latter is a consequence of the fact that a RF does only consider a single feature vector for classification (cf. Equations (3.1) and (3.2)). That means in effect, that a feature vector is classified without taking the order of phases into account.

The trained model achieved an accuracy of around 69% for the 7 classes using cross-validation with a leave-one-out iterator. Classes with similar characteristics (which differ only in the sequence of occurrence) can not be distinguished. In [SPG+16] the authors also get comparable results for a simplified 7-phase hip replacement surgery with a high confusion for phases which are highly discriminative to the order of phases.

This is a prototypical behavior of a classifier that does not take the sequence of feature vectors into account. Therefore this model is, out of the box, not suited regarding the constituents of the problem. Nevertheless, to reduce the conceptional drawback, such a model can be embedded into a sequential model. One simple form of such a model is, e.g., a deterministic automaton.

In [KSW+16] this concept (cf. Figure 3.1) is used on two application examples: Firstly, a pancreatic resection (removal of the pancreas) comprising 12 classes and a training set of 11 surgeries. Secondly a adrenalectomy (removal of the adrenal glands) with 9 classes and a training set of 5 surgeries. Considered features are the use of a specific instrument, the action performed and the anatomical structure.

The use of this sequential framework (cf. Figure 3.1) is like shifting a window over a workflow (cf. Figure 2.1) comprising the current phase, and additionally,

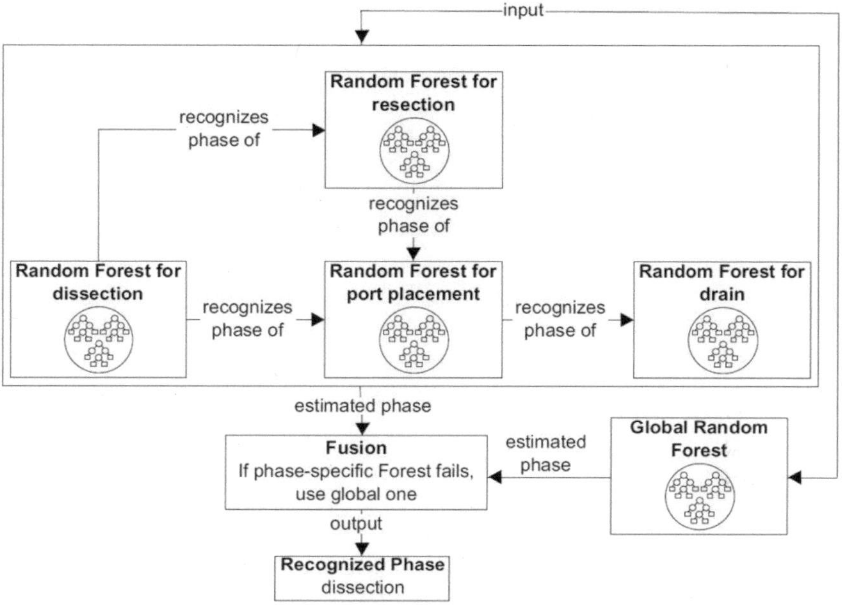

Figure 3.1: Figures depicts the utilization of a random forest (RF) embedded into a simple sequential model. A RF is used to predict the current and possible next phases. (e.g. dissection with possible next phases resection and port placement). If a next phase is predicated, a transition is made. As a result, another RF is used to discriminate between the new current phase and possible next phases. If a transition is made by mistake, the model tends to get lost. Therefore a global RF is used to discriminate between all possible phases in order to be able to reset the sequential model. Modified from [KSW$^+$16].

possible next phases. A window-specific classifier then discriminates between the phases inside the window [Phi16, Phi17]. The window is shifted forward as soon as a next phase is predicted.

The modeling approach in [KSW$^+$16] achieved an accuracy around 70%. Drawback is the use of deterministic transitions, which makes it necessary to implement strategies to reset the sequential model (cf. Figure 3.1).

3.2 Stochastic Petri Net (SPN)

There are a whole range of reasons for considering Petri Nets [Pet62] as a modeling tool for dynamic aspects of a process [vdA96, vdA98]. With respect to the application example, Petri Nets can be of use because of their formal semantics and the abundance of analysis techniques.

The net structure [Rei13b] of a Petri Net is given by the tupel

$$NST = (\mathcal{P}, \mathcal{T}, \mathcal{F}),$$

where $\mathcal{P}$ is the set of places and $\mathcal{T}$ is the set of transitions

$$\mathcal{P} = \{p_i : i = 1, \ldots, |\mathcal{P}|\},$$
$$\mathcal{T} = \{t_i : i = 1, \ldots, |\mathcal{T}|\},$$

so that

$$\mathcal{P} \cap \mathcal{T} = \emptyset.$$

The flow relation $\mathcal{F}$ reflects the connection of places and transitions (and vice versa):

$$\mathcal{F} \subseteq (\mathcal{P} \times \mathcal{T}) \cup (\mathcal{T} \times \mathcal{P}).$$

Consequently, the net structure NST of a Petri Net is a directed bipartite graph (see Figure 3.2). To model the dynamic behavior of the system, so called "tokens" are introduced (black dot in Figure 3.2). The distribution of tokens on the set of places represents the state of the Petri Net. It is also called marking [Rei13b].

A Stochastic Petri Net (SPN) is defined as a tuple

$$SPN = (NST, \Lambda),$$

whereby $\Lambda = \{\lambda_i : i = 1, \ldots, |\mathcal{T}|\}$ is the set of shifting rates λ_i which are assigned to transitions t_i. These shifting rates are distributed exponentially [Mol81].

Figure 3.2 depicts a SPN on the left. Circles represent places p_i and squares represent transitions t_i. The state of the SPN is given by the current distribution of tokens (marking). In the reachability graph the states are represented by vectors, whereby each entry i represent the number of tokens at a place p_i. That means,

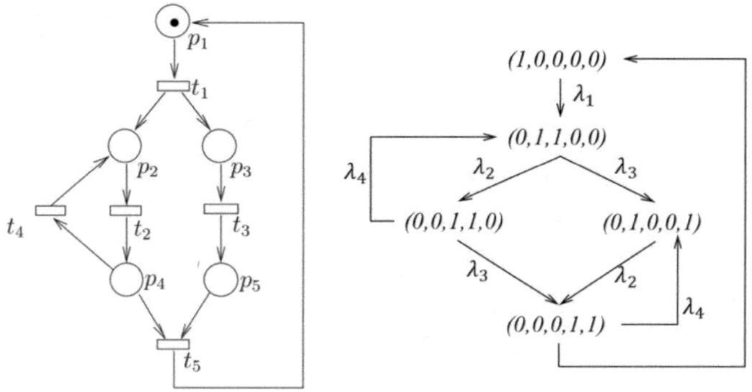

Figure 3.2: Figure depicts a SPN on the left. Circles represent places p_i and squares represent transitions t_i. The state of the SPN is given by the current distribution of tokens (marking). In the reachability graph the states are represented by vectors, whereby each entry i represent the number of tokens at a place p_i. The Figure visualizes that a SPN represents a Markov Process whereby, inter alia, the firing rates λ_i of states Z_i of the reachability graph corresponds to the transition probabilities a_{ij} of a (discrete) Markov Process. Modified from [B$^+$02].

the state $(1, 0, 0, 0, 0)$ of the reachability graph represents the state of the SPN depicted on the left. Figure 3.2 visualizes the fact that a SPN actually represents a Markov Process. I.e. the states of the reachability graph of the SPN correspond to the states of a Markov Process and the firing rates λ_i of states Z_i of the reachability graph correspond to the transition probabilities a_{ij} of a (discrete) Markov Process. That is, inter alia, because the firing rates are exponentially distributed (cf. memorylessness) and therefore the Markov Property is satisfied [B$^+$02].

The use of Markov Models with observable states is suitable in cases where the states of the modeled system are directly accessible. E.g. in [PFHB15a] a decision support system for the diagnosis of two complex cancerous diseases is modeled using Petri Nets. The involved dialog system allows for a direct access to the necessary features. Clearly, this model can also be used as sequential model to embed a model like a RF instead of a deterministic automaton (cf. Section 3.1). Nevertheless, with respect to the constituents of the problem, this model has to be extended, e.g. by introducing hidden states.

3.3 Hidden Markov Model (HMM)

A Hidden Markov Model (HMM) [RJ86] is a Markov Model using a Markov Process with unobserved (i.e. hidden) states. That means, in contrast to Markov Processes, where the state of the model at a time step t is known for certain (i.e. directly observable), in a HMM an observer can only access emissions which are generated by a hidden (i.e. not observable) state. To enable this, state transition probabilities and furthermore emission probabilities are part of a HMM.

Formally, a (discrete) HMM is defined as a 5-tuple

$$\lambda = (S, V, A, B, \pi),$$

whereby $S = \{s_1, \ldots, s_n\}$ is the set of hidden states and $V = \{v_1, \ldots, v_m\}$ is the set of emissions for each hidden state (i.e. output vocabulary). Moreover, there is a transition matrix $A \in \mathbb{R}^{n \times n}$ encoding the transition probabilities from a current state s_i to a next state s_j by the matrix entry (a_{ij}). Matrix $B \in \mathbb{R}^{n \times m}$ encodes the emission probabilities of a state s_i by the corresponding row entries $(a_{ij}) : j = 1, \ldots, m$. Finally, $\pi \in \mathbb{R}^n$ encodes the initial state probabilities, i.e. the probability that a state is the starting state.

The use of a HMM for a medical phase detection has been elaborated in [BPFN08] by the application example of a cholecystectomy (removal of the gall-bladder). 14 phases are considered in context of this surgery. The training set comprises 12 surgical interventions. Nominal features are the use of 17 specific instruments (yes/no). The authors present a 14-state HMM and a merged HMM. In the latter, similar states are transformed into one single state. The models achieved an accuracy of around 86% and 93% respectively, using a complete cross-validation.

In [PBF$^+$08] a cholecystectomy comprising 14 phases is considered, too. The training set comprises 11 surgical interventions. Nominal features are the use of 18 specific instruments (yes/no) including the state of an optical device (inserted/not inserted). The best accuracy achieved using a complete cross-validation is around 92% – but for computing this value, a tolerance of 5 seconds before and after the ground truth definition of a phase is set. Additionally. the authors state that phases with very short durations are poorly recognized which is a result of the inertia of the model.

A HMM can be seen as a common sequential model considering the constituents of the problem (cf. Section 2). Indeed, it can be a suitable model for problems where data is not independent and identically distributed, i.e. a feature vector $\boldsymbol{x}$ does depend on the feature vectors seen before. Nevertheless, the structure of this model is not well suited to include expert knowledge about emission probabilities. That is because, inter alia, the corresponding probability distribution can not be factorized and therefore grows exponentially with the number of possible emissions. To overcome this drawback, the generalization of a HMM, namely a Dynamic Bayesian Network can be used.

3.4 Dynamic Bayesian Network (DBN)

A Bayesian Network (BN) is a probabilistic graphical model (PGM), combining graph theoretic approaches with approaches of probability theory. Consequently, a BN over random variables $X^{0:N} := X^0, \ldots, X^N$ is given by a pair

$$B = (G, P)\,.$$

Whereby G corresponds to a directed, acyclic graph

$$G = (V, E)\,,$$

and

$$P(X^{0:N}) = \prod_{n=0}^{N} P(X^n | \mathrm{Pa}(X^n))\,,$$

corresponds to a joint probability distribution [KF09].

Graph G is used to define dependencies between random variables $X^{0:N}$. It is also known as the structure of the BN. The vertex set V represents the set of random variables, while a directed edge $V_i \to V_j$ of the set of edges E represents a direct dependency between two variables. A missing edge symbolizes the independence of these two variables.

The joint probability distribution is given by the product of all conditional probability distributions associated with the vertices of G. It is also known as the parameters of the BN. Here, $\mathrm{Pa}(X^n)$ denotes the set of parents of a random variable X^n. Graphically, this corresponds to vertices having a directed edge pointing to

X^n's vertex. Please note, if Pa$(X^n) = \emptyset$, a random variable X^n is a root node of the BN, and $P(X^n|\,\emptyset) = P(X^n)$ gives the a-priori probability.

A Dynamic Bayesian Network (DBN) is an extension of a BN, also taking the temporal dependencies of variables into account [Mur02]. A DBN is given by a pair

$$\text{DBN} = (B_0, B_{\rightarrow}),$$

where the BN B_0 uses $P(X_0^{0:N})$ to specify the a-priori probability distribution over random variables $X^{0:N}$ in a time step with index 0.

Furthermore, $B_{\rightarrow}$ specifies the conditional probability distribution over discrete time steps t by using

$$P(X_t^{0:N}|X_{t-1}^{0:N}) = \prod_{n=0}^{N} P(X_t^n|\text{Pa}(X_t^n)).$$

Thereby Pa(X_t^n) denotes the set of X_t^n's parents in the corresponding graph. The parents can be in the same time slice (e.g. representing instantaneous causation) or the previous one (i.e., we assume the model to be fist-order Markov). In the latter case, arcs point to time slices with ascending index, reflecting the causal flow of time [Mur02].

Figure 3.3 depicts on the left a DBN structure that represents a HMM. Thereby the root node represents a surgical phase and the child node represents the emission of feature vectors $\boldsymbol{x}_t$ given a phase, i.e. $P(\boldsymbol{x}_t|\textit{Phase}_t)$. By introducing a conditional independence between the feature values (cf. Figure 3.3, right side), a naive DBN can be constructed. The corresponding probability distribution of the children is given by $\prod_{n=1}^{N} P(\boldsymbol{x}_t^n|\textit{Phase}_t)$. It can easily be seen that in the first case the number of parameters grows exponentially, whereas in the second case the number of parameters grows linearly. For example, let's assume that there are 7 distinct phases to predict and there is a feature vector $\boldsymbol{x}_t$ with dimension $D = 3$ having discrete feature values with 4 different characteristics. Then, the corresponding conditional probability $P(\boldsymbol{x}_t|\textit{Phase}_t)$ of a HMM is given by $(4 \cdot 4 \cdot 4) \cdot 7 = 448$ parameters from which 441 have to specified because the probabilities some up to 1. But $\prod_{n=1}^{N} P(\boldsymbol{x}_t^n|\textit{Phase}_t)$ is given by $(4+4+4) \cdot 7 = 84$ parameters from which 63 parameters have to specified. Further details can also be found in [PFB17].

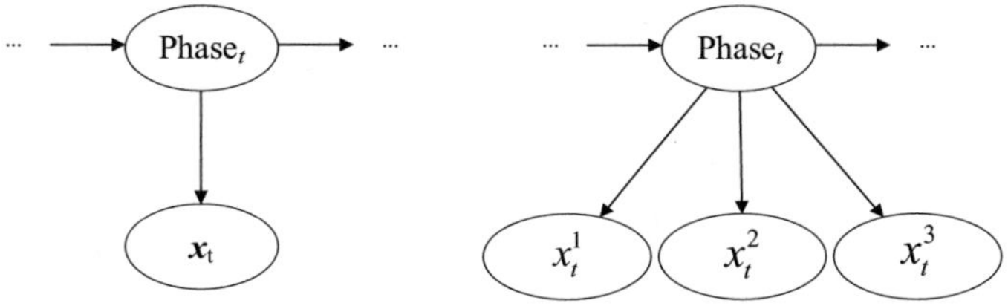

Figure 3.3: Figure shows on the left a HMM represented by a DBN structure. There is a root node representing the surgical phases and a child node representing the emissions given a phase. The parameters needed to specify a conditional probability distribution of this child node grow exponentially with the number of used features, i.e. with the size of the feature vector $\boldsymbol{x}_t$. On the right side of the figure a DBN structure is shown which takes advantage of conditional independence of feature values x_n^t to reduce the growing of parameters: in the depicted case the number of parameters linearly grows with the size of $\boldsymbol{x}_t$.

This reduction of parameters can be useful in case only a small amount of training data is available [KF09]. Furthermore, the special structure of the network supports expert-based parametrization and therefore to incorporate the knowledge of experts into the models – which also can be useful when dealing with small amount of training data and in context of translation and/or fusion mechanisms of workflow models [PFHB15b, PFHB16, PFB17].

In [PSG$^+$16] a DBN model is elborated by using the application example of a simplified total hip replacement. 7 phases are considered in context of this surgery and the training set comprises 12 surgical interventions. Features are the positioning of the sergeants (position A / position B), the number of used instruments (0/1/2) as well as the number of persons at the operating table (0/1/2/3/4). Using a complete cross-validation, the model achieves an accuracy around 85%. Concerning an earlier publication using RF [SPG$^+$16] the sequence modeling greatly reduces confusion of time depended feature values.

4 Overview

The model approaches discussed in Section 3 are briefly summarized in Table 4.1. Thereby a Random forest (RF) shows prototypical behavior of a model which omits the sequence of feature vectors $\boldsymbol{x}_t$ during classification. Although this drawback can be addressed, e.g. by embedding such a classifier into a sequential model, a RF can generally categorized as non-sequential. Subsequently RF do no allow to model hidden states, which can be necessary to represent the fact that an observer can not directly access the state of a modeled system (cf. Section 2). Furthermore a RF is a discriminative model and allows for an online classification. The latter is necessary to be able to provide a phase detection on the fly (cf. Section 2). The model allows for a data-driven training but lacks of a suitable interface to incorporate expert knowledge which can be especially of use if only a small amount of training data is available.

A Stochastic Petri Net (SPN) represents a Markov Process (cf. Section 3.2). This model is suited for representing sequential dependencies for systems in which internal states are visible to an observer (e.g. Dialogue Systems). Furthermore, SPN is an generative approach allowing for an online classification. A data-driven training is possible, e.g. by using genetic algorithms. Finally, a knowledge-based parametrization of a SPN is possible, too – in practice the size of the model can cause limitations. In such a case, an extension of the model by using additional concepts, e.g. Coloured Petri Nets, can become necessary.

A Hidden Markov Model (HMM) can be seen as a common and well researched sequential model. A HMM allows for a direct modeling of hidden states which suits the considered application example (cf. Section 2). It is an generative approach and is able to classify online. Nevertheless, the structure of this model is not well suited to incorporate expert knowledge about the emission probabilities. That is because, inter alia, the corresponding probability distribution can not be factorized and therefore grows exponentially with the number of possible emissions.

To overcome this drawback, the generalization of a HMM, namely a Dynamic Bayesian Network (DBN) can be used. It extends the model by the ability to express the state space in a factored form and not only as a single random variable. This allows for the reduction of parameters and consequently facilitates the improvement of modularity and interpretability. This opens up a practicable way to incorporate expert knowledge into a DBN. Furthermore, concerning Kalman Filter Models, a DBN allows for arbitrary probability distributions (not only for

	RF	SPN	HMM	DBN
Sequential Model	□	■	■	■
Hidden States	□	□	■	■
Generative Approach	□	■	■	■
Online Classification	■	■	■	■
Data-driven Training	■	■	■	■
Knowledge-based Parametrization	□	■	□	■

Table 4.1: The Table briefly compares different modeling approaches discussed in this work. The symbols ■ / □ are used to specify if a property is present / not present.

unimodal linear-Gaussians). A DBN is a promising approach because it combines a reasonable tradeoff between expressiveness and complexity, and includes probabilistic models that have proved to be successful in practice (e.g. HMM).

5 Outlook

Recently, the use of Artificial Neural Networks is elaborated. E.g. a Convolutional Neural Network (CNN) for a medical phase detection is used in [LZL+16] by the application example of a resuscitation with only 3 phases. The training set comprises 20 workflows. Features are extracted from depth image recordings and from sound recordings. Furthermore, the model is embedded into a simple sequential model represented by thresholds which is similar to a finite automaton. Nevertheless, the model achieved an accuracy of 80%.

In [TSM+17] a cholecystectomy comprising 7 phases is considered. The training set comprises 80 surgical interventions. The authors use a CNN to extract features from video recordings of endoscope. The model is embedded into a HMM, which achieved an accuracy of 82%. Finally, in [LZZ+17] the authors elaborated the application example of a resuscitation with 35 classes and a training set of 42 video recordings. Also a CNN is used for feature extraction – in this case, the CNN is combined with a recurrent neural network using long-short term memory (LSTM). Features are extracted from depth image records, sound recordings and via a passive RFID (radio-frequency identification) system which tracks the medical instruments. The model achieves an accuracy of around 94%.

In view of these results, a further study of Artificial Neural Networks with respect to the constituents of the problem (cf. Section 2) can be considered as useful. Further elaboration is needed e.g. concerning the incorporation of expert knowledge (cf. [HML+16, PBFB17]) into the models, the challenge of a small amount of available data for training and the explainability of the models output [RSG16].

6 Conclusion

In this work, we discussed notable modeling approaches for a surgical phase detection. The models have different characteristics and are differently suited concerning the constituents of the problem. Considering a small amount of training data and a preferably expert-based modeling, Dynamic Bayesian Networks seems to be a suited and long-standing solution. Nevertheless, upcoming approaches, facilitating Artificial Neural Networks, have recently shown promising classification results in the field of surgical phase detection. To trim these models to be accessible to expert-based knowledge and be able to deal with the fact that typically only a small amount of real training data is available, could be a good starting point for approaches which enrich the current state of the art.

Bibliography

[B+02] Falko Bause et al. *Stochastic Petri nets – An introduction to the theory*. Citeseer, 2002.

[BPFN08] Tobias Blum, Nicolas Padoy, Hubertus Feußner, and Nassir Navab. Modeling and online recognition of surgical phases using hidden Markov models. In *International Conference on Medical Image Computing and Computer-Assisted Intervention*, pages 627–635. Springer, 2008.

[Bre01] Leo Breiman. Random forests. *Machine learning*, 45(1):5–32, 2001.

[FL92] E Field and K Lohr. *Guidelines for Clinical Practice: From Development to Use*. National Academies Press, 1992.

[Her03] C Herfarth. Lean surgery through changes in surgical work flow. *British Journal of Surgery*, 90(5):513–514, 2003.

[HML+16] Zhiting Hu, Xuezhe Ma, Zhengzhong Liu, Eduard Hovy, and Eric Xing. Harnessing deep neural networks with logic rules. *arXiv:1603.06318*, 2016.

[JL83] Joseph P Joyce and George W Lapinsky. A history and overview of the safety parameter display system concept. *IEEE Transactions on Nuclear Science*, 30(1):744–749, 1983.

[KF09] Daphne Koller and Nir Friedman. *Probabilistic graphical models: principles and techniques*. MIT press, 2009.

[KSF+13] Michael Kranzfelder, Christoph Staub, Adam Fiolka, Armin Schneider, Sonja Gillen, Dirk Wilhelm, Helmut Friess, Alois Knoll, and Hubertus Feussner. Toward increased autonomy in the surgical OR: needs, requests, and expectations. *Surgical endoscopy*, 27(5):1681–1688, 2013.

[KSW+16] Darko Katić, Jürgen Schuck, Anna-Laura Wekerle, Hannes Kenngott, Beat Peter Müller-Stich, Rüdiger Dillmann, and Stefanie Speidel. Bridging the gap between formal and experience-based knowledge for context-aware laparoscopy. *International journal of computer assisted radiology and surgery*, 11(6):881–888, 2016.

[KWN+15] HG Kenngott, M Wagner, F Nickel, AL Wekerle, A Preukschas, M Apitz, T Schulte, R Rempel, P Mietkowski, F Wagner, et al. Computer-assisted abdominal surgery: new technologies. *Langenbeck's Archives of Surgery*, 400(3):273–281, 2015.

[LDC+13] Cristian A Linte, Katherine P Davenport, Kevin Cleary, Craig Peters, Kirby G Vosburgh, Nassir Navab, Pierre Jannin, Terry M Peters, David R Holmes III, Richard A Robb, et al. On mixed reality environments for minimally invasive therapy guidance: systems architecture, successes and challenges in their implementation from laboratory to clinic. *Computerized Medical Imaging and Graphics*, 37(2):83–97, 2013.

[LZL+16] Xinyu Li, Yanyi Zhang, Mengzhu Li, Shuhong Chen, Farneth R Austin, Ivan Marsic, and Randall S Burd. Online process phase detection using multimodal deep learning. In *Ubiquitous Computing, Electronics & Mobile Communication Conference (UEMCON), IEEE Annual*, pages 1–7. IEEE, 2016.

[LZZ+17] Xinyu Li, Yanyi Zhang, Jianyu Zhang, Shuhong Chen, Ivan Marsic, Richard A Farneth, and Randall S Burd. Concurrent activity recognition with multimodal CNN-LSTM structure. *arXiv preprint arXiv:1702.01638*, 2017.

[McW17] Andrew McWilliams. Medical robotics and computer-assisted surgery: The global market. *BCC Research*, HLC036G, 2017.

[Mol81] Michael Karl Molloy. *On the integration of delay and throughput measures in distributed processing models*. University of California, Los Angeles, 1981.

[Mur02] Kevin Patrick Murphy. *Dynamic Bayesian networks: representation, inference and learning*. PhD thesis, University of California, Berkeley, 2002.

[OMG11] OMG. OMG Unified Modeling Language(OMG UML) Superstructure Version 2.4.1, 2011.

[PBF+08] Nicolas Padoy, Tobias Blum, Hubertus Feussner, Marie-Odile Berger, and Nassir Navab. On-line recognition of surgical activity for monitoring in the operating room. In *AAAI*, pages 1718–1724, 2008.

[PBFB17] Patrick Philipp, Johannes Bleier, Yvonne Fischer, and Jürgen Beyerer. Towards a surgical phase detection using Markov logic networks. *Radermacher, Klaus (Ed.): CAOS*

2017, 17th Annual Meeting of the International Society for Computer Assisted Orthopaedic Surgery. Papers. Online resource: June 14-17, 2017, Aachen, Germany. (EPiC Series in Health Sciences 1), pp. 288-294, 2017.

[Pet62] Carl Adam Petri. *Kommunikation mit Automaten*. PhD thesis, Universität Bonn, 1962.

[PFB17] Patrick Philipp, Yvonne Fischer, and Jürgen Beyerer. Expert-based probabilistic modeling of workflows in context of surgical interventions. *CogSima 2017, IEEE Conference on Cognitive and Computational Aspects of Situation Management*, 2017.

[PFHB15a] Patrick Philipp, Yvonne Fischer, Dirk Hempel, and Jürgen Beyerer. Framework for an Interactive Assistance in Diagnostic Processes Based on the Translation of UML Activities into Petri Nets. In *Proceedings of ISHI 2015 – International Symposium on Health Informatics and Medical Systems: CSCI 2015. International Conference on Computational Science and Computational Intelligence*, pages 732–737. IEEE Conference Publishing Services, 2015.

[PFHB15b] Patrick Philipp, Yvonne Fischer, Dirk Hempel, and Jürgen Beyerer. Modeling of clinical practice guidelines for interactive assistance in diagnostic processes. In *WorldComp 2015, World Congress in Computer Science, Computer Engineering, and Applied Computing : HIMS 2015, International Conference on Health Informatics and Medical Systems, july 27-30, Las Vegas, Nevada, USA*, pages 3–9. CSREA Press, 2015.

[PFHB16] Patrick Philipp, Yvonne Fischer, Dirk Hempel, and Jürgen Beyerer. Framework for an interactive assistance in diagnostic processes based on probabilistic modeling of clinical practice guidelines. In *Emerging Trends in Applications and Infrastructures for Computational Biology, Bioinformatics, and Systems Biology*, pages 371–390. Elsevier, 2016.

[Phi16] Patrick Philipp. Framework for modeling medical guidelines based on the translation of UML activities into YAWL. Technical report, KIT Scientific Publishing, Karlsruhe, 2016.

[Phi17] Patrick Philipp. Combining YAWL and DBNs for surgical phase detection. Technical report, KIT Scientific Publishing, Karlsruhe, 2017.

[PSG+16] Patrick Philipp, Luzie Schreiter, Johannes Giehl, Yvonne Fischer, Joerg Raczkowsky, Markus Schwarz, Heinz Woern, and Jürgen Beyerer. Situation detection for an interactive assistance in surgical interventions based on dynamic Bayesian networks. *CRAS 2016, 6th Joint Workshop on New Technologies for Computer/Robot Assisted Surgery,*, 2016.

[Rei13b] Wolfgang Reisig. *Understanding Petri Nets*. Springer, Heidelberg, 2013.

[RJ86] Lawrence Rabiner and B Juang. An introduction to hidden Markov models. *ieee assp magazine*, 3(1):4–16, 1986.

[Rok10] Lior Rokach. *Pattern classification using ensemble methods*, volume 75. World Scientific, 2010.

[RSG16] Marco Tulio Ribeiro, Sameer Singh, and Carlos Guestrin. Why should I trust you?: Explaining the predictions of any classifier. In *Proceedings of the 22nd ACM SIGKDD International Conference on Knowledge Discovery and Data Mining*, pages 1135–1144. ACM, 2016.

[SGM+11] Earl Steinberg, Sheldon Greenfield, Michelle Mancher, et al. *Clinical Practice Guidelines We Can Trust*. National Academies Press, 2011.

[SOP+14] Ralf Stauder, Aslı Okur, Loïc Peter, Armin Schneider, Michael Kranzfelder, Hubertus Feussner, and Nassir Navab. Random forests for phase detection in surgical workflow analysis. In *International Conference on Information Processing in Computer-Assisted Interventions*, pages 148–157. Springer, 2014.

[SPG+16] Luzie Schreiter, Patrick Philipp, Johannes Giehl, Yvonne Fischer, Joerg Raczkowsky, Markus Schwarz, Jürgen Beyerer, and Heinz Woern. Situation detection for an interactive assistance in surgical interventions based on random forests. *in Proceedings of International Journal of Computer Assisted Radiology and Surgery (CARS),*, pages 115–116, 2016.

[TSM+17] Andru P Twinanda, Sherif Shehata, Didier Mutter, Jacques Marescaux, Michel de Mathelin, and Nicolas Padoy. Endonet: A deep architecture for recognition tasks on laparoscopic videos. *IEEE transactions on medical imaging*, 36(1):86–97, 2017.

[vdA96] Wil van der Aalst. Three good reasons for using a Petri-net-based workflow management system. In *Proceedings of the International Working Conference on Information and Process Integration in Enterprises*, pages 179–201. World Scientific, 1996.

[vdA98] Wil van der Aalst. The application of Petri nets to workflow management. *Journal of circuits, systems, and computers*, 8(01):21–66, 1998.

[Zho12] Zhi-Hua Zhou. *Ensemble methods: foundations and algorithms*. CRC press, 2012.

Deep Learning based Vehicle Detection in Aerial Imagery

Lars Sommer

Vision and Fusion Laboratory
Institute for Anthropomatics
Karlsruhe Institute of Technology (KIT), Germany
lars.sommer@kit.edu

Technical Report IES-2017-06

Abstract: Detecting vehicles in aerial images is an important task for many applications like traffic monitoring or search and rescue work. In recent years, several deep learning based frameworks have been proposed for object detection. However, these detection frameworks were developed and optimized for datasets that exhibit considerably differing characteristics compared to aerial images, e.g. size of objects to detect. In this report, we demonstrate the potential of Faster R-CNN, which is one of the state-of-the-art detection frameworks, for vehicle detection in aerial images. Therefore, we systematically investigate the impact of adapting relevant parameters. Due to the small size of vehicles in aerial images, the most improvement in performance is achieved by using features of shallower layers to localize vehicles. However, these features offer less semantic and contextual information compared to features of deeper layers. This results in more false alarms due to objects with similar shapes as vehicles. To account for that, we further propose a deconvolutional module that up-samples features of deeper layers and combines these features with features of shallower layers.

1 Introduction

Vehicle detection in aerial images is an important task for many applications like traffic monitoring or search and rescue work. Conventional approaches applied to detect vehicles in aerial images are generally comprised of hand-crafted features and a classifier within a sliding window approach [LM15, CH16, MM14]. In recent years, several authors applied convolutional neural networks (CNNs) to extract features at each sliding window position [CXLP14, KPF16]. In [CXLP14], improved results are achieved for vehicle detection in satellite images by applying convolutional features instead of hand-crafted features. However, the computation of convolutional features for each candidate window separately is computational expensive [Gir15].

In recent years, deep learning based detection frameworks like Faster R-CNN [RHGS15], which achieves top performing results on common detection benchmark datasets, have been proposed to reduce the computational effort. Therefore, a convolutional feature map is computed for the entire image at once and shared for all candidate windows [Gir15, RHGS15]. However, such detection frameworks are developed and optimized for common detection benchmark datasets that exhibit considerably differing characteristics compared to aerial images, e.g. size of objects to detect.

In the context of this report, we demonstrate the applicability of Faster R-CNN for vehicle detection in aerial images. Therefore, several adaptions are performed to account for the characteristics of the aerial images and the impact on the detection performance is evaluated. The DLR 3K Munich Vehicle Aerial Image Dataset [LM15] that comprises objects in the range of 15×30 pixels is used for all experiments.

The main improvement is achieved by adapting the resolution of the output of the last convolutional layer, which is used as feature map to localize and classify objects. The resolution of the standard feature map is only 1/16 of the input image and consequently insufficient for object sizes between 15 and 30 pixels. To provide a sufficient feature map resolution, the output of shallower convolutional layers is used as feature map. However, these features offer less semantic and contextual information compared to features of deeper layers. This results in more false alarms due to objects with similar shapes as vehicles. To account for that, we further propose a deconvolutional module that up-samples features of deeper layers and combines these features with features of shallower layers.

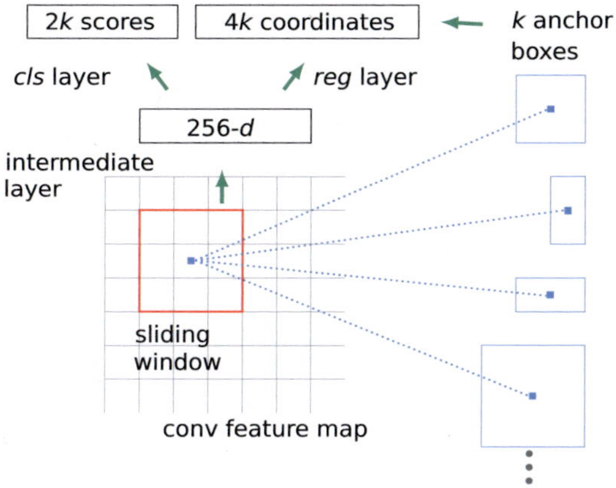

Figure 2.1: Schematic illustration of the Region Proposals Network (RPN) used to generate a set of candidate regions that are likely to contain an object.

2 Faster R-CNN

In the following, the functional principle of the Faster R-CNN detection framework as proposed by Ren et al. [RHGS15] is introduced. Faster R-CNN is comprised of two modules: an initial deep learning based object proposals method called Region Proposals Network (RPN) and the subsequent Fast R-CNN module [Gir15] used to classify the generated proposals. Both the RPN and the Fast R-CNN module share the convolutional layers to reduce the computational effort.

Figure 2.1 shows schematically the RPN. The RPN uses the output of the last convolutional layers as feature map. Then, a small network is shifted over the feature map to generate a set of candidate regions. The small network comprises a 3×3 convolutional layer followed by a classification layer (*cls* layer) and a bounding box regression layer (*reg* layer). The classification layer outputs a confidence score at each position, which is used to rank the proposals. The bounding box regression layer is used to compute the corresponding coordinates. For this, a set of fixed scaled anchor boxes *k* are used as bounding box reference.

The top 300 region proposals (highest confidence score) are forwarded to the Fast R-CNN module. The Fast R-CNN module classifies each region proposal into various object classes or background. Therefore, each region proposal is projected onto the feature map. Then, the corresponding features are extracted by the so called Region of Interest (RoI) pooling layer to generate a vector of fixed length as required for the subsequent fully connected layers. After a sequence of fully connected layers, a classification layer and a bounding box regression layer are used for classification and to refine the coordinates of the corresponding candidate region, respectively.

3 Adaption to Aerial Images

The detection performance is mainly affected by adapting the resolution of the feature map used to compute proposals and for classification and by adapting the parameters of the RPN.

The original Faster R-CNN utilizes VGG-16 [SZ14] as base architecture. The VGG-16 comprises 13 convolutional layers with a kernel size of 3×3 followed by 3 fully-connected layers. To reduce the amount of parameters and to make the network invariant to small translations of the input, max-pooling layers are inserted after the 2nd (conv1_2), 4th (conv2_2), 7th (conv3_3), 10th (conv4_3), and 13th (conv5_3) convolutional layer. In case of Faster R-CNN, the output of the last convolutional layer is used as feature map. As illustrated in Figure 3.1, the dimensions of the feature map are only 1/16 of the dimensions of the input image. Thus, the feature map resolution is insufficient to accurately localize objects in the range of 15 to 30 pixels or even smaller. To account for that, we replace the initially used VGG-16 architecture by a network architecture optimized for handling small instances. The network is inspired by the network proposed in [HWB16] and comprises 4 convolutional layers followed by 3 fully connected layers. Max-pooling layers are inserted after the 1st, 2nd, and 4th convolutional layer. We performed optimization of all relevant network parameters including number of layers, number of filters per layer, kernel size and dropout. Analogous to the original Faster R-CNN, the output of the last convolutional layer is used as feature map. As depicted in Figure 3.2, the dimensions of the feature map are 1/4 of the dimensions of the input image. Thus, a finer localization of small objects is feasible due to the higher resolution of the feature map.

In addition to increasing the feature map resolution, adapting the parameters of the RPN mainly affects the detection performance. The benchmark datasets used

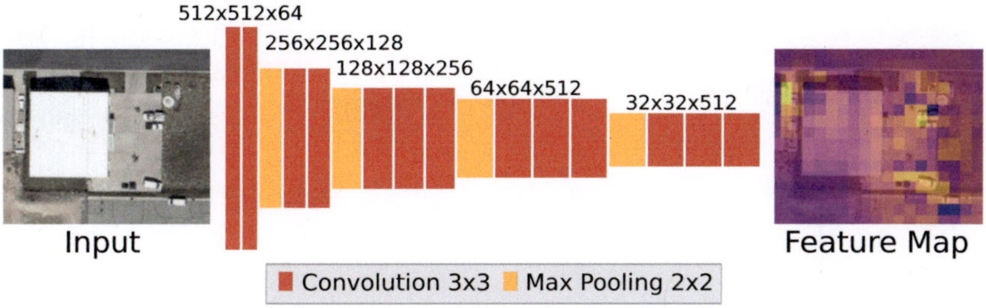

Figure 3.1: Schematic illustration of the convolutional part of VGG-16 and the resulting feature map.

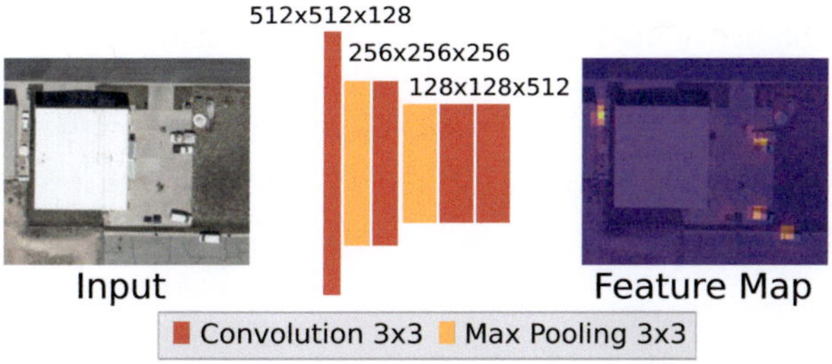

Figure 3.2: Schematic illustration of the convolutional part of the proposed network architecture optimized for handling small objects and the resulting feature map.

for developing Faster R-CNN contain objects that are generally in the range between 50 and 200 pixels. Thus, the parameters of the RPN are adjusted for these object dimensions. First, we reduce the minimal height and width of considered proposals (RPN_MI_SIZE) from 16 to 4, in order to account for the smaller object sizes in case of aerial images. Initially, the top 300 region proposals are considered for classification. This is enough to localize objects in the benchmark datasets, which generally contain only one or a few objects per image. Multiple proposals are typically located around the same object. Aerial images can contain clearly more objects per image and furthermore can contain more potentially disturbing objects, e.g. trailers or solar cells on buildings. Therefore, we set the number of proposals considered for classification to 2,000. As

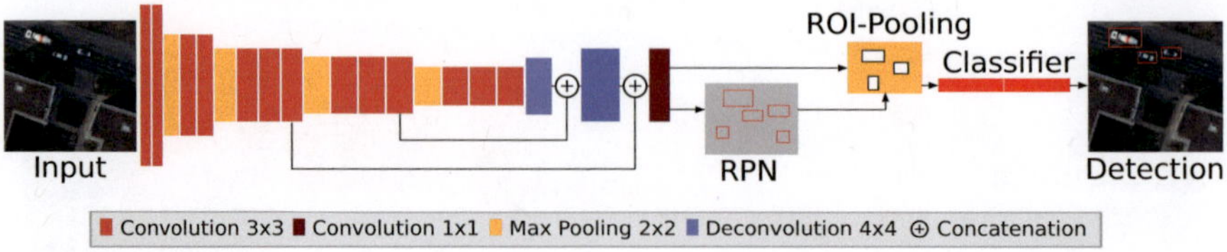

Figure 4.1: Schematic illustration of the Faster R-CNN extended by the deconvolutional module (DFRCNN).

described in Section 2, anchor boxes are used as reference for bounding box regression. The initially used anchor scales are chosen to account for the size of objects in the benchmark datasets. The ANCHOR_BASE_SIZE is set to 16 and the ANCHOR_SCALE factors are set to 8, 16 and 32, which results in anchor boxes with dimensions in the range between 128 and 512 pixels. We set the ANCHOR_BASE_SIZE to 2 while the ANCHOR_SCALE factors are kept unchanged.

4 Deconvolutional Module

To achieve a higher feature map resolution that is sufficient to localize small objects as in case of aerial images, small networks as described in Section 3 or shallow layers of standard architectures like VGG-16 are applicable. However, high-resolution feature maps offer less semantic and contextual information compared to features of deeper layers. The less semantic and contextual information make the detection framework more prone to false alarms due to objects with shapes similar to vehicles.

In order to achieve a high-resolution feature map and semantic and contextual informative features, we extend the Faster R-CNN by a deconvolutional module. The deconvolutional module up-samples low-dimensional feature maps of deep layers and combines the up-sampled features with the features of shallow layers while the feature map resolution is kept sufficiently high to localize small objects. The network architecture of the Faster R-CNN extended by the deconvolutional module (DFRCNN) is schematically illustrated in Figure 4.1. We use VGG-16 as base network architecture. First, the features of conv5_3 are up-sampled by a factor of 2 and then concatenated with the features of conv4_3. Then, thc combined features are up-sampled by a factor of 2 and then concatenated with the features of conv3_3. Thus, the features of conv4_3 and conv5_3 are up-sampled by a factor of 2 and 4, respectively. We use deconvolutional layers with a kernel size of 4×4 and a stride of 2 to up-sample the features. The combined features of conv3_3, conv4_4 and conv5_3 are used as feature map. The feature map dimensions are 1/4 of the dimensions of the input image. To adapt the number of output channels of the feature map required as input for the fully connected layers, we insert an additional convolutional layer with kernel size 1×1.

5 Evaluation

In the following section, we evaluate the impact of the adaptions described in Section 3 and of the deconvolutional module proposed in Section 4. We use Average Precision (AP) computed as defined in [EVGW+10], precision and recall as evaluation metrics. Ground truth (GT) objects are considered as recalled, if the Pascal-overlap criterion [EVGW+10] is satisfied. For all experiments, we use the publicly available DLR 3K Munich Vehicle Aerial Image Dataset. The dataset comprises 20 aerial images with a resolution of 5616×3744 pixels and a ground sampling distance (GSD) of approximately 13 cm. Due to the limited memory capacity of the used GPUs, each image is divided into tiles of 936×624 pixels. Image sections are exemplarily depicted in Figure 5.1. We further align the provided GT annotations at image edges as required for the Faster R-CNN detection framework.

5.1 Adaption to Aerial Images

The impact of increasing the feature map resolution on the detection performance is shown in Figure 5.2. The blue line corresponds to the precision-recall curve for an IoU threshold value of 0.5 used to accept GT objects as recalled (PASCAL-criterion). In case of using the VGG-16 architecture (feature map 1/16), both precision and recall are considerably worse compared to using the optimized network architecture (feature map 1/4). Precision values close to 1 and recall values

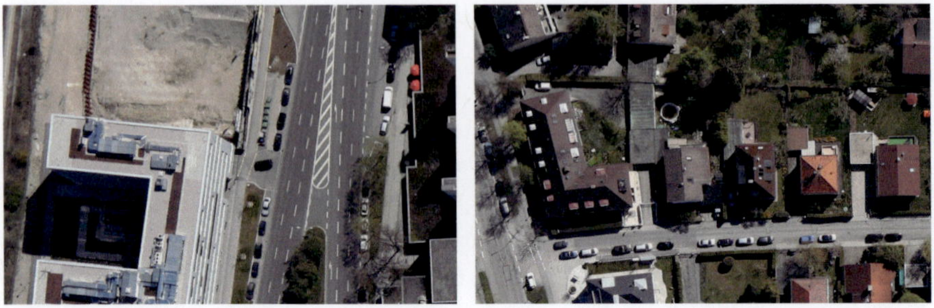

Figure 5.1: Image sections of the DLR 3K Munich Vehicle Aerial Image Dataset [LM15]

above 0.95 are achieved for the optimized network architecture. Reason for the improved performance is the higher feature map resolution as the detections are better localized around the GT elements. The better localization of the detections is illustrated in Figure 5.2 by plotting precision-recall curves for various IoU threshold values used to accept GT objects as recalled. For a resolution of 1/4 of the input image, the performance is only slightly decreasing with increasing IoU thresholds up to 0.5, which indicates a good localization of the detections. In contrast, the performance for lower resolutions decreases stronger with increasing IoU threshold values. The worse localization results in worse classification into object or background though the features comprise more semantic and contextual information. To highlight the difference in localization quality, qualitative detection examples are given for both feature map resolutions (see Figure 5.3 and Figure 5.4, respectively). For a resolution of 1/16 of the input image, the bounding box positions of the detections (red boxes) clearly differ from the GT annotations (green boxes). Furthermore, multiple detections are often generated due to the poor localization. In contrast, the detections for a feature map resolution of 1/4 of the input image overlap very well with the GT annotations.

The impact of adapting the RPN is illustrated in Figure 5.5 and Figure 5.6. Figure 5.5 depicts the proposals' quality for various anchor box sizes. Therefore, we plot the recall achieved for the proposals with respect to the IoU threshold value used to accept the GT objects as recalled. The mean anchor box dimensions are given in the legend. Reducing the anchor box sizes clearly improves the proposals' quality. For anchor box dimensions in the range between 14 and 28 pixels, which is roughly the size of present objects, the best recall values are

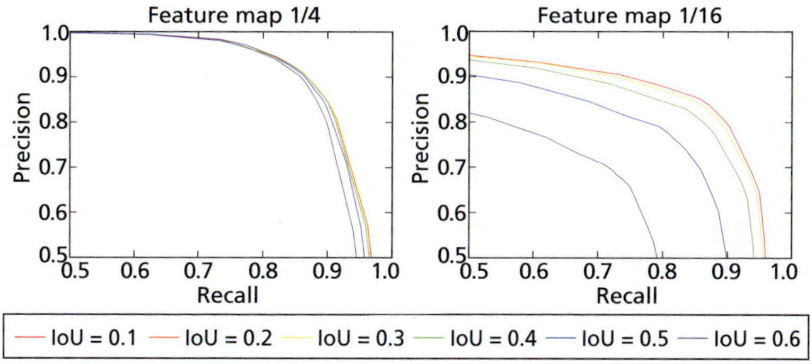

Figure 5.2: Precision-recall curves for various IoU threshold values used to accept GT objects as recalled. Higher feature map resolutions result in better localization quality as the performance decreases clearly less with increasing threshold values.

Figure 5.3: Qualitative detections (red boxes) and corresponding GT annotations (green boxes) for a feature map resolution of 1/16 of the input image. The detections show a relatively poor overlap with the GT annotations and multiple detections are often generated for one GT object.

achieved. The relation between proposals' quality and detection performance is shown in Figure 5.6. Therefore, we plot AP with respect to Average Best Overlap

Figure 5.4: Qualitative detections (red boxes) and corresponding GT annotations (green boxes) for a feature map resolution of 1/4 of the input image. The detections overlap very well with the GT annotations.

(ABO), which is an evaluation metric for the localization quality. ABO is calculated by averaging the best overlap between each GT annotation $g_i \in G$ and the corresponding set of object proposals L:

$$ABO = \frac{1}{|G|} \sum_{g_i \in G} \max_{l_j \in L} IoU(g_i, l_j) \, .$$

The best ABO is achieved for anchor box sizes in the range of present objects. The best AP is achieved for anchor boxes in the range of present objects as well. Thus, we assume that better proposals result in better detection performance.

To sum up the impact of the adaptions, the detection performance for both adaptions and the original Faster R-CNN is given in Figure 5.7. The performance of the original Faster R-CNN is poor. Both precision and recall are clearly less than 1. Applying the adapted RPN results in clearly improved precision and recall (VGG-16 adapted). However, the detection performance is still poor. Replacing the VGG-16 architecture with the optimized network architecture and consequently increasing the feature map resolution results in a significantly improved detection performance. It is to mention, that both adaptions are necessary to achieve the best detection results.

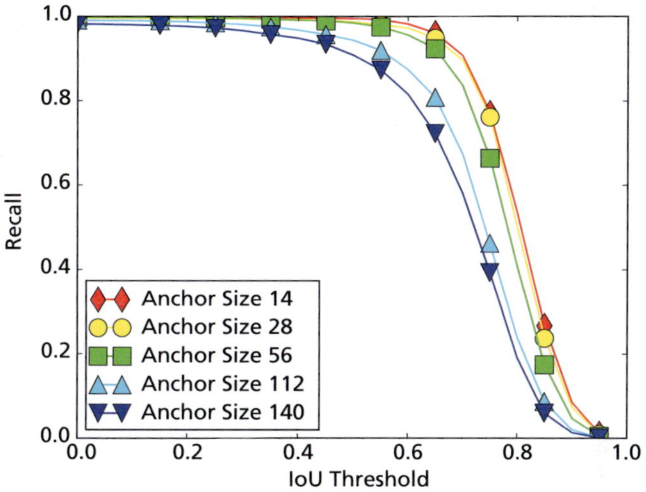

Figure 5.5: Recall-IoU curves for various anchor box sizes used as bounding box reference. The mean anchor box dimensions are given in the legend.

5.2 Deconvolutional Module

The impact of our proposed deconvolutional module on the detection performance is given in Table 5.1. We compare the detection results of our proposed Deconvolutional Faster R-CNN (DFRCNN) to baselines on the DLR 3K dataset for various GSDs. For this, we re-scaled the input images for training and testing by factors 1, 0.75, and 0.5. As baseline, we consider Faster R-CNN with different convolutional layers of VGG-16 used as feature map. For each GSD, the anchor box sizes are adapted for all Faster R-CNNs to the size of present objects. As discussed above increasing the feature map resolution from 1/16 of the input image (VGG-16 – conv5_3) to 1/4 of the input image (VGG-16 – conv3_3) clearly improves the detection performance especially for tiny objects as for a GSD of 26 cm. The performance is improved though the used features are less semantically and contextually informative. To account for the smaller receptive fields and less semantic information, we use our DFRCNN which combines features of conv3_3, conv4_3, and conv5_3 as described in Section 4. The performance is improved for all GSD especially for a GSD of 26 cm and consequently smaller

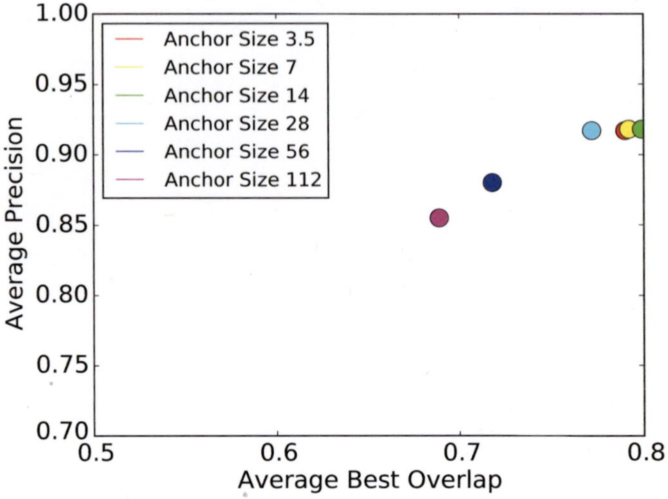

Figure 5.6: Average Precision (AP) w.r.t. Average Best Overlap (ABO) for various anchor box sizes used as bounding box reference. Applying region proposals with better ABO results in higher AP.

objects. In case of GSD 26, the number of false positive detections is reduced by a factor of 33.4% compared to VGG-16 — conv3_3, while the number of false negative detections remains almost unchanged.

To illustrate the impact of adding more semantic information, qualitative detection examples for Faster R-CNN using conv3_3 as feature map (left column) and

Table 5.1: Average Precision of our proposed DFRCNN compared to baselines on the DLR 3K dataset for various GSDs (in cm).

Method	GSD 13	GSD 19.5	GSD 26
VGG-16 — conv5_3	0.770	0.558	0.207
VGG-16 — conv4_3	0.967	0.896	0.601
VGG-16 — conv3_3	0.979	0.944	0.836
DFRCNN	**0.980**	**0.957**	**0.864**

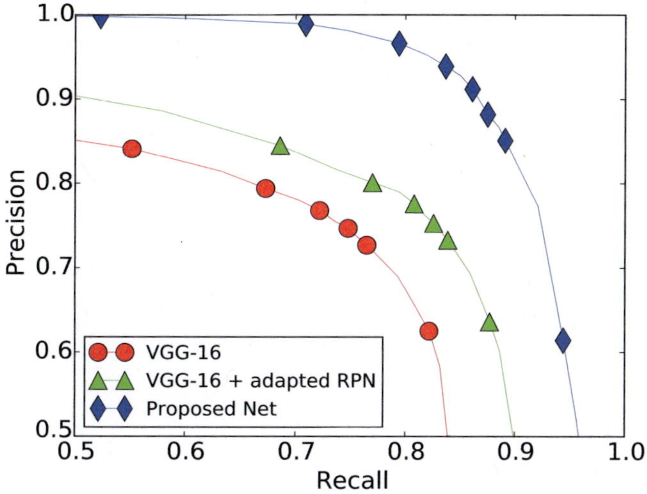

Figure 5.7: Precision-recall curves of the original Faster R-CNN and for both adaptions.

our proposed DFRCNN (right column) are given in Figure 5.8. Therefore, we use a classification threshold value of 0.5. For Faster R-CNN using conv3_3, several false positive detections are caused by objects with shapes similar to vehicles such as solar cells or chimneys on buildings. Integrating more semantic information clearly reduces the number of false positive detections caused by such objects.

6 Summary

In this report, the applicability of Faster R-CNN for vehicle detection in aerial images was demonstrated. Therefore, we have systematically evaluated the impact of adapting relevant parameters of Faster R-CNN to the characteristics of aerial images. The most improvement in detection performance was achieved by adapting the size of the anchor boxes used for bounding box regression and by increasing the feature map resolution as the initial resolution is insufficient to localize small objects. To achieve high feature map resolutions that are sufficient to localize small objects, small networks or shallow layers of standard architectures

Figure 5.8: Qualitative detections (red boxes) and corresponding GT (green boxes) for Faster R-CNN using *conv3_3* (left column) and our proposed DFRCNN (right column) on DLR 3K indicate that false alarms due to objects with shapes similar to vehicles are reduced by integrating more semantic information.

like VGG-16 are applicable, which offer less semantic and contextual information compared to features of deeper layers. In order to overcome this drawback, we extended the original Faster R-CNN by a deconvolutional module. Therefore, features of deeper layers are up-sampled and combined with features of shallower layers. The detection performance is improved by integrating features with more semantic information especially for tiny objects as the number of false positive detections due to objects with shapes similar to vehicles is reduced.

Bibliography

[CH16] Gong Cheng and Junwei Han. A survey on object detection in optical remote sensing images. *ISPRS Journal of Photogrammetry and Remote Sensing*, 117:11–28, 2016.

[CXLP14] Xueyun Chen, Shiming Xiang, Cheng-Lin Liu, and Chun-Hong Pan. Vehicle detection in satellite images by hybrid deep convolutional neural networks. *IEEE GRSL*, 11(10):1797–1801, 2014.

[EVGW+10] Mark Everingham, Luc Van Gool, Christopher KI Williams, John Winn, and Andrew Zisserman. The pascal visual object classes (voc) challenge. *International journal of computer vision*, 88(2):303–338, 2010.

[Gir15] Ross Girshick. Fast R-CNN. In *Proceedings of the IEEE International Conference on Computer Vision*, pages 1440–1448, 2015.

[HWB16] Christian Herrmann, Dieter Willersinn, and Jürgen Beyerer. Low-resolution convolutional neural networks for video face recognition. In *Advanced Video and Signal Based Surveillance*. IEEE, 2016.

[KPF16] Georgy V Konoplich, Evgeniy O Putin, and Andrey A Filchenkov. Application of deep learning to the problem of vehicle detection in UAV images. In *Soft Computing and Measurements (SCM), 2016 XIX IEEE International Conference on*, pages 4–6. IEEE, 2016.

[LM15] K. Liu and G. Mattyus. Fast multiclass vehicle detection on aerial images. *GRSL, IEEE*, PP(99):1–5, 2015.

[MM14] Thomas Moranduzzo and Farid Melgani. Detecting cars in UAV images with a catalog-based approach. *IEEE Transactions on Geoscience and Remote Sensing*, 52(10):6356–6367, 2014.

[RHGS15] Shaoqing Ren, Kaiming He, Ross Girshick, and Jian Sun. Faster R-CNN: Towards real-time object detection with region proposal networks. In *Advances in neural information processing systems*, pages 91–99, 2015.

[SZ14] Karen Simonyan and Andrew Zisserman. Very deep convolutional networks for large-scale image recognition. *arXiv preprint arXiv:1409.1556*, 2014.

Karlsruher Schriftenreihe zur Anthropomatik
(ISSN 1863-6489)

Herausgeber: Prof. Dr.-Ing. habil. Jürgen Beyerer

Band 1 Jürgen Geisler
Leistung des Menschen am Bildschirmarbeitsplatz. 2006
ISBN 3-86644-070-7

Band 2 Elisabeth Peinsipp-Byma
Leistungserhöhung durch Assistenz in interaktiven Systemen zur Szenenanalyse. 2007
ISBN 978-3-86644-149-1

Band 3 Jürgen Geisler, Jürgen Beyerer (Hrsg.)
Mensch-Maschine-Systeme. 2010
ISBN 978-3-86644-457-7

Band 4 Jürgen Beyerer, Marco Huber (Hrsg.)
Proceedings of the 2009 Joint Workshop of Fraunhofer IOSB and Institute for Anthropomatics, Vision and Fusion Laboratory. 2010
ISBN 978-3-86644-469-0

Band 5 Thomas Usländer
Service-oriented design of environmental information systems. 2010
ISBN 978-3-86644-499-7

Band 6 Giulio Milighetti
Multisensorielle diskret-kontinuierliche Überwachung und Regelung humanoider Roboter. 2010
ISBN 978-3-86644-568-0

Band 7 Jürgen Beyerer, Marco Huber (Hrsg.)
Proceedings of the 2010 Joint Workshop of Fraunhofer IOSB and Institute for Anthropomatics, Vision and Fusion Laboratory. 2011
ISBN 978-3-86644-609-0

Band 8 Eduardo Monari
Dynamische Sensorselektion zur auftragsorientierten Objektverfolgung in Kameranetzwerken. 2011
ISBN 978-3-86644-729-5

Die Bände sind unter www.ksp.kit.edu als PDF frei verfügbar oder als Druckausgabe bestellbar.

Band 9 Thomas Bader
Multimodale Interaktion in Multi-Display-Umgebungen. 2011
ISBN 3-86644-760-8

Band 10 Christian Frese
Planung kooperativer Fahrmanöver für kognitive Automobile. 2012
ISBN 978-3-86644-798-1

Band 11 Jürgen Beyerer, Alexey Pak (Hrsg.)
Proceedings of the 2011 Joint Workshop of Fraunhofer IOSB and Institute for Anthropomatics, Vision and Fusion Laboratory. 2012
ISBN 978-3-86644-855-1

Band 12 Miriam Schleipen
Adaptivität und Interoperabilität von Manufacturing Execution Systemen (MES). 2013
ISBN 978-3-86644-955-8

Band 13 Jürgen Beyerer, Alexey Pak (Hrsg.)
Proceedings of the 2012 Joint Workshop of Fraunhofer IOSB and Institute for Anthropomatics, Vision and Fusion Laboratory. 2013
ISBN 978-3-86644-988-6

Band 14 Hauke-Hendrik Vagts
Privatheit und Datenschutz in der intelligenten Überwachung: Ein datenschutzgewährendes System, entworfen nach dem „Privacy by Design" Prinzip. 2013
ISBN 978-3-7315-0041-4

Band 15 Christian Kühnert
Data-driven Methods for Fault Localization in Process Technology. 2013
ISBN 978-3-7315-0098-8

Band 16 Alexander Bauer
Probabilistische Szenenmodelle für die Luftbildauswertung. 2014
ISBN 978-3-7315-0167-1

Band 17 Jürgen Beyerer, Alexey Pak (Hrsg.)
Proceedings of the 2013 Joint Workshop of Fraunhofer IOSB and Institute for Anthropomatics, Vision and Fusion Laboratory. 2014
ISBN 978-3-7315-0212-8

Die Bände sind unter www.ksp.kit.edu als PDF frei verfügbar oder als Druckausgabe bestellbar.

Band 18 Michael Teutsch
Moving Object Detection and Segmentation for Remote Aerial Video Surveillance. 2015
ISBN 978-3-7315-0320-0

Band 19 Marco Huber
Nonlinear Gaussian Filtering: Theory, Algorithms, and Applications. 2015
ISBN 978-3-7315-0338-5

Band 20 Jürgen Beyerer, Alexey Pak (Hrsg.)
Proceedings of the 2014 Joint Workshop of Fraunhofer IOSB and Institute for Anthropomatics, Vision and Fusion Laboratory. 2014
ISBN 978-3-7315-0401-6

Band 21 Todor Dimitrov
Permanente Optimierung dynamischer Probleme der Fertigungssteuerung unter Einbeziehung von Benutzerinteraktionen. 2015
ISBN 978-3-7315-0426-9

Band 22 Benjamin Kühn
Interessengetriebene audiovisuelle Szenenexploration. 2016
ISBN 978-3-7315-0457-3

Band 23 Yvonne Fischer
Wissensbasierte probabilistische Modellierung für die Situationsanalyse am Beispiel der maritimen Überwachung. 2016
ISBN 978-3-7315-0460-3

Band 24 Jürgen Beyerer, Alexey Pak (Hrsg.)
Proceedings of the 2015 Joint Workshop of Fraunhofer IOSB and Institute for Anthropomatics, Vision and Fusion Laboratory. 2016
ISBN 978-3-7315-0519-8

Band 25 Pascal Birnstill
Privacy-Respecting Smart Video Surveillance Based on Usage Control Enforcement. 2016
ISBN 978-3-7315-0538-9

Band 26 Philipp Woock
Umgebungskartenschätzung aus Sidescan-Sonardaten für ein autonomes Unterwasserfahrzeug. 2016
ISBN 978-3-7315-0541-9

Band 27 Janko Petereit
Adaptive State × Time Lattices: A Contribution to Mobile Robot Motion Planning in Unstructured Dynamic Environments. 2017
ISBN 978-3-7315-0580-8

Band 28 Erik Ludwig Krempel
Steigerung der Akzeptanz von intelligenter Videoüberwachung in öffentlichen Räumen. 2017
ISBN 978-3-7315-0598-3

Band 29 Jürgen Moßgraber
Ein Rahmenwerk für die Architektur von Frühwarnsystemen. 2017
ISBN 978-3-7315-0638-6

Band 30 Andrey Belkin
World Modeling for Intelligent Autonomous Systems. 2017
ISBN 978-3-7315-0641-6

Band 31 Chettapong Janya-Anurak
Framework for Analysis and Identification of Nonlinear Distributed Parameter Systems using Bayesian Uncertainty Quantification based on Generalized Polynomial Chaos. 2017
ISBN 978-3-7315-0642-3

Band 32 David Münch
Begriffliche Situationsanalyse aus Videodaten bei unvollständiger und fehlerhafter Information. 2017
ISBN 978-3-7315-0644-7

Band 33 Jürgen Beyerer, Alexey Pak (Eds.)
Proceedings of the 2016 Joint Workshop of Fraunhofer IOSB and Institute for Anthropomatics, Vision and Fusion Laboratory. 2017
ISBN 978-3-7315-0678-2

Band 34 Jürgen Beyerer, Alexey Pak and Miro Taphanel (Eds.)
Proceedings of the 2017 Joint Workshop of Fraunhofer IOSB and Institute for Anthropomatics, Vision and Fusion Laboratory. 2018
ISBN 978-3-7315-0779-6

Die Reform der Bestechungsdelikte

Europäische Hochschulschriften
Publications Universitaires Européennes
European University Studies

Reihe II
Rechtswissenschaft

Série II Series II
Droit
Law

Bd./Vol. 4283

PETER LANG
Frankfurt am Main · Berlin · Bern · Bruxelles · New York · Oxford · Wien

Michael Köhler

Die Reform der Bestechungsdelikte

Reformgeschichte und Reformperspektiven unter besonderer Berücksichtigung der subjektiven Tatumstände der §§ 331 ff. StGB

PETER LANG
Europäischer Verlag der Wissenschaften

Bibliografische Information Der Deutschen Bibliothek
Die Deutsche Bibliothek verzeichnet diese Publikation in der Deutschen Nationalbibliografie; detaillierte bibliografische Daten sind im Internet über <http://dnb.ddb.de> abrufbar.

Zugl.: Frankfurt (Main), Univ., Diss., 2005

D 30
ISSN 0531-7312
ISBN 3-631-54435-9

www.peterlang.de

Vorwort

Die Arbeit hat dem Fachbereich Rechtswissenschaft der Johann Wolfgang Goethe-Universität Frankfurt am Main im Wintersemester 2002/2003 als Dissertation vorgelegen. Schrifttum und Rechtsprechung sind bis Juni 2002 berücksichtigt.

Ich danke Herrn Professor Dr. Cornelius Prittwitz für die Betreuung der Arbeit und mancherlei Anregung.

Ich widme meine Arbeit meiner Frau Carola, die mich tatkräftig unterstützt hat, und meiner kleinen Tochter Lilly. Im Gedenken an meinen 1995 verstorbenen Vater Werner danke ich auch meiner Mutter Irmgard Katharina für die seelische Unterstützung.

Berlin, 2. Juni 2005 Michael Köhler

Inhaltsverzeichnis

Abkürzungsverzeichnis XVII

Einleitung 1

I. Ausgangslage und Reformbestrebungen 1
II. Problem- und Fragestellungen 2
III. Stand der wissenschaftlichen Diskussion 5
IV. Aufbau der Untersuchung 7

Teil A Die subjektiven Tatbestandserfordernisse der Bestechungsdelikte 9

Erster Abschnitt : Die Rechtsentwicklung unter dem RStGB von 1871 bis zum EGStGB von 1974 13

I. Das Rechtsgut der Bestechungsdelikte 13

1. Die Auffassungen im Schrifttum 13

a) Schutz vor „Verfälschung des Staatswillens“ 13
b) Schutz des „Vertrauens der Öffentlichkeit“ 15

2. Die Auffassung in der Rechtsprechung 15

a) Das Urteil RGSt 39, 193 vom 5.10.1906 15
b) Das Urteil BGHSt 15, 88 vom 25.7.1960 16

3. Eine erste Stellungnahme zur Bestimmung des geschützten Rechtsguts 16

II. Die subjektiven Elemente der Tathandlungen der §§ 331-333 17

1. Annahme eines Vorteils (§§ 331 und 332) 17
2. Gewähren eines Vorteils (§ 333) 18
3. Fordern (§§ 331,332), Anbieten und Versprechen eines Vorteils (§ 333) 19
4. Sichversprechenlassen (§§ 331, 332) 20
5. Zusammenfassende Bewertung 21

III. Die subjektiven Bestandteile des Äquivalenzverhältnisses der §§ 331-333 22

1. Definition 22
2. Das Äquivalenzverhältnis bei den Tathandlungen „Annehmen“ und „Sichversprechenlassen“ (§§ 331,332) 22

a) Auffassung der Rechtsprechung 23

aa) Frühere Entscheidungen des RG 23

aaa) RGSt 51, 87 23

bbb) RGSt 65, 52 23
ccc) RGSt 65, 277 23

bb) Korrektur der subjektiven Taterfordernisse durch die spätere Rechtsprechung 23

aaa) RGSt 74, 251 23
bbb) RGSt 77, 75 24
ccc) BGHSt 11, 125 24

b) Auffassung des Schrifttums 24

aa) Voraussetzung einer vertragsmäßigen Willensübereinstimmung 25

aaa) Die Position von E. Schmidt 25
bbb) Die Gegenposition von Fuhrmann 26

bb) Voraussetzung des Willens, die (pflichtwidrige) Amtshandlung zu begehen 26

aaa) Die Argumente von E. Schmidt 26
bbb) Die Argumentation von R. Schmitt 27
ccc) Das Argument von Klug 28
ddd) Die Argumente von Fuhrmann und von Kirschbaum und Schmitz gegen die Position von E. Schmidt 28

cc) Voraussetzung der inneren Entschließungsfreiheit beim Ermessensbeamten 29

aaa) Die Pflichtwidrigkeit von Ermessensentscheidungen 29

aaaa) RGSt 77, 75 29
bbbb) Das BGH-Urteil vom 27.10.1959 30
cccc) Die Kritik des Schrifttums 30
dddd) Die BGH-Urteile 15, 88 und 15, 239 aus dem Jahr 1960 32

bbb) Ergebnis 32

3. Das Äquivalenzverhältnis bei der Tathandlung „Fordern“ 33

a) Die Entwicklung der Rechtsprechung 33

aa) Die Auffassung des RG 33
bb) Die Auffassung des BGH 34

b) Die Auffassung des Schrifttums 34

aa) Die Position von E. Schmidt 34
bb) Die Gegenposition von Baumann, Kirschbaum/Schmitz und Fuhrmann 35

cc) Zusammenfassende Bewertung 35

4. Das Äquivalenzverhältnis im Hinblick auf die Deliktsabsicht des § 333 36

a) (Bedingter) Vorsatz genügt nicht für die Deliktsabsicht 37
b) Tatrichterliche Feststellung der Deliktsabsicht 37

5. Zusammenfassung 38

IV. Vorsatz- und Irrtumsfragen 40

1. Das BGH-Urteil 2, 194 40
2. Vorsatz und Irrtum bei § 331 42
3. Vorsatz und Irrtum bei § 332 43
4. Vorsatz und Irrtum bei § 333 43

V. Zwischenergebnis 44

Zweiter Abschnitt : Die Rechtsentwicklung unter dem EGStGB von 1974 47

I. Neubestimmung des Rechtsguts der Bestechungsdelikte 47

1. Die Begründung des Gesetzgebers zum EGStGB 48
2. Die Auffassung der Rechtsprechung 48
3. Die neueren Auffassungen im Schrifttum 49

a) „Verfälschung des Staatswillens" 50

aa) Jaques 50
bb) Dölling 51

b) „Vertrauen der Allgemeinheit" 51
c) Verknüpfung beider Schutzzwecke im Sinne eines „komplexen" Rechtsguts 51

aa) Bauchrowitz 52
bb) Graupe 52
cc) Loos 52
dd) Gribl 52
ee) Hardtung 52
ff) Schwieger 53
gg) Überhofen 53

d) Eigene Stellungnahme 53

II. Die gesetzlichen Änderungen des EGStGB 55

1. Die Neuregelung des Äquivalenzverhältnisses 56

a) Begründung des Gesetzgebers 56
b) Reaktion des BGH 57

c) Auffassung der Literatur 57
d) Eigene Auffassung 58

2. Die gesetzliche Festschreibung der vom BGH entwickelten Grundsätze zur Vollendung der Tat beim Ermessensbeamten 62

a) Problemstellung 62
b) Ansatzpunkt „Schutzgut" 64

3. Subjektive Einbruchstelle beim neu aufgenommenen Abs. 3 des § 334? 66

a) Neuregelung des § 334 Abs. 3 66
b) Objektive Verkürzung des Tatbestandes 66
c) Unechte Zweiaktigkeit der Tathandlung 67
d) Inhalt der Versuchshandlung des § 334 Abs. 3 67

aa) Objektive Voraussetzungen 67
bb) Subjektive Voraussetzungen 67

e) Eigene Auffassung 68

aa) Verstoß gegen Bestimmtheitsgrundsatz? 68

aaa) Rückschlüsse vom objektiven auf den subjektiven Tatbestand 69
bbb) Prüfung der Plausibilität 69
ccc) Nachweis von Irrtümern auf der Tatsachenseite 69

bb) Systematischer Ansatz verfehlt? 70
cc) Anknüpfungspunkt Rechtsgut 71

III. Zwischenergebnis 72

Dritter Abschnitt : Die Rechtsentwicklung unter dem KorrBekG von 1997 73

I. Die strafrechtlichen Änderungen des KorrBekG, die keiner vertieften Prüfung unterzogen werden 74

1. Amtsträgerbegriff 74
2. Neuformulierung des § 333 74
3. Strafverschärfungen 75
4. Vermögensstrafe, Erweiterter Verfall (§§ 302, 338) 75
5. Bestechlichkeit und Bestechung im geschäftlichen Verkehr (§§ 299-302) 76
6. Wettbewerbsbeschränkende Absprachen bei Ausschreibungen (§ 298) 77
7. Keine Kronzeugenregelung für die Bestechungsdelikte 79

II. Die näher zu prüfenden materiell-rechtlichen Änderungen des KorrBekG 79

1. Drittvorteile 79

a) Begründung des Gesetzgebers 80

b) Begründung des Schrifttums 81

aa) Dölling 81
bb) Möhrenschlager 81
cc) Schaupensteiner 82

c) Eigene Auffassung 82

2. Unrechtsvereinbarung 83

a) Die Lösung des Gesetzgebers 83

aa) Begründung des Vorschlags „für die Dienstausübung" 83
bb) Begründung des Vorschlags „im Zusammenhang mit dem Amt" 84

b) Die Meinungen im Schrifttum 85

aa) Dölling 85
bb) Möhrenschlager 85
cc) Volk 86
dd) Schaupensteiner und Schaefer 86
ee) Schlicht, Lüderssen und König 87
ff) Hettinger und Ransiek 87

c) Eigene Auffassung 88

aa) „Im Zusammenhang mit dem Amt" 89
bb) „Für die Dienstausübung" 90

aaa) Erster Schritt: Definition und Begriffsbestimmung durch Gesetzgeber 90
bbb) Zweiter Schritt: Bisherige BGH-Rspr. 90
ccc) Dritter Schritt: Nur ein gradueller Unterschied zwischen alter und neuer Gesetzesfassung? 91
ddd) Lockerung der Unrechtsvereinbarung ein richtiger Schritt? 93

III. Strafrechtliche Regelungen zur internationalen Korruptionsbekämpfung und Rechtsvergleich nationaler Rechtsordnungen im Hinblick auf die Rechtsgutsfrage und die Unrechtsvereinbarung 94

1. Strafrechtliche Regelungen zur internationalen Korruptionsbekämpfung 94

a) EUBestG 94
b) IntBestG 95
c) Stellungnahme 96

2. Rechtsvergleich nationaler Rechtsordnungen im Hinblick auf die Rechtsgutsfrage und die Unrechtsvereinbarung 97

a) Ansatzpunkte für einen Rechtsgüterschutz 97

aa) Verallgemeinerungsfähiger Grundgedanke? 97

aaa) Italien 97
bbb) Österreich 98
ccc) Frankreich 98
ddd) Spanien 98
eee) Griechenland 98
fff) Portugal 98
ggg) Türkei 99
hhh) Niederlande 99
iii) Japan 99
jjj) USA 99
kkk) China, Russland und Polen 100
lll) Schweden 100

bb) Ergebnis 100

b) Konzeptioneller Ansatz bezüglich des Tatmerkmals der Unrechtsvereinbarung 101

aa) Fragestellung 101

aaa) Italien 102
bbb) Österreich 102
ccc) Frankreich 102
ddd) Spanien 103
eee) Griechenland 103
fff) Portugal 104
ggg) Türkei 104
hhh) Niederlande 104
iii) Japan 104
jjj) USA 105
kkk) China, Russland und Polen 105
lll) Schweden 106

bb) Ergebnis 106

IV. Ergebnis Teil A 108

Teil B Die Auswirkungen des KorrBekG 111

Erster Abschnitt: Die strafrechtliche Subsumtion 111

I. Die Fälle 111

1. Fall A 111
2. Fall B 112
3. Fall C 112

II. Bewertung 112

1. Bewertung außerhalb der Strafrechtsordnung 112

a) Definitionen und Abgrenzungen 113

aa) Sponsoring 113
bb) Drittmittelforschung 113
cc) Spenden und Schenkungen 114
dd) Fallzuordnung 114

b) Billigung durch den Gesetzgeber 114

aa) Sponsoring 114
bb) Drittmittelforschung 116

c) Zwischenergebnis 117

2. Prüfung der Strafbarkeit nach § 331 117

a) Sanktionsbedürftigkeit? 119

aa) Gewandeltes Staatsverständnis 119
bb) Schutzgut des Vertrauens der Bevölkerung in die Integrität der Verwaltung ein verlässliches Kriterium zur Erfassung korruptiven Unrechts? 121

aaa) Fall A 121

aaaa) Geschehensablauf (Was passiert wirklich?) 121
bbbb) Betrachtung von außen 121
cccc) Ergebnis 122

bbb) Fall B 122

aaaa) Geschehensablauf 122
bbbb) Betrachtung von außen 123
cccc) Ergebnis 124

ccc) Fall C 124

aaaa) Geschehensablauf 124
bbbb) Betrachtung von außen 124
cccc) Ergebnis 126

b) Tatbestandliche Begutachtung 126

aa) Fall A 126

aaa) Tatbestandliche Fragestellung 126

aaaa) Der Vorteilsbegriff des § 331 127
bbbb) „Für die Dienstausübung“ 128

cccc) Tatbestandliche Einbruchstelle 133

bbb) Ergebnis 134

bb) Fall B 134

aaa) Tatbestandliche Fragestellung 134

aaaa) Vorteil aus Vertrag 135

aaaaa) BGHSt 31, 264 135
bbbbb) Kritik des Schrifttums 136
ccccc) Eigene Auffassung 137

bbbb) Vorteil aus Überkompensation 139
cccc) Immaterielle Vorteile 142
dddd) Tatbestandliche Einbruchstelle 143

bbb) Ergebnis 144

cc) Fall C 145

aaa) Tatbestandliche Fragestellung 145

aaaa) Vorteil aus Vertrag 145
bbbb) Vorteil aus faktischer Verfügung über die Sponsorengelder 147
cccc) Immaterielle Vorteile 148
dddd) „Für die Dienstausübung" 149
eeee) Tatbestandliche Einbruchstelle 149

bbb) Ergebnis 150

dd) Konsequenzen aus den Fallergebnissen? 150

Zweiter Abschnitt : Die strafrechtlichen Korrektive zur Eingrenzung der Strafbarkeit der Vorteilsannahme 153

I. Bereits nach altem Recht vorhandene Instrumentarien 153

1. Institut der Sozialadäquanz 153
2. Institut der Genehmigung nach § 331 Abs. 3 154

II. Auf dem 61. DJT vorgeschlagene Alternative der „Eignung" des Vorteils 155

1. Auffassung von Lüderssen 156
2. Auffassung von Volk 156
3. Eigene Auffassung 157

III. Eingrenzungsversuche auf der Grundlage des geltenden Rechts 158

1. Der Ansatz von Zieschang 158
2. Der Ansatz von Cramer 160
3. Der Ansatz von Dauster 160
4. Der Ansatz des BGH 161
5. Eigene Auffassung 162

a) Ausgangspunkt Rechtsgut 162
b) Rechtsgut korrespondiert mit der objektiven Rechtsordnung 163
c) Begrenzung des tatbestandlichen Geltungsbereichs 164

IV. Ergebnis Teil B 165

Teil C Das öffentliche Dienstrecht als rechtliche Alternative zum Strafrecht? 167

I. Meinungen im Schrifttum 170

1. E. Schmidt 170
2. Wagner 170
3. Hamm 171
4. Hettinger 171
5. Möhrenschlager 172
6. Dölling 172
7. Zwischenergebnis 173

II. Öffentlich-rechtlicher Strafanspruch 174

1. Strafzwecke 174
2. Zwecke des Disziplinarrechts 176

a) Meinung des Bundesdisziplinaranwalts 176
b) Urteil des BVerwG vom 30.8.2000 176
c) Stellungnahme 177

aa) Gesetzlich dokumentierter Reinerhaltungszweck 177
bb) Generalpräventiver Zweck und Vergeltungsgedanke 178
cc) Erziehungszweck 179

3. Vergleich der Strafzwecke mit den Zwecken des Disziplinarrechts 180
4. Ergebnis 182

III. Unterschiedlicher Rechtsgüterschutz? 182

1. Wirkbereich 183
2. Schutzzweck des Disziplinarrechts 184
3. Schutzzweck des § 70 BBG 184
4. Ergebnis 186

IV. Sind die verfügbaren Disziplinarmaßnahmen als Sanktionsmittel im Vergleich zu den strafrechtlichen Sanktionen ausreichend? 187

1. Verweis und Geldbuße 187

2. Kürzung der Dienstbezüge 187
3. Zurückstufung 188
4. Entfernung aus dem Beamtenverhältnis 188
5. Ergebnis 189

V. Verfahrensrechtliche Unterschiede des neuen BDG im Vergleich zum Strafverfahrensrecht; Vollzugsproblematik 189

1. Legalitätsprinzip 189
2. Opportunitätsprinzip 190
3. Beschleunigungsgrundsatz 192
4. Neugestaltung des Bundesdisziplinarrechts 193

a) Bezug zur Strafprozessordnung 194
b) Verfahrenssystematik 194

aa) Einheitliches Verwaltungsverfahren 194
bb) Zuständigkeit der Verwaltungsgerichtsbarkeit 195

c) Abschaffung der Institution des Bundesdisziplinaranwalts 197
d) Bedeutsame Einzelvorschriften im Hinblick auf die Korruptionsbekämpfung 197

aa) § 14 BDG 197
bb) § 80 BDG 198
cc) Wegfall des § 28 Abs. 2 BDO 199
dd) § 27 BDG 200

5. Stellungnahme 200

VI. Ergebnis Teil C 205

VII. Zusammenfassung der Ergebnisse aus Teil A, B und C 206

Anhang 1 209

Anhang 2 210

Anhang 3 213

Literaturverzeichnis 217

Abkürzungsverzeichnis

a. A.	andere Auffassung
ABl. EG	Amtsblatt der Europäischen Gemeinschaft
Abs.	Absatz
Abt.	Abteilung
a. F.	alte Fassung
Amtl.	Amtliche bzw. Amtlicher bzw. Amtliches bzw. Amtlichen
Anm.	Anmerkung
Aufl.	Auflage
AuslG	Ausländergesetz
Az.	Aktenzeichen
BAnz.	Bundesanzeiger
BAT	Bundesangestelltentarifvertrag
BB	Betriebsberater
BBG	Bundesbeamtengesetz
Bd.	Band
BDO	Bundesdisziplinarordnung
BDG	Bundesdisziplinargesetz
BDHE	Entscheidungen des Bundesdisziplinarhofes
BDiszNOG	Gesetz zur Neuordnung des Bundesdisziplinarrechts
BGB	Bürgerliches Gesetzbuch
BGBl.	Bundesgesetzblatt
BGH	Bundesgerichtshof
BGHSt	Entscheidungssammlung des Bundesgerichtshofs in Strafsachen
BKA	Bundeskriminalamt
BMF	Bundesminister/-ministerium der Finanzen
BMI	Bundesminister/-ministerium des Innern
BR	Bundesrat
BReg.	Bundesregierung
BR-Drs.	Bundesratsdrucksache
BRRG	Beamtenrechtsrahmengesetz
BT	Besonderer Teil
BT-Drs.	Bundestagsdrucksache
BtMG	Betäubungsmittelgesetz
BVerfG	Bundesverfassungsgericht
BVerfGE	Entscheidungen des Bundesverfassungsgerichts
BVerwG	Bundesverwaltungsgericht
BVerwGE	Entscheidungen des Bundesverwaltungsgerichts
bzgl.	bezüglich
bzw.	beziehungsweise
CDU	Christlich Demokratische Union
CSU	Christlich Soziale Union
DJT	Deutscher Juristentag
d. h.	das heißt
DÖD	Der Öffentliche Dienst

Dok.Ber.	Dokumentarische Berichte
E	Entwurf
EG	Europäische Gemeinschaft
EGStGB	Einführungsgesetz zum Strafgesetzbuch
Einl.	Einleitung
EStG	Einkommensteuergesetz
EU	Europäische Union
EUBestG	Gesetz zu dem Protokoll vom 27. 9. 1996 zum Übereinkommen über den Schutz der finanziellen Interessen der Europäischen Gemeinschaften (EU-Bestechungsgesetz)
f.	folgende bzw. folgender bzw. folgendes
ff.	fortfolgend
FDP	Freie Demokratische Partei
Fn.	Fußnote
GA	Goltdammer's Archiv für Strafrecht
GG	Grundgesetz für die Bundesrepublik Deutschland
ggf.	gegebenenfalls
GKÖD	Gesamtkommentar Öffentliches Dienstrecht
GmbH	Gesellschaft mit beschränkter Haftung
GMBl.	Gemeinsames Ministerialblatt
GSlg.	Gesetz-Sammlung für die Preußischen Staaten
GSSt	Großer Strafsenat
GWB	Gesetz gegen Wettbewerbsbeschränkungen
h. L.	herrschende Lehre
h. M.	herrschende Meinung
HRG	Hochschulrahmengesetz
i. d. F.	in der Fassung
IntBestG	Gesetz zu dem Übereinkommen vom 17. 12. 1997 über die Bekämpfung der Bestechung ausländischer Amtsträger im internationalen Geschäftsverkehr (Gesetz zur Bekämpfung internationaler Bestechung)
i. S.	im Sinne
i. S. d.	im Sinne des/der
JR	Juristische Rundschau
Jura	Juristische Ausbildung
JuS	Juristische Schulung, Zeitschrift für Studium und Ausbildung
JZ	Juristenzeitung
KorrBekG	Gesetz zur Bekämpfung der Korruption
LK	Leipziger Kommentar
MedR	Medizinrecht
MDR	Monatsschrift für deutsches Recht

m.w.N.	mit weiteren Nachweisen
NJW	Neue Juristische Wochenschrift
nlStGB	Niederländisches Strafgesetzbuch
Nr.	Nummer
NStZ	Neue Zeitschrift für Strafrecht
NVwZ-RR	Neue Zeitschrift für Verwaltungsrecht - Rechtsprechungsreport
OECD	Organization for Economic Cooperation and Development
OLG	Oberlandesgericht
polnStGB	Polnisches Strafgesetzbuch
Prot.	Protokoll
RegE	Regierungsentwurf
RG	Reichsgericht
RGBl.	Reichsgesetzblatt
Rn.	Randnummer
RGSt	Entscheidungen des Reichsgerichts in Strafsachen
Rspr.	Rechtsprechung
RStGB	Reichsstrafgesetzbuch
S.	Seite
s.	siehe
s. o.	siehe oben
st. Rspr.	ständige Rechtsprechung
s. u.	siehe unten
SK	Systematischer Kommentar
sog.	sogenannte bzw. sogenannter bzw. sogenanntes
SoldG	Soldatengesetz
SPD	Sozialdemokratische Partei Deutschlands
StGB	Strafgesetzbuch
StPO	Strafprozessordnung
StrafFo	Strafverteidiger Forum
StrRG	Gesetz zur Reform des Strafrechts
StV	Strafverteidiger
u.	unter
u.a.	unter anderem
UWG	Gesetz gegen den unlauteren Wettbewerb
v. Chr.	vor Christus
vgl.	vergleiche
Vh.	Verhandlungen
VwGO	Verwaltungsgerichtsordnung
VwVfg	Verwaltungsverfahrensgesetz
WaffG	Waffengesetz
WDO	Wehrdisziplinarordnung
WissR	Wissenschaftsrecht
Wistra	Zeitschrift für Wirtschaft, Steuer, Strafrecht

WRP	Wettbewerb in Recht und Praxis
z. B.	zum Beispiel
ZBR	Zeitschrift für Beamtenrecht
ZStW	Zeitschrift für die gesamte Strafrechtswissenschaft

Einleitung

I. Ausgangslage und Reformbestrebungen

Die Reformbedürftigkeit der Bestechungstatbestände steht seit Jahren angesichts der stetigen Zunahme dieses Deliktsbereichs[1] im Mittelpunkt der Diskussion. Der durch Korruption entstandene Schaden geht in die Milliarden[2]. Zahlreiche komplexe Bestechungsskandale in der Bundesrepublik[3] und inzwischen beachtliche Vorkommnisse auch in der Europäischen Gemeinschaft[4] nähren auf den ersten Blick den Verdacht, dass die Korruption nach Art und Umfang neue Dimensionen anzunehmen beginnt. Die Tatintensität nimmt dort beträchtlich zu, wo sich mehrere Täter bis hin zur länderübergreifenden organisierten Kriminalität mit dem Ziel zusammenschließen, im Rahmen von Absprachekartellen verbotswidrig öffentliche Aufträge zu erhalten. Die mit spektakulären Verhaftungen und Durchsuchungen verbundene Aufdeckung von schlagzeilenträchtigen Bestechungstaten entfaltet dabei keine generalpräventive Wirkung, ganz im Gegenteil wie die „Frankfurter Fälle" beweisen[5]. Ob deshalb als Strategie zur Bekämpfung der Korruption der Einsatz vermeintlich bewährter Instrumentarien wie eine Ausweitung der Straftatbestände unter Anhe-

---

1 In Deutschland nimmt die Belastung von Wirtschaft und Gesellschaft durch Korruption weiter zu, Süddeutsche Zeitung vom 6.4.2000: „Korruption wird immer mehr zur Alltagspraxis"; die Kriminalitätsanalyse der Wiesbadener Polizeizentrale registriert einen Anstieg der Korruptionsstraftaten im Jahr 2000 gegenüber dem Vorjahr um 38,6 Prozent und eine Erhöhung der Zahl der Tatverdächtigen um 12,5 Prozent, Die Welt vom 12.3.2002, S.4; die Polizeiliche Kriminalstatistik weist für das Jahr 2001 einen Anstieg der Korruptionsdelikte um über 90 Prozent gegenüber dem Vorjahr aus, Handelsblatt vom 3./4.5.2002, S.4.

2 Der Spiegel 1/1999, S. 58/59; zu den Ursachen der Korruption siehe Dölling, Gutachten zum 61. DJT 1996, C 30 ff.; zu empirischen Fakten Killias in Festschrift für H.J. Schneider, S. 239 ff.

3 Genannt seien nur die sogenannten „Frankfurter Fälle" mit 1.500 Ermittlungsverfahren zwischen 1987 und 1994, Claussen, Korruption im öffentlichen Dienst, S. 7 und 8; im Einzelnen Herbig, Korruptionsfälle in der Stadtverwaltung Frankfurt, in: Claussen, S. 55 ff.; ferner die „Münchener Fälle", Claussen, S. 8; siehe auch in: Der Spiegel 1/1999, S. 58/59, u.a. zum Neubau des Terminals am Frankfurter Flughafen Rhein/Main.

4 Zum erstenmal in der Geschichte der EG hat die Polizei Anfang 1996 zwei EU-Beamte wegen Korruptionsverdacht verhaftet, Süddeutsche Zeitung vom 20.2.1996: „Mit dem Fallschirm ins gemachte Nest springen"; die alte EU-Kommission unter Jacques Santer war im März 1999 unter dem Druck des Verdachts möglicher Misswirtschaft und Korruption zurückgetreten; von Anfang 1998 bis Ende 1999 sind laut EU-Kommission 26 Disziplinarverfahren gegen EU-Beamte eingeleitet worden, die unter Korruptionsverdacht standen, Die Welt vom 15.5.2000: „EU-Kommission will keine Untersuchung von Korruption".

5 Vgl. Claussen (Fn. 3), S. 16.

bung des Strafrahmens[6], Restriktionen in der StPO[7] oder eine Verschärfung der dienstrechtlichen Verbotstatbestände[8] unter Einbeziehung des Disziplinarrechts[9] ein probates Mittel darstellen kann, darf zumindest bezweifelt werden, wenn man sich die Ursachen der Korruption wie eine schwindende Loyalität der Staatsbürger vor Augen hält[10].

II. Problem- und Fragestellungen

Die besonderen Schwierigkeiten bei der Aufklärung korruptiver Zusammenhänge haben ihre Ursache darin, dass alle Beteiligten Täter oder zumindest doch Teilnehmer an der Tat sind. Praktisch jede Anzeige eines involvierten Mitwissers gerät so zur Selbstanzeige. Hierzu korrespondiert der Aspekt der Geheimhaltung, da Bestecher und Bestochener als „Gefahrengemeinschaft" auf die gegenseitige Verschwiegenheit angewiesen sind. Hinzu kommt, dass es sich bei den Tathandlungsalternativen der §§ 331 ff. StGB[11] („Fordern", „Sichversprechenlassen", „Annehmen", „Anbieten", „Versprechen" und „Gewähren") um kommunikative Akte und damit Willenserklärungen handelt[12]. Dabei muss der intendierte Gehalt des Kommunikationsaktes zumindest objektiv erkennbar sein[13]. Es lässt sich leicht erahnen, wie schwer im Einzelfall dieser Inhalt und die Willensbedeutung einer zwischen zwei Parteien stattfindenden Kommunikationsbeziehung nachzuweisen ist. Den eigentlichen Kern der Tathandlungen nach den §§ 331 ff. bildet die sogenannte Unrechtsvereinbarung[14], die wiederum das Bezugsobjekt für die Tathandlungsalternativen darstellt[15]. Die in dieser Unrechtsvereinbarung liegende kausale Verknüpfung von Vorteil und Dienstausübung muss zudem von einem kognitiven Element umspannt sein[16], welches

---

6 Vgl. Abschnitt 1 Artikel 1 (Änderung des StGB) des KorrBekG vom 13.8.1997, BGBl. I, S. 2038/2039.

7 Vgl. Abschnitt 1 Artikel 3 (Änderung der StPO) des KorrBekG, BGBl. I, S. 2040.

8 Vgl. Abschnitt 2 Artikel 9 und 10 (Änderung des BRRG und des BBG) des KorrBekG, BGBl. I, S. 2041.

9 Vgl. Abschnitt 2 Artikel 11 (Änderung der BDO) des KorrBekG, BGBl. I, S. 2041.

10 Vgl. zu den Ursachen der Korruption Miller, Die Verwaltung 1990, S. 227 (231 ff.).

11 §§ ohne Gesetzesangabe sind solche des StGB.

12 Kuhlen, NStZ 1988, S. 433.

13 Kuhlen, NStZ 1988, S. 433 (434).

14 Dies gilt – wenn auch in abgeschwächter Form – auch auf der aktuellen Grundlage des KorrBekG, vgl. Schönke/Schröder/Cramer, § 331 Rn. 3 und 26-28; ferner Jescheck, LK, vor § 331 Rn. 17; Tröndle/Fischer, § 331 Rn. 15 ff.; vgl. auch BGHSt 33, 336 (339).

15 Kuhlen, NStZ 1988, S. 433.

16 So jedenfalls ständige BGH-Rechtsprechung seit BGHSt 15, 239 (252), nach der beide Seiten sich bewusst sein müssen, dass der geforderte, versprochene oder gewährte Vorteil eine Gegenleistung für eine (pflichtwidrige) Diensthandlung oder für die Unterlassung einer dienstlichen Handlung sein soll. Zu den Änderungen durch das KorrBekG s. S. 84 ff.

in seinen psychologisch denkbaren Fallgestaltungen zur Bejahung oder Verneinung des Straftatbestandes der §§ 331 ff. führen kann[17].

Aus diesen summarischen Ausführungen wird bereits deutlich, worin die Probleme der Strafrechtspraxis bestehen. Die strafprozessuale Feststellung der subjektiven Tatbestandselemente bereitet erhebliche Schwierigkeiten. Vor dem Hintergrund der durch das KorrBekG überarbeiteten Straftatbestände der §§ 331 ff.[18] ist die Vermutung nicht abwegig, dass die als „normative Schwachstelle" der Bestechungsdelikte bezeichnete subjektive Tatseite[19] in ihren Beweisanforderungen abgeschwächt werden sollte. Denn das Merkmal der Unrechtsvereinbarung begnügt sich nach der neuen Rechtslage mit dem Bezug des Bewusstseins zu irgendeiner nicht näher zu konkretisierenden Gegenleistung (Dienstausübung) des Beamten[20]. Der objektive Geschehensablauf wird dennoch vielfach nicht den Nachweis der inneren Tatseite erbringen können, der Amtsträger habe den Vorteil für die Dienstausübung angenommen. Ein äußerer Zusammenhang zwischen dem Geschäftsbereich des Vorteilsgebers und der Dienstzuständigkeit des Vorteilsnehmers wäre kein ausreichendes Indiz für eine Verurteilung. Die subjektive Tatseite scheint damit als „normative Schwachstelle" in ihrem nach neuem Recht abgeschwächten Anforderungsprofil erhalten zu bleiben.

Ein zweiter Punkt betrifft die Abgrenzung zum beamtenrechtlichen Verbot der Geschenkannahme.[21] Diese Abgrenzung ist mit der Neuausrichtung der §§ 331 ff. schwieriger geworden. Denn beim Geschenkannahmeverbot des § 70 BBG wird ein Bezug auf das Amt vorausgesetzt, der dann vorliegt, wenn die Amtsstellung für die Zuwendung der entscheidende Anlass war[22]. Der wesentliche Unterschied zwischen Straf- und Disziplinarunrecht begrenzt sich mithin auf das Vorliegen und den Nachweis der subjektiven Tatseite, dass über die Amtsstellung hinaus die Vorteilshingabe für die Dienstausübung des Amtsträgers erfolgt ist. Zwischen Kriminal- und Disziplinarunrecht besteht jetzt nur noch ein minimaler subjektiv-gradueller Unterschied. Der näheren Untersuchung bedarf die Frage, ob der primäre Beweggrund des Gesetzgebers für diese Angleichung von Kriminal- und Disziplinarunrecht tatsächlich auf die Strafbedürftigkeit der erfassten Lebenssachverhalte zielte, oder stärker auf die Beseitigung

17 Je nachdem, ob sich das Wissen beim Vorteilsempfänger nachweisen lässt, dass der Vorteil für die Dienstausübung in der Vergangenheit oder Zukunft zugewendet worden ist oder unterhalb dieser Strafbarkeitsschwelle eben nur als „Dankeschön für gute Zusammenarbeit" oder zur „Klimapflege" erfolgt ist.

18 BGBl. I (1997), S. 2038 ff.

19 Fätkinhäuer, der kriminalist, S. 285 (286).

20 Schönke/Schröder/Cramer, § 331 Rn. 7.

21 Für Bundesbeamte ist dies der § 70 BBG, der ebenfalls durch das KorrBekG neu gefasst worden ist, s. BGBl. I (1997), S. 2041.

22 Claussen (Fn. 3), S. 35; enger noch Köhler/Ratz, BDO, B II 10, Rn. 44.

tatrichterlicher Beweisschwierigkeiten beim Nachweis der Unrechtsvereinbarung gerichtet war.

Im Ergebnis sind mit der Neubestimmung der gegenüber der bisherigen Regelung „abgeschwächten“ Unrechtsvereinbarung durch das KorrBekG die strafrichterlichen Anforderungen an den Nachweis der nach dem objektiv wahrnehmbaren Tatgeschehen selten zweifelsfrei feststellbaren subjektiven Tatseite nach dem EGStGB von 1974 ein weiteres Mal zurückgeführt worden[23]. Im Gesetzgebungsverfahren des KorrBekG wurde sogar der Verzicht auf die Unrechtsvereinbarung mit der Begründung diskutiert[24], dass schon durch die bloße Beziehung von Vorteil und Dienst die mögliche Käuflichkeit des Amtsträgers offenbar und eine Ungleichbehandlung der Bürger wahrscheinlich werde[25]. Spätestens an dieser Stelle müssen Zweifel laut werden, ob denn jede im Zusammenhang mit dem Amt erfolgende nicht nur geringwertige[26] Zuwendung den Eindruck der Käuflichkeit erweckt und ob das Vertrauen in die Sachlichkeit der Amtsführung[27] in allen lebensnahen Fallgestaltungen mit der Folge beeinträchtigt wird, dass das Strafrecht als ultima ratio eingreifen müsste. Die Gefahr einer Überdehnung der Straftatbestände der §§ 331, 333 besteht durchaus[28]. Gerade dort, wo das Gesetz Absichten, Motive und Vorstellungen, also subjektive Strafbarkeitselemente voraussetzt, sind die Strafbarkeitsgrenzen durch präzise Tatbestandsfestlegungen exakt zu bestimmen. Anhand von Lebenssachverhalten ist daher zu ermitteln, ob die gegenwärtige Normfassung des § 331 eine hinreichend sichere Abgrenzung strafbedürftiger von nicht strafbedürftigen Verhaltensweisen noch gewährleistet[29]. Bei dieser Untersuchung ist der berechtigten gesellschaftspolitischen Forderung nach Entbürokratisierung der öffentlichen Verwaltung und Annäherung an privatwirtschaftliche Verhaltensmaßstäbe sowie dem gesellschaftlichen Verständnis eines effizient ausgerichteten Staatsapparats Rechnung zu tragen.

---

23 Es wird Aufgabe der Untersuchung sein, dies im Einzelnen zu belegen.

24 So ist Schaupensteiner für eine übereinstimmende Reichweite der dienstrechtlichen Verbotsnorm mit der des strafrechtlichen Tatbestands eingetreten, Kriminalistik 1994, S. 514 (522); ebenso der Gesetzentwurf des Bundesrates vom 3.11.1995, BR-Drs. 298/95, Anlage, S.2/3.

25 BR-Drs. 298/95, Anlage, S. 10.

26 Also außerhalb sozialüblicher Zuwendungen wie z.B. dem Weihnachtsgeld für den Briefträger.

27 Zum Rechtsgut der §§ 331ff. vgl. u. S. 13 ff.

28 Vgl. Lüderssen, JZ 1997, S. 112 (115/116).

29 Auch Dölling (Fn. 31), der sich ausführlich mit der Problematik auseinander setzt, äußert sich zwar kritisch zum Vorschlag des Verzichts auf die Unrechtsvereinbarung, bleibt aber mit seinem Vorschlag einer jetzt vom Gesetzgeber übernommenen abgeschwächten Unrechtsvereinbarung die Antwort schuldig, Gutachten C, C 62-66.

Die soziologische Entwicklung der letzten Jahrzehnte von Staat und Verwaltung im Hinblick auf die ökonomische Bedeutung eines wirtschaftsnahen Zusammenwirkens mit Industrie und Wirtschaft verbindet beide Seiten immer mehr zu einer Gestaltungsgemeinschaft, die nur in ihrer funktionsnotwendigen Wechselwirkung volkswirtschaftlich erfolgreich sein kann. Unzählige gemeinsame Projektarbeiten zwischen Wirtschaft und Staat dokumentieren dies. Der Staat selbst als wichtiger Wirtschaftsfaktor und bedeutender Auftraggeber tritt heute durch zahlreiche Privatisierungsmaßnahmen als Marktkonkurrent auf. Von seinen Bediensteten erwartet er betriebswirtschaftliches Denken bei der Erfüllung ihrer Aufgaben. Weitreichende Kontakte zur Privatwirtschaft haben das Gestaltungsprofil des Staatsapparats verändert. Heute ist von Verwaltungsmanagement und Verwaltungsmodernisierung die Rede, kaum mehr von einer bürokratisch ausgerichteten und vom Wirtschaftsleben abgeschirmten Staatsautorität.

Ein weiterer wichtiger Punkt betrifft den ultima ratio-Gedanken des Strafrechts. Dieser beinhaltet die Notwendigkeit des Nachweises, dass das öffentliche Dienstrecht/Disziplinarrecht als alternative rechtliche Handhabe zum Strafrecht entsprechend seiner Zweckbestimmung als angemessenere Reaktion dem Strafrecht nicht vorzuziehen ist. Unter das Dienstrecht/Disziplinarrecht fallen nämlich Sachverhalte, die zwar ein sozialschädliches Verhalten im Sinne strafbaren Unrechts nicht erkennen lassen, aber dienstrechtliche Verstöße enthalten und daher insoweit gemaßregelt werden können. Besonderes Augenmerk ist dabei auf die verfahrensrechtliche Seite zu richten, denn der Vorwurf eines beim dienstrechtlichen Geschenkannahmeverbot bestehenden Vollzugsdefizits[30] wirft die Frage nach der Anwendungspraxis des Disziplinarrechts insgesamt auf.

III. Stand der wissenschaftlichen Diskussion

Mit dem durch das KorrBekG von 1997 überarbeiteten Korruptionsstrafrecht ist – wenngleich eine Beruhigung in der Diskussion eingetreten ist – kein Schlusspunkt in der wissenschaftlichen Auseinandersetzung um den Einsatz des Strafrechts bei der Bekämpfung der Korruption erreicht worden.

Dölling, der mit seinem Gutachten zum 61. DJT maßgeblich an der Reform der Bestechungstatbestände mitgewirkt hat[31], vertritt dabei die Auffassung, die Gesetzesänderungen hätten zu einer „sachgerechten Erfassung des Unrechts der

---

30 Hierzu vgl. Hettinger, NJW 1996, S. 2263 (2272); Vahlenkamp/Knauß, Korruption – hinnehmen oder handeln?, S. 235 f.

31 Gutachten C zum 61. DJT mit der Fragestellung „Empfehlen sich Änderungen des Straf- und Strafprozeßrechts, um der Gefahr von Korruption in Staat, Wirtschaft und Gesellschaft wirksam zu begegnen?“.

Korruption geführt“[32]. Zur Begründung verweist er auf die durch die Neuregelung erfolgte Änderung des Merkmals der Unrechtsvereinbarung, nach der sich der Vorteil nicht mehr auf eine „Diensthandlung“, sondern nur noch auf die „Dienstausübung“ als solche beziehen muss. Mit dieser Neuerung seien erhebliche Beweisschwierigkeiten in der Strafverfolgungspraxis und bestehende Strafbarkeitslücken beseitigt worden[33].

Auf dem 61. DJT wurden in der Abteilung Strafrecht mehrere Alternativen zur Abschwächung der Anforderungen an das Merkmal der Unrechtsvereinbarung kontrovers diskutiert. Durchsetzen konnte sich die Auffassung, nach der die §§ 331,333 bereits dann eingreifen sollten, wenn der Vorteil für die dienstliche Tätigkeit gewährt wird oder gewährt werden soll[34]. Inhaltlich ist dieser auch von Dölling favorisierte Vorschlag in abgeänderter sprachlicher Formulierung Gesetzestext geworden. Die Alternativen, auf die Zuwendung „im Zusammenhang mit dem Amt“ und damit auf einen weitgehenden Verzicht der Unrechtsvereinbarung abzustellen bzw. an das Merkmal der Eignung des Vorteils anzuknüpfen, den Amtsträger bei der Wahrnehmung seiner Dienstgeschäfte zu beeinflussen, konnten sich weder in der wissenschaftlichen Diskussion, noch im Rahmen des parlamentarischen Gesetzgebungsverfahrens durchsetzen[35].

Nach Dölling ist eine Verbesserung der Gesetzeslage zudem mit der auch vom 61. DJT befürworteten Einbeziehung von Drittvorteilen in die Neufassung der §§ 331 ff. erfolgt. Damit entfielen Abgrenzungsprobleme im Hinblick auf die Unterscheidung von vom früheren Gesetz bereits erfassten mittelbaren Vorteilen des Amtsträgers zu den davon abzugrenzenden Drittvorteilen[36]. Allerdings – und damit spricht Dölling einen „wunden Punkt“ der Reformgesetze an – könnte durch die Verknüpfung der Auflockerung der Unrechtsvereinbarung mit der Einbeziehung von Drittvorteilen eine Ausdehnung des Tatbestandes mit der Folge neuer Abgrenzungsprobleme zwischen strafbarem und straflosem Verhalten eingetreten sein[37].

Fragwürdig ist auch die Herleitung der Strafbedürftigkeit einzelner in den erweiterten Strafbarkeitsbereich der Vorteilsannahme nach § 331 fallenden Verhaltensweisen. Dabei ist die nach dem Inkrafttreten des KorrBekG immer noch umstrittene Frage nach dem Rechtsgut der Bestechungsdelikte weiter ungeklärt.

32 Dölling, ZStW 112 (2000), S. 334 (354).
33 Dölling, ZStW 112 (2000), S. 334 (343/344).
34 Beschlüsse der Abteilung Strafrecht des 61. DJT 1996, Vh., Bd. II/2, L 189.
35 Zu den Einzelheiten s. u. ab S. 83.
36 Dölling, ZStW 112 (2000), S. 334 (345).
37 Dölling, ZStW 112 (2000), S. 334 (345); zu den von Dölling angesprochenen Themenbereichen „Drittmittelforschung“ und „Sponsoring“ s. Teil B.

Dölling vertritt hier die vermittelnde Schrifttumsmeinung, die das objektive Element der Sachlichkeit der Amtsführung als primär schützenswert ansieht, dem subjektiven Element des Vertrauens der Allgemeinheit in die Unkäuflichkeit des Amtsträgers aber immerhin mittelbare Schutzwirkung beimisst[38].

In der wissenschaftlichen Diskussion um die tatbestandlichen Voraussetzungen der Bestechungstatbestände ist auffallend, dass ein näheres Eingehen auf die Wirkungszusammenhänge der subjektiven Tatelemente unterbleibt. Dabei kommt der subjektiven Tatseite mit ihren beweisrechtlichen Auswirkungen weitaus größere Bedeutung zu als den objektiven Tatbestandserfordernissen. Der vorerst nicht vom Gesetzgeber übernommene Vorschlag eines weitgehenden Verzichts auf das Merkmal der Unrechtsvereinbarung kann durchaus als Versuch gewertet werden, sich der Problematik der Nachweisbarkeit subjektiver Tatelemente auf diese Weise zu entledigen. Die Tatbestände der §§ 331 ff. verdienen aber über die Unrechtsvereinbarung hinaus eine Auseinandersetzung mit den subjektiven Normzusammenhängen, um die historische Entwicklung der Bestechungstatbestände und die bis heute anhaltenden Reformbestrebungen in ihren Ansätzen wie z.B. dem der Rechtsgutbestimmung nachvollziehen zu können.

IV. Aufbau der Untersuchung

Die vorliegende Arbeit verfolgt das Ziel, den gegenwärtigen vom Gesetzgeber erreichten Status Quo zum Einsatz des Strafrechts gegen korruptive Verhaltensweisen auf seine Auswirkungen zu durchleuchten und darüber hinaus herauszufinden, ob sich der verstärkte präventive und repressive Einsatz des Dienst- und Disziplinarrechts gegenüber dem Strafrecht als vorzugswürdige Alternative erweisen könnte[39].

Diesem Ziel folgend ist zunächst die historische Entwicklung und die vor allem in den Sechziger Jahren heftig geführte Diskussion über die subjektiven Tatbestandserfordernisse der Bestechungsdelikte nachzuzeichnen, um Aufschluss über die Frage zu erhalten, ob und ggf. aus welchen Überlegungen heraus ein schrittweiser Abbau der Anforderungen an die subjektiven Tatelemente vollzogen wurde (Teil A der Untersuchung).

---

[38] Dölling, ZStW 112 (2000), S. 334 (335); im Einzelnen hierzu s. u. S. 13 ff. und 47 ff.

[39] Vgl. Pressekonferenz des Frankfurter Arbeitskreises Strafrecht, auf der vor dem Missbrauch des Strafrechts gewarnt wurde; das Strafrecht sei kein Mittel zur gesellschaftlichen Steuerung und dürfe nur das allerletzte Mittel sein; der Gesetzgeber müsse wieder stärker auf Vorbeugung setzen und unterhalb des Strafrechts steuernd eingreifen; je mehr der Gesetzgeber als erstes an das Strafrecht denke, desto eher wiege er sich in falsche Sicherheit und desto weniger Phantasie bleibe für eine wirklich effektive Vorbeugung übrig, Bonner General-Anzeiger vom 8. Juli 1997.

Auf dieser Untersuchungsgrundlage soll der Frage nachgegangen werden, in welcher Weise das KorrBekG die historische Entwicklung fortschreibt und ob das Gesetz in der Rechtswirklichkeit Abgrenzungsprobleme zwischen strafwürdigem (strafbarem) und nicht strafwürdigem (straflosem) Verhalten auslöst. Verschiedene Lebenssachverhalte sind daraufhin in der strafrechtlichen Subsumtion zu überprüfen (Teil B der Untersuchung).

Im abschließenden Teil der Arbeit ist der Frage nachzugehen, ob das Ziel der Bekämpfung der Korruption in Teilbereichen menschlichen Fehlverhaltens nicht auch unterhalb der Schwelle strafrechtlicher Verantwortung effektiver mit den Mitteln des Dienstrechts/Disziplinarrechts erreicht werden kann und daher eine Zurückdrängung des Strafrechts begründen könnte. Den Maßstab für diese Untersuchung liefert das zum 1.1.2002 in Kraft getretene BDG[40], das die BDO[41] ablöst und das Disziplinarverfahrensrecht neu regelt (Teil C der Untersuchung).

40 BGBl. I (2001), S. 1510.

41 In der Fassung der Bekanntmachung vom 20.7.1967, BGBl. I, S. 750 (984), zuletzt geändert durch Artikel 19 Abs. 3 des Gesetzes vom 29.6.1998, BGBl. I, S. 1666.

Teil A : Die subjektiven Tatbestandserfordernisse der Bestechungsdelikte

Zu allen Zeiten und bei allen Kulturvölkern, die über eine mehr oder weniger stark ausgeprägte Verwaltung verfügten, hat es Bestechungskriminalität gegeben[42]. Die Verbote reichen daher weit zurück. Seit dem frühen römischen Zwölftafelrecht (451 v. Chr.)[43] entwickelten sich Rechtsquellen, die bereits die aktive und passive Richter- und Zeugenbestechung verboten[44]. Der Richter als wichtiger Entscheidungsträger und unparteiischer Dritter sollte nicht Gefahr laufen, Zweifel an seiner Neutralität und an der Objektivität seines Urteils aufkommen zu lassen.

Neben dem Schutzbedürfnis vor Rechtsbeugung trat im Zuge der zunehmenden staatlichen Reglementierung das Verlangen nach Schutz vor der Bedrückung der Bürger durch die ihre Machtfülle ausnutzenden Beamten. Die Repetundengesetze und hier insbesondere die „Lex Julia de repetundis" aus dem Jahr 59 v. Chr. sollten die um sich greifende Bestechlichkeit der Beamten bekämpfen. Mit ihr wurde den Beamten die Annahme von (Geld-)Geschenken untersagt[45]. Dass man sich nicht damit begnügte, nur das repressive Fordern von Geschenken zu untersagen, sondern die Vorteilsannahme generell verbot, war wohl Ausfluss der Erkenntnis, dass es dann nicht mehr auf den Nachweis des „Forderns" bzw. der Bedrängung des Gebers zur Schenkung, mithin auf eine Unterscheidung der von der Einstellung des Täters geprägten Tathandlung ankam[46]. Da auch nicht der Nachweis einer wie auch immer gearteten Beziehung zwischen Vorteil und Amt geführt werden musste, war die römische Gerichtsbarkeit noch nicht den Beweisschwierigkeiten heutiger Korruptionsstrafprozesse ausgesetzt. Mit der Bestrafung der nach objektiven Tatmerkmalen unter Außerachtlassung subjektiver Beweggründe feststellbaren Vorteilsannahme verfolgte die Repetundengesetzgebung erkennbar den Zweck, den in der Annahme von Geschenken liegenden Gefährdungen des Nehmers im Vorfeld von Bestechlichkeit und Rechtsbeugung zu begegnen[47].

---

42 Vgl. Geerds, Über den Unrechtsgehalt der Bestechungsdelikte und seine Konsequenzen für Rechtsprechung und Gesetzgebung, S. 8 und S. 93.

43 Dazu Mommsen, Römisches Strafrecht, S. 668.

44 Vgl. Mommsen (Fn. 43), S. 674 f., wonach die Annahme eines Vorteils verboten war, der zum Zwecke der Rechtsbeugung hingegeben wurde.

45 Geerds (Fn. 42), S. 6; die aktive Beamtenbestechung war nach römischem Recht nicht strafbar, Mommsen (Fn. 43), S. 717 f.

46 Vgl. Mommsen (Fn. 43), S. 714 ff.

47 Vgl. Stock, Entwicklung und Wesen der Amtsverbrechen, S. 63; zu den Ausnahmen vom allgemeinen Verbot der Geschenkannahme s. Mommsen (Fn. 43), S. 715 f.

Die Korruption verbreitete sich im Laufe der Zeit in Abhängigkeit von der jeweiligen Entwicklung der einzelnen Kulturen und Staatswesen. So findet man im kanonischen Recht den Kauf von geistlichen Ämtern[48]. Im späten Mittelalter wurde neben der Bestechlichkeit des Richters[49] und Beamten[50] teilweise auch schon die aktive Bestechung bestraft[51].

Anfang bis Mitte des 19. Jahrhunderts bildeten sich dann schärfere tatbestandliche Konturen. So wurde jetzt die Entgegennahme eines in Beziehung auf die Amtsausübung, d.h. zum Zwecke der Einwirkung auf eine Amtshandlung, dargebotenen Vorteils als strafwürdig angesehen[52] und damit der vom Willen gesteuerten Zielrichtung des Täterverhaltens ausdrücklich Bedeutung zuerkannt. Der Vorsatz bezog sich beim Bestochenen auf das wissentliche Annehmen des Vorteils und die Absicht, sich diesen zuzueignen[53], beim Bestechenden auf „das wissentliche Darbringen oder Anbieten des Vortheils" in der „Absicht, sich den Staatsdiener in der Ausübung seines Amtes geneigt zu machen"[54]. Um Beweisschwierigkeiten zu entgehen, wurde beim Bestochenen eine Anzeigepflicht unter Strafandrohung und die Zulässigkeit seiner Zeugenstellung vor Gericht begründet[55], beim Bestechenden für eine Anzeige des be-

---

48 Hofmeister,Die Bestechung, S. 10.

49 Die Constitutio Criminalis Carolina aus dem Jahre 1532 richtet sich in Artikel 205 im Interesse einer sachlichen Entscheidung des Richters gegen jeden Anschein einer Parteilichkeit, Geerds (Fn. 42), S. 7.

50 Mit zunehmender Ausdehnung auf alle Beamtengruppen.

51 Geerds (Fn. 42), S. 7 m.w.N.

52 Feuerbach, Themis, S. 230-232; im Gesetz von 1807 heißt es zur Strafbarkeit des Bestechenden:„Wer, um einen Staatsdiener zu einem Mißbrauche seiner Amtsgewalt zu verleiten, oder denselben in einer gegenwärtigen oder künftigen Amtsangelegenheit sich selbst oder einem Dritten geneigt zu machen, diesem Staatsdiener selbst oder dessen Angehörigen irgend ein Geschenk, oder was immer für einen Vortheil oder Genuß anbietet, verspricht, gibt, anbieten, versprechen oder geben läßt, wird hiedurch des Verbrechens der Bestechung schuldig und nach folgenden Gesezen bestraft." Zur Strafbarkeit des Bestochenen heißt es: „ Der Staatsbeamte selbst vollendet auch von seiner Seite das Verbrechen der Bestechung, wenn er das Dargebotene wirklich in Empfang genommen, oder sich zur Annahme des Versprochenen bereit erklärt, ... hat."

53 Feuerbach (Fn. 52), S. 213.

54 Feuerbach (Fn. 52), S. 214.

55 Feuerbach (Fn 52), S. 219 ff.; als möglicher Zeuge konnte der Staatsbeamte grundsätzlich nur dienen, wenn er den Bestechungsversuch zurückgewiesen hatte und daher selbst prozessual nicht Mitbeschuldigter war, S. 223; die Glaubwürdigkeit eines solchen Zeugen, der sich wohl regelmäßig postwendend einer Beschuldigung der Bestechlichkeit durch den Angezeigten ausgesetzt sah und damit nachträglich in die Rolle eines Mitbeschuldigten gedrängt wurde, erscheint zumindest fragwürdig; allgemein zur Problematik des Tausches der Beschuldigten- zur Zeugenrolle siehe Prittwitz, Der Mitbeschuldigte im Strafprozeß.

stochenen Staatsdieners eine Aberkennung der gesetzlichen Strafe bei zusätzlicher Belohnung in Aussicht gestellt[56].

In diesen Anfängen einer differenzierteren Normgestaltung wurde kognitiven und voluntativen Tatelementen bei allen daraus für die tatrichterliche Feststellungsseite folgenden Konsequenzen zunehmend Bedeutung beigemessen. Dies darf aber nicht darüber hinwegtäuschen, dass sowohl das preußische Strafgesetzbuch von 1851, welches bereits detaillierte Vorschriften über die Staatsdiener und die Amtsdelikte enthielt[57], und das nach preußischem Vorbild konzipierte Strafgesetzbuch für das Deutsche Reich von 1871 (RStGB)[58] noch vom Vergeltungsgedanken bestimmt waren, der seine Rechtfertigung aus der vorrangigen Bedeutung der Verletzung des geschützten Handlungsobjekts und damit des Taterfolgs bezog. Die subjektiven Tatmerkmale, der Wille und die Motive des Täters fanden allenfalls nachgeordnet Berücksichtigung[59].

---

56 Feuerbach (Fn. 52), S. 234.

57 GSlg., S. 101 ff. (§§ 309 ff., S. 164 f.).

58 RGBl. I, S. 127 (191).

59 Jescheck, LK, Einleitung Rn. 59.

Erster Abschnitt : Die Rechtsentwicklung unter dem RStGB von 1871[60] bis zum EGStGB von 1974

I. Das Rechtsgut der Bestechungsdelikte

Die Diskussion um die Bestechungsdelikte (insbesondere bezüglich der Tatbestände der passiven Bestechung, §§ 331 und 332) entflammte in den Sechziger Jahren und wurde von Eberhard Schmidt mit seiner Monographie aus dem Jahre 1960 angeführt[61]. Die Auseinandersetzung in Rechtsprechung und Schrifttum galt u.a. der Frage des geschützten Rechtsguts bzw. der geschützten Rechtsgüter dieser Delikte.

Eine bedeutsame Rolle im Zusammenhang mit der Erörterung subjektiver Tatelemente spielte die Rechtsgutproblematik bei der Frage, ob der Beamte die pflichtwidrige Amtshandlung tatsächlich beabsichtigt haben müsse[62], um den Tatbestand des § 332 zu erfüllen. Zwei Auffassungen standen sich gegenüber[63], ohne dass Einigung erzielt worden wäre[64].

1. Die Auffassungen im Schrifttum

a) Schutz vor „Verfälschung des Staatswillens"

Ausgehend von dem Tatbestandserfordernis der pflichtwidrigen Amtshandlung im § 332 vertraten die Anhänger der Lehre von der „Verfälschung des Staatswillens"[65] die Meinung, § 332 bezwecke den Schutz vor einer Verfälschung des Staatswillens durch die Pflichtwidrigkeit seiner Organe[66]. § 331 erweise sich demgegenüber als „abstraktes Gefährdungsdelikt"[67], da der Beamte mit der An-

---

60 Die einschlägigen §§ sind im Anhang 1 abgedruckt; soweit §§ ohne Gesetzesangabe unter diesem Abschnitt zitiert werden, handelt es sich um die Fassung des RStGB.

61 E. Schmidt, Die Bestechungstatbestände in der höchstrichterlichen Rechtsprechung von 1879 bis 1959.

62 Hierzu s. u. S. 26.

63 Darüber hinaus wurden vereinzelt Ansichten vertreten, die allenfalls einen Teilaspekt des geschützten Rechtsguts erfassten wie „Die Reinheit der Amtsausübung", „Die Unentgeltlichkeit der Amtshandlung", „Die Ordnung des staatlichen Gebühren- und Abgabenwesens"; vgl. Darstellung und Kritik dieser „älteren Auffassungen" bei Graupe, Die Systematik und das Rechtsgut der Bestechungsdelikte, S. 76 ff. und S. 95.

64 Zusammenfassend vgl. Loos, Festschrift für Hans Welzel, S. 879 ff.

65 E. Schmidt (Fn. 61), S. 81; Baumann, Zur Problematik der Bestechungstatbestände, S. 7-12 und S. 30 f.; Henkel, JZ 1960, S. 507 (508-509); Kaufmann, JZ 1959, S. 375 ff.; Klug, JZ 1960, S. 724 ff.; Bockelmann, ZStW 72 (1960), S. 251 (257).

66 Kaufmann, JZ 1959, S. 375 (377).

67 Kaufmann, JZ 1959, S. 375 (377); E. Schmidt (Fn. 61), S. 149.

nahme[68] eines Vorteils für eine pflichtgemäße Amtshandlung sich immer auch in die Gefahr begebe, künftig mit Blick auf den Vorteil auch pflichtwidrige Handlungen vorzunehmen[69]. Nach diesem Rechtsgutverständnis ist die Absicht, die pflichtwidrige Amtshandlung tatsächlich vorzunehmen, Voraussetzung zur Erfüllung des Tatbestands des § 332[70]. Die Verletzung des in § 332 geschützten Rechtsguts trete ein, wenn die Vornahme der Amtshandlung im Bewusstsein und mit dem Willen, eine Amtspflichtverletzung zu begehen, erfolge[71].

Ausgehend von der Grundthese, dass alle von § 332 erfassten Fälle hinsichtlich des Unrechts- und Schuldgehalts vergleichbar sein müssten[72], sei Vorsatz „nicht nur Vorstellung, sondern Tatverwirklichungswille“[73]. Wenn schon der Tatbestand des § 332 die Ausführung der pflichtwidrigen Amtshandlung nicht verlange und damit die Tatvollendung bereits vorverlegt werde, müsse dann aber im Hinblick auf die hohe Strafandrohung[74] zumindest der Wille des Beamten zur Vornahme der pflichtwidrigen Amtshandlung vorliegen[75]. Der „Wertungsunterschied“ zu § 331 bestehe darin, dass dort die Amtsführung immerhin korrekt verlaufe, während sie bei § 332 „depraviert“ werde und den Staatswillen verfälsche oder nach dem Täterwillen verfälschen solle[76].

Nach Baumann liegt die „Steigerung des Unrechtsgehaltes in § 332“ in „dem Angriff gegen die Richtigkeit des Staatswillens“[77]. Daher genüge die bei fehlendem Tatverwirklichungswillen vorliegende bloße „Vortäuschung einer Gefährdung“ noch nicht, um dem in § 332 manifestierten Unrechtsgehalt der Gefährdung oder Verletzung des Staatswillens zu entsprechen[78].

Nach Henkel erfolgt bei § 332 neben einer schon von § 331 erfassten Verletzung des Grundsatzes der Unentgeltlichkeit staatlicher Amtshandlungen eine vom Unrechts- und Schuldgehalt viel schwerer wiegende „Preisgabe des Staatswillens an den Willen des bestechenden Käufers“[79]. Dabei handele es

---

68 Zur Vereinfachung im Text werden die anderen Handlungsmodalitäten nur erwähnt, soweit Differenzierungen erforderlich werden.

69 Kaufmann, JZ 1959, S. 375 (377).

70 E. Schmidt (Fn. 61), S. 81; Baumann (Fn. 65), S. 30 f.

71 Henkel, JZ 1960, S. 507 (509); E. Schmidt (Fn. 61), S. 79.

72 In Bezug auf bereits ausgeführte pflichtwidrige Amtshandlungen wie auch auf künftig zu begehende, E. Schmidt (Fn. 61), S. 79.

73 E. Schmidt (Fn. 61), S. 80.

74 § 332 RStGB sah noch die Zuchthausstrafe vor.

75 E. Schmidt (Fn. 61), S. 79/80.

76 E. Schmidt (Fn. 61), S. 81; ähnlich Baumann (Fn. 65), S. 31.

77 Baumann (Fn. 65), S. 31.

78 Baumann (Fn. 65), S. 31.

79 Henkel, JZ 1960, S. 507 (508).

sich bei § 332 um einen gegenüber § 331 selbständigen, nicht nur qualifizierten Tatbestand[80].

b) Schutz des „Vertrauens der Öffentlichkeit“

Die Anhänger dieses Schutzgutgedankens sehen in jeder Vorteilsannahme, gleichgültig ob sie im Zusammenhang mit einer pflichtmäßigen oder pflichtwidrigen Amtshandlung steht, eine Gefährdung der Funktionsfähigkeit der Verwaltung durch Erschütterung des Vertrauens der Öffentlichkeit in die Sachlichkeit der Verwaltungsentscheidungen[81]. Ausreichend ist nach dieser Ansicht der Anschein der Käuflichkeit pflichtwidriger Amtshandlungen. Auf den Willen des Täters zur Vornahme der pflichtwidrigen Amtshandlung, egal ob er diesen Willen wirklich hat oder nur vortäuscht, kommt es nicht an[82].

Nach Schröder steht im Mittelpunkt der Bestechungstatbestände die Geschenkannahme, nicht die Verfälschung des Staatswillens und auch nicht die Pflichtwidrigkeit der Amtshandlung[83]. Folgerichtig leite sich der Schutzgedanke der §§ 331 und 332 aus „der Wirkung der Geschenkannahme auf die Öffentlichkeit und der dadurch hervorgerufenen generellen Gefährdung des Staatsapparates“ ab[84]. Mithin sanktionierten die §§ 331,332 gleichartiges Unrecht, wobei § 332 eine Qualifizierung gegenüber § 331 darstelle[85].

2. Die Auffassung in der Rechtsprechung

a) Das Urteil RGSt 39, 193 vom 5.10.1906

Das RG hat in dieser Entscheidung erklärt, „daß es für den Tatbestand der passiven Bestechung gleichgültig ist, ob der Beamte den Willen hat, die Pflichtwidrigkeit zu verüben, oder sich insgeheim vorbehalten hat, das Erklärte nicht zu wollen“[86]. Das Gericht begründet dies u.a. mit dem geschützten Rechtsgut des Anscheins der Käuflichkeit von Amtshandlungen[87].

---

80 Henkel, JZ 1960, S. 507 (509).
81 So Schröder, GA 1961, S. 289 (292); Fuhrmann, ZStW 72 (1960), S. 535 (537); Kirschbaum/Schmitz, GA 1960, S. 321 (343 ff.).
82 Schröder, GA 1961, S. 289 (297).
83 Schröder, GA 1961, S. 289 (291).
84 Schröder, GA 1961, S. 289 (291).
85 Schröder, GA 1961, S. 289 (292).
86 RGSt 39, 193 (201 f.).
87 RGSt 39, 193 (201); bestätigt später durch RGSt 77, 75 (78).

b) Das Urteil BGHSt 15, 88 vom 25.7.1960

Der BGH beschreibt in seiner Entscheidung das geschützte Rechtsgut wie folgt: „Die Makellosigkeit des Amtes nach außen soll gesichert werden; mit der Ehrenhaftigkeit und vor allem Unbestechlichkeit der Beamten soll die Grundlage für das Vertrauen der Bevölkerung erhalten werden, dessen die Staatsverwaltung für eine gedeihliche Wirksamkeit bedarf."[88] Der BGH hält daher daran fest, dass der Wille des Beamten, die angesonnene Pflichtwidrigkeit zu begehen, nicht zum Tatbestand des § 332 gehört[89].

3. Eine erste Stellungnahme zur Bestimmung des geschützten Rechtsguts

Übereinstimmend mit der These Schröders, dass nur eine Klärung der Grundstruktur der Bestechungstatbestände und deren Schutzobjekt Klarheit bei der Lösung tatbestandlicher Detailfragen bringen könne[90], verneint das heute überwiegend auf den Schutzgedanken des „Vertrauens der Allgemeinheit in die Sachlichkeit dienstlicher Tätigkeit und damit in die Nichtkäuflichkeit von Diensthandlungen" abstellende Schrifttum die Frage, ob bei noch ausstehender Amtshandlung der Wille des Beamten, die (pflichtwidrige) Handlung zu begehen, vorhanden sein müsse und damit eine Mentalreservation beachtlich wäre[91]. Teilweise wird die Bedeutungslosigkeit dieses Tatverwirklichungswillens damit erklärt, dass die Frage der Beeinträchtigung des geschützten Rechtsguts an anderer Stelle des Tatbestandes geklärt werden könne, nämlich bei der Unrechtsvereinbarung[92].

Andererseits wird vorgetragen, dass gerade im Falle der Bestechungstatbestände die Klärung der Grundstruktur erhebliche Probleme bereitet und daher eine teleologische Auslegung der einzelnen Tatbestandsmerkmale anhand eines zuvor eindeutig umgrenzten Rechtsgutes nicht zielführend erscheint[93]. So gerät die Interpretation einzelner Gesetzesmerkmale in Gefahr, den Schutzzweck nach dem möglicherweise kriminalpolitisch wünschenswerten Ergebnis hin auszulegen und zu bestimmen[94]. Dieser Gesichtspunkt wirft die weitergehende Frage auf, ob von solchermaßen problematischer

---

88 BGHSt 15, 88 (96 f).

89 BGHSt 15, 88 (97).

90 Schröder, GA 1961, S. 289.

91 Schönke/Schröder/Cramer, § 331 Rn. 5 und 30; Rudolphi, SK, § 331 Rn. 17a; Tröndle/Fischer, § 331 Rn. 22; Jescheck, LK, § 331 Rn. 14.

92 Jescheck, LK, § 331 Rn. 14.

93 Baumann (Fn. 65), S. 11.

94 E. Schmidt (Fn. 61), S. 81/82, der auf den vom Gesetzgeber festgelegten Wertungsunterschied zwischen § 331 und § 332 hinweist und daher die Begründung für die Bedeutungslosigkeit des Tatverwirklichungswillens über eine entsprechende Rechtsgutbestimmung in Zweifel zieht.

Rechtsgutargumentation überhaupt eine Lösung für die Auslegung einzelner Tatbestandsmerkmale zu erwarten ist[95]. Loos geht soweit, dass er diese Frage sogar für die Bestimmung der Schnittstelle zwischen § 331 und § 332 verneint und folgerichtig andere Erwägungen wie z.B. tatrichterliche Fragen der Erweislichkeit als zulässige Begründung für die Ausdehnung des Anwendungsbereichs des § 332 für denkbar hält[96].

Für die nachfolgende Untersuchung der subjektiven Tatumstände der Bestechungsdelikte ergeben sich aus dem voran Gesagten drei Fragestellungen, deren Klärung Rückschlüsse auf die Überzeugungskraft der den Vertrauensgedanken tragenden Argumente zulässt:

- Ist die Heranziehung des Vertrauensgedankens bei der Schutzgutbestimmung der Bestechungsdelikte auch bei der Auslegung der subjektiven Tatelemente durchgängig eingehalten worden?

- Führt die Berücksichtigung dieses Vertrauenskriteriums im Hinblick auf kognitive und voluntative Tatelemente zu einer (ungewollten) extensiven Auslegung des Gesetzes?

- Lässt die aktuelle Diskussion um den Schutzzweck der Bestechungsdelikte neue, überzeugendere Ansatzpunkte erkennen im Hinblick auf den Veränderungsprozess der staatlichen Aufgabenstellung bei zunehmender Einflechtung ins Wirtschaftsleben?[97]

II. Die subjektiven Elemente der Tathandlungen der §§ 331-333

1. Annahme eines Vorteils (§§ 331 und 332)

Unter Annahme ist das tatsächliche Empfangen, die Entgegennahme des Vorteils zu verstehen[98]. Dabei wird der Wille des Empfängers, den Vorteil behalten und im eigenen Interesse verwenden zu wollen, für erforderlich gehalten und ein „Annehmen" i.S.d. §§ 331,332 in den Fällen verneint, in denen der Beamte z.B. das Bestechungsgeld nur zwecks Überführung des Gebers entgegengenommen hat[99]. Im Gegensatz zur Unbeachtlichkeit des Willens zur Vornahme der (pflichtwidrigen) Amtshandlung[100] wird hier die tatrichterliche Feststellung

95 Verneinend Loos (Fn. 64), S. 879 (892).
96 Loos (Fn. 64), S. 879 (894/895).
97 Allen drei Fragen wird im Verlauf dieser Arbeit nachzugehen sein.
98 Rudolphi, SK, § 331 Rn. 26.
99 RGSt 58, 263 (266/267); BGH NJW 1960, S. 2154 (2155).
100 S. o. unter Fn. 91 für die Vertreter des „Vertrauensgedankens".

des Willens auf Einverleibung des Vorteils verlangt[101]. Dies überrascht deshalb, weil aus der Sicht der Vertreter des „Vertrauensgedankens“ auch hier ein Verzicht auf den Tatverwirklichungswillen mit der schon in der Entgegennahme des dargebotenen Vorteils liegenden Beeinträchtigung des Vertrauens in die Nichtkäuflichkeit von Diensthandlungen hätte begründet werden können[102]. Das Schutzgutverständnis i.S. einer „Vertrauensgefährdung“ wird an dieser Stelle nicht in Ansatz gebracht, anderenfalls hätte die Unbeachtlichkeit des Tatverwirklichungswillens hinsichtlich einer bereits durch äußeres Verhalten manifestierten Tathandlung (Entgegennahme) festgestellt werden müssen[103]. Der im Rahmen der Rechtsgutdiskussion von der Rspr. herangezogene Gedanke des Vertrauensschutzes hätte konsequent auch hier in Fällen der Überführungsabsicht des Nehmers zu einer Ausdehnung der Strafbarkeit führen müssen. Die Abkehr von diesem Vertrauensschutzgedanken im Einzelfall vermittelt den Eindruck einer bislang nicht überzeugend und bei der Auslegung der Tatbestandsmerkmale widerspruchsfrei belegten Rechtsgutkonzeption[104].

2. Gewähren eines Vorteils (§ 333)

„Gewähren“ bedeutet die tatsächliche Hingabe, Zuwendung, Übergabe oder Aushändigung des Vorteils und korrespondiert daher mit dem „Annehmen“[105]. Auch das „Gewähren“ beinhaltet einen Kommunikationsakt[106] dergestalt, einen Vorteil in den Verfügungsbereich des Beamten überführen zu wollen. Diese Intention muss objektiv erkennbar sein[107], was voraussetzt, dass – wenn nicht der Empfänger selbst – so doch ein durchschnittlich kompetenter Dritter in der konkreten Situation des Empfängers den mit dem Vollzug der Handlung transportierten Inhalt (Hingabe als Vorteil) verstehen kann[108]. Die einseitige

---

101 Zustimmend insoweit auch E. Schmidt (Fn. 61), S. 68/69, der darauf hinweist, dass mit der faktischen Entgegennahme des Vorteils nur „der erste äußere Ansatz für den Nachweis der Tatbestandserfüllung gewonnen“ sei.

102 Die Entscheidung RGSt 58, 263 ist aber diesbezüglich nicht kritisiert worden.

103 So argumentiert grundsätzlich auch das RG in RGSt 58, 263 (266 f.); dass es für den speziellen Fall der Überführungsabsicht des Nehmers eine Ausnahme macht, lässt darauf schließen, dass kriminalpolitische Erwägungen im Vordergrund standen; Baumann stellt in Kritik zu dieser Entscheidung unabhängig von der Rechtsgutfrage auf eine wenig überzeugende Einengung des Begriffs der „Annahme“ durch das RG ab, (Fn. 65), S. 19.

104 Ähnlich Loos (Fn. 64), S. 880 f.; E. Schmidt hält das durch die §§ 331 ff. geschützte Rechtsgut für „alles andere als über jeden Zweifel erhaben“, (Fn. 61), S. 81; Baumann (Fn. 65), S. 11, spricht von möglicherweise spekulativen Erwägungen bei der Frage nach dem geschützten Rechtsgut.

105 Unstreitig, vgl. E. Schmidt (Fn. 61), S. 123; Schönke/Schröder/Cramer, § 333 Rn. 3.

106 S. unter Fn. 12.

107 Kuhlen, NStZ 1988, S. 433 (434).

108 Kuhlen, NStZ 1988, S. 433 (434); weitergehend E. Schmidt, der verlangt, dass der Beamte selbst das Gewährte als einen ihm zugewendeten Vorteil versteht, (Fn. 61),

Willensbetätigung des Gebers reicht demnach für ein „Gewähren" nicht aus, hinzukommen muss die Annahme des Vorteils durch den anderen Teil[109]. In dieser Annahme liegt in aller Regel die zumindest konkludente Willensbetätigung des Empfängers, das Dargebotene als Vorteil anzunehmen.

3. Fordern (§§ 331,332), Anbieten und Versprechen eines Vorteils (§ 333)

Beim „Fordern" einer Leistung, beim „Anbieten" einer gegenwärtigen Leistung und beim „Versprechen" einer künftigen Leistung handelt es sich um Tathandlungsalternativen, deren Bedeutung aus dem Sinngehalt der ihnen innewohnenden Erklärungen erwächst[110]. Die drei Tatbestandsformen sind auf den Abschluss einer Unrechtsvereinbarung gerichtet[111] und daher einseitige, empfangsbedürftige Willenserklärungen, die zur Kenntnis des Empfängers gelangen müssen[112]. Uneinigkeit herrscht hier bei der Frage, ob beim Kenntnis nehmenden Adressaten der Erklärung auch ein Verstehen des Erklärungsinhalts erwartet werden muss[113]. Ohne diese Streitfrage an dieser Stelle abschließend zu begutachten[114], soll hier die Entscheidung des BGH[115] erwähnt werden, nach der der Sinn einer in verschleierter Form vorgetragenen Forderung dem Empfänger nicht einmal erkennbar gewesen zu sein braucht. Aus dieser Entscheidung könnte leicht der Schluss gezogen werden, für die Tatvollendung reiche auch eine dem Adressaten zur Kenntnis gelangte mehrdeutige, unklare oder verschlüsselte Forderungserklärung aus, die von ihrem Sinngehalt her nicht einmal von einem durchschnittlich kompetenten Dritten in der konkreten Situation des Forderungsempfängers richtig interpretiert werden könnte. Damit wäre aber der Schutzbereich der §§ 331 ff. auch für die Vertreter des „Vertrauensschutzgedankens" bereits verlassen. Aus einem objektiv nicht zu verstehenden Forderungsinhalt kann nicht der vorwerfbare Eindruck der Käuflichkeit von Diensthandlungen entstehen. Daher ist zumindest die objektive Erkennbarkeit des Sinngehalts der Forderung zu verlangen[116]. Dabei muss der

---

S. 124; einschränkend BGHSt 10, 237 (241) für das „Fordern", wo nicht einmal die objektive Erkennbarkeit der Handlungsbedeutung verlangt wird.

109 RGSt 29, 413 (413/414); Jescheck, LK, § 333 Rn. 4.

110 E. Schmidt (Fn. 61), S. 71 und 119.

111 BGHSt 15, 88 (102).

112 RGSt 70, 166 (171); E. Schmidt (Fn. 61), S. 71 und 120; Jescheck, LK, § 331 Rn. 4 und § 333 Rn. 4.

113 Bejahend E. Schmidt (Fn. 61), S. 98 ff. und S. 122/123; verneinend u.a. RGSt 26, 424 (426); 70, 166 (171/172); BGHSt 10, 237 (241).

114 Im Rahmen der Erörterung der Tathandlungen der §§ 331-333 geht es zunächst nur um den Erklärungsinhalt der jeweiligen Tatbestandsform; die Fragestellung erweitert sich bei der Prüfung des Äquivalenzverhältnisses um die Frage des Zusammenhangsverständnisses zwischen Vorteil und Amtshandlung; daher wird auf die Streitfrage erst dort näher eingegangen, s. u. S. 33.

115 BGHSt 10, 237 (240 f.).

116 Jescheck, LK, § 331 Rn. 4; Kuhlen, NStZ 1988, S. 433 (434).

einseitig Erklärende den Willen haben, dass der Adressat den Sinn seiner Erklärung versteht und seine Absicht erkennt[117]. Dagegen muss das Ansinnen des Erklärenden für die Beurteilung der Tatvollendung und damit seiner Strafbarkeit nicht erfolgreich verlaufen sein, d.h. eine Willensbeeinflussung des Adressaten ist nicht erforderlich[118].

4. Sichversprechenlassen (§§ 331, 332)

Die Tathandlung des „Sichversprechenlassen" i.S.d. §§ 331 und 332 setzt zunächst ein Angebot auf der Gegenseite voraus und beinhaltet die Annahme dieses Angebots[119]. Zwischen dem den Vorteil Versprechenden und dem das Versprechen Annehmenden muss ein Einverständnis hinsichtlich künftiger Leistung und des Empfangs dieser Leistung bestehen[120]. Tatvollendung tritt erst ein, wenn der Beamte durch entsprechendes Verhalten dem Anbietenden zu erkennen gibt, dass er das Anerbieten annehme[121]. Auch für die Tatbestandsmäßigkeit des „Sichversprechenlassen" wird wie für die Tatbestandsform des „Annehmen" darauf abgestellt, dass der Beamte den Willen hat, den ihm versprochenen Vorteil später entgegenzunehmen[122]. Ferner soll für das „Sichversprechenlassen" nicht ausreichen, dass das Versprechen in dem Bewusstsein angenommen wird, der Versprechende sei gar nicht willens, das Versprechen zu erfüllen[123]. Im Unterschied zum ersten Fall, bei dem ein Willensmangel auf Seiten des Versprechensempfängers besteht, liegt im zweiten Fall ein solcher Mangel auf Seiten des Versprechenden vor. Beide Vorbehalte ändern aber nichts an der nach außen dokumentierten Übereinkunft eines Versprechens. Die Vertreter des Vertrauensschutzgedankens könnten gut begründen, dass eine Beeinträchtigung des Vertrauens der Allgemeinheit in die Sachlichkeit bzw. Unkäuflichkeit amtlicher Tätigkeit bereits durch die Kundgabe eines vom Gegenüber angenommenen – wenn auch mit einseitigen oder beidseitigen Willensmängeln behafteten – Vorteilsversprechens eintrete[124]. Mit gleicher Argumentation wird der Wille des Beamten, die (pflichtwidrige) Amtshandlung nicht zu begehen, für unbeachtlich erklärt[125], während im Gegensatz hierzu der Wille des Beamten, den entgegengenommenen Vorteil sich auch einverleiben zu wollen, für erforderlich gehalten wird[126].

---

117 Jescheck, LK, §§ 331 und 333 jeweils Rn. 4.
118 RGSt 26, 424 (426); Rudolphi, SK, § 333 Rn. 8.
119 Schönke/Schröder/Cramer, § 331 Rn. 23.
120 E. Schmidt (Fn. 61), S. 70.
121 RGRspr. 7, 285.
122 OLG Hamm, MDR 1973, S. 68.
123 E. Schmidt (Fn. 61), S. 70.
124 Eine Beeinträchtigung des Schutzgutes einer „Verfälschung des Staatswillens" wird in diesen Fällen kaum angenommen werden können.
125 Vgl. o. unter Fn. 91.
126 Vgl. o. unter Fn. 99 und Fn. 103/104.

5. Zusammenfassende Bewertung

Die Rechtsfolgen bei nicht auf Irrtümern beruhenden Willens- oder Verständnisdefiziten innerhalb der Kommunikationstathandlungen zwischen Vorteilsnehmer und Vorteilsgeber fallen bei den Vertretern des Vertrauensschutzgedankens teilweise widersprüchlich aus. Einmal wird die Tatvollendung trotz des insoweit fehlenden Willens, die (pflichtwidrige) Amtshandlung zu begehen, nicht ausgeschlossen. Andererseits soll ein Willensdefizit bei der Inempfangnahme des Vorteils tatbestandsausschließende Wirkung entfalten, wenn der Vorteilsnehmer den Vorteil nur (vorläufig) entgegengenommen hat, um den Geber überführen zu können[127]. Handelt es sich bei letzterem Fall um einen Fall der Tatüberführung, bei dem der Anbietende auf die Probe gestellt werden soll, ob er den Vorteil tatsächlich aushändigt, könnte auch der erste Fall so gestaltet werden, dass der den Vorteil fordernde Beamte den Angesprochenen lediglich auf die Probe stellen will, selbst aber zu keinem Zeitpunkt beabsichtigt, die in Aussicht gestellte (pflichtwidrige) Amtshandlung tatsächlich auszuführen. Eine Gleichbehandlung des in beiden Fällen fehlenden Tatvollendungswillens hätte unter dem Gesichtspunkt des Vertrauensschutzes nahe gelegen, zunächst unabhängig von den rechtlichen Folgerungen, die daraus zu ziehen wären.

Hier besteht ein erstes Anzeichen für die These, dass die Heranziehung des Rechtsgutsgedankens des Vertrauensschutzes bei den Bestechungsdelikten nicht durchgängig konsequent, sondern fallbezogen und mitunter kriminalpolitisch motiviert erfolgt ist[128]. Diese fallbezogene Widersprüchlichkeit fällt bei den subjektiven Tatelementen der Tathandlungsalternativen der §§ 331 ff. besonders ins Gewicht, weil grundsätzlich Willens- oder Verstehensmängel der nur den objektiven Geschehensablauf wahrnehmenden Außenwelt vorenthalten bleiben und daher bei der Frage nach der Beeinträchtigung des Vertrauensverhältnisses Bürger-Staat keine objektiv bewertbaren Anhaltspunkte liefern können. Bezeichnenderweise hat der BGH bei der Tatbestandsalternative des „Forderns" aus Rechtsgutserwägungen die Feststellung getroffen, dass es auf die Erkennbarkeit des Forderungsinhaltes für den Aufgeforderten nicht ankomme[129]. Hieran knüpft die Frage an nach einer Harmonisierung eines die weitgehende Unbeachtlichkeit bestehender Willens- oder Verständnismängel einbindenden Rechtsgüterschutzes[130].

---

127 Wobei im Einzelfall offen bleibt, ab welcher zeitlichen Grenze die Vermutung für ein entgültiges Behalten spricht und ob dem späteren Herausgeben des Vorteils nicht ein Behaltenwollen vorausgegangen ist, vgl. zu den Beweisschwierigkeiten E. Schmidt (Fn. 61), S. 69, dort unter Fn. 187.

128 Das Schutzgutelement des „Vertrauens" eröffnet dabei die Möglichkeit von Strafbarkeitserweiterungen, vgl. Baumann (Fn. 65), S. 11.

129 BGHSt 10, 237 (241).

130 Zur weiteren Diskussion über das Rechtsgut der §§ 331 ff. s. u. S. 47 ff.

III. Die subjektiven Bestandteile des Äquivalenzverhältnisses der §§ 331-333

Aus der tatbestandlichen Erwähnung „für" eine in sein Amt einschlagende Handlung in den §§ 331 und 332 wird ein Beziehungsverhältnis zwischen Vorteil und Amtshandlung als notwendige Tatbestandsvoraussetzung hergeleitet, das bereits in RGSt 2,129 erwähnt wird[131].

1. Definition

In RGSt 19, 19 (22) wird das Äquivalenzverhältnis wie folgt erläutert: „... nicht jeder aus Anlaß oder bei Gelegenheit einer Amtshandlung angenommene Vorteil" muss „als für die Amtshandlung gegeben angesehen werden ..., sondern ... für letztere Feststellung" muss „noch ein ausdrücklicher Zusammenhang zwischen der Annahme des Vorteiles und der Amtshandlung vorhanden sein ..., welcher erkennen läßt, daß der Vorteil als Gegenleistung für die Amtshandlung erscheine, und daß die Feststellung dieses Zusammenhanges die Grundlage des bezüglichen Thatbestandsmerkmales zu bilden hat". Dieser RG-Entscheidung ist zu entnehmen, dass ein rein kausaler Zusammenhang zwischen Vorteil und Amtshandlung nicht ausreichend sein kann, sondern eine aufgrund der Vorstellungen und Willensbildung der Beteiligten begründete Beziehung zwischen der Tathandlung und der vom Vorteilsgeber in Aussicht genommenen Amtshandlung bestehen muss. Welches sind aber nun die weiteren, insbesondere subjektiven Anforderungen an diesen vom RG erwähnten „Zusammenhang" im Hinblick auf die Tathandlungsalternativen der §§ 331-333?

2. Das Äquivalenzverhältnis bei den Tathandlungen „Annehmen" und „Sichversprechenlassen" (§§ 331,332)

Die Tatbestandsalternativen „Annehmen" und „Sichversprechenlassen" können hier gemeinsam begutachtet werden, da sie insoweit einen vergleichbaren Grundtypus bilden. Bei ihnen werden korrespondierende Willensbetätigungen zwischen Vorteilsgeber und Vorteilsnehmer vorausgesetzt, während sich hiervon die Handlungsalternative des „Forderns" als einseitige Willensbetätigung des Beamten unterscheidet und daher eine Differenzierung erforderlich macht[132].

---

131 RGSt 2, 129 (131/132).
132 Vgl. RGSt 39, 193 (198).

a) Auffassung der Rechtsprechung

aa) Frühere Entscheidungen des RG

aaa) RGSt 51, 87

In RGSt 51, 87 heißt es, der Tatbestand des § 331 erfordere, „daß das Geschenk nach dem übereinstimmenden Willen des Gebers sowohl wie des Empfängers eine Gegenleistung für die Amtshandlung sein soll“[133].

bbb) RGSt 65, 52

Ergänzend fügt RGSt 65, 52 (53) hinzu: „Zum Wesen der Bestechung gehört die vertragsmäßige Willensübereinstimmung der Beteiligten dahin, daß dem Beamten – als Gegenleistung für eine Amtshandlung – ein Vorteil zufließen soll. Fehlt es an diesem übereinstimmenden Willen auf der einen oder anderen Seite, so entfällt die Bestechung“.

ccc) RGSt 65, 277

Die vom Gericht betonte vertragsmäßige Beziehung wird dann in RGSt 65, 277 interpretiert: „Die Bestechung setzt ... einen ... auf das Abkaufen der Amtshandlung gerichteten Vertrag voraus“. Nach dieser Rechtsprechung kommt es auf die Vorstellung und den übereinstimmenden Willen der Beteiligten an. Zwischen diesen muss ein „Unrechtsgeschäft“ vereinbart sein, das auf Käuflichkeit einer Amtshandlung abzielt[134].

bb) Korrektur der subjektiven Taterfordernisse durch die spätere Rechtsprechung

aaa) RGSt 74, 251

In RGSt 74, 251 (255) heißt es: „Zum Tatbestande des § 332 StGB. gehört nur, daß der Vorteilgeber von dem Beamten als Gegenleistung für den Vorteil eine pflichtwidrige Amtshandlung erwartet und daß der Beamte das erkennt und gleichwohl den Vorteil oder das Versprechen eines solchen mit Willen entgegennimmt, nicht auch, daß das Unternehmen der Bestechung Erfolg hat, daß der Beamte eine Amtspflichtwidrigkeit begeht, ja nicht einmal, daß er innerlich zu einem solchen Handeln bereit ist".

---

[133] Mit gleichem Wortlaut RGSt 58, 203 (204).

[134] E. Schmidt spricht von „Koinzidenz der beiderseitigen Vorstellungen und Willen“, (Fn. 61), S. 78.

bbb) RGSt 77, 75[135]

RGSt 77, 75 (78) fügt den Ausführungen von RGSt 74, 251 in Bezug auf das Äquivalenzverhältnis noch folgende Aussage hinzu: „Zum Tatbestande der schweren Bestechlichkeit nach dem § 332 StGB. gehört nicht, daß sich der Beamte innerlich entschlossen hat, sich in der Freiheit seines Ermessens durch die Vorteile beeinflussen zu lassen".

Von der ehemals geforderten einverständlichen Willensgemeinschaft im Hinblick auf das Beziehungsverhältnis zwischen Vorteil und Amtshandlung, einer Unrechtsvereinbarung im eigentlichen Sinn, weichen die beiden RG-Entscheidungen nicht unerheblich ab. Sie verzichten darauf, dass zwischen dem (Ermessens-)Beamten und seinem Gegenpart ein Einverständnis und eine Willensgemeinschaft bezüglich dieses Äquivalenzverhältnisses bestehen. Nach diesen Entscheidungen reicht für die Tatbestandserfüllung, wenn der Beamte den Vorteil annimmt oder sich versprechen lässt, ohne dass er dies in Beziehung zu einer Verletzung seiner Amtspflichten setzt oder setzen will; er muss sich nur vorstellen oder für möglich halten, dass sein Gegenüber von ihm eine pflichtwidrige Amtshandlung erwartet.

ccc) BGHSt 11, 125

Der BGH hat in dieser Entscheidung aus dem Jahre 1957 ganz im Sinne von RGSt 77, 75 Stellung genommen[136]. Gleiches gilt für spätere Entscheidungen[137].

b) Auffassung des Schrifttums

Um die Tragweite dieser Rspr. in ihren Einzelkomponenten richtig deuten und interpretieren zu können, empfiehlt sich eine Aufgliederung der Einzelfragen wie sie vom Schrifttum vorgenommen worden ist:

---

135 RGSt 74, 251 und RGSt 77, 75 behandeln den Fall des Ermessensbeamten, der im Gegensatz zum „gebundenen" Beamten bei seinen Entscheidungen ein Auswahlermessen besitzt – näher hierzu R. Schmitt, ZStW 73 (1961), S. 414 (425 ff.); die einschlägigen RG- und BGH-Entscheidungen betreffen fast ausnahmslos den Ermessensbeamten, weil bei ihm die Probleme der subjektiven tatbestandlichen Anforderungen besonders deutlich hervortreten; soweit nicht mit der Besonderheit des Status eines Ermessensbeamten verbunden, gelten die Erörterungen aber auch für den gebundenen Beamten.

136 BGHSt 11, 125 (129/130).

137 BGH GA 1959, 374; BGH NJW 1960, S. 830 (831).

aa) Voraussetzung einer vertragsmäßigen Willensübereinstimmung

Es geht hier um die Frage, wie weit die inhaltliche Übereinstimmung in der Vorstellung und dem Willen der Beteiligten reichen muss, d.h. welchen tatbestandsbezogenen Sachverhalt der vom Vorteilsgeber und -nehmer getragene Konsens beinhalten muss. Unterschiedlich sind die Auffassungen in Bezug auf die Vereinbarung der Pflichtwidrigkeit der Amtshandlung bei § 332.

aaa) Die Position von E. Schmidt

Die Kritik E. Schmidts an der weitgehenden Preisgabe der subjektiven Bestandteile des Äquivalenzverhältnisses seit RGSt 74, 251 fällt eindeutig und massiv aus[138]. Als Konsequenz dieser Rspr. des RG entfalle das bis dato als „Kernstück des § 332 angesehene Tatbestandselement, das Moment nämlich, daß für den Beamten der zuteilgewordene oder zugesagte Vorteil im Äquivalentsverhältnis zu einer von ihm erkannten und gewollten Amtspflichtwidrigkeit steht und daß der Beamte seine auf den Vorteil bezügliche Verhaltensweise in diesem Sinne versteht und will“[139]. Nach Auffassung von E. Schmidt könnten die Beteiligten nach der Rspr. des RG „völlig aneinander vorbeidenken und ganz verschiedener Meinung sein“[140]. Auf die Vereinbarung einer Amtspflichtwidrigkeit könne aber nicht verzichtet werden, wolle man nicht gänzlich auf das Bezugsverhältnis zwischen Vorteil und pflichtwidriger Amtshandlung verzichten[141]. E. Schmidt plädiert daher für eine Rückkehr zur älteren Rspr. des RG, die eine auf Käuflichkeit einer Amtshandlung gerichtete Unrechtsvereinbarung zwischen Vorteilsgeber und Vorteilsnehmer vorausgesetzt habe. Es müsse „eine Koinzidenz der beiderseitigen Vorstellungen und Willen bestehen“[142]. Eine sog. „äußere Konnivenz“ genüge nicht, um die in den §§ 331 und 332 getroffene Unterscheidung zwischen pflichtgemäßer und pflichtwidriger Amtshandlung deutlich werden zu lassen[143].

---

138 E. Schmidt spricht von einem „Fehlschluss“, (Fn. 61), S. 89.

139 E. Schmidt (Fn. 61), S. 89.

140 E. Schmidt (Fn. 61), S. 90.

141 E. Schmidt (Fn. 61), S. 89; ihm folgend Bockelmann, ZStW 72 (1960), S. 251 (256).

142 E. Schmidt (Fn. 61), S. 78; nach Berresheim beinhaltet eine Unrechtsvereinbarung „das korrespondierende Wissen des konkret gewollten Unrechts“, Die Korruption aus der Sicht des Verteidigers, S. 26.

143 E. Schmidt, NJW 1960, S. 802 (804). Im Ergebnis E. Schmidt folgend: Berresheim (Fn. 142), S. 26; Bockelmann, ZStW 72 (1960), S. 251 (256); Schmidt-Leichner, NJW 1960, S. 846 (848 f.); Henkel, JZ 1960, S. 507 (509 f.); Klug, JZ 1960, S. 724 (725/726) m.w.N. dort unter Fn. 28.

bbb) Die Gegenposition von Fuhrmann

Zwar setzt auch Fuhrmann für die Annahme eines Äquivalenzverhältnisses voraus, dass bei der Annahme des Vorteils bzw. des Versprechens Vorteilsgeber und -nehmer darüber einig sind, der Vorteil solle die Belohnung für eine pflichtmäßige oder pflichtwidrige Amtshandlung sein[144]. Dieses vertragliche Beziehungsverhältnis dürfe aber nicht so verstanden werden, dass „damit ein Austausch gegenseitiger Leistungen erreicht werden soll“[145]. Es bestehe zwischen den Beteiligten nur eine einseitig auf die Handlung des Beamten ausgerichtete Abhängigkeit von der Leistung des Vorteilsgebers. Dementsprechend müsse die Pflichtwidrigkeit der angesonnenen Amtshandlung nur dem Beamten bewusst geworden sein, eine gegenseitige Willensübereinstimmung sei insoweit nicht erforderlich[146].

bb) Voraussetzung des Willens, die (pflichtwidrige) Amtshandlung zu begehen

Die Rechtsprechung hat den Willen des Beamten im Hinblick auf die Begehung der (pflichtwidrigen) Amtshandlung für unbeachtlich erklärt[147]. Diese Frage wird heute auch in der Literatur so entschieden[148]. Im Schrifttum der frühen sechziger Jahre nahm diese Frage eine zentrale Stellung in der Kontroverse um die vor allem von E. Schmidt behauptete unzulässige Ausweitung der Strafbarkeit der Bestechungstaten ein. Dabei wurden neben Rechtsgutserwägungen zahlreiche andere Argumente vorgebracht.

aaa) Die Argumente von E. Schmidt

E. Schmidt vertritt die Ansicht, dass bei noch bevorstehender Amtshandlung der Beamte nicht nur das Bewusstsein der Pflichtwidrigkeit, sondern auch den Willen haben müsse, die pflichtwidrige Handlung zu begehen[149]. Anderenfalls würden vom Tatbestand des § 332 Fälle mit unterschiedlichem Unrechts- und Schuldgehalt erfasst, nämlich sowohl diejenigen, in denen der Beamte eine pflichtwidrige Amtshandlung bereits begangen habe, als auch diejenigen, in denen diese Amtshandlung noch bevorstehe, aber mangels Tatwillen nicht einmal beabsichtigt werde[150]. Unabhängig von der Frage des Tatverwirklichungs-

---

144 Fuhrmann, ZStW 72 (1960), S. 534 (559/560).

145 Fuhrmann, ZStW 72 (1960), S. 534 (560).

146 Fuhrmann, ZStW 72 (1960), S. 534 (560), der seine Auffassung durch Entscheidungen des RG gestützt sieht.

147 S. unter Fn. 86-89.

148 Schönke/Schröder/Cramer, § 333 Rn. 5 und 30; Tröndle/Fischer, § 332 Rn. 22.

149 E. Schmidt (Fn. 61), S. 79; die Frage stellt sich auch bei einer pflichtgemäßen Amtshandlung, allerdings nicht mit der gleichen Tragweite.

150 E. Schmidt (Fn. 61), S. 79.

willens werde schon durch den Verzicht auf die tatsächliche Vornahme der pflichtwidrigen Amtshandlung wie Binding[151] formuliert habe „die Vollendung tief in das Versuchsstadium zurückgeschoben“[152]. Deshalb müsse wie beim Versuch der Wille des Beamten die Vornahme der pflichtwidrigen Amtshandlung einbeziehen[153]. Wenn sich der Beamte bei fehlendem Willen überhaupt keine Vorstellungen über die Pflichtwidrigkeit der Amtshandlung mache, sei sein Vorsatz allenfalls auf die Verwirklichung des § 331 gerichtet[154]. Auch im Hinblick auf die bei § 332 angedrohte Zuchthausstrafe müsse die Amtspflichtverletzung zumindest in Aussicht genommen, also gewollt werden[155].

bbb) Die Argumentation von R. Schmitt

R. Schmitt stellt auf den Zusammenhang ab zwischen dem Nachweis der Beeinflussung der Willensbildung beim der Bestechlichkeit beschuldigten Ermessensbeamten, und dem Willen des Beamten in Bezug zur Pflichtwidrigkeit der Amtshandlung. Bestehe beim Ermessensbeamten „doch die Pflichtwidrigkeit allein in der Beeinflußtheit des Willens“[156]. Soweit man wie das RG in seinen Entscheidungen RGSt 74, 251 und RGSt 77, 75 den Einfluss des Vorteils auf die Ermessensbildung unwiderleglich vermute[157], wäre es widersprüchlich, gleichzeitig noch Feststellungen über den – insoweit bereits beeinflussten – Willen des Beamten bezüglich der Pflichtwidrigkeit der in Aussicht stehenden Amtshandlung treffen zu wollen[158]. Verlange man wie der BGH in seiner das RG insoweit korrigierenden Entscheidung BGHSt 15, 88 den Nachweis des konkreten Einflusses des Vorteils auf die Willensbildung[159], dann sei erst mit der tatrichterlichen Überzeugung dieses Nachweises auch der Wille zur Pflichtwidrigkeit dokumentiert. Erörterungen des BGH zur auch von ihm vertretenen Unbeachtlichkeit dieses Willens seien dann zumindest überflüssig[160].

151 Binding, Lehrbuch, Besonderer Teil Bd. II 2, S. 726.
152 E. Schmidt (Fn. 61), S. 80.
153 E. Schmidt (Fn. 61), S. 80; ebenso Baumann (Fn. 65), S. 33.
154 E. Schmidt (Fn. 61), S. 80.
155 E. Schmidt (Fn. 61), S. 81; ihm folgend Bockelmann, ZStW 72 (1960), S. 251 (257); Baumann (Fn. 65), S. 33/34; Henkel, JZ 1960, S. 507 (510), der sich wie bereits E. Schmidt (Fn. 61), S. 82 ff., mit der umstrittenen Begründung des RG-Urteils RGSt 39, 193 (201) auseinandersetzt, die den Willen des Beamten, eine pflichtwidrige Amtshandlung vorzunehmen, als „dolus ex re“ interpretiert, der nur durch Gegenbeweis ausgeschlossen werden könne.
156 R. Schmitt, ZStW 73 (1961), S. 414 (432/433).
157 RGSt 74, 251 (255) und RGSt 77, 75 (78).
158 Daher konsequent, wenn das RG in seinen Entscheidungen den Willen zur Amtspflichtwidrigkeit für irrelevant erklärt, R. Schmitt, ZStW 73 (1961), S. 414 (433).
159 BGHSt 15, 88 (91 ff.).
160 R. Schmitt, ZStW 73 (1961), S. 414 (435/436).

ccc) Das Argument von Klug

Nach Klug widerspricht der Verzicht auf den Tatverwirklichungswillen des Beamten „dem rechtsstaatlichen Verbot einer Schuldvermutung im Strafrecht“[161]. Der Strafrichter könne von seiner Aufgabe, den verbrecherischen Willen des Täters festzustellen, nicht einfach befreit werden. Beweisschwierigkeiten dürften nicht als Grund für die Preisgabe subjektiver Strafbarkeitsvoraussetzungen herhalten[162].

ddd) Die Argumente von Fuhrmann und von Kirschbaum und Schmitz[163] gegen die Position von E. Schmidt

Die Genannten verneinen das Erfordernis eines auf die Vornahme der Amtspflichtwidrigkeit bezogenen Willens und lassen ausreichen, dass der Beamte die Zweckbestimmung der Vorteilshingabe erkennt und zumindest mit der Möglichkeit einer auf die Vornahme einer pflichtwidrigen Handlung gerichteten Erwartungshaltung des Gebers rechnet[164]. Fuhrmann hält E. Schmidt entgegen, dessen Forderung nach Ausweitung des Äquivalenzverhältnisses erschwere die Beweisführung und könne sich zudem nicht auf eine 80 Jahre gewachsene Rechtsprechung stützen[165]. Weiter wird E. Schmidt entgegengehalten, der Gesetzgeber habe im Tatbestand des § 332 das Erfordernis eines erfolgsbezogenen Willens nicht zum Ausdruck gebracht und damit auf die Voraussetzung der Vornahme der pflichtwidrigen Amtshandlung wie auf die diesbezügliche Absicht verzichtet[166]. Ausgehend von den Materialien zum preußischen Strafgesetzbuch von 1851 versucht Fuhrmann nachzuweisen, dass der damalige Gesetzgeber die seitdem unverändert gebliebene Gesetzesfassung der schweren Bestechlichkeit in bewusster Ausgrenzung der Beachtlichkeit des infrage stehenden Willens verfasst habe[167]. Kirschbaum/Schmitz ergänzen diese Argumentation um die Schlussfolgerung, dass beim Täter kein entsprechender Wille zu verlangen sei, wenn die Vornahme der pflichtwidrigen Handlung nicht zum Tatbestand gehöre. Dennoch gehe auch ohne diesen Tatverwirklichungswillen der Vorsatz des Täters im Hinblick auf sein Bewusstsein, der

161 Klug, JZ 1960, S. 724 (727).

162 Klug, JZ 1960, S. 724 (727).

163 Ihnen folgend Stein, NJW 1961, S. 433 (435 f.); Krönig, NJW 1960, S. 2083, der mit dem Rechtsgedanken des § 116 I BGB für die Unbeachtlichkeit einer Mentalreservation argumentiert.

164 Fuhrmann, ZStW 72 (1960), S. 534 (567); Kirschbaum/Schmitz, GA 1960, S. 321 (343 ff.).

165 Fuhrmann, ZStW 72 (1960), S. 534 (565/566 und 572 ff.); dies gelte mit einer Ausnahme für alle Entscheidungen des RG zu dieser Frage, S. 574.

166 Fuhrmann, ZStW 72 (1960), S. 534 (568); Kirschbaum/Schmitz, GA 1960, S. 321 (344).

167 Fuhrmann, ZStW 72 (1960), S. 534 (570/571).

Vorteilsgeber gebe die Belohnung für eine pflichtwidrige Amtshandlung, über einen „reinen" Betrugsvorsatz hinaus[168].

cc) Voraussetzung der inneren Entschließungsfreiheit beim Ermessensbeamten

Die oben schon zitierte Entscheidung RGSt 77, 75 enthält u.a. die Feststellung, dass zum Tatbestand der schweren Bestechlichkeit nicht der Entschluss des Beamten gehört, sich durch die Vorteile in der Freiheit des Auswahlermessens beeinflussen zu lassen[169]. E. Schmidt hat die mit dieser Aussage verbundenen Konsequenzen eindrucksvoll verdeutlicht, indem er den Fall eines Ermessensbeamten schildert, der zunächst nach ausschließlich sachlichen Gesichtspunkten bestimmte Entscheidungen fällt, dann eine Zuwendung erhält und nunmehr auch weiterhin nach den gleichen korrekten Erwägungen seine Entscheidungen wie zuvor trifft. Seine innere von sachfremden Erwägungen frei gebliebene Einstellung im Hinblick auf die Entscheidungsfindung führe nach dem Urteil des RG allein durch die Annahme der Zuwendung zwingend zur Pflichtwidrigkeit der ihr nachfolgenden amtlichen Tätigkeit[170]. Damit werde das Beziehungsverhältnis im Sinne einer einverständlichen Willensgemeinschaft neben dem Tatverwirklichungswillen eines weiteren subjektiven Moments beraubt[171].

Um diesen Entscheidungssatz des RG in seiner Bedeutung und Tragweite richtig einordnen zu können, müssen die zur Pflichtwidrigkeit der Amtshandlung getroffenen Urteilsfeststellungen zunächst genauer begutachtet werden.

aaa) Die Pflichtwidrigkeit von Ermessensentscheidungen[172]

aaaa) RGSt 77, 75[173]

Nach Auffassung des RG handelt ein Ermessensbeamter pflichtwidrig, „wenn er sich nicht ausschließlich von sachlichen Gesichtspunkten leiten läßt", indem er z.B. den versprochenen Vorteil bei seinen Entscheidungen berücksichtigt, er also „an die Entscheidungen nicht unbefangen, sondern mit der inneren Belas-

---

168 Kirschbaum/Schmitz, GA 1960, S. 321 (344/345).

169 RGSt 77, 75 (78).

170 E. Schmidt (Fn. 61), S. 88/89.

171 E. Schmidt (Fn. 61), S. 89.

172 Es geht dabei vor allem um diejenigen nach außen hin fehlerfreien Ermessensentscheidungen, bei denen der Beamte sein Ermessen – vom Vorteil beeinflusst oder nicht – innerhalb des Ermessensspielraums ausgeübt hat und zu einer von mehreren möglichen und daher objektiv zulässigen Entscheidung gekommen ist. Dass aber auch eine vom Vorteil mitbeeinflusste im Rahmen des Ermessensspielraums bleibende Amtshandlung pflichtwidrig ist, hat das RG schon früh entschieden, vgl. RGSt 1, 404 (405); 4, 101 (103).

173 Vorher bereits RGSt 74, 251.

tung herangeht, die für ihn in dem gewährten oder erwarteten Vorteile liegt; denn durch eine solche Belastung“ werde „sein Urteil regelmäßig getrübt“[174]. Das RG bediente sich hier zur Begriffsbestimmung der Amtspflichtverletzung eines die strafprozessuale Feststellung ersetzenden Erfahrungssatzes und erzeugte damit zumindest den Anschein, den jahrzehntelang für gültig erklärten Grundsatz des Verbots antizipierter Beweiswürdigung aufgeben zu wollen[175].

bbbb) Das BGH-Urteil vom 27.10 1959

Der BGH ist dieser Rspr. des RG zunächst gefolgt[176], hat in einer Entscheidung aus dem Jahre 1959 sogar noch hinzugefügt, die Pflichtwidrigkeit liege beim Ermessensbeamten bereits darin, dass er „infolge der Beschenkung an seine Ermessensentscheidung nicht mehr unbefangen herangehen kann, sondern nur – möglicherweise ganz unbewußt – mit der inneren Belastung, die für ihn in den gewährten Geschenken liegt und durch die sein Urteil regelmäßig getrübt wird“[177].

cccc) Die Kritik des Schrifttums

E. Schmidt und weite Teile des Schrifttums haben sich energisch gegen diese Rspr. gewandt[178]. Als Gründe für den behaupteten Wechsel der Rspr. zu einer extensiven Anwendung des § 332 werden nicht selten Beweisschwierigkeiten bei der Feststellung der subjektiven Tatelemente genannt[179].

Henkel sieht den wesentlichen Unterschied obiger Urteile zur älteren Rspr. des RG darin, dass der zur Ermessensentschließung hinführende Abwägungsvorgang, also die reale auf die Einräumung von Rücksichten auf den Vorteilsgeber projizierte Willensbildung des Beamten keiner richterlichen Feststellung mehr bedürfe, sondern die Pflichtwidrigkeit der Amtshandlung mit der in der Vorteilsannahme liegenden Makelhaftigkeit unwiderleglich begründet werde[180].

---

174 RGSt 77, 75 (78); RGSt 74, 251 (255).

175 Hierzu vgl. RGSt 75, 11.

176 Vgl. BGHSt 11, 125 (129 f); ferner BGH GA 59, 176 (177).

177 BGH NJW 1960, S. 830 (831).

178 E. Schmidt (Fn. 61), S. 56 ff. und NJW 1960, S. 802 f.; Henkel, JZ 1960, S. 507 (507/510); Klug, JZ 1960, S. 724 (726 f.); Bockelmann, ZStW 72 (1960), S. 251 (255 f.); a.A. Kirschbaum/Schmitz, GA 1960, S. 321 (334 ff.); zurückhaltender Fuhrmann, ZStW 72 (1960), S. 534 (551 ff.).

179 Bockelmann, ZStW 72 (1960), S. 251 (258); Klug, JZ 1960, S. 724 (727); E. Schmidt (Fn. 61), S. 58; Baumann (Fn. 65), S. 29; Berresheim (Fn. 142), S. 17; Schmidt-Leichner, NJW 1960, S. 846 (848); unerwartet deutlich auch RGSt 74, 251 (256) und nachfolgend BGHSt 15, 88 (99/100).

180 Henkel, JZ 1960, S. 507.

Bockelmann argumentiert, die praktische Umsetzung der neueren Rspr. des RG führe dazu, dass die in der Annahme einer Belohnung liegende Pflichtwidrigkeit zugleich die Pflichtwidrigkeit der belohnten Amtshandlung begründe. Es sei aber immer noch ein Unterschied, ob man sich durch die Annahme einer Belohnung „der Versuchung aussetzt, einen pflichtwidrigen Entschluß zu fassen und auszuführen, oder ob man ihn wirklich faßt". Diesen Unterschied, der die Grenze zwischen § 332 und § 331 markiere, habe das RG preisgegeben[181].

Schmidt-Leichner und Berresheim bilden die Formel: „Ermessensbeamter + Vorteilsnahme = schwere Bestechung"[182]. Die vom RG eingeschlagene Entwicklung führe dazu, dass das beamtenrechtliche Geschenkannahmeverbot unter Streichung des § 331 nunmehr als „Verbrechen" bestraft werde[183]. Die Kritiker führen aus, kriminalpolitische Überlegungen hätten dazu geführt, die Beweisnot durch Einebnung vor allem der subjektiven Tatbestandserfordernisse zu beseitigen. Dabei sei man sogar bereit gewesen, auf tatbestandliche Fiktionen bei gleichzeitigem Verzicht auf tatrichterliche Feststellungen zurückzugreifen[184].

Für E. Schmidt ist mit dem BGH-Urteil von 1959 „die äußerste Grenze des juristisch Unerträglichen erreicht", denn nach diesem Urteil werde nicht nur auf tatrichterliche Feststellungen zur Beeinflusstheit des Ermessensbeamten verzichtet, sondern selbst dann noch die Pflichtwidrigkeit seiner Entscheidungen erklärt, wenn er „tatsächlich ganz unbefangen" bleibe, weil er sich einer „inneren Belastung" gar „nicht bewußt" gewesen sei[185].

Klug ergänzt die von E. Schmidt vorgetragenen strafrechtsdogmatischen Argumente um psychologische Gesichtspunkte. Ein psychisches Gesetz oder ein psychologischer Erfahrungssatz, der die These stütze, jede Vorteilsgewährung stelle eine „innere Belastung" dar und führe dazu, dass der Ermessensbeamte

---

181 Bockelmann, ZStW 72 (1960), S. 251 (254/255).

182 Schmidt-Leichner, NJW 1960, S. 846 (847); Berresheim (Fn. 142), S. 16.

183 Schmidt-Leichner, NJW 1960, S. 846 (848); im Ergebnis genauso E. Schmidt (Fn. 61), S. 91.

184 Vgl. Schmidt-Leichner, NJW 1960, S. 846 (848); Berresheim (Fn. 142), S. 17 ff.; R. Schmitt, ZStW 73 (1961), S. 414 (427/428) hält den Begriff „Fiktion" für zu weitgehend, vielmehr handele es sich bei den Formulierungen des RG im Ergebnis um eine unwiderlegliche Vermutung unter Verzicht auf die Feststellung einer motivationsbeeinflussenden Wirkung des Vorteils auf die Entschließungsfreiheit des Beamten.

185 E. Schmidt, NJW 1960, S. 802 (803); a.A. Kirschbaum/Schmitz, GA 1960, S. 321 (334-339), nach denen es auf das Bewusstsein der inneren Belastung des Beamten überhaupt nicht ankomme, wobei ihre darauf aufbauende Abgrenzung zwischen § 331 und § 332 nicht überzeugt, weil auch sie hier nicht auf eine innerhalb der Unrechtsvereinbarung subjektiv vom Beamten zu treffende Unterscheidung zwischen pflichtwidriger und pflichtgemäßer Amtshandlung verzichten können.

nicht mehr unbefangen an seine Entscheidungen herangehen könne, gebe es nicht[186].

dddd) Die BGH-Urteile 15, 88 und 15, 239 aus dem Jahr 1960

Der BGH distanziert sich in diesen Urteilen von der vom RG aufgestellten Behauptung der unwiderleglichen Vermutung des Vorteilseinflusses auf die Entscheidungsfindung des Ermessensbeamten. Im Leitsatz von BGHSt 15, 239 heißt es: „Allein durch die Annahme eines Vorteils macht sich auch ein Ermessensbeamter nicht der schweren Bestechlichkeit schuldig ... Die Feststellung dieser Unrechtsvereinbarung kann nicht ersetzt werden durch den allgemeinen Hinweis auf die innere Belastung, in der sich ein Ermessensbeamter befindet, dem ein Vorteil gewährt oder versprochen worden ist". Mit dieser Kurskorrektur hat sich der BGH gegen die Beweisvermutungsregeln des RG ausgesprochen und ist zur rechtsstaatlichen Forderung nach tatrichterlicher Feststellung und Beweisführung der inneren Tatsachen zurückgekehrt[187]. Allerdings hält er daran fest, dass der Tatbestand der Bestechung nicht voraussetzt, „daß der Beamte die Pflichtwidrigkeit begeht oder auch nur den Willen dazu hat"[188].

bbb) Ergebnis

Mit den Urteilen RGSt 74, 251 und RGSt 77, 75 hat das RG den Verzicht auf die konkrete Feststellung des inneren Willensbildungsprozesses des Beamten im Hinblick auf eine denkbare, auf Bevorzugung des Vorteilsgebers gerichtete Beeinflussung durch die Vorteilsannahme erklärt und das Vorhandensein einer solchen Beeinflussung für regelmäßig gegeben erachtet. Mit dieser Festlegung konnte es auf eine tatrichterliche Prüfung des inneren Entschlusses des Beamten, sich im Rahmen seines Ermessensspielraums durch den Vorteil beeinflussen zu lassen, nicht mehr ankommen; denn für diese Beeinflussung bestand nun eine unwiderlegliche Vermutung. Der BGH hat – nachdem er vorübergehend dem RG gefolgt war – später den Nachweis des konkreten Vorteilseinflusses verlangt. Er setzt damit für die Annahme der schweren Bestechlichkeit nach § 332 im Einzelfall die tatrichterliche Feststellung der Beeinflussung der Entschließungsfreiheit des Ermessensbeamten voraus. Diese Voraussetzung sei erfüllt, wenn der Beamte „durch seine ausdrückliche oder stillschweigende Erklärung" die Bereitschaft kundgibt, „bei seiner künftigen Entscheidung nicht ausschließlich sachliche Gesichtspunkte walten zu lassen, sondern der Rücksicht auf den Vorteil Raum zu geben"[189].

---

186 Klug, JZ 1960, S. 724 (726/727).
187 Vgl. BGHSt 15, 239 (249).
188 BGHSt 15, 239 (242).
189 BGH NJW 1961, S. 469.

3. Das Äquivalenzverhältnis bei der Tathandlung „Fordern“

Im Unterschied zu den Handlungsalternativen „Annehmen“ und „Sichversprechenlassen“ wird beim „Fordern“ als einseitiger Willenserklärung[190] keine Willensbetätigung auf der Seite des Angesprochenen vorausgesetzt. Unstreitig braucht es daher bei dieser Tatbestandsalternative zu einer das Beziehungsverhältnis[191] umfassenden einvernehmlichen Willensgemeinschaft nicht zu kommen. Streitig ist dagegen, ob auf beiden Seiten der am Forderungsaustausch Beteiligten eine Wissensgemeinschaft um die zwischen Vorteil und Amtshandlung bestehende Verknüpfung vorauszusetzen ist, d.h. ob der die Forderungserklärung zur Kenntnis nehmende Adressat den Inhalt der Äußerung verstehen muss, ob dieser Inhalt für ihn zumindest erkennbar gewesen sein muss oder ob die generelle Erkennbarkeit aus der Sicht eines mit der Situation vertrauten Dritten genügt[192].

a) Die Entwicklung der Rechtsprechung

aa) Die Auffassung des RG

Die früheren Entscheidungen des RG zu dieser Frage sind nicht eindeutig in der Beurteilung, ob allein schon die akustische Wahrnehmung der Äußerung des Beamten beim Adressaten bereits für die Tatvollendung ausreichend sein soll, unabhängig davon, ob diesem das in der Forderung zum Ausdruck kommende Zusammenhangsverhältnis zwischen Leistung und Gegenleistung bewusst war oder wenigstens hätte bewusst werden können.

So wird in RGSt 39, 193 (199) dieses Bewusstsein des Äußerungsadressaten für unbeachtlich erklärt, andererseits aber von der Beschaffenheit des Forderungsinhalts verlangt, „daß das Wesen des geforderten Vorteils als eines von einem Beamten verlangten Entgelts für seine Amtshandlung daraus hervorgeht“.

RGSt 70, 166 (171 f.) führt dann schon genauer die Voraussetzung aus, dass der Forderungsadressat aus der Forderungserklärung oder den Gesamtumständen den vom Beamten mit seinem Vorteilsbegehren zum Ausdruck gebrachten

---

190 Schönke/Schröder/Cramer, § 331 Rn. 22.

191 Zwischen gefordertem Vorteil und (pflichtwidriger) Amtshandlung.

192 Für die Frage, ob der Beamte im Zeitpunkt der Forderungserklärung den Willen haben muss, eine (pflichtwidrige) Amtshandlung im Falle der Erfüllung seiner Forderung zu begehen, gelten die gleichen Ausführungen wie zu den Tatalternativen „Annehmen“ und „Sichversprechenlassen“, oben S. 26 ff.

Zusammenhang mit der Inaussichtstellung einer Amtshandlung erkennen konnte[193].

Da das RG von dem Erfordernis des Bewusstseins des Vorteilsgebers absieht, ihm werde etwas als Vorteil für eine Amtshandlung abverlangt, bleibt hinsichtlich der gleichwohl für erforderlich erachteten „Erkennbarkeit" die Frage, ob diese für den konkret betroffenen Forderungsempfänger in der vorgefundenen Situation zu ermitteln ist oder generalisierend für einen sog. durchschnittlich kompetenten Dritten.

bb) Die Auffassung des BGH

Der BGH erweitert in einer früheren Entscheidung[194] in Abkehr von RGSt 77, 75 die Voraussetzungen für die Handlungsvariante des „Forderns" dadurch, dass er über die Erkennbarkeit des Forderungsinhalts hinaus auf beiden Seiten der am Forderungsaustausch Beteiligten das „Wissen" verlangt, „daß das Geforderte die Gegenleistung für jene Amtshandlung sein soll". Die damit geschaffene subjektive Verstehensbeziehung des Forderungsadressaten zum Forderungsinhalt wird aber wenig später vom BGH in BGHSt 10, 237 wieder fallengelassen. Im Unterschied zu den reichsgerichtlichen Entscheidungen legt sich der BGH im Hinblick auf die Erkennbarkeit des Forderungsinhalts jetzt sogar darauf fest, dass diese beim Aufgeforderten nicht vorliegen müsse[195]. Zur Begründung führt er an, dass das geschützte Rechtsgut der „Reinheit der Amtsausübung" beim „Fordern" schon dann verletzt sei, wenn der Beamte mit dem (bedingten) Willen, der andere werde sich dieses Zusammenhangs bewusst, von diesem einen Vorteil für eine Amtshandlung einfordere[196].

b) Die Auffassung des Schrifttums

aa) Die Position von E. Schmidt

E. Schmidt vertritt die Meinung, der Forderungsadressat müsse den Inhalt und Zusammenhang des an ihn herangetragenen Ansinnens nicht nur akustisch wahrnehmen, sondern auch verstehen[197]. Er begründet seine Auffassung einmal mit dem Verständnis des bei Äußerungsdelikten wie z.B. der Beleidigung zu fordernden Verstehens des Inhalts der an den Adressaten gerichteten einseitigen Willenserklärung. Zum anderen bezweifelt er die Eignung des Schutzzweckes der „Reinheit der Amtsführung", strafrechtlich relevantes von nur

193 Ähnlich auch RGSt 77, 75 (76).
194 BGHST 8, 214 (215).
195 BGHSt 10, 237 (241).
196 BGHSt 10, 237 (241/242).
197 E. Schmidt (Fn. 61), S. 105 ff.

dienstrechtlich erheblichem Verhalten abzugrenzen. Außerdem werde mit dem Verzicht auf eine Wissensgemeinschaft zwischen Forderndem und Angesprochenem eine Kommunikationsbeziehung negiert und damit die dem Verbrechen der Bestechlichkeit innewohnende „Gegenseitigkeitsbeziehung“ aufgegeben[198]. Im Übrigen wäre der auch von der Rspr. verlangte Wille des Beamten, der Forderungsadressat solle sich des Zusammenhangs zwischen Vorteil und Amtshandlung bewusst werden, bei Verzicht der Voraussetzung eines tatsächlichen Verstehens des Forderungsinhaltes nur schwer einzuordnen. Ordne man diesen Willen dem allgemeinen Vorsatz zu, so würde dieser über die Merkmale hinausgehen, die die Tathandlung umfassten[199].

bb) Die Gegenposition von Baumann, Kirschbaum/Schmitz und Fuhrmann

Das sich mit den Argumenten von E. Schmidt auseinandersetzende Schrifttum hält seiner Ansicht entgegen, die gesamte höchstrichterliche Judikatur sei bis auf die Ausnahme von BGHSt 8, 214 darin einig gewesen, dass ein Verstehen der Forderung durch den Empfänger der Erklärung für die Tatvollendung der §§ 331 ff. bedeutungslos sei[200]. Die Argumentation von E. Schmidt zum Wesen der Äußerungsdelikte sei nicht überzeugend, da das „Fordern“ als Handlungsalternative rechtssystematisch einer zum Status der vollendeten Tat erhobenen Versuchshandlung entspreche[201]. Es könne auch nicht von der Auffassungsgabe des Forderungsadressaten abhängig sein, ob den Beamten, der sich mit der Forderungserklärung käuflich zeige, die hohe Strafdrohung des § 332 treffe[202]. Baumann stellt darauf ab, dass das „Fordern“ nur ein „einseitiges Handeln“ und dementsprechend kein Verstehen auf der anderen Seite voraussetze[203].

cc) Zusammenfassende Bewertung

Die Kontroverse um die Voraussetzungen der Tatalternative des „Forderns“ offenbart die eigentliche, hinter Einzelerwägungen stehende Problematik um den bis heute umstritten gebliebenen Schutzzweck der Bestechungsdelikte[204].

Die Begründung des BGH, die auf dem Schutzgut der „Reinheit der Amtsführung“ aufbaut, erfolgt nicht durchgängig konsequent; denn bereits vor Zugang der Forderung beim Adressaten, den auch der BGH voraussetzt, wird die Reinheit der Amtsführung durch die Abgabe der Forderungserklärung als sol-

---

198 E. Schmidt (Fn. 61), S. 105/106.

199 E. Schmidt (Fn. 61), S. 108.

200 Kirschbaum/Schmitz, GA 1960, S. 321 (349/350); Fuhrmann, ZStW 72 (1960), S. 534 (581 ff.); Baumann (Fn. 65), S. 20.

201 Kirschbaum/Schmitz, GA 1960, S. 321 (350).

202 Kirschbaum/Schmitz, GA 1960, S. 321 (352).

203 Baumann (Fn. 65), S. 21.

204 Dazu s. unten S. 47 ff.

che verletzt. Wenn also ein zeitlich nachgelagertes individuelles Verstehen des Forderungsinhalts durch den Empfänger aus besagten Rechtsschutzüberlegungen nicht für erforderlich gehalten wird, so dürfte es auch nicht auf den Zugang und damit die formale Entgegennahme des Forderungsinhalts ankommen. Eine ausufernd interpretierbare und unpräzise Grenzziehung des geschützten Rechtsgutsbereichs birgt die Gefahr, zunächst das einzelne Tatbestandsmerkmal in Augenschein zu nehmen, um aus dem erzielten Auslegungsergebnis die Vereinbarkeit mit dem definierten Schutzbereich herzustellen.

Der BGH hat sich in der Wechselwirkung der Tatbestandserfordernisse zum erklärten Schutzzweck gleichsam verfangen, denn aus seinem damaligen Rechtsgutsverständnis heraus hätte er den Zeitpunkt der Vollendung der Tathandlung des „Forderns" weiter auf den Zeitpunkt der Abgabe der Forderungserklärung vorverlegen müssen. Gleiches gilt, wenn man als Schutzgut das Vertrauen der Allgemeinheit in die Sachlichkeit amtlicher Tätigkeit heranzieht[205]. Denn auch hier reicht es in aller Regel für eine Beeinträchtigung dieses Vertrauens aus, dass eine ihrem Inhalt nach objektiv verständliche Erklärung eines Beamten die an einen Dritten gerichtete Forderung „Vorteil gegen Amtshandlung" enthält, ohne dass es auf den erfolgreichen Zugang der Erklärung beim anvisierten Empfänger letztlich ankäme.

Die Folgen einer mit Hilfe des Rechtsschutzgedankens extensiv betriebenen Interpretation der Tatbestandsmerkmale werden bei Zuspitzung denkbarer Fallgestaltungen offen gelegt. Denn was bliebe tatsächlich von der für die §§ 331 ff. geforderten Unrechtsvereinbarung bei der Tatalternative des „Forderns" noch übrig, wenn man – obigem Rechtsschutzgedanken folgend – eine Kommunikationsbeziehung zwischen Vorteilsgeber und -nehmer überhaupt nicht mehr für erforderlich halten würde wie im Falle des von dritten Personen gelesenen, aber noch nicht an den Adressaten abgesandten Briefs des Beamten mit entsprechendem Forderungsinhalt? Der schwelende Zielkonflikt zwischen der Berücksichtigung schützenswerter Interessen und der Vermeidung einer Überdehnung des tatbestandlichen Wirkbereichs kann augenscheinlich jedenfalls nicht durch den Verzicht auf subjektive Tatelemente gelöst werden. Hier soll im Verlauf der Untersuchung eine Lösung aufgezeigt werden.

4. Das Äquivalenzverhältnis im Hinblick auf die Deliktsabsicht des § 333

Die aktive Bestechung des § 333 steht nach ihrem Wortlaut in unverkennbarer Beziehung zur schweren Bestechlichkeit des § 332. Nach dem Wortlaut müssen die Tathandlungsalternativen ausgeführt werden, „um" den Beamten „zu einer

---

205 Zur aktuellen Diskussion über den Inhalt des Schutzguts bei den Bestechungsdelikten s. u. S. 47 ff.

Handlung, die eine Verletzung einer Amts- oder Dienstpflicht enthält, zu bestimmen"[206]. Der damalige Gesetzgeber verstand demnach die Tathandlung als Mittel zur Bestimmung des Beamten zur Amtspflichtwidrigkeit. Damit stellt sich die Frage nach dem Inhalt und der Verknüpfung dieser Deliktsabsicht mit dem Äquivalenzverhältnis für die Beurteilung der Strafbarkeit des Täters nach § 333.

a) (Bedingter) Vorsatz genügt nicht für die Deliktsabsicht

Der BGH hat der Tendenz in der Lehre, die fehlende Absicht des Täters z.B. in Bezug auf die Pflichtwidrigkeit der Amtshandlung, zu der der Beamte bestimmt werden sollte, durch bedingten Vorsatz zu ersetzen, eine Absage erteilt. Er hat insoweit die pflichtwidrige Amtshandlung als „Zweck" der Tathandlung bezeichnet, demzufolge könne die Bestimmungsabsicht des Täters nicht durch unbedingten oder bedingten Vorsatz erfüllt werden[207].

b) Tatrichterliche Feststellung der Deliktsabsicht

Die Bestechungsabsicht als zentraler subjektiver Unrechtsbestandteil der aktiven Bestechung konfrontierte den Tatrichter mit der schwierigen Aufgabe, alle den Tatbestand des § 333 nicht erfüllende, aber vom Täter vorgetragene Beweggründe und Motive auf Schutzbehauptungen zu überprüfen und ihm die tatsächlich vorhandene Absicht zur Bestimmung einer pflichtwidrigen Amtshandlung nachzuweisen. Keine Absicht i.S.d. § 333 lag in den Fällen vor, in denen das Handlungsmotiv des Vorteilsgebers in der Erfüllung gesellschaftlicher Pflichten und Konventionen bestand oder der Schaffung einer guten Arbeitsatmosphäre mit den Staatsbediensteten diente. So hat das RG nicht bei jedem „aus Anlaß oder bei Gelegenheit einer Amtshandlung angenommene(n) Vorteil" diesen „als für die Amtshandlung gegeben" betrachtet, sondern tatbestandsausschließende „Regeln des sozialen Verkehres und der gewöhnlichen Höflichkeit" anerkannt, deren darauf gerichtete Absicht nicht der des § 333 entsprach[208].

Das Tatgericht hatte es daher im Einzelfall nicht leicht, das Äquivalenzverhältnis zwischen Vorteil und pflichtwidriger Amtshandlung und einer darauf gerichteten Bestimmungsabsicht des Täters festzustellen. Der Sinnzusammenhang des Äquivalenzverhältnisses musste von der subjektiven Vorstellung des Täters her bestimmt werden. Auch das RG tat sich mitunter schwer, diesen von

---

206 S. Anhang 1.

207 BGH-Urteil vom 22.1.1953, 4 StR 345/52.

208 RGSt 19, 19 (22).

der subjektiven Seite zu ermittelnden Bedeutungszusammenhang differenziert im Hinblick auf strafbares oder nicht strafbares Verhalten zu bewerten[209].

Der BGH hat dann 1953 entschieden, dass die Absicht des Vorteilsgebers, „sich lediglich das allgemeine Wohlwollen und ein geneigtes Verhalten des Beamten zu sichern", nicht der Deliktsabsicht des § 333 entspreche[210].

Die Gefahr der Heranziehung zweifelhafter Beweiswürdigungsregeln lag nahe, z.B. je nach der Werthaltigkeit des Vorteils auf die Deliktsabsicht des Zuwendenden zu schließen. Bei geringwertigen Geschenken könnte man diese als aus Höflichkeit und bei Gelegenheit hingegeben betrachten, bei hochwertigen Präsenten dagegen einen deliktsbejahenden Zusammenhang zwischen Vorteil und konkreter Amtshandlung annehmen[211].

Besonders problematisch geriet die Festlegung der Voraussetzungen der Deliktsabsicht, wenn sie sich auf die Amtshandlung eines Ermessensbeamten bezog. Denn da dieser nach der Rspr. des RG aufgrund der Zuwendung des Vorteils regelmäßig gar nicht mehr anders als unsachlich erwägen und daher pflichtwidrig handeln konnte[212], hätte es für die Annahme einer darauf gerichteten Absicht des Gebers an sich genügt, ihm dieses Wissen um die (rechtliche) Folge der Hingabe eines Vorteils an einen Ermessensbeamten nachzuweisen, um hieraus die Absicht zu folgern, er habe die Entschließungsfreiheit des Beamten in diesem Sinne beeinträchtigen wollen[213]. Die Erforschung der individuellen subjektiven Tatsachenbasis im Rahmen der Deliktsabsicht des § 333 dürfte die Tatrichter nicht selten vor große, unüberbrückbare Beweisschwierigkeiten gestellt haben.

5. Zusammenfassung

Im Unterschied zu den an die Deliktsabsicht der aktiven Bestechung nach § 333 gestellten Anforderungen, nach denen die Tathandlung vom zweckgerichteten Willen getragen sein musste, den Beamten zu einer konkreten pflichtwidrigen Amtshandlung zu bestimmen und allein die Vorstellung des Täters von einer Zusammenhangsbeziehung zwischen Vorteilshingabe und pflicht-

---

209 Instruktiv RGSt 2, 129 für den Fall, wo Eltern aus Dankbarkeit für die Lehrtätigkeit dem Lehrer ein Geschenk überreichten und RGSt 16, 42 für den Fall, wo zwar seitens des Beamten eine Amtspflichtwidrigkeit begangen worden war, zu dieser aber der Vorteil in keinem Äquivalenzverhältnis gestanden hatte und auch die Bestimmungsabsicht diesbezüglich fehlte.

210 BGH-Urteil vom 25.6.1953, 3 StR 608/5.

211 Vgl. die Ausführungen von E. Schmidt (Fn. 61), S. 134 ff.

212 Vgl. oben u. Fn. 174.

213 Diese Gefahr sieht auch E. Schmidt (Fn. 61), S. 126.

widriger Amtshandlung für nicht ausreichend angesehen wurde[214], hat die Rspr. des RG und nachfolgend des BGH auf der Seite der Staatsbediensteten weitaus geringere Anforderungen an die subjektiven Erfordernisse in Bezug auf das Äquivalenzverhältnis vor allem im Rahmen der schweren Bestechlichkeit nach § 332 gestellt.

So ist die anfänglich vom RG formulierte „vertragsmäßige Willensübereinstimmung“ zwischen Vorteilsgeber und -nehmer, der Vorteil werde für eine (pflichtwidrige) Amtshandlung hingegeben, später dahingehend korrigiert worden, es genüge für die Tathandlung der Bestechlichkeit, dass der Beamte erkennt oder davon ausgeht, der andere gebe den Vorteil für eine vom Beamten bereits vorgenommene oder noch vorzunehmende pflichtwidrige Amtshandlung hin. Dabei sei weder der tatsächliche Wille des Beamten zur Vornahme der Amtshandlung erforderlich noch komme es überhaupt auf eine das Beziehungsverhältnis zwischen Vorteil und Amtshandlung umfassende Willensübereinstimmung an.

Bezeichnend ist in diesem Zusammenhang die von der Rspr. einseitig auf die Vorstellungswelt des Beamten reduzierte Kommunikationsbeziehung bei der Tathandlungsalternative des „Forderns“. Indem die Rspr. darauf verzichtete, dass der Forderungsadressat den Inhalt der Forderungserklärung überhaupt verstand, vernachlässigte sie sogar die einer Willensübereinstimmung vorgelagerte Voraussetzung einer Wissensgemeinschaft über den Beziehungszusammenhang zwischen Vorteil und Amtshandlung.

Beim Ermessensbeamten hatte das RG sogar eine unwiderrufliche Vermutung dafür aufgestellt, dass der Beamte bereits mit der Annahme des Vorteils in seiner Entschließungsfreiheit beeinträchtigt sei und seine Entscheidung daher nicht mehr vom Vorteil unbeeinflusst getroffen werden könne. Demzufolge könne es auf eine innere Entschließung des Beamten, sich nicht vom Vorteil beeinflussen zu lassen, gar nicht mehr ankommen. Der BGH hat diese Rspr. des RG insoweit korrigiert, als er den tatrichterlichen Nachweis für eine Vorteilsbeeinflussung verlangt hat.

Ein Teil des Schrifttums und allen voran E. Schmidt haben die Entwicklung der Rspr. heftig kritisiert. Der Vorwurf traf insbesondere die richterlichen Anforderungen an die subjektiven Tatelemente, die nach Ansicht der Kritiker nach und nach aus dem Tatbestand der §§ 331 und 332 eliminiert worden seien und damit eine Überdehnung der Tatbestände nach sich gezogen hätten. Die Ursache dieser Entwicklung habe – wie die Gerichte zum Teil selbst eingeräumt

---

214 A.A. einzelne Vertreter des Schrifttums, vgl. Nachweise bei E. Schmidt (Fn. 61), S. 125.

hätten – in den bestehenden Beweisschwierigkeiten bei der tatrichterlichen Aufklärung der Beweggründe und Absichten der Beteiligten bestanden.

IV. Vorsatz- und Irrtumsfragen

Die Vorsatz- und Irrtumsfragen im Zusammenhang mit den Bestechungsdelikten sind für die Untersuchung insoweit von Bedeutung, als sich ein unmittelbarer Zusammenhang zwischen der Zurückdrängung subjektiver Tatbestandsvoraussetzungen dieser Delikte und den Anforderungen auf der Vorsatzseite nachweisen lässt. Auf diese Frage soll hier eingegangen werden. Zuvor erfolgt ein kurzer Überblick über die vom Großen Senat in Strafsachen in seiner bedeutsamen Entscheidung vom 18.3.1952[215] festgelegten, nunmehr in den §§ 15 -17 StGB materiell-rechtlich geregelten Grundlagen für die subjektive Tatseite von Straftatbeständen. Die dortigen Ausführungen bilden das Fundament für alle Zweifelsfragen, die im Zusammenhang mit dem Wissen und Willen des Täters im Hinblick auf die Verwirklichung der Tatbestandsmerkmale bestehen können.

1. Das BGH-Urteil 2, 194

Die Entscheidung des GSSt des BGH war von grundlegender Bedeutung für das Verständnis aller Schuld- und Irrtumsprobleme. Dem BGH stellten sich neben dem Problem der subjektiven Zurechenbarkeit die Fragen nach Inhalt und Form des Verschuldens sowie nach der Notwendigkeit und dem Inhalt des Unrechtsbewusstseins einschließlich dessen Stellung innerhalb des Schuldbegriffs.

Während man um die Jahrhundertwende noch von einem „psychologischen" Schuldverständnis ausging, das sich mit dem Vorliegen von Vorsatz und Fahrlässigkeit begnügte[216], ging der BGH von einem normativen Schuldbegriff aus:

„Strafe setzt Schuld voraus. Schuld ist Vorwerfbarkeit. Mit dem Unwerturteil der Schuld wird dem Täter vorgeworfen, daß er sich nicht rechtmäßig verhalten ... hat, obwohl er sich ... für das Recht hätte entscheiden können. Der innere Grund des Schuldvorwurfes liegt darin, daß der Mensch auf freie, verantwortliche, sittliche Selbstbestimmung angelegt und deshalb befähigt ist, ... sein Verhalten nach den Normen des rechtlichen Sollens einzurichten ..."[217].

---

215 BGHSt 2, 194.

216 Vgl. Achenbach, Historische und dogmatische Grundlagen der strafrechtlichen Schuldlehre, S. 62 ff.

217 BGHSt 2, 194 (200); vgl. auch BVerfGE 20, 323 (331); ferner Kaufmann, Das Schuldprinzip, S. 127 ff.

Die Abhängigkeit der Freiheit des Menschen zur Selbstbestimmung von Anlage und Umwelt führt letztlich zu einer Wertentscheidung der Vorwerfbarkeit. Es ist grundsätzlich von der Fähigkeit des Menschen zur Selbstbestimmung und damit von strafrechtlicher Verantwortlichkeit auszugehen, es sei denn, dass äußere oder innere Umstände (unüberwindliche Determinanten) dieser Annahme entgegenstehen[218].

Hinsichtlich der Verschuldensformen geht es um den Grad des Verschuldens im Sinne von Vorsätzlichkeit oder Fahrlässigkeit je nach Graduierbarkeit der kognitiven[219] und voluntativen[220] Beziehungen des Täters zu seiner Tat[221].

Der BGH sah sich nun wegen Fehlens einer zum Entscheidungszeitpunkt dem § 17 StGB vergleichbaren Norm über den Verbotsirrtum den Fragen ausgesetzt, ob das Unrechtsbewusstsein eine notwendige Schuldvoraussetzung ist und wenn ja, welche Konsequenzen sein Fehlen nach sich zieht.

Während das RG aus Gründen einer damals noch selbstverständlichen Jedermannspflicht, die Strafgesetze zu kennen, den Rechtsirrtum über strafrechtliche Rechtssätze losgelöst von Vorsatz und Schuldurteil für unbeachtlich hielt[222], hat sich der BGH unter dem Einfluss der politischen Reformbestrebungen und des die Rspr. des RG fast einhellig ablehnenden Schrifttums[223] für die prinzipielle Beachtlichkeit des Unrechtsbewusstseins als verfassungsrechtliche und strafrechtsdogmatische Forderung des Schuldprinzips ausgesprochen[224]. Entscheidender Maßstab für den Inhalt des Unrechtsbewusstseins, das sich auf die konkrete Tat beziehen muss[225], ist der Widerspruch zur Rechtsordnung, denn der Täter muss „... in einer seiner Gedankenwelt entsprechenden allgemeinen Wertung das Unrechtmäßige der Tat erkennen oder bei gehöriger Gewissensanspannung erkennen können“[226]. Im Rahmen der Erörterung des systemkonformen Standortes des Unrechtsbewusstseins hat sich der BGH unter Ableh-

---

218 Ausdruck hat dieser Gedanke in § 20 StGB gefunden; vgl. ferner Henkel, Die Selbstbestimmung des Menschen als rechtsphilosophisches Problem, Larenz-Festschrift, S. 19 ff.

219 Wissenselement: Kenntnis und Vorstellungen des Täters von den Umständen und Folgen seines Verhaltens.

220 Wollenselement: Das Interesse am Vorliegen oder Eintritt bestimmter Umstände und Folgen.

221 Zur Grenzziehung von (bedingtem) Vorsatz und (bewusster) Fahrlässigkeit vgl. Roxin, Jus 1964, S. 53.

222 BGHSt 2, 194 (197/198); den außerstrafrechtlichen Rechtsirrtum stellte das RG dem vorsatzausschließenden Tatirrtum gleich.

223 BGHSt 2, 194 (200).

224 BGHSt 2, 194 (202, 204 f.).

225 H.L. vgl. Rudolphi, SK § 17 Rn. 7; BGHSt 2, 194 (209): „...wenn er das Unrecht dieser Tatbestandsverwirklichung kannte...“.

226 BGHSt 2, 194 (202).

nung der noch vom RG vertretenen Vorsatztheorie[227] für die sogenannte Schuldtheorie[228] entschieden, die mit dem 2. Strafrechtsreformgesetz durch § 17 StGB kodifiziert wurde.

Nach den §§ 15 - 17 StGB muss sich der Tatvorsatz lediglich auf die unrechtsbegründenden Tatumstände erstrecken, so dass ein mangelndes Unrechtsbewusstsein infolge Verbotsirrtums den Tatvorsatz des Täters grundsätzlich unberührt lässt[229]. Der Mangel des Unrechtsbewusstseins kann aber sowohl auf tatsächlichen wie auf Wertungsirrtümern beruhen. Der BGH hat daher auf der Grundlage der Schuldtheorie eine Einschränkung insofern vorgenommen, als er den Fall des Irrtums über einen Sachverhalt, der die Annahme eines Rechtfertigungsgrundes nach sich zieht, entsprechend § 16 StGB als Tatirrtum behandelt[230].

2. Vorsatz und Irrtum bei § 331

Nach der Rechtslage bis zum EGStGB von 1974 umfasste der Vorsatz des Täters die objektiven Tatbestandsmerkmale des § 331 alter Fassung, d.h. der Täter musste wissen, dass er „Beamter“ war, dass sich sein Handeln z.B. als „Annehmen“ eines „Geschenks“ oder „anderen Vorteils“ darstellte[231]. Darüber hinaus musste er sich vorstellen, dass die Handlung eine „in sein Amt einschlagende“ war und der Vorteil ein Entgelt für diese Amtshandlung war, zu ihr also im Äquivalenzverhältnis stand. Die Vorstellung, nur privat tätig geworden zu sein, ließ den Vorsatz entfallen.

Nach den Grundsätzen von BGHSt 2, 194 kam Verbotsirrtum in Betracht, wenn der Beamte irrig von einer Genehmigung des Vorgesetzten ausging oder fälschlicherweise der Meinung war, seine Annahme eines Vorteils entspreche einer allgemeinen Verkehrssitte. Die Vermeidbarkeit eines solchen Verbotsirrtums hängt von den Umständen des Einzelfalles ab[232].

---

227 Nach dieser Theorie werden Tatbestandsirrtum und Verbotsirrtum gleichmäßig nach § 16 I StGB behandelt, weil das Bewusstsein der Rechtswidrigkeit als Bestandteil des Vorsatzes gewertet wird; im Sinne einer modifizierten Vorsatztheorie immer noch Otto, § 15 Rn. 10 f.; ferner auch Schmidhäuser, 7/89; zur Kritik des BGH siehe BGHSt 2, 194 (205-207), für den der Hauptablehnungsgrund die bei Anwendung dieser Theorie kriminalpolitisch für bedenklich erachteten Strafbarkeitslücken waren.

228 BGHSt 2, 194 (208/209); die Schuldtheorie begreift das Bewusstsein der Rechtswidrigkeit als ein vom Vorsatz getrenntes selbständiges Schuldelement.

229 Unvermeidbarkeit des Verbotsirrtums schließt die Schuld des Täters aus, Vermeidbarkeit führt zur Strafmilderung, § 17 S. 2 StGB.

230 BGHSt 3, 105 (106/107); im Sinne dieser „eingeschränkten Schuldtheorie“ auch die h.L.

231 Zur „Bedeutungskenntnis“ bei normativen Tatbestandsmerkmalen vgl. E. Schmidt (Fn. 61), S. 111 f.

232 Hierzu E. Schmidt (Fn. 61), S. 146 f.

3. Vorsatz und Irrtum bei § 332

Bei § 332 musste der Täter im Unterschied zu § 331 zusätzlich die Vorstellung haben, dass die Amtshandlung durch Missachtung oder Verletzung der ihr für die dienstliche Ausführung zugrunde liegenden Vorschriften pflichtwidrig ist. E. Schmidt verlangt denn auch in konsequenter Verfolgung seiner Rechtsauffassung zur Strafbarkeit des Ermessensbeamten, dass sich der Beamte seiner unsachgemäßen, dem Vorteil Berücksichtigung einräumenden Erwägungen bewusst ist; bei irriger Nichtkenntnis der die Pflichtwidrigkeit begründenden Umstände liege ein Vorsatz ausschließender Tatbestandsirrtum vor mit der Folge einer allenfalls dienstrechtlichen Ahndung[233].

Die Rspr. nahm dagegen - wie E. Schmidt zu Recht kritisierte - eine bedenkliche Rechtsposition ein, wenn sie zunächst aus der Vorteilshingabe die „regelmäßige" Befangenheit des Ermessensbeamten und daraus die Vermutung der Pflichtwidrigkeit seiner Entscheidungen folgerte und bei der Vorsatzfrage dann zur Vermeidung von Widersprüchen auch noch das Wissen des Beamten um diese die Pflichtwidrigkeit begründenden Umstände unterstellen musste[234].

Im Rahmen des Äquivalenzverhältnisses musste der Beamte den konkreten Bezug und die Zweckrichtung des zugewendeten Vorteils zur pflichtwidrigen Amtshandlung erkennen. Glaubte er fälschlicherweise, die Zuwendung sei zu anderen Zwecken hingegeben, z.B. um sein allgemeines Wohlwollen zu erwerben, entfiel der Vorsatz. Ein untauglicher Versuch nach § 332 konnte vorliegen, wenn der Beamte dagegen irrig annahm, der Vorteil werde für eine bestimmte pflichtwidrige Handlung hingegeben, während er in Wirklichkeit zu anderen Zwecken nämlich aus Dankbarkeit oder Höflichkeit übergeben wurde[235].

4. Vorsatz und Irrtum bei § 333

Heftig umstritten war bei der Deliktsabsicht des § 333 die Frage, ob für ihre Annahme bereits ausreichend sein sollte, wenn der Täter irrig die Vorstellung hatte, den Beamten zu einer pflichtwidrigen Amtshandlung zu bestimmen, während er den tatsächlichen Umständen nach diesen bloß zu einer rein privaten Tätigkeit aufgefordert hatte. Von den Befürwortern wurde dies begründet mit der subjektiven Ausrichtung des Tatbestandes, bei dem die nicht erforderliche objektive Verwirklichung (Amtshandlung) nur in der Vorstellung des

---

233 E. Schmidt (Fn. 61), S. 113/114; zu diesem Ergebnis gelangt man nur, wenn das Verhältnis der §§ 331 und 332 zueinander als aliud-aliud-Verhältnis aufgefasst wird und demgemäß für § 331 eine objektiv pflichtgemäße Amtshandlung vorauszusetzen ist; für aliud-aliud-Verh. auch BGHSt 12, 146; anders jetzt BGH NStZ 1984, S. 24.

234 Vgl. BGH GA 1959, 176 (177).

235 Hierzu und zur Fallgestaltung eines Verbotsirrtums siehe E. Schmidt (Fn. 61), S. 116.

Täters Gestalt annehmen müsse[236]. Richtigerweise hätte mit der Gegenmeinung auf der Grundlage von BGHSt 2, 194 von einem Wahndelikt oder aber von einem untauglichen Versuch ausgegangen werden müssen, je nachdem ob es sich um eine irrige rechtliche Bewertung der vorgestellten Tatumstände oder um eine Verkennung des tatsächlichen Geschehensablaufs handelte.

V. Zwischenergebnis

Die Darstellung der Entwicklung der Auffassungen von Rspr. und Schrifttum zu der seit 1871 bis zum EGStGB von 1974 gültigen Gesetzesfassung der Bestechungsdelikte hat die überragende Bedeutung der subjektiven Tatelemente offengelegt.

Die Diskussion um den Schutzzweck der Normen fokussiert sich auf das subjektive Kriterium des „Vertrauens" der Allgemeinheit in die Sachlichkeit amtlicher Entscheidungen, das von der herrschenden Meinung als Kernelement des Rechtsgüterschutzes herangezogen wurde. Als erster Schritt in Richtung einer weitreichenden Auslegung der Bestechungstatbestände wurde unter dem Postulat des Vertrauensschutzes der fehlende Tatverwirklichungswille des Beamten ebenso tatbestandlich für unbeachtlich erklärt wie der Umstand, dass der Adressat den Inhalt der den Tathandlungen des „Forderns" und „Sichversprechenlassens" zugrundeliegenden Erklärungen nicht verstand. Mit dem Verdacht einer Gefährdung dieses durch die Bestechungstatbestände geschützten Vertrauens konnte eine tendenziell einhergehende Vorverlagerung der Strafbarkeit gerechtfertigt werden.

Unbestritten war bei der damaligen Gesetzesfassung, dass erst mit der Verknüpfung von Vorteil und Amtshandlung strafrechtlich relevantes Unrecht begründet werden konnte. Dementsprechend richtete sich das Augenmerk auf dieses Äquivalenzverhältnis. Und hier vollzog sich dann der zweite bedeutsame Schritt einer aus dem Verzicht auf subjektive Wissens- und Willenselemente folgenden Ausweitung der Strafbarkeitsgrenzen. Das subjektive Wesensmerkmal dieser anfangs noch einem Vertragsverhältnis mit gegenseitiger Willensübereinstimmung gleichgestellten Unrechtsbeziehung wurde seiner Sonderstellung innerhalb der nachzuweisenden Unrechtsvereinbarung beinahe vollständig beraubt, indem es auf den allgemeinen Tatvorsatz zurückgeführt wurde. Die einseitige Vorstellung des Beamten, der Vorteilsgeber erwarte von ihm eine pflichtwidrige Amtshandlung als Gegenleistung für den Vorteil, sollte ausreichen. Der sich in einer Übereinstimmung der Handlungsabsichten beider Seiten niederschlagende Vereinbarungscharakter einer Unrechtsbeziehung ging verloren und wurde durch dem Tatvorsatz entnommene Wissenselemente ersetzt. E. Schmidt hat diese Rechtsentwicklung heftig kritisiert nicht zuletzt auf-

---

236 Nachweise bei E. Schmidt (Fn. 61), S. 138/139.

grund der Überzeugung, dass kriminalpolitische Erwägungen für die von den Gerichten vorgenommene Ausdehnung des Strafbarkeitsbereichs ursächlich waren. Die Probleme der tatrichterlichen Beweisführung waren evident. Besonders verdeutlicht sich dies an der Problematik der Strafbarkeit von Ermessensbeamten. Dort half sich die Rspr. vorübergehend sogar damit, dass sie in der Vorteilsannahme eine unwiderlegliche Vermutung der Amtspflichtwidrigkeit unter Verzicht auf den tatsächlichen Nachweis der Vorteilsbeeinflussung beim Beamten erkannte.

Der folgende Abschnitt soll den weiteren Weg dieser Rechtsentwicklung aufzeigen.

Zweiter Abschnitt: Die Rechtsentwicklung unter dem EGStGB von 1974[237]

Während dem Reichsstrafgesetzbuch von 1871 – bestimmt vom Gedanken der Gleichsetzung der Straftat mit der Verletzung des geschützten Handlungsobjekts und der damit verbundenen Überbewertung des Taterfolgs – noch ein streng objektivistisches, auf den vom Täter verursachten Schaden ausgerichtetes Konzept der Voraussetzungen der Strafbarkeit zugrunde lag, verlangte das Anfang des 20. Jahrhunderts zunehmend sozialethische Verständnis der Straftat die Berücksichtigung des Willens und der Motive des Täters. Es führte so zu einer Hervorhebung der subjektiven Momente unter den Voraussetzungen des deliktischen Handelns[238]. Dass dem aus diesen Gründen bereits um die Jahrhundertwende eingeleiteten Strafrechtsreformbestreben zunächst kein bleibender Erfolg beschieden war, lag an der Ungunst der politischen Verhältnisse zweier Weltkriege. Nach dem zweiten Weltkrieg wurde die Strafrechtsreform von der Großen Strafrechtskommission unter Vorsitz des damaligen Bundesjustizministers Dr. Neumayer wieder aufgenommen. Auf der Grundlage der Beschlüsse dieser Kommission wurde der Entwurf 1960 (E 1960) erstellt, der nach den Beratungen einer Länderkommission als Entwurf 1962 (E 1962) dem Bundestag vorgelegt wurde. Die Beratungen des Sonderausschusses für die Strafrechtsreform unter Einbeziehung eines 1968 von der Fraktion der FDP im Bundestag eingebrachten Alternativ-Entwurfes eines Strafgesetzbuches mündeten in der Neufassung des Allgemeinen Teils und in der Reform zahlreicher Partien des Besonderen Teils des Strafgesetzbuches[239]. Eine weitergehende Reform des Besonderen Teils, insbesondere auch der Bestechungstatbestände, hat dann das Einführungsgesetz zum Strafgesetzbuch (EGStGB) vom 2.3.1974[240] vorgenommen.

I. Neubestimmung des Rechtsguts der Bestechungsdelikte

Der E 1960 benennt als Rechtsgut der Bestechungstatbestände die „Reinheit des öffentlichen Dienstes“[241] und das „Vertrauen der Allgemeinheit in dessen

---

237 Gesetzesfassung s. Anhang 2; soweit §§ ohne Gesetzesangaben unter diesem Abschnitt zitiert werden, handelt es sich um die bis zur Neufassung durch das KorrBekG vom 13.8.1997 gültige Gesetzesfassung des StGB.

238 Deutlich wird dies durch die Anerkennung subjektiver Unrechtsmerkmale und dem Aufbau der normativen Schuldlehre mit den Konsequenzen für die Irrtumsproblematik; vgl. hierzu BGHSt 2, 194 ff. (dazu oben S. 40 ff.).

239 1. und 2. StrRG vom 25.6.1969 (BGBl. I, S. 645) und vom 4.7.1969 (BGBl. I, S. 717).

240 BGBl. I (1974), S. 469 (496); die neugefassten §§ 331 – 335a traten am 1.1.1975 in Kraft.

241 So bereits vorher RGSt 72, 174 (175) und BGHSt 10, 237 (241) in der Formulierung „Reinheit der Amtsausübung“.

Unantastbarkeit“[242]. Schon der E 1962 enthielt Abweichungen von dieser Rechtsgutsbestimmung, denn einmal spricht er vom Schutz der Lauterkeit des öffentlichen Dienstes, die es durch Bekämpfung der Verkäuflichkeit von Diensthandlungen und der vorteilsbelasteten Befangenheit der Amtsträger zum Schutz vor Verfälschung des Staatswillens zu bewahren gelte[243]. Zum anderen sollte zugleich das Vertrauen der Allgemeinheit in die Unbefangenheit der Amtsträger und in die sachliche Richtigkeit ihrer Handlungen geschützt werden[244]. Nach der amtlichen Begründung von 1973 zum Entwurf des EGStGB wurde zwar der erstgenannte Schutzzweck des E 1962 wieder aufgegriffen, der zweitgenannte blieb jetzt aber dahingestellt[245].

1. Die Begründung des Gesetzgebers zum EGStGB

Nach der Begründung zum EGStGB glaubte der Gesetzgeber, auf das Schutzgut „Vertrauen der Allgemeinheit“ in die Lauterkeit des öffentlichen Dienstes und damit in die Unbefangenheit der Bediensteten und in die sachliche Richtigkeit ihrer Handlungen verzichten zu können[246], weil schon der Gesichtspunkt des Schutzes des „Staatswillens vor einer Verfälschung“ den Strafschutz gegen Korruption hinreichend gewährleiste[247]. Strafwürdig sei bereits die durch die nach außen gezeigte Bereitschaft zu einer pflichtwidrigen Handlung ausgelöste Gefahr einer Verfälschung des Staatswillens, mag der Amtsträger innerlich auch gar nicht zur Pflichtwidrigkeit bereit sein und mag es auch zu der Handlung überhaupt nicht kommen[248]. Dieser vom Gesetzgeber vertretene Schutzgutgedanke stellt beim Schutz vor Beeinträchtigung sachlichen staatlichen Handelns vor allem auf die Pflichtwidrigkeit seiner Organe ab und hat damit die Verletzung der Dienstpflicht im Blickfeld. Danach wäre § 332 ein konkretes, § 331 ein abstraktes Gefährdungsdelikt[249].

2. Die Auffassung der Rechtsprechung

Der BGH hält seit der Entscheidung BGHSt 10, 237 grundsätzlich an dem Schutzgutgedanken „Vertrauen der Allgemeinheit“ auch nach der Neufassung der §§ 331ff. fest, wobei die Bezeichnung des Bezugsgegenstandes des „Vertrauens“ häufiger gewechselt hat. So sprach er früher von der „Reinheit der Amtsführung und das Vertrauen der Öffentlichkeit in dieselbe“[250] und von der

---

242 E 1960, BT-Drs. 2150, S. 607.
243 BT-Drs. IV/650, S. 648.
244 BT-Drs. IV/650, S. 649.
245 BT-Drs. 7/550, S. 269.
246 Anders noch die Begründungen zum E 1962, BT-Drs. IV/650, S. 649.
247 BT-Drs. 7/550, S. 269/270.
248 BT-Drs. 7/550, S. 270.
249 Vgl. E. Schmidt (Fn. 61), S. 147-149; Kaufmann, JZ 1959, S. 377.
250 BGHSt 10, 237 (241); BGHSt 15, 352 (354).

„Makellosigkeit des Amtes nach außen“[251] und dem „Vertrauen der Bevölkerung in die Lauterkeit des öffentlichen Dienstes“[252], später dann von dem „Schutz des Vertrauens der Allgemeinheit in die Sachlichkeit staatlicher Entscheidungen“[253].

Genau besehen vertritt der BGH in seinen Entscheidungen durch die Verknüpfung der Gesichtspunkte der Lauterkeit des öffentlichen Dienstes (objektiver Teilaspekt) und des Vertrauens der Allgemeinheit in diese Lauterkeit (subjektiver Teilaspekt) ein zweidimensional ausgestaltetes Schutzgut[254]. Damit nähert sich der BGH den Vertretern eines „komplexen“ Rechtsguts an[255].

3. Die neueren Auffassungen im Schrifttum[256]

Aufgabe dieser Untersuchung ist es nicht, sich vorrangig in einer dogmatischen Diskussion mit dem Rechtsgutsbegriff des Strafrechts auseinander zu setzen[257], um hierauf aufbauend den Versuch einer Neubestimmung des geschützten Rechtsguts der Bestechungsdelikte zu unternehmen[258]. Ziel dieser Arbeit ist es, zunächst die neueren Untersuchungen zum Rechtsgut der Bestechungsdelikte

---

251 BGHSt 15, 88 (96 f.).

252 BGHSt 15, 88 (96 f.); BGHSt 30, 46 (48); NStZ 1984, 24 (25); NJW 1987, 1340 (1342).

253 BGH NJW 1990, 2074 (2075); zuletzt in NJW 2002, 2801 (2803) spricht der BGH von „Vertrauen in die Sachgerechtigkeit“.

254 Deutlich in NStZ 1985, 497 (499).

255 S. u. Fn. 265.

256 Zu den weitgehend älteren Auffassungen zum Strafrechtsgut wie Dienstpflichtverletzung“, „Reinheit der Amtsausübung“, „Unentgeltlichkeit“, „Ungestörtes Funktionieren der Staatsverwaltung“, „Verletzung der Ordnung des staatlichen Abgaben- und Gebührenwesens“ ausführlich Jaques, Die Bestechungstatbestände unter besonderer Berücksichtigung des Verhältnisses der §§ 331 ff. StGB zu § 12 UWG, S. 36-41; zu der von Wagner vertretenen Meinung, der das Rechtsgut je nach der Handlungsmodalität festlegt, s. Amtsverbrechen, S. 233-236; Wagner unterscheidet dabei zwischen Staatszurechnungs und Nichtstaatszurechnungsdelikten: zu den Nichtstaatszurechnungsdelikten zählt er dann die Handlungsformen des „Sichversprechenlassens“ und des „Annehmens“ bei der Vorteilsannahme (Rechtsgut: Schutz bestimmter staatlicher Rechtsgüter wie die Ordnung des staatlichen Abgaben- und Gebührenwesens, S. 273) und die Bestechlichkeit (Rechtsgut: generelle Gefährdung der gesamten Staatstätigkeit, S. 277), zu den individualrechtsgutverletzenden Nichtstaatszurechnungsdelikten die Handlungsform des „Forderns“ bei der Vorteilsannahme (Rechtsgut: Individualrechtsgut der persönlichen Handlungsfreiheit, S. 234); zur Kritik an dieser differenzierenden Betrachtungsweise vgl. Hirsch, ZStW 88 (1976), S. 772 (778/779), der Zweifel an der Ergiebigkeit dieser Differenzierung äußert.

257 Hierzu vgl. Jaques (Fn. 256), S. 23 ff. und Schwieger, Der Vorteilsbegriff in den Bestechungsdelikten, S. 38 ff.

258 Hierzu gibt es einschlägige neuere Untersuchungen, vgl. die Arbeiten von Jaques (Fn. 256), S. 60 ff. und von Schwieger (Fn. 257), S. 74 ff.

gegenüber zu stellen und die Frage zu prüfen, ob sich grundlegend neue Erkenntnisse gegenüber den beiden Grundpositionen „Verfälschung des Staatswillens“ und „Vertrauen der Allgemeinheit“ herausgebildet haben. Im Anschluss an eine Begutachtung der einzelnen Auffassungen unter Einschluss der Neuerungen durch das KorrBekG von 1997 sowie einer vergleichenden Betrachtung ausländischer Rechtsordnungen wird es Aufgabe des zweiten Teils (B) dieser Untersuchung sein, die für die Gerichts-Praxis bedeutsame, bis heute vorherrschend gebliebene Auffassung vom primär geschützten „Vertrauen der Allgemeinheit“ auf ihre problematische Rolle im Zusammenhang mit der Bestimmung und Eingrenzung strafbaren Verhaltens bei den Bestechungsdelikten zu hinterfragen. Eine wichtige Fragestellung wird dabei sein, ob der Vertrauensschutzgedanke nicht zu einer ungewollten Überdehnung der Straftatbestände führt und eine hinreichend exakte Abgrenzung strafwürdigen Verhaltens von nicht strafwürdigem Verhalten verhindert.

a) „Verfälschung des Staatswillens“

Nachfolgende Verfasser haben auch nach der Neufassung der Bestechungsdelikte noch den Schutzzweck-Gedanken der „Verfälschung des Staatswillens“ vertreten:

aa) Jaques

Nach Jaques stellen die „Rechtsinstitute, derer sich der Staat als Organisationsstrukturen zur Übertragung seiner Aufgaben bedient“ das Strafrechtsgut der §§ 331 ff. dar[259]. Die gegenüber dem Staat bestehenden Pflichten zur Wahrnehmung der übertragenen Aufgaben würden bei eigennützigen Motiven der Bediensteten dazu führen, dass die staatlichen Aufgaben nicht mehr bürgergerecht wahrgenommen würden. Sie wären damit letztlich nicht mehr übertragbar und der Staat in der von der Verfassung vorgegebenen Form so nicht mehr organisierbar. Ohne die Möglichkeit der Aufgabenübertragung auf der Basis geeigneter Organisationsstrukturen würde unsere Massengesellschaft nicht mehr funktionieren. Jaques selbst sieht in seiner Auffassung eine weitgehende Übereinstimmung mit dem Schutzgut „Verfälschung des Staatswillens“[260].

---

259 Jaques (Fn. 256), S. 90.

260 Jaques (Fn. 256), S. 90/91; Jaques schlägt im Ergebnis seiner Überlegungen vor, das Gebot der Gleichbehandlung der Amtsträger- und Angestellten-Bestechung durch Einführung eines Grundtatbestands umzusetzen, der auf die Voraussetzung der Amtsträgereigenschaft verzichtet, vgl. S. 243-246.

bb) Dölling

Dölling sieht den Strafgrund im – den Gedanken der Staatswillensverfälschung einschließenden – „Schutz korrekter Amtsführung gegen die sich aus der Geschenkannahme für Diensthandlungen ergebenden Gefahren“[261]. Von der in der Vorteilsannahme nach § 331 liegenden Käuflichkeit von Diensthandlungen gingen bereits Gefahren für die Sachlichkeit der Amtsführung aus, woraus wiederum eine Beeinträchtigung des „Vertrauens der Allgemeinheit“ resultieren könne. Daher sei in diesem Gefährdungszusammenhang der Unrechtskern der Bestechungsdelikte zu erblicken. Das „Vertrauen der Allgemeinheit“ genieße aber nur mittelbaren strafrechtlichen Schutz[262].

b) „Vertrauen der Allgemeinheit“

Ein Teil der Literatur sieht heute in dem Vertrauen der Allgemeinheit in die Unkäuflichkeit von Diensthandlungen und in die Sachlichkeit staatlicher Entscheidungen das maßgebliche Schutzgut[263]. Im Gegensatz zum Schutzgut der „Verfälschung des Staatswillens“ soll sich hier aus jeder Vorteilsannahme, egal ob diese zu einer pflichtgemäßen oder pflichtwidrigen Amtshandlung in Beziehung steht, eine generelle Gefährdung des Staatsapparates ergeben, da in jedem dieser Fälle das Vertrauen der Allgemeinheit in die Sachlichkeit staatlicher Entscheidungen beeinträchtigt werde. § 332 sei so ein erschwerter (qualifizierter) Fall des § 331, bei dem bereits eine Erschütterung dieses Vertrauens der Allgemeinheit begründet werde[264].

c) Verknüpfung beider Schutzzwecke im Sinne eines „komplexen“ Rechtsguts

Bei den neueren Untersuchungen zum Schutzzweck der Bestechungsdelikte fällt auf, dass die Verfasser im Ergebnis vielfach für ein „komplexes“ Rechtsgut plädieren, wobei die einzelnen Meinungen nur im Detail differieren, letztlich aber alle in einer Verknüpfung der oben genannten Grundpositionen bestehen[265].

---

261 Dölling, JuS 1981, S. 570 (574) und Gutachten C zum 61. DJT, C 49/50.

262 Dölling, Gutachten C, C 49; im Ergebnis tritt er damit wie die Mehrheit der Verfasser neuerer Untersuchungen letztlich auch für ein „komplexes“ Rechtsgut ein, vgl. C. 50/51.

263 Schönke/Schröder/Cramer, § 331 Rn. 3; Jescheck, LK, Vor § 331, Rn. 17; Ricks, Ökonomische Analyse der Wirtschaftskriminalität unter besonderer Berücksichtigung der Korruption und Bestechung, S. 201; Pelke, Die strafrechtliche Bedeutung der Merkmale „Übel“ und „Vorteil“, S. 105.

264 Schönke/Schröder/Cramer, § 331, Rn. 3; Jescheck, LK, Vor § 331, Rn. 16 und 17.

265 Graupe (Fn. 63), S. 116; Schönherr, Vorteilsgewährung und Bestechung als Wirtschaftsstraftaten, S. 24 f.; Gribl, Der Vorteilsbegriff bei den Bestechungsdelikten, S. 73 f.; Hardtung, Erlaubte Vorteilsannahme, S. 44-47; Schwieger (Fn. 257), S. 90f.;

aa) Bauchrowitz

Bauchrowitz kombiniert nur beide Grundpositionen, indem er ihnen nebeneinander gleiche Bedeutung zumisst[266].

bb) Graupe

Genauso verfährt Graupe, wobei er zwar in anderer Reihung, inhaltlich aber deckungsgleich die Kernelemente „Funktionsfähigkeit staatlicher Verwaltung“, „Vertrauen der Allgemeinheit in die Sachlichkeit staatlicher Verwaltung“ und „Verfälschung des Staatswillens“ miteinander verknüpft[267].

cc) Loos

Loos wiederum sieht – ebenfalls kombinierend – in der „expressiven Bedeutung“ der einzelnen Bestechungshandlung die generelle (abstrakte) Geeignetheit, sowohl das „Amtsethos“ der Beamtenschaft als auch das Vertrauen der Bevölkerung in die staatliche Verwaltung zu erschüttern. Die Institution der staatlichen Verwaltung in ihren inneren und äußeren Funktionsbedingungen werde aber erst durch eine Vielzahl solcher Bestechungsakte beeinträchtigt[268].

dd) Gribl

Gribl dagegen argumentiert in einem Stufenverhältnis. Primär sei die Makellosigkeit der Amtsführung und damit die „formelle und materielle Gesetzmäßigkeit des externen Funktionsbereiches des öffentlichen Dienstes" zu schützen. Erst in zweiter Linie komme es auf die "Integrität des öffentlichen Dienstes unter dem Aspekt des Vertrauens in die Wahrung der formellen und materiellen Gesetzmäßigkeit“ an[269].

ee) Hardtung

Ähnlich wie Gribl stellt Hardtung den Gedanken der Staatswillensverfälschung in den Mittelpunkt seiner Schutzzweckerwägungen und misst dem Vertrauensgedanken nur ergänzende Bedeutung zu[270].

Bauchrowitz, Der immaterielle Vorteilsbegriff der Bestechungsdelikte im StGB, S. 95 ff.; Letzgus, NStZ 1987, S. 309 (310); ferner Rudolphi, SK, § 331 Rn. 4; Lackner/Kühl, § 331 Rn. 1; Blei BT, S. 454-456.

266 Bauchrowitz (Fn. 265), S. 103.

267 Graupe (Fn. 63), S. 116.

268 Loos (Fn. 64), S. 891 f.

269 Gribl (Fn. 265), S. 74-77.

270 Hardtung (Fn. 265), S. 45 und 47.

ff) Schwieger

Schwieger differenziert nach der zeitlichen Reihenfolge von Unrechtsvereinbarung und Amtshandlung. Nur wenn erstere der Amtshandlung vorausgehe, sei die „Sachlichkeit ... der Amtsführung bestimmter Funktionsträger" geschützt. Dagegen sei bei allen Tatalternativen der Bestechungsdelikte das „Vertrauen der Allgemeinheit in eben diesen objektiven Zustand" vom Schutzzweck umfasst[271].

gg) Überhofen

Überhofen sieht den zu gewährleistenden Schutz im „Vertrauen der Allgemeinheit in die ordnungsgemäße Amtsführung" und in der „Integrität des Staates"[272]. Er ist der Auffassung, Korruption könne nur dann wirksam bekämpft werden, wenn auch der „böse Schein" im Hinblick auf das Vertrauen der Allgemeinheit unter Strafe gestellt werde. Jeden diesbezüglich nicht auszuschließenden Anscheinsverdacht will er auch im Vorfeldbereich korruptiver Handlungsweisen der Strafbarkeit unterfallen lassen[273]. Das Postulat der ultima ratio-Funktion des Strafrechts sieht er nicht in Gefahr[274].

Andererseits bewertet Überhofen die Bestechungstatbestände als bis „an die noch vertretbare Grenze ausgedehnt"[275]. Eine weitere Ausdehnung hält er für unverhältnismäßig[276]. Den Lösungsweg sucht er daher über eine „strafbewehrte Meldepflicht für nicht geringwertige Zuwendungen"[277]. Auch die Heranziehung von die Strafbarkeit vorverlegenden „Inkompatibilitätstatbeständen"[278] hält er für überlegenswert[279].

d) Eigene Stellungnahme

Man kann schwerlich behaupten, dass die neueren Untersuchungen Überraschendes zu Tage gefördert hätten. Mit dem Rückgriff auf das zumindest

271 Schwieger (Fn. 257), S. 91.
272 Überhofen, Korruption und Bestechungsdelikte im staatlichen Bereich, S. 81.
273 Überhofen (Fn. 272), S. 82.
274 Überhofen (Fn. 272), S. 52.
275 Überhofen (Fn. 272), S. 468.
276 Überhofen (Fn. 272), S. 82.
277 Überhofen (Fn. 272), S. 469; die Grenze soll „alternativ oder kumulativ etwa 1.000 DM" betragen.
278 Wie sie in Frankreich bestehen, Überhofen (Fn. 272), S. 397 ff.; Zweck dieser „abgeleiteten Korruptionstatbestände" ist es, im Vorfeld eigentlichen Korruptionsunrechts Interessenkollisionen und damit Korruptionsgefahren durch Verquickung amtlicher mit privaten Interessen zu begegnen.
279 Überhofen (Fn. 272), S. 468.

kriminalpolitisch begrüßenswerte Schutzgut des „Vertrauens“ werden tatbestandliche Unschlüssigkeiten und Auslegungsprobleme eingeebnet, ohne dass die hieraus resultierende Gefahr einer Überdehnung des tatbestandlichen Geltungsbereichs argumentativ als Gegengewicht in die Waagschale geworfen würde[280].

Ein besonderer Verdienst in der aktuellen Diskussion kommt daher Dölling zu, der in eindrucksvoller Weise davor warnt, mit dem Gesichtspunkt des Vertrauensschutzes als „kriminalpolitische Zauberformel“ die Strafbarkeit „nahezu jeder unkorrekten Verhaltensweise eines Amtsträgers zu legimitieren“[281]. Dölling vermeidet dabei, den Vertrauensgedanken völlig zu verdrängen, da diesem für die Funktionsfähigkeit der Verwaltung erhebliche Bedeutung zukomme. Grundsätzlich sei aber schon mit dem Schutz der korrekten Amtsführung auch das Vertrauen in diese ausreichend geschützt[282].

Als Ausgangspunkt der Überlegungen stellt sich die Frage, ob der Aspekt des Vertrauensschutzes überhaupt als Rechtsgut tragbar ist, weil man Vertrauen in alles und jeden haben kann und damit die tatbestandsbeschränkende Funktion eines Strafrechtsguts[283] kaum verwirklicht werden kann. Wie angreifbar der Vertrauensschutzgedanke ist, zeigt sich auch bei einem Blick in die Statistik. Nach einer Spiegel-Umfrage glaubten 1992 45% der Bundesbürger aus den alten und sogar 55% aus den neuen Bundesländern, dass sich Beamte bestechen lassen[284]. Kann nicht mehr bestehendes Vertrauen strafgesetzlich überhaupt noch geschützt werden? Woraus resultiert dieser Vertrauensverlust? Ersichtlich doch nur aus bereits bekannt gewordenen Bestechungsfällen, bei denen korrekte staatliche Tätigkeit durch korruptes Verhalten einzelner Staatsbediensteter diskreditiert wurde. Es kann aber auch sein, dass das Vertrauen ohne tatsächlich bestehenden Grund aufgrund eines irrtümlich angenommenen Fehlverhaltens eines Amtsträgers beeinträchtigt wurde. Auch in diesem Fall liegt ein Vertrauensdefizit vor. Es existiert aber kein vernünftiger Grund, diesen falsch entstandenen Eindruck unter den Schutzmantel des Strafrechts zu stellen[285]. Als schützenswert könnte man nur noch das bestehende Restvertrauen in der Bevölkerung oder eben ein von der Realität inzwischen konterkariertes abstrakt unterstelltes Vertrauen heranziehen. Es scheint aber eher gerechtfertigt, erst aus der Verletzung anderer Strafrechtsgüter, wie der Funk-

---

280 Instruktiv Schwieger, der wohl meint, den Schutzgegenstand der Bestechungsdelikte endgültig festgelegt zu haben, ohne im Ergebnis wirklich Neues zu verkünden; denn auch er hebt insoweit unkritisch wesentlich auf den Vertrauensgedanken ab, um tatbestandliche Zweifelsfälle erfassen zu können, (Fn. 257), S. 91-95.

281 Dölling, Gutachten C, C 50.

282 Dölling, Gutachten C, C 51; ebenso Ransiek, StV 1996, S. 446 (450).

283 Vgl. hierzu Hassemer, NStZ 1989, S. 553 (557).

284 Der Spiegel, Nr. 31 aus 1993, S. 43.

285 Ebenso Ransiek, StV 1996, S. 446 (450).

tionsfähigkeit der Staatsverwaltung und der damit verbundenen sachgemäßen Aufgabenerledigung, den mittelbar damit verbundenen Vertrauenstatbestand[286] in den Schutzbereich denknotwendig, aber nicht strafbarkeitsbegründend mit einzubeziehen. Dabei wird das Vertrauen nicht um seiner selbst willen geschützt, sondern untersteht dem primären Schutzzweck der objektiven Funktionsfähigkeit staatlichen Verwaltens. Die Konsequenz einer primären Heranziehung des Vertrauensgedankens birgt zudem die Gefahr, an tatbestandlichen Einbruchstellen subjektive Tatelemente aus dem Tatbestand der Bestechungsdelikte zu verdrängen. Wie die Darstellung der Rspr. des RG und teilweise auch des BGH gezeigt hat, kann der Vertrauensschutzgedanke wenig Hilfe dabei leisten, im Grenzbereich strafbaren Verhaltens eindeutig nicht strafwürdige Sachverhalte im Rahmen von Schutzzweckerwägungen aus dem Strafbarkeitsbereich herauszulösen[287].

II. Die gesetzlichen Änderungen des EGStGB

Während der E 1960 noch einen Systemaufbau nach Tätergruppen vorsah[288], enthielt bereits der E 1962 und in der Folge der Entwurf zum EGStGB einen weitaus übersichtlicheren Aufbau der Vorschriften nach Taten[289]. Einen weiteren Vorzug sah man in der klaren Gegenüberstellung der wesensunterschiedlichen Vorteilsannahme (§ 331) und Vorteilsgewährung (§ 333) einerseits und der schwerer wiegenden Bestechlichkeit (§ 332) und Bestechung (§ 334) andererseits[290].

Bereits in dem E 1960 waren die bisher in den §§ 2 bis 4 der „Verordnung gegen Bestechung und Geheimnisverrat nichtbeamteter Personen“[291] enthaltenen Tatbestände wegen der wachsenden Bedeutung der Aufgabenwahrnehmung im öffentlichen Dienst durch Nicht-Amtsträger eingearbeitet[292].

Eine weitere wichtige inhaltliche Änderung gegenüber dem damals geltenden Recht enthielt der E 1960 mit der erstmals strafrechtlich verankerten Regelung einer vorherigen als auch nachträglichen Genehmigung der zuständigen Behörde zur Annahme des Vorteils[293]. Während aber die Entwürfe 1960 und 1962 in einer wirksamen Genehmigung noch einen Rechtfertigungsgrund erkann-

---

286 Vertrauensverlust resultiert aus gestörter Funktionsfähigkeit.
287 Zu einzelnen Falluntersuchungen unter diesem Aspekt siehe Teil B der Arbeit.
288 BT-Drs. 2150, S. 84/85.
289 BT-Drs. IV/650, S. 87/88 und 649 sowie BT-Drs. 7/550, S. 270.
290 BT-Drs. 7/550, S. 270.
291 I.d.F. der Bekanntmachung vom 22.5.1943, BGBl. III 2034-1.
292 BT-Drs. IV/650, S. 649.
293 BT-Drs. 2150, S. 84 und 609 (§ 460 Abs. 3 StGB a.F.); im Beamtenrecht gab es bereits eine die Genehmigung behandelnde Vorschrift, § 70 BBG für die Bundesbeamten und § 43 BRRG als Rahmenvorschrift für die übrigen Beamten.

ten[294], überließ der Entwurf zum EGStGB ohne dogmatische Festlegung die Entscheidung der Frage der rechtlichen Beurteilung der Rspr. und Wissenschaft[295].

1. Die Neuregelung des Äquivalenzverhältnisses

a) Begründung des Gesetzgebers

Der Gesetzgeber hat die Formulierung „als Gegenleistung dafür" gewählt, um das zwischen der bereits erfolgten oder noch ausstehenden Diensthandlung oder ihrer bewussten Unterlassung und dem Vorteil geforderte Beziehungsverhältnis tatbestandlich zu umschreiben. Er wollte damit einmal das Verhältnis von Leistung und Gegenleistung im Sinne eines „do ut des" zum Ausdruck bringen, und zum anderen diejenigen Diensthandlungen ausscheiden, die in keiner inneren Beziehung zum Vorteil stehen[296]. Daher konnte ein objektiver Kausalzusammenhang zwischen Vorteil und Diensthandlung nicht ausreichen[297], vielmehr musste ein subjektives Moment hinzutreten, welches dem Beziehungsverhältnis den bezweckten subjektiven Einschlag verlieh[298].

Mit dem Begriff „Gegenleistung" sollte klargestellt werden, dass der Vorteil im Hinblick auf eine bestimmte Diensthandlung oder zumindest auf einen bestimmten Kreis von Diensthandlungen angeboten oder angenommen werden musste[299]. Nicht genügen konnte demnach, „wenn sich der Vorteilgeber mit dem Geschenk lediglich allgemeines Wohlwollen und Geneigtheit des Beamten sichern" wollte[300].

Der Gesetzgeber hat mit der Gesetzesformulierung die bis dahin herausgebildete BGH-Rspr. weitestgehend nachvollzogen.

---

294 BT-Drs. 2150, S. 609 und BT-Drs. IV/650, S. 651; nach dem E 1962 sollte bei der korrespondierenden Vorteilsgewährung die dem Vorteilsempfänger nachträglich erteilte Genehmigung (§ 462 Abs. 4 StGB a.F.) beim Vorteilsgeber nur einen persönlichen Strafaufhebungsgrund darstellen, BT-Drs. IV/650, S. 655.

295 BT-Drs. 7/550, S. 272; vgl. zu dieser Fragestellung ausführlich die Untersuchung von Merges, Die Strafausschließungsgründe der Bestechungsdelikte, S. 43 ff.

296 BT-Drs. 7/550, S. 271.

297 So auch die Begründung, BT-Drs. 7/550, S. 271.

298 Dazu näher u. S. 58.

299 BT-Drs. 7/550, S. 271.

300 Vgl. BGHSt 15, 217 (223).

b) Reaktion des BGH

Im Anschluss an das Urteil aus dem Jahre 1960[301], in dem der BGH die Regeln der Höflichkeit und des sozialen Verkehrs als Begründung dafür heranzieht, dass nicht jeder bei Gelegenheit einer Amtshandlung dargereichte Vorteil <u>für</u> eine Amtshandlung hingegeben sein muss, spricht er in Entscheidungen nach 1973 teilweise von einem „Beziehungsverhältnis", nach dem der Vorteil der Amtsperson als Gegenleistung für ihr Verhalten zufließen soll[302], teilweise von einem Entgeltcharakter des Vorteils und von einem „Äquivalenzverhältnis" zwischen Vorteil und Diensthandlung[303], an anderer Stelle wiederum von einer „Unrechtsvereinbarung"[304]. Letztlich lässt er die Entscheidung offen, ob ein echtes „do ut des"-Verhältnis im Sinne des „Ich gebe dir etwas, damit du mir etwas gibst" besteht[305].

c) Auffassung der Literatur

Die Überlegungen des Schrifttums zur Gesetzesformulierung „als Gegenleistung dafür" stimmen insoweit überein, als eine Beziehung zwischen Vorteil und Diensthandlung, mithin ein innerer Zusammenhang zwischen diesen Komponenten angenommen wird. Unterschiedlich fallen die Meinungen zur Konkretisierung dieses Beziehungsverhältnisses aus, also zu der Frage, wie diese Beziehung im Einzelnen ausgestaltet sein muss.

Geerds spricht von einem Äquivalenzverhältnis, dessen Grundlage die Unrechtsvereinbarung bilde, die wiederum in ihrem objektiven und subjektiven Gehalt zu unterscheiden sei. Die objektiv „für" eine Diensthandlung festzustellende Vorteilszuwendung müsse subjektiv von den Beteiligten in ihrer Bedeutung als Gegenleistungsverhältnis erkannt werden[306].

Kuhlen spricht von einer asymetrischen Äquivalenzbeziehung zwischen Diensthandlung und Vorteil[307]. Asymetrisch, weil nur der Vorteil als Äquivalent oder Gegenleistung für eine Diensthandlung vereinbart werden könne, nicht auch umgekehrt die Diensthandlung als Äquivalent für den zu gewährenden Vorteil[308]. Ein „do ut des"-Verhältnis komme dabei nur für das Anbieten und Vereinbaren künftiger Diensthandlungen in Betracht, da hier anders

301 BGHSt 15, 239 (251 f.).
302 BGH wistra 1986, S. 218 (219).
303 BGH NStZ 1987, S. 326 (327).
304 BGH wistra 1991, S. 220 (221).
305 BGH wistra 1994, S. 104.
306 Geerds, JR 1993, S. 211 (212).
307 Kuhlen, NStZ 1988, S. 433 (438).
308 Kuhlen, NStZ 1988, S. 433 (438).

als bei schon vollzogener Diensthandlung die künftige Diensthandlung das Mittel zur Erlangung der Gegenleistung sein solle[309].

Andere Verfasser fordern schlicht ein Austauschverhältnis im Sinne eines „do ut des" zwischen Vorteil und Diensthandlung[310].

d) Eigene Auffassung

Ausgehend von dem in der Literatur unterschiedlich gedeuteten Inhalt des in der Gesetzesformulierung zum Ausdruck gebrachten Beziehungsverhältnisses stellt sich hier vor allem die Frage nach den subjektiven Anforderungen bezüglich der dem Beziehungsverhältnis zugrunde liegenden sog. Unrechtsvereinbarung zwischen Nehmer und Geber. Wie ist die Interpretation dieser Vereinbarung bei den Tathandlungsalternativen zu verstehen, wenn man davon ausgeht, dass beim „Fordern" des Vorteils die Unrechtsvereinbarung angestrebt, beim „Sichversprechenlassen" geschlossen und beim „Annehmen" realisiert wird? Der BGH vertritt die Auffassung, eine Unrechtsvereinbarung könne nicht vorliegen, „wenn auf der einen oder anderen Seite – der des Vorteilsgebers oder des Amtsträgers – der Wille fehlt, daß der Vorteil dem Beamten als Gegenleistung für eine Diensthandlung zufließen soll"[311]. Mehrere Fragen bleiben dabei unbeantwortet: Wie verträgt sich diese BGH-Auffassung mit der Entscheidung des BGH, der innere Vorbehalt des Beamten, die angekündigte pflichtwidrige Handlung nicht zu begehen, sei unbeachtlich[312]? Dem Beamten fehlt in diesem Fall doch regelmäßig der für eine Unrechtsvereinbarung für maßgeblich erachtete, auf das Austauschverhältnis gerichtete Wille. Und umgekehrt sähe sich der BGH für den Fall der Verneinung einer Unrechtsvereinbarung mangels Tatwillens mit der Frage konfrontiert, wie dieses Ergebnis dann noch mit seiner Auffassung vom Strafgrund der Bestechungsdelikte konform gehe[313]. Denn der Amtsträger, der z.B. für eine vorgetäuschte (pflichtwidrige) Amtshandlung einen Vorteil entgegennimmt[314], besitzt nicht den vom Gegenüber vorausgesetzten Willen zum Austausch des Vorteils gegen die Diensthandlung, hat aber andererseits durch die Annahme des Vorteils bereits den Anschein von Käuflichkeit erweckt und damit das Vertrauen der Allgemeinheit in die Makellosigkeit der Amtsführung erschüttert. Aus Rechtsschutzerwägungen müsste der BGH hier die Tatbestandsmäßigkeit bejahen,

309 Kuhlen, NStZ 1988, S. 433 (438/439).

310 Geppert, Jura 1981, S. 42 (47).

311 BGHSt 39, 45 (48); zuvor schon in BGHSt 10, 237 (241); dem BGH folgend die überwiegende Meinung der Literatur vgl. Tröndle/Fischer, § 331 Rn. 15; Lackner/Kühl, § 331 Rn. 10; Rudolphi, SK,§ 331Rn. 28; ferner Jescheck, LK, § 331 Rn. 13.

312 So BGHSt 15, 88 (97).

313 Nämlich der „Makellosigkeit des Amtes" und dem korrespondierenden „Vertrauen der Bevölkerung", BGHSt 15, 88 (96 f).

314 S. hierzu den Fall BGH, NJW 1980, S. 2203.

wegen fehlender Unrechtsvereinbarung sie gleichzeitig aber wieder verwerfen[315].

Bei genauer Unterscheidung und Abgrenzung der erforderlichen, aber auch ausreichenden subjektiven Bestandteile einer Unrechtsvereinbarung könnten diese sich widersprechenden Ergebnisse vermieden werden[316]. Folgende, abgestufte Anforderungen an diese Unrechtsvereinbarung sind denkbar:

1.
Beidseitig mit übereinstimmendem Willen getroffene Absprache, dass die Vorteilshingabe für die von beiden vorgestellte, konkret ins Auge gefasste Amtshandlung erfolgt (do-ut-des-Verhältnis im Sinne von „Du gibst mir was, damit ich Dir etwas gebe").

2.
Beidseitig übereinstimmende Vorstellung von dem Zusammenhangsverhältnis zwischen Vorteil und ins Auge gefasster Amtshandlung unter Inkaufnahme des Zustandekommens einer diesbezüglichen (Unrechts-)Vereinbarung trotz möglicherweise fehlendem Tatausführungswillen (echtes Korrespondenzverhältnis).

3.
Einseitige Vorstellung von dem Zusammenhangsverhältnis und Erkennbarkeit dieser Vorstellung beim Gegenüber (unechtes Korrespondenzverhältnis).

4.
Einseitige Vorstellung von dem Zusammenhangsverhältnis.

5.
Nach außen tretendes konkludentes Verhalten im Hinblick auf ein Zusammenhangsverhältnis (unechter Willensbekundungsakt oder objektivierte Unrechtsvereinbarung).

Wo nun die Grenzziehung notwendiger, aber auch ausreichender Voraussetzungen für die Annahme einer Unrechtsvereinbarung nach der Gesetzeslage bis zum Inkrafttreten des KorrBekG von 1997 hätte verlaufen müssen, beurteilt sich zunächst nach der Wortinterpretation des Merkmals „Unrechtsverein-

---

315 So verneint der BGH in NJW 1980, S. 2203, die Strafbarkeit wegen Vorteilsannahme und Bestechlichkeit, begründet dies aber mit dem Wortlaut der §§ 331,332; die Fragen des Vorliegens einer Unrechtsvereinbarung und der Rechtsgutverletzung lässt er ungeprüft.

316 Geerds wirft zu Recht Rechtspraxis und Wissenschaft vor, es bis dato unterlassen zu haben, Klarheit über das strafrechtlich relevante Beziehungsverhältnis zu erzielen, JR 1993, S. 211 (213).

barung“ und dem Zweck, dem diese dient. Unzweifelhaft erlangt die Formulierung „als Gegenleistung dafür“ in ihrem Sinnzusammenhang mit den Merkmalen „Vorteil“ und „Diensthandlung“ erst durch die individuellen Vorstellungen von Geber und Nehmer Aussagekraft in Bezug auf ein Zusammenhangsverhältnis[317]. Von diesem subjektiven Einschlag losgelöst könnte ein Zusammenhangsverhältnis zwischen Vorteil und Amtshandlung nur als kausale Verknüpfung objektiver Geschehensabläufe angenommen werden, was für den Nachweis einer strafbaren (Unrechts-)Vereinbarung schon vom Wortsinn nicht ausreichend wäre.

Ob und in welcher Weise ein Beziehungsverhältnis zwischen Vorteil und Amtshandlung zustande gekommen ist, hängt zunächst vom für den jeweiligen Gegenpart erkennbaren Zweck des Handelns und den Beweggründen des Verhaltens des Gegenüber ab[318]. Diesbezüglich korrespondierende Überlegungen auf Geber- und Nehmerseite – Vorteil und Amtshandlung sind individualisiert und in Abhängigkeit zueinander als Austauschobjekte erkannt – bilden eine ausreichende Wissensgrundlage für die Annahme einer den Vorstellungen entsprechenden Austauschbeziehung (echtes Korrespondenzverhältnis). Eine Willensübereinstimmung ist insoweit nicht erforderlich[319]. Hat z.B. der Vorteilsgeber erkannt, dass der Beamte die Diensthandlung in Abhängigkeit von der Gewährung des Vorteils vornehmen will, und bringt der Geber sein Einverständnis hierzu ausdrücklich oder konkludent zum Ausdruck, obwohl ihn diese verwerfliche Absicht des Beamten in Wahrheit gar nicht interessiert, weil er tatsächlich aus anderen Beweggründen ohne jede Bestimmungsabsicht handelt[320], so fehlt ihm selbst zwar der (Vollendungs-)Wille im Hinblick auf die vom Amtsträger beabsichtigte Unrechtsverwirklichung, nicht aber das Wissen und die Akzeptanz um die eine solche Vereinbarung begründenden Tatumstände. Wenn er den Vorteil in Kenntnis der Einstellung des Beamten dennoch hingibt, so mag sein fehlender Wille bezüglich der Verknüpfung von Vorteil und Diensthandlung die Frage seines Tatvorsatzes aufwerfen, im Rahmen des Zustandekommens einer Unrechtsvereinbarung ist die korrespondierende Kenntnis der Umstände ausreichend. Der in Kenntnis aller Voraussetzungen einer Unrechtsbeziehung handelnde Vorteilsgeber nimmt die äußeren und inneren Geschehensabläufe in Kauf, mögen seine eigenen, seine Strafbarkeit betreffenden Beweggründe auch andere sein.

---

317 Maiwald spricht von Motivation als maßgeblichem Kriterium, NStZ 1994, S. 489.

318 Instruktiv BGHSt 39, 45 (48), wo der BGH eine Unrechtsvereinbarung verneint, weil der Vorteil nicht für die Diensthandlung selbst gewährt worden sei, sondern für die Art und Weise, in der sie erbracht wurde.

319 Zumindest missverständlich daher der BGH, der auf den beidseitigen Willen abstellt, BGHSt 39, 45 (48).

320 Zum Beispiel aus Dankbarkeit.

Der BGH entscheidet im Ergebnis ebenso, wenn er auf Seiten des Vorteilsnehmers den möglicherweise nur vorgetäuschten, aber nicht wirklich bestehenden Willen zur Vornahme der pflichtwidrigen Amtshandlung für die Vollendung der Tat durch den Vorteilsnehmer für unbeachtlich ansieht[321]. Denn im Rahmen der Unrechtsvereinbarung kommt es nur darauf an, dass der Vorteilsnehmer in Korrespondenz mit den Absichten seines Gegenüber das Zusammenhangsverhältnis zwischen Vorteil und erwarteter Diensthandlung erkennt[322].

Nicht ausreichend für die Annahme einer Unrechtsübereinkunft[323] ist danach ein unechtes Korrespondenzverhältnis zwischen Geber und Nehmer, bei dem die eine Seite die verwerfliche Absicht der anderen Seite nicht erkannt hat, diese aber aus den äußeren Umständen hätte erkennen können. Hier fehlt es an dem Nachweis einer tatsächlich bestehenden Wissensgemeinschaft, die Mindestvoraussetzung für die Annahme verabredeten Handlungsunrechts ist. Das Abstellen auf die Prüfung der Erkennbarkeit der die Unrechtsübereinkunft beinhaltenden Umstände würde die Vereinbarung bzw. Übereinkunft ihres subjektiven Wesensmerkmals berauben, das in der begriffsnotwendigen intellektuellen Korrespondenz der Beteiligten liegt.

Tätereigene (geheime) Vorbehalte verhindern damit nicht die Verwirklichung einer Unrechtsübereinkunft. Andererseits setzt sie das Wissen um alle Unrechtsmerkmale im Zusammenhang mit der Austauschbeziehung und der in Bezug genommenen Austauschobjekte voraus.

Wenn Cramer[324] demgegenüber für die Bejahung einer Unrechtsvereinbarung genügen lassen will, dass jedenfalls aus dem Verhalten des Vorteilsnehmers erkennbar wird, er verknüpfe Vorteil und Diensthandlung im Sinne eines Gegenleistungsverhältnisses, während es auf den Willen und die Vorstellungen beim Geber nicht ankomme, so verkennt er die der Sinnbedeutung einer Unrechtsvereinbarung immanenten kognitiven Anforderungen sowohl auf Geber- wie auch auf Nehmerseite.

Nicht zu verwechseln hiermit ist die Frage nach der individuell zu beurteilenden Strafbarkeit des Vorteilsgebers und des Vorteilsnehmers entsprechend ihrem Tatvorsatz. Dies ergibt sich aus der Gegenüberstellung der Tatbestände der §§ 331-334, die in ihren tatbestandlichen Voraussetzungen allerdings erst

---

321 BGHSt 15, 88 (96 f.).

322 Der BGH hat in seiner Grundsatzentscheidung BGHSt 15, 88 (96 f.) allerdings vorrangig Rechtsschutzerwägungen als Begründung herangezogen; richtiger Ansatzpunkt wäre aber die Unrechtsvereinbarung gewesen.

323 Diese Formulierung wird anstelle des Begriffs der Unrechtsvereinbarung vorgeschlagen, weil sie das Erfordernis einer Wissensgemeinschaft, nicht Willensgemeinschaft, besser zum Ausdruck bringt.

324 Schönke/Schröder/Cramer, § 331 Rn. 4 und 29 d.

mit dem KorrBekG von 1997 deutlich erkennbare Spiegelbildlichkeit aufweisen[325].

Das hier gefundene Ergebnis betreffend die subjektiven Voraussetzungen einer Unrechtsübereinkunft hält auch kriminalpolitischen Erwägungen stand. Damit wird die im Rahmen der Neufassung der Bestechungsdelikte durch das KorrBekG geführte Diskussion um den völligen Verzicht oder die Lockerung der Voraussetzungen der Unrechtsvereinbarung keineswegs vorweg genommen[326]. Für die Tatgerichte ist es zugegeben schwer, eine Willensgemeinschaft bezüglich des Austauschverhältnisses strafprozessual nachzuweisen und von bloßen Schutzbehauptungen abzugrenzen. Nach der hier vertretenen Auffassung kann der Nachweis eines echten Korrespondenzverhältnisses im Sinne einer Wissensgemeinschaft im Hinblick auf die objektiven, rekonstruierbaren Tatumstände viel eher gelingen und es werden damit keine überzogenen Beweisanforderungen gestellt.

2. Die gesetzliche Festschreibung der vom BGH[327] entwickelten Grundsätze zur Vollendung der Tat beim Ermessensbeamten

a) Problemstellung

Der Abs. 3 des § 332 ist mit dem EGStGB neu aufgenommen worden[328]. Dieser Absatz bedarf deshalb besonderer Begutachtung, weil selbst nach der Kodifizierung der Rspr. des BGH die Schwierigkeit der exakten Bestimmung der subjektiven Anforderungen an die Tatseite bestehen geblieben ist.

Nach § 332 Abs. 3 ist die Tathandlung zweiaktig. Sie besteht einmal im Fordern, Sichversprechenlassen oder Annehmen eines Vorteils als Gegenleistung für eine Dienstpflichtverletzung, zum anderen in dem ausdrücklichen oder stillschweigenden Sichbereitzeigen, eine Dienstpflichtverletzung zu begehen. Abs. 3 stellt klar, dass mit der Pflichtwidrigkeit, auf die sich das Bereitzeigen bezieht, die künftige, durch den Vorteil belastete Vornahme oder Unterlassung der Diensthandlung gemeint ist, nicht schon die Vorteilsannahme als solche. Nach Abs. 3 ist es für die Vollendung der Tat unerheblich, ob es zu der mit dem Vorteil im Äquivalenzverhältnis stehenden Gegenleistung tatsächlich

---

325 Dazu näher S. 74 f.

326 Auch nach der Neufassung der §§ 331 ff. wird eine wenn auch gelockerte Unrechtsvereinbarung tatbestandlich vorausgesetzt (vgl. S. 83 ff.), so dass die hier geführte Diskussion um die subjektiven Anforderungen auch weiterhin Aktualität besitzt.

327 BGHSt 15, 239.

328 Geppert sieht darin eine Auslegungsregel, Jura 1981, S. 42 (50); ebenso Wintrich, Neue Polizei 1976, S. 82 (84); in der Amtl. Begründung wird offen gelassen, ob es sich um eine Auslegungsregel oder eine Tatbestandserweiterung zu Abs. 1 handelt, BT-Drs. 7/550, S. 274.

kommt und wenn dies der Fall ist, ob die Handlung tatsächlich pflichtwidrig ist bzw. die Ermessensentscheidung tatsächlich durch den Vorteil beeinflusst ist, ob sie letztlich sachgerecht oder sachwidrig getroffen wurde. Mit dem Wort „schon" wird klargestellt, dass Tatvollendung mit dem Sichbereitzeigen eintritt. Abs. 3 Nr. 2 geht beim Ermessensbeamten davon aus, dass die Ermessensausübung schon dann pflichtwidrig ist, wenn ihr ein Sichbereitzeigen vorausgegangen ist, dem Vorteil ein Gewicht bei der Ausübung des Ermessens einzuräumen, auch wenn die Ermessenshandlung dann tatsächlich sachgerecht vorgenommen wird[329].

Aus dieser Gesetzeslage kann sich für den Tatrichter folgende nur schwer zu beherrschende Beweissituation ergeben:

Bei der Tatmodalität der „Annahme" eines Vorteils ist der innere Vorbehalt des Amtsträgers nach der Rspr. dann beachtlich und der Tatbestand nicht erfüllt, wenn er den Vorteil nicht behalten will, auch wenn er ihn zunächst entgegennimmt[330]. Der BGH verneint dann eine „Annahme" i.S.d. §§ 331 ff.[331].

In § 332 Abs. 3 ist die Strafbarkeit vorverlegt und an die auf die Pflichtwidrigkeit (Nr. 1) bzw. Beeinflussbarkeit (Nr. 2) abzielende Erklärung des Amtsträgers gebunden. Diese Erklärung des Sichbereitzeigens muss zu der Annahme des Vorteils hinzukommen, um die Tathandlung zu erfüllen, d.h. die Annahme des Vorteils in dem Bewusstsein, dass eine Beziehung zu der künftigen Diensthandlung besteht und der Vorteilsgeber eine Pflichtwidrigkeit erwartet, genügt allein noch nicht (Zweiaktigkeit der Tathandlung).

Welche Anforderungen sind an das Merkmal des „Sichbereitzeigens" zu stellen? Oftmals wird der Tatrichter neben der Feststellung der Annahme des Vorteils durch den Amtsträger keine dokumentierten Erklärungen des Vorteilsnehmers seiner Beweiswürdigung unterziehen können. Wie soll er die Überlegungen und Gedanken des Amtsträgers ausforschen? Die äußeren Tatumstände werden selten zur weiteren Aufklärung mit der für eine gerichtliche Verwertbarkeit erforderlichen Beweissicherheit beitragen können. Er hat oftmals nur die Möglichkeit, bereits in der Annahme des Vorteils und dem dadurch nach außen erweckten „bösen" Anschein die konkludente, stillschweigende Erklärung des Ermessensbeamten zu entnehmen, dieser lasse sich bei der Ausübung seines Ermessens durch den Vorteil beeinflussen[332]. Ein hier bestehender ge-

329 Zur Gesetzesbegründung im Einzelnen siehe BT-Drs. 7/550, S. 273/274.

330 S. o. unter Fn. 99.

331 Ähnliches soll gelten für das Vorliegen des Merkmals „Sichversprechenlassen", das den Willen des Beamten zur Entgegennahme voraussetze, Schönke-Schröder/Cramer, § 331 Rn. 23, unter Hinweis auf OLG Hamm MDR 1973, S.68.

332 Vgl. Maiwald in JuS 1977, S. 353 (354) und Wintrich, Neue Polizei 1976, S. 82 (84).

heimer Vorbehalt des Amtsträgers, sich tatsächlich bei der Ausübung des Ermessens nicht beeinflussen zu lassen, wäre unbeachtlich[333].

Der Tatrichter muss in diesen Fällen das Tatmerkmal der „Annahme“ unter unterschiedlichen Blickwinkeln würdigen. Einmal unter dem Gesichtspunkt des ggf. beachtlichen geheimen Vorbehalts, den Vorteil nicht endgültig behalten zu wollen. Zum anderen unter dem Aspekt, ob in der tatsächlichen Entgegennahme des Vorteils ein wenn auch nur konkludentes „Sichbereitzeigen“ geschlussfolgert werden kann und letztlich unter dem Blickwinkel des ggf. unbeachtlichen geheimen Vorbehalts des Amtsträgers, sich tatsächlich in der Ermessensausübung durch die Annahme der Zuwendung nicht beeinflussen zu lassen.

Die mit unterschiedlichen strafrechtlichen Konsequenzen versehenen geheimen Vorbehalte und konkludenten Willensbekundungen, die ausschließlich aus dem Tatmerkmal der Annahme des Vorteils „herausgelesen“ werden müssen, erscheinen nicht nur im Hinblick auf die Beachtlichkeit vorsatzausschließender Willensmängel fragwürdig. Die Überzeugung des Gerichts kann sich bei der Erforschung der Absichten und Beweggründe des Amtsträgers regelmäßig nur an der „Einaktigkeit“ der Annahme-Handlung ausrichten, wobei diese nicht nur den Prüfgegenstand für etwaige geheime Vorbehalte bildet, sondern zugleich auch das wesentliche Indiz für den Nachweis des zweiten Akts des „Sichbereiterklärens“ liefert.

Man kann sich leicht vorstellen, auf welcher prozessrechtlich problematischen Grundlage die Beweiswürdigung des Tatrichters in bestimmten Fallkonstellationen erfolgen wird. Die Gefahr des Rückfalls in die alte Rspr. des RG, die noch in der Annahme eines Vorteils beim Ermessensbeamten eine unwiderlegliche Vermutung für seine unrechtsbegründende Befangenheit annahm[334], besteht akut, wenn der Tatrichter sich nicht mit allen im Geschehenszusammenhang mit der faktischen Annahme des Vorteils liegenden Interpretationsalternativen gerade auch im Hinblick auf behauptete Willensmängel auseinandersetzt. Die einseitige Bezugnahme auf die Tathandlung der „Annahme“ birgt die Gefahr einer Verkürzung der Zweiaktigkeit der Tathandlung des § 332 Abs. 3 nicht zuletzt deshalb, weil eine verwerfliche Motivlage beim Täter substanziell mit der Entgegennahme des Vorteils verbunden erscheint.

b) Ansatzpunkt „Schutzgut“

Die oben genannte Problematik wirft die Frage auf, warum der von der Annahme des Vorteils ausgehende unrechtsbehaftete böse Anschein für widerlegbar gehalten wird, soweit er das endgültige Behaltenwollen betrifft, dagegen

---

333 BT-Drs. 7/550, S. 273.

334 RGSt 74, 251 (255) und 77, 75 (78).

trotz (geheimen) Vorbehalts als unwiderlegbar gilt, soweit er auf das Sichbereiterklären zur Vornahme einer pflichtwidrigen Diensthandlung (beeinflusste Ermessensentscheidung) hindeutet. Eine Erklärung könnte in kriminalpolitischen Überlegungen liegen, dem Täter seine ansonsten kaum widerlegbare Behauptung abzuschneiden, er habe sich im Hinblick auf seine Entscheidung nicht beeinflussen lassen. Der Nachweis des behaupteten Nichtbehaltenwollens kann dagegen leichter anhand der tatsächlichen, der Vorteilsannahme nachgelagerten Geschehensabläufe geführt werden. Mögen solche beweisökonomischen Überlegungen auch verständlich sein, in der Konsequenz führen sie zu den aufgezeigten prozessualen Verwerfungen.

Schutzzweckerwägungen könnten da schon eher einen widerspruchsfreien Erklärungsansatz liefern. Nach der hier vertretenen Auffassung des vorrangig anhand des Maßstabs der objektiven Funktionsfähigkeit der staatlichen Verwaltung und der damit immanent verbundenen sachgemäßen Aufgabenerledigung einzugrenzenden Schutzbereichs[335] bestimmt sich die Gefährdungslage in den oben genannten Fallgestaltungen unterschiedlich. Die nur zum Schein erfolgte Entgegennahme eines Vorteils kann das fehlerfreie und von unlauteren Erwägungen unbeeinflusste Funktionieren des Staatsapparats nicht ernsthaft gefährden, fehlt hier doch erkennbar der Wille des Amtsträgers, mit der nachweisbar zeitlich befristeten Entgegennahme eines Vorteils staatliches Handeln zu diskreditieren[336]. Anders liegt das im Fall des geheimen Vorbehalts des Amtsträgers, sich nicht durch den Vorteil bei der Ausübung seines Ermessens beeinflussen zu lassen. Hier ist er schon tief in die Tathandlung verstrickt, da die Entgegennahme des Vorteils nicht nur vorübergehend erfolgt und nur noch aufzuklären ist, ob aus der Annahme des Vorteils im Rahmen der Tatumstände ein zumindest konkludentes Sichbereiterklären i.S.d. Strafnorm resultiert. Selbst wenn der Amtsträger Tatvorbehalte glaubhaft vortragen kann und damit ein ihn entlastendes Indiz für die Gesamtwürdigung schafft, unterliegt er dem Einfluss der Erwartung des Gebers bezüglich der eingeforderten Gegenleistung. Ob es dem Vorteilsnehmer dabei gelingt, sich dieser Erwartungshaltung tatsächlich innerlich derart zu widersetzen, dass ein Sichbereitzeigen nicht bejaht werden könnte, hängt letztlich von den nachweisbaren weiteren Geschehensabläufen ab. Die Grenze, ab der eine Gefährdung für das frei von äußeren Einwirkungen und damit regelgerechte und fehlerfreie Funktionieren der staatlichen Verwaltung anzunehmen ist, dürfte dabei schnell überschritten sein. Denn der sich in einer bloßen Behauptung ohne tatsächliche Belege erschöpfende geheime Vor-

---

335 S. o. S. 53 ff.

336 Anders sähe wohl die Beurteilung aus, wenn man den Vertrauensgedanken als Schutzgut heranzieht; in diesem Fall liegt nahe, bereits in der – wenn auch nur vorübergehenden – Entgegennahme des Vorteils zumindest eine Gefährdungssituation im Hinblick auf das Vertrauen der Allgemeinheit in die Lauterkeit des Öffentlichen Dienstes anzunehmen.

behalt des Amtsträgers könnte den Eintritt der geschilderten Gefährdungssituation nicht mehr verhindern.

Mit dem hier vertretenen Verständnis vom Schutzgut der Bestechungsdelikte lässt sich die inzwischen kodifizierte Rspr. des BGH widerspruchsfrei nachvollziehen.

Die Vertreter des Vertrauensschutzgedankens werden sich dagegen schwer tun, die Fallkonstellationen ebenso widerspruchsfrei herzuleiten[337].

3. Subjektive Einbruchstelle beim neu aufgenommenen Abs. 3 des § 334?

Diese Frage stellt sich bei näherer Betrachtung der rechtlichen Konstruktion dieses Absatzes. Die nachhaltige Bekämpfung der Bestechungskriminalität hängt entscheidend von der Nachweisbarkeit gerade der subjektiven Strafbarkeitsvoraussetzungen ab. Stellen sich hier Beweisschwierigkeiten ein, liegt die prozessuale Versuchung nahe, vom Beschuldigten vorgetragene entlastende Indizien als Schutzbehauptungen für unbeachtlich zu bewerten. Nun könnte der Gesetzgeber zur Vermeidung solcher Beweissituationen sich des Erfordernisses objektiver Tatbestandsmerkmale zur exakten Bestimmung der Strafbarkeitsgrenzen bedienen. Wie ist er bei § 334 Abs. 3 verfahren?

a) Neuregelung des § 334 Abs. 3

Die Vorschrift des § 334 Abs. 3 ist das Gegenstück zu § 332 Abs. 3 und regelt diejenigen Fälle, in denen der Täter den Vorteil für eine künftige Handlung anbietet, verspricht oder gewährt. Die Tathandlung ist zweiaktig und besteht neben der eigentlichen Tathandlung – z.B. Anbieten des Vorteils als Gegenleistung für eine künftige Diensthandlung – in einer Versuchshandlung, die auf eine Pflichtverletzung des Amtsträgers gerichtet ist[338]. Mit dem Wort „schon" wird verdeutlicht, dass die Vollendung der Tat bereits mit der Versuchshandlung eintritt[339].

b) Objektive Verkürzung des Tatbestandes

Nach der Fassung des § 334 Abs. 3 ist es für die Vollendung der Tat unerheblich, ob es zu der vom Täter gewünschten Gegenleistungs-Handlung kommt, und wenn dies doch der Fall sein sollte, ob die Handlung pflichtwidrig bzw. die Ermessensentscheidung tatsächlich durch den Vorteil beeinflusst ist

---

337 Vgl. unter Fn. 336.
338 BT-Drs. 7/550, S. 276.
339 BT-Drs. 7/550, S. 276.

und ob sie letztlich sachgerecht oder sachwidrig erfolgt ist[340]. Der Gesetzgeber hat damit die Strafbarkeit des Täters nicht vom Eintritt des Bestimmungserfolges abhängig gemacht und den Tatbestand auf die Versuchshandlung verkürzt.

c) Unechte Zweiaktigkeit der Tathandlung

Wenn der Gesetzgeber von Zweiaktigkeit der Tathandlung spricht[341], so darf dies nicht zu dem Missverständnis führen, die Tathandlung könne nicht auch in einem Akt dergestalt zusammenfallen, dass z.B. im Anbieten eines Vorteils zugleich auch das Ansinnen des Anbieters in Bezug auf die Diensthandlung konkludent zum Ausdruck kommt[342]. Wenn demnach, was in den Geschehensabläufen häufig der Fall sein dürfte, die Versuchshandlung des § 334 Abs. 3 bereits in einer der Tathandlungsalternativen des Abs. 1 konkludent oder stillschweigend mitangelegt ist, welches sind dann die gesonderten Anforderungen an diese Versuchshandlung, die allein als Prüfungsmaßstab in Abs. 3 verbleibt?

d) Inhalt der Versuchshandlung des § 334 Abs. 3

aa) Objektive Voraussetzungen

Für das Ansinnen des Bestimmungsversuchs ist es nicht erforderlich, dass es zur späteren Vornahme der gewünschten Amtshandlung kommt und dass diese dann pflichtwidrig wäre[343]. Damit beschränkt sich die Beurteilung der Strafbarkeit nach Abs. 3 auf die Prüfung des Inhalts der möglicherweise nur konkludent zum Ausdruck kommenden Bestimmungshandlung, mithin auf die Vorstellungen des Täters.

bb) Subjektive Voraussetzungen

Hier soll genügen, dass sich der Täter das angesonnene künftige Verhalten seines Gegenübers als eine Pflichtwidrigkeit vorstellt[344], so dass Strafbarkeit entfällt, wenn der Täter das seinem Gegenüber angesonnene Verhalten nicht für pflichtwidrig hält, selbst wenn bei rechtlicher Bewertung das dienstliche Handeln des Amtsträgers pflichtwidrig wäre[345].

---

340 BT-Drs. 7/550, S. 276.

341 BT-Drs. 7/550, S. 276.

342 Auch der Gesetzgeber geht hiervon aus, indem er es ausreichen lässt, dass der zweite Akt sich stillschweigend aus den Umständen ergibt, BT-Drs. 7/550, S. 276.

343 BT-Drs. 7/550, S. 276.

344 BT-Drs. 7/550, S. 276; Schönke/Schröder/Cramer, § 334 Rn. 10.

345 Schönke/Schröder/Cramer, § 334 Rn. 10; Lackner/Kühl, § 334 Rn. 4, § 332 Rn. 6.

Aus dieser Rechtsmeinung folgt die Konsequenz, dass für die Strafbarkeit nach § 334 Abs. 3 bei Verzicht auf einen objektiven Handlungserfolg die irrige Vorstellung des Täters genügt, den Unrechtsbereich des § 334 betreten zu haben, und umgekehrt ein entsprechender Wertungsirrtum seine Straflosigkeit begründet, obwohl der Deliktsbereich nach rechtlicher Bewertung betreten wurde. Es wird einzig und allein auf die Vorstellungswelt des Täters abgestellt.

Die Kritiker dieser Auffassung stellen daher nur insoweit auf die Vorstellung des Täters ab, als es um die Individualisierung der vom Beamten gewünschten Handlung als solche geht. Die Charakterisierung dieser Handlung als Amtshandlung und als Amtspflichtverletzung erfolgt dann auf objektiver Beurteilungsgrundlage[346].

e) Eigene Auffassung

aa) Verstoß gegen Bestimmtheitsgrundsatz?

Zurückkehrend zur Ausgangsfrage lässt sich feststellen, dass der Gesetzgeber in § 334 Abs. 3 eindeutig subjektive Normerfordernisse für die Ausgestaltung der Strafbarkeitsgrenzen gewählt hat, unter Inkaufnahme der daraus resultierenden Nachteile für die prozessuale Beweisführung. Dem Täter wird es in aller Regel nicht schwer fallen, seine Einlassung zum Vorwurf des Bestimmungsversuchs auf kaum zu widerlegende entlastende Behauptungen zu stützen. Dem Richter wiederum fehlen belastbare objektive Prüfelemente, die er als Indizien zur Beweisführung heranziehen kann.

Es bestehen daher ernsthafte Zweifel, ob die Absätze 3 der §§ 332, 334 in Verbindung mit den jeweiligen Absätzen 1 noch hinreichend bestimmt sind und dem Bestimmtheitsgebot entsprechen, das eine zuverlässige Grundlage für die Rspr. erfordert[347]. Dies könnte hier zweifelhaft sein, weil dem Tatrichter bei der Prüfung der Voraussetzungen des Tatbestandes innerhalb seiner Beweiswürdigung vielfach nur der Rückgriff auf allgemeine Erfahrungssätze verbleibt. Drei denkbare Gefahrenquellen für Verstöße gegen den Bestimmtheitsgrundsatz lassen sich offen legen:

---

346 So E. Schmidt (Fn. 61), S. 139/140.

347 Vgl. Schönke/Schröder/Eser, § 1 Rn. 20 ff.; ferner zum verfassungsrechtlichen Bestimmtheitsgebot i.S.d. Normklarheit und Justitiabilität vgl. BVerfGE 21, 73 (79); auch der betroffene Bürger soll aus der hinreichend eindeutigen gesetzlichen Bestimmung die Rechtslage erkennen und sein Verhalten danach einrichten können.

aaa) Rückschlüsse vom objektiven auf den subjektiven Tatbestand

Wenn man mit Kuhlen die Ansicht vertritt, dass die kommunikativen Handlungen der Bestechungstatbestände, wie z.B. die „Annahme“ und das „Gewähren“, wirklich vollzogen werden müssen[348], kann aus der bloßen faktischen Entgegennahme des Vorteils eben noch nicht auf das Vereinbaren einer Vorteilsgewährung, also auf die erforderliche Unrechtsvereinbarung selbst geschlossen werden[349]. Der Verständigungsinhalt der Unrechtsvereinbarung, auf den es als zentralen Unrechtsbestandteil ankommt, muss gesondert belegt werden[350]. Hier liegt eine Gefahr für Zirkelschlüsse, nach allgemeinen Erfahrungssätzen Schlüssigkeitsprüfungen anzustellen, die auf keiner Tatsachenfeststellung zu diesem Verständigungsinhalt, sondern nur auf der äußerlich wahrnehmbaren Übergabe und Entgegennahme des Vorteils beruhen.

bbb) Prüfung der Plausibilität

Die Ermittlung des Verständigungsinhalts einer Unrechtsvereinbarung kann bei strategisch geschicktem Schweigen der Tatverdächtigen allenfalls durch eine Bewertung des konkludent durch die Tathandlung Erklärten erfolgen. Der Tatrichter müsste fragen, ob es neben dem Interesse des Amtsträgers an dem Erhalt des Vorteils noch andere plausible Erklärungen für die Vornahme der infrage stehenden Diensthandlung gibt[351]. Wenn dies zu bejahen wäre, müsste im Zweifel zu Gunsten des Tatverdächtigen entschieden werden. Auch hier tritt das Spannungsverhältnis beim Nachweis der subjektiven Tatseite zutage, dem sich der Tatrichter bei der Beweiswürdigung ausgesetzt sieht. Im Rahmen der Denkgesetze, Erfahrungssätze und Schlüssigkeitserwägungen muss er den Bedeutungsgehalt des von beiden Seiten stillschweigend Erklärten verifizieren und vom nur indiziellen Charakter des objektiv Geschehenen abgrenzen. Darin besteht das eigentliche Problem der Feststellung der subjektiven Tatsachen.

ccc) Nachweis von Irrtümern auf der Tatsachenseite

Vertieft wird das Problem der Nachweisbarkeit der subjektiven Tatelemente in Irrtumsfällen. Irrt der Betroffene über den Bedeutungsgehalt seiner Erklärungen oder seines Handelns, würde dieser Irrtum bei tatrichterlicher Bestätigung

348 Kuhlen, NStZ 1988, S.433 (434); Kuhlen sieht in den Merkmalen „Vorteil“, „Diensthandlung“ und „als Gegenleistung“ nur unselbständige Elemente des Tatbestandes, dagegen in den Tathandlungsalternativen die wesentlichen Merkmale des objektiven Tatbestandes mit der Folge, dass es entscheidend auf das Vorliegen der die unselbständigen Elemente umfassenden Unrechtsvereinbarung ankommt.

349 Nach Kuhlen kann der Erhalt des Vorteils das Vereinbaren der Vorteilsgewährung nicht ersetzen, NStZ 1988, S. 433 (436).

350 Zur Plausibilitätsprüfung s. u. unter bbb).

351 Vgl. Kuhlen, NStZ 1988, S. 433 (438).

erhebliche Bedeutung in den Fällen des nach allgemeinen Grundsätzen vorsatzausschließenden Tatbestandsirrtums erlangen. Mögliche Schutzbehauptungen in Bezug auf irrige Vorstellungen über den der Unrechtsvereinbarung zugrundeliegenden Verständigungsinhalt sind für den Tatrichter solange von Relevanz, als er nach Plausibilitätsgesichtspunkten einen derartigen Tathergang von vornherein nicht auszuschließen vermag.

Die Absätze 3 der §§ 332, 334 erschweren die richterliche Ausforschung nicht unwesentlich, da allein die subjektive Tatseite des „Sichbereiterklärens“ und die Versuchshandlung des „Bestimmens“ den Anknüpfungspunkt für die richterliche Beweiswürdigung bilden. Auch wenn man den Ausweg über die Würdigung des insofern nur konkludent interpretierbaren Erklärungsinhalts mit dem Bezugspunkt der objektiv nachweisbaren Annahme des Vorteils sucht, kann dieser Rückschluss vom Objektiven auf das Subjektive allein niemals ausreichend sein. Er kann nur als einzelnes Indiz der Gesamtwürdigung unterliegen.

Es bleiben somit gewichtige Zweifel an der hinreichenden Bestimmtheit der im Kontext der Bestechungstatbestände stehenden Absätze 3 der §§ 332, 334 bestehen, deren Strafbarkeitsvoraussetzungen neben dem allgemeinen Tatvorsatz auf subjektiven Tatelementen wie der anvisierten Unrechtsvereinbarung, dem Sichbereiterklären oder dem Bestimmungsversuch beruhen. Die Wahrheitsfindung durch den Tatrichter bezüglich dieser Tatmerkmale wird selten ohne Rückgriff auf Erfahrungssätze und Plausibilitätserwägungen gelingen, was wiederum die prozessrechtliche Erfüllung des Gebots der Gewährung gleicher Rechtsanwendung erschwert.

bb) Systematischer Ansatz verfehlt?

Mag der Gesetzgeber in § 334 Abs. 3 im Hinblick auf dessen Qualität als Auffangtatbestand im Einzugsbereich eigentlichen Bestechungsunrechts, das eine Unrechtsvereinbarung im Sinne eines echten Korrespondenzverhältnisses erfordert[352], seinen Blick vorrangig auf das Erfordernis einer entsprechenden Regelung zu § 332 Abs. 3 gerichtet haben. Systematisch verfährt er aber unterschiedlich. Bei § 332 Abs. 3 hält er beim tatbestandlichen Anknüpfungspunkt des „Sichbereiterklärens“ die Vorstellungen des Täters für unbeachtlich, wenn diese den objektiv feststellbaren oder konkludent z.B. in der Annahme des Vorteils zum Ausdruck gekommenen Geschehensabläufen widersprechen (Unbeachtlichkeit des geheimen Vorbehalts). Beim Anknüpfungspunkt des § 334 Abs. 3 soll es dagegen unabhängig von einer rechtlichen Einordnung des vor-

[352] S. o. S. 58 ff.; bei § 334 Abs. 3 ist nicht erforderlich, dass der Amtsträger das mit dem Vorteil verfolgte Ansinnen des Bestechers erkennt, BT-Drs. 7/550, S. 276 unter Hinweis auf BGHSt 15, 88 (102) und 184 (185).

gestellten Tatverlaufs allein auf diese – möglicherweise eben auch schutzbehaupteten – Tätervorstellungen ankommen. Diese in Folge der gesetzgeberischen Rechtsetzung auftretenden Interpretationsunterschiede können aber nicht allein unter Berufung auf das kriminalpolitisch Wünschenswerte[353] gerechtfertigt werden.

cc) Anknüpfungspunkt Rechtsgut

Die Vorverlegung der Strafbarkeit in § 334 Abs. 3 muss Rechtsschutzerwägungen standhalten. Bei der Bestimmung des geschützten Rechtsguts der Bestechungsdelikte war der Gesetzgeber 1973 immer noch unentschlossen[354].

Nach der hier vertretenen Auffassung zum geschützten Rechtsgut[355] ist Prüfungsgegenstand für die Frage nach dem Grund einer Vorverlagerung der Strafbarkeit in § 334 Abs. 3 das Täterverhalten, das bereits im Versuchsstadium zumindest eine Gefährdung der objektiven Funktionsfähigkeit der staatlichen Verwaltung nach sich ziehen muss. Um diesen Gefährdungsmaßstab zu erfüllen, müsste das Vorstellungsbild des (Versuchs-)Täters nach einer rechtlichen Bewertung des angesonnenen dienstlichen Handelns des Amtsträgers auf eine Bestechung im Sinne des § 334 Abs. 1 gerichtet sein. Der Täter, der irrig eine nach beamtenrechtlichen Grundsätzen korrekte Diensthandlung für dienstpflichtwidrig hält, kann mit einem darauf gerichteten Bestimmungsversuch die fehlerfreie Aufgabenerledigung der Verwaltung und damit die Funktionsfähigkeit des Staates auch nicht versuchsweise gefährden. Die Strafbarkeit an einer subjektiv verwerflichen Rechtsinterpretation des Täters festzumachen, würde ein strafrechtsdogmatisch als Wahndelikt eingestuftes Verhalten außerhalb einer erkennbaren Rechtsgutsgefährdung in den Strafbarkeitsbereich verlegen[356].

Daher muss Prüfungsgrundlage für § 334 Abs. 3 eine objektive Bewertung des Vorstellungsinhalts des Bestimmungsversuchs des Täters sein, mag dieser auch nur konkludent in einer der Tathandlungsalternativen des Abs. 1 zum Ausdruck kommen.

---

353 Vgl. nur BT-Drs. 7/550, S. 274 zu § 332 Abs. 3 Nr. 2, wo der Gesetzgeber die systematische Zuordnung „Tatbestandserweiterung oder Auslegungsregel" offen lässt und es als seine vorrangige Aufgabe betrachtet, das kriminalpolitisch gewünschte Ergebnis sicherzustellen.

354 Er legt sich nicht fest, indem er die Schutzwürdigkeit des „Vertrauens der Allgemeinheit" dahinstehen lässt, BT-Drs. 7/550, S. 269.

355 S. o. S. 53 ff.

356 Zum vergleichbaren Ergebnis kommt Baumann beim § 333 RStGB, BB 1961, S. 1057 (1066).

III. Zwischenergebnis

Nach der Intention des Gesetzgebers strebte dieser mit der Neufassung der Bestechungsdelikte durch das EGStGB von 1974 keine grundlegende Neuausrichtung an, sondern kam zum einen der kriminalpolitisch erhobenen Forderung nach Ausdehnung der Strafbarkeit aktiver Bestechungshandlungen in dem von ihm für geboten gehaltenen Umfang nach[357]. Zum anderen wollte der Gesetzgeber in der Vergangenheit aufgetretene Streitfragen unter Einbeziehung der dazu ergangenen BGH-Rspr. verbindlich klären.

Dabei ist er dem BGH in der Bestimmung des geschützten Rechtsguts „Lauterkeit des öffentlichen Dienstes" nicht vollständig gefolgt. Die bezüglich der Rechtsgutsfrage zwischen Gesetzgeber, Rspr. und Schrifttum differierenden Meinungen erschweren nach wie vor die Klärung der Strafbarkeitsgrenzen der Bestechungsdelikte. So sind mit der Beseitigung alter rechtlicher Kontroversen neue Auslegungsschwierigkeiten entstanden. Insbesondere bei den beiden Absätzen 3 der §§ 332, 334, die jetzt zwar die Zweiaktigkeit der Tathandlungen herausstellen, treten neue Abgrenzungsprobleme im Zusammenhang mit der Frage der Beachtlichkeit oder Unbeachtlichkeit der Vorstellungen des Täters auf.

Die bereits für die Rechtsentwicklung vor dem EGStGB nachgezeichnete Ausweitung der Strafbarkeitsgrenzen setzt sich auch nach 1974 fort. Das erklärtermaßen kriminalpolitisch Wünschenswerte steht im Mittelpunkt der gesetzgeberischen Absichten. Soweit nunmehr aber subjektive Tatelemente wie das „Sichbereiterklären" und der „Bestimmungsversuch" in die Tatbestandsfassungen aufgenommen wurden, ergeben sich dort Auslegungs- und prozessrechtliche Nachweisschwierigkeiten.

Darüber hinaus steht die Einhaltung des Bestimmtheitsgebots infrage, da die Bestechungstatbestände mit ihrer seit 1974 noch stärker vorgenommenen subjektiven Ausprägung Gefahr laufen, keine justitiable, tatbestandlich exakt fixierte Prüfungsgrundlage für tatrichterliche Feststellungen abzubilden.

Bei der ebenfalls bislang ungelösten Frage nach den subjektiven Anforderungen an das Äquivalenzverhältnis hat der BGH in ihren Auswirkungen zumindest missverständliche Festlegungen getroffen, die mit der hier vertretenen Auffassung vom echten Korrespondenzverhältnis vermieden werden können.

Im nachfolgenden Abschnitt sollen die offen gebliebenen Streitfragen auf der aktuellen Gesetzesgrundlage begutachtet werden.

---

357 BT-Drs. 7/550, S. 270.

Dritter Abschnitt: Die Rechtsentwicklung unter dem KorrBekG von 1997[358]

Dem am 20.8.1997 in Kraft getretenen KorrBekG ist eine lebhafte Diskussion vor allem bei den Beratungen der Strafrechtlichen Abteilung des 61. DJT im Herbst 1996 vorausgegangen[359].

Den parlamentarischen Beratungen lagen Gesetzentwürfe des Bundesrates[360] und der Bundesregierung[361] sowie eine Beschlussempfehlung des Rechtsausschusses des Bundestages[362] zugrunde, der zudem eine Expertenanhörung durchgeführt hatte[363].

Das KorrBekG enthält neben Änderungen im materiellen Strafrecht einen dienstrechtlichen Teil, in dem die §§ 43 BRRG, 70 BBG und 19 SoldG neu gefasst[364] und eine Art Kronzeugenregelung im Disziplinarrecht für aus dem Dienst entfernte Amtsträger eingeführt wurden[365].

Mit einem gesonderten „Zweiten Nebentätigkeitsbegrenzungsgesetz“[366] wollte der Gesetzgeber verdeutlichen, dass es verfehlt wäre, Nebentätigkeiten generell in einen Zusammenhang mit Korruption zu bringen[367].

---

358 BGBl. I, S. 2038; Gesetzesfassung siehe Anhang 3; soweit §§ ohne Gesetzesangaben unter diesem Abschnitt zitiert werden, handelt es sich um die aktuelle Gesetzesfassung.

359 Vh. des 61. DJT, Bd. II, L 8 ff.; das Gutachten zum Thema “Empfehlen sich Änderungen des Straf- und Strafprozeßrechts, um der Gefahr von Korruption in Staat, Wirtschaft und Gesellschaft wirksam zu begegnen ?“ erstellte Dieter Dölling, Gutachten C zum 61. DJT 1996.

360 BR-Drs. 298/95 (Beschluss) und BT-Drs. 13/3353.

361 BT-Drs. 13/6424; ferner ein mit dem RegE inhaltsgleicher Koalitionsentwurf von CDU/CSU und FDP, BT-Drs. 13/5584; ferner siehe Anträge der SPD-Fraktion, BT-Drs. 13/742, 13/1717, 13/4118, 13/8083 und 13/8084 sowie der Fraktion von Bündnis 90/Die Grünen, BT-Drs. 13/617.

362 BT-Drs. 13/8079.

363 Prot. Nr. 13/82 des BT-Rechtsausschusses.

364 Laut Koalitionsentwurf von CDU/CSU und FDP ist die Neufassung lediglich deklaratorischer Natur, durch die das grundsätzliche Verbot jeder Annahme von Belohnungen und Geschenken verdeutlicht werden soll, BT-Drs. 13/5584, S. 8.

365 §§ 11a BDO, 58a WDO; näher zu diesem Komplex „Dienstrechtlicher Teil“ Schaller, Recht im Amt 1998, S. 9 (13/14); Vahle, Verwaltungsrundschau 1998, S. 325 (327); Korte, NJW 1997, S. 2556 (2557).

366 BGBl. I (1997), S. 2294.

367 Vgl. BT-Drs. 13/8079, S.14; im Einzelnen zu den Änderungen siehe Vahle, Verwaltungsrundschau 1998, S. 325 (327/328); Korte, NJW 1997, S. 2556 (2557/2558).

I. Die strafrechtlichen Änderungen des KorrBekG, die keiner vertieften Prüfung unterzogen werden

1. Amtsträgerbegriff

Die Bestechungstatbestände knüpfen an den Begriff des „Amtsträgers“[368] an, so dass mit der Begriffsbestimmung des § 11 Abs. 1 Nr. 2 über strafbares Verhalten aus diesen Tatbeständen entschieden wird. Nach einem Urteil des BGH von 1992, mit dem die Geschäftsführer einer landeseigenen Wohnungsbaugesellschaft in der Rechtsform einer GmbH vom Vorwurf der Bestechlichkeit wegen fehlender Amtsträgereigenschaft freigesprochen wurden[369], sah sich der Gesetzgeber zu einer gesetzlichen Ergänzung des § 11 Abs. 1 Nr. 2c und damit zur Klarstellung veranlasst, dass es für den Begriff der „Aufgabe der öffentlichen Verwaltung“ auf die gewählte Organisationsform nicht ankommt, sondern allein die Art der Aufgabe maßgebend ist[370].

2. Neuformulierung des § 333

Der Gesetzgeber des EGStGB war 1974 noch davon überzeugt, dass die Gewährung eines Vorteils für eine ordnungsgemäße Diensthandlung nichts Verfängliches sei, sondern im allgemeinen Bewusstsein als ein Akt des Wohlwollens oder der Dankbarkeit angesehen werde[371]. Der Gesetzgeber von 1997 hat zumindest für die Gewährung von Vorteilen größeren Ausmaßes eine Bewusstseinsänderung in der Bevölkerung ausgemacht[372]. War somit bisher von § 333 a.F. nur das Gewähren von Vorteilen für künftige, im Ermessen des Amtsträgers stehende Diensthandlungen erfasst[373], bildet der § 333 neuer Fassung den § 331 spiegelbildlich ab, indem jede Dienstausübung erfasst wird ohne Einschränkung hinsichtlich des Zeitpunkts ihrer Vornahme und ohne Rücksicht darauf, ob es sich um eine Ermessenshandlung handelt oder nicht.

---

368 Ausführlich zu den Voraussetzungen Dölling, Gutachten C, C 53 ff.

369 BGHSt 38, 199; nach dem Urteil des BGH spreche bei der Wahl der Privatrechtsform für die Geltung privatrechtlicher Grundsätze, wenn das Unternehmen am Markt gleichberechtigt neben anderen stehe, S. 203/204.

370 Vgl. BT-Drs. 13/5584, S. 12; dazu Dölling, Gutachten, C 58/59; König, JR 1997, S. 397/398; Vahle, Verwaltungsrundschau 1998, S. 325 (326); kritisch Wolters, JuS 1998, S. 1100 (1104).

371 BT-Drs. 7/550, S. 274.

372 BT-Drs. 13/5584, S. 17; so auch Dölling, Gutachten C, C 68/69.

373 Nicht strafbar war also auch das Gewähren eines Vorteils für eine künftige Handlung eines gebundenen Amtsträgers.

Mit dem Hinweis auf die Auffangfunktion des § 333 für Fälle, in denen die Pflichtwidrigkeit einer Amtshandlung nicht bewiesen werden kann[374], betritt der Gesetzgeber den umstrittenen Bereich der Unrechtsvereinbarung. Die Begründung für die tatbestandliche Ausweitung des § 333 auf die Schwierigkeit der Nachweisbarkeit der Unrechtsvereinbarung in § 334 zu stützen und damit erweiterte strafrechtliche Eingriffsbefugnisse zu legitimieren, erscheint im Zusammenhang mit der Beantwortung der Frage nach der Strafwürdigkeit deliktischen Verhaltens sehr problematisch[375]. Der Gesetzgeber hätte daher gut daran getan, auf diesen Aspekt seiner Begründung zu verzichten.

3. Strafverschärfungen

Der Gesetzgeber verschärfte die Strafrahmen sowohl der aktiven als auch der passiven Bestechungstatbestände aus generalpräventiven Gründen[376]. Das Gesetz sieht für den Grundtatbestand der Vorteilsannahme nach § 331 Abs. 1 nun Freiheitsstrafe bis zu drei (bisher: zwei) Jahren oder Geldstrafe, für die Qualifizierung nach § 331 Abs. 2 Freiheitsstrafe bis zu fünf (bisher: drei) Jahren oder Geldstrafe vor. Gleiches gilt für den nun spiegelbildlich zu § 331 aufgebauten § 333. Die bisherigen Strafrahmen bei den §§ 332, 334 bleiben unverändert, dafür wurde mit § 335 eine Vorschrift für „besonders schwere Fälle der Bestechlichkeit und Bestechung“ mit erhöhtem Strafrahmen eingeführt, deren Regelbeispiele in Abs. 2 einer tatbestandsspezifischen Interpretation bedürfen[377].

4. Vermögensstrafe, Erweiterter Verfall (§§ 302, 338)

Alle an der Korruption Beteiligten streben in der Regel einen materiellen Vorteil an. Die Vorschriften zur Vermögensstrafe (§ 43 a) und zum Erweiterten Verfall (§ 73 d), die der Gewinnabschöpfung vor allem in den Fällen des gewerbs- und bandenmäßigen Vorgehens dienen, hat der Gesetzgeber mit Blick

---

374 BT-Drs. 13/5584, S. 17; richtig wäre hier die Formulierung gewesen: „..., in denen das Beziehungsverhältnis zu einer pflichtwidrigen Dienstausübung nicht festgestellt werden kann.“; entscheidend ist nämlich die Unrechtsvereinbarung als Bezugspunkt für die Pflichtwidrigkeit; ferner vgl. Entwurf des BR, BT-Drs. 13/3353, S. 12.

375 Zur Bewältigung von Beweisschwierigkeiten durch Ausdehnung des materiellen Strafrechts siehe Weigend, Bewältigung von Beweisschwierigkeiten durch Ausdehnung des materiellen Strafrechts?, Festschrift für Triffterer, S. 695 ff.

376 BT-Drs. 13/5584, S. 16; ebenso Entwurf des BR, BT-Drs. 13/3353, S. 8; siehe aber Dölling, Gutachten C, C 75, der bezweifelt, dass nach den Ergebnissen der empirischen Generalpräventionsforschung allgemein davon ausgegangen werden könne, dass mit höheren Strafen eine ins Gewicht fallende Abschreckungswirkung korrespondiere.

377 BT-Drs. 13/5584, S. 17; § 335 Abs. 2 Nr. 1 entspricht seinem Wortlaut nach dem Regelbeispiel des § 300 S. 2 Nr. 1, was nicht bedeutet, dass damit in der Rechtspraxis dieselbe Auslegung vorzunehmen ist; zur Problematik der auch beim Strafzumessungsgrund des § 335 betroffenen „Strafzumessungsregeltechnik“ siehe König, JR 1997, S. 397 (400).

auf vergleichbare Vorschriften über die Gewinnabschöpfung bei anderen Straftaten, die einen engen Bezug zur organisierten Kriminalität aufweisen[378], insoweit zur Anwendung gebracht, als er bei gewerbs- oder bandenmäßiger Bestechung oder Bestechlichkeit bzw. Angestelltenbestechung die Anwendung der erweiterten Verfallsbestimmungen des § 73 d vorsieht (§§ 302, 338).

Für den Fall der bandenmäßigen Bestechung ist außerdem die Vermögensstrafe nach § 43 a vorgesehen (§§ 302 Abs. 2 Satz 1, 338 Abs. 2 Satz 1). Der Gesetzgeber hält die Vermögensstrafe aus Gründen ihres spezialpräventiven Zwecks, dem Täter die Mittel für einen künftigen (erneuten) Aufbau einer verbrecherischen Organisation zu entziehen, nur für den Vorteilsgeber, nicht aber auch für den Vorteilsnehmer für anwendbar[379].

5. Bestechlichkeit und Bestechung im geschäftlichen Verkehr (§§ 299-302)

Aus Gründen einer einheitlichen Korruptionsbekämpfung und zur Schärfung des Bewusstseins in der Bevölkerung, dass Korruptionshandlungen im Geschäftsverkehr nicht nur ein die Wirtschaft treffendes Unrecht darstellen, sondern Ausdruck eines allgemein sozialethisch missbilligten Verhaltens sind[380], hat der Gesetzgeber den § 12 UWG als Tatbestände gegen die aktive und passive Bestechung im geschäftlichen Verkehr (§ 299) in das Kernstrafrecht eingefügt[381].

Die sog. Angestelltenbestechung ist jetzt kein reines Antragsdelikt mehr. Die Staatsanwaltschaft kann bei besonderem öffentlichen Interesse die Strafverfolgung aufnehmen (§ 301). Hintergrund dieser Regelung ist die Überzeugung, dass antragsberechtigte Mitbewerber oftmals keine Strafanträge stellen, weil sie

---

378 Vgl. §§ 181 c, 256 Abs. 2, 261 Abs. 7 Sätze 3 und 4, 286 Abs. 1, ferner Beschlussempfehlung Rechtsausschuss, BT-Drs. 13/8079, S. 14 und 16.

379 Beschlussempfehlung Rechtsausschuss, BT-Drs. 13/8079, S. 14 und 16; allgemein zu den Nebenstrafnormen der §§ 43 a, 73 d s. BGH, NJW 1995, S. 1367 und S. 470.

380 BT-Drs. 13/5584, S. 15.

381 Diese Übernahme war zwischen BR und BReg streitig, s. Stellungnahme des BR zum Entwurf der BReg, BT-Drs. 13/6424, S. 7; der BR kann als Argument für sich verbuchen, dass eine Bewusstseinsschärfung unter Hinweis auf durchaus im Bewusstsein der Bevölkerung verankerte Tatbestände im Nebenstrafrecht - BtMG, WaffG, AuslG - eine solche Übernahme ins Kernstrafrecht nicht erfordert hätte und durch diese Übernahme zudem im Kontext der Korruptionsbekämpfung stehende andere Tatbestände des UWG - z.B. § 17 - in ihrer Gesamtbedeutung auseinander gerissen wurden; kritisch ebenso König, JR 1997, S. 397 (401) und Wolters, JuS 1998, S. 1100 (1103); zur Gesamtthematik s. Dölling, Gutachten C, C 84 ff.

wirtschaftliche Beschädigung oder die Offenlegung von Betriebsvorgängen befürchten[382].

Im Gegensatz zu den Bestechungstatbeständen der §§ 331-334 bleiben bei der Angestelltenbestechung weiterhin nur zukünftige Zuwendungen strafbar, hingegen korrespondieren die Erweiterung auf Drittvorteile und die Regelungen zur Vermögensstrafe und zum Erweiterten Verfall (§ 302) mit den §§ 331 ff. Auch die Strafrahmen wurden entsprechend angehoben und Fälle von besonderer Schwere (§ 300)[383] geregelt.

6. Wettbewerbsbeschränkende Absprachen bei Ausschreibungen (§ 298)

Der als Kernstück des neuen Abschnitts „Straftaten gegen den Wettbewerb" bezeichete § 298[384] stellt die Angebotsabgabe nach unzulässiger Preis- oder Kartellabsprache unter Strafe. Eine jahrzehntelange Diskussion um die Frage der Strafbarkeit des „Ausschreibungs- oder Submissionsbetrugs" fand mit der Hochstufung eines Teilbereichs der bislang nach § 38 Abs. 1 Nr. 1 und Nr. 8 GWB erfassten Kartellordnungswidrigkeiten zu Straftaten ihr Ende. Der wachsenden Bedeutung von Ausschreibungen im Wirtschaftsleben sollte die strafrechtliche Verankerung Rechnung tragen, zumal Submissionsabsprachen häufig im Zusammenhang mit der Korruption von Amtsträgern stehen. Mit solchen Absprachen bei Ausschreibungen werden überhöhte Preise zum Nachteil der öffentlichen Hand erwirkt. Daher stellte sich bisher die Frage des Vorliegens eines sogenannten Submissionsbetruges nach § 263 Abs. 1. Die Problematik der Feststellung eines Vermögensschadens konnte auch nach der BGH-Entscheidung im sogenannten „Rheinausbaufall"[385] nicht behoben werden. Die vom BGH geforderte Ermittlung des regelmäßig über dem mit dem Anbieter vereinbarten Preis liegenden hypothetisch erzielbaren Wettbewerbspreises gelang in der Praxis der Tatgerichte vielfach nicht.

Der Gesetzgeber hat sich bei der Ausgestaltung des Straftatbestandes nicht am Vorschlag des Bundesrates orientiert, der den Unrechtskern in der Verheimlichung der getroffenen Absprache dem Veranstalter der Ausschreibung gegen-

---

382 So vor allem die Begründung des BR zum eigenen Gesetzentwurf, BT-Drs. 13/3353, S. 13, und in seiner Stellungnahme zum Gesetzentwurf der BReg, BT-Drs. 13/6424, S. 8.

383 Zu dem Regelbeispiel des „großen Ausmaßes" siehe Wolters, JuS 1998, S. 1100 (1103), der bei der Bestimmung des Grenzbetrages, ab dem das Regelbeispiel vorliege, auf die Orientierung am einzelnen Tatbestand abstellt.

384 Ausführlich zum Tatbestand König, JR 1997, S. 397 (401) und Wolters, JuS 1998, S. 1100 (1101).

385 BGHSt 38, 186; der BGH hat in dieser Entscheidung die Anforderungen an die Feststellung eines Vermögensschadens gelockert; zur uneinheitlichen Schrifttumsmeinung siehe Nachweise bei Dölling, Gutachten C, C 93.

über und dementsprechend das vorrangig geschützte Rechtsgut im Vermögen des Veranstalters sieht[386]. Er hat sich für den Vorschlag der Bundesregierung[387] entschieden, der den freien Wettbewerb als primär geschütztes Rechtsgut deklariert und das Vermögen des Veranstalters einer Ausschreibung nur als mitgeschützt ansieht. Der Tatbestand des § 298 geht somit über die Schaffung eines abstrakten Gefährdungsdelikts im Vorfeld des Betruges hinaus, dessen wesentliches Merkmal gerade das betrügerische Element ist[388].

Zweifelhaft bleibt nach der neuen Rechtslage, ob ein strafrechtliches Schutzgut des „freien Wettbewerbs" hinreichend bestimmbare Konturen aufweist, um eine Kriminalisierung von Absprachen legitimieren zu können[389]. Die Zulässigkeit der Reichweite des Strafrechts könnte infrage stehen[390]. Auch in der Begründung des Regierungsentwurfs zur Einführung des GWB hieß es noch, weite Kreise der Betroffenen würden eine Zuwiderhandlung gegen das Gesetz nur als kaufmännisch unlauteres Verhalten und als Verstoß gegen gewisse Ordnungsprinzipien auffassen. Eine Sanktionierung derartiger Verstöße mit Strafbestimmungen sei nicht angemessen[391]. Die jetzige Aufwertung von Teilbereichen des § 38 GWB a.F. basiert offenkundig auf einer allgemeinen Bewusstseinsänderung wie sie bereits bei der Tatbestandserweiterung des § 333 tatbestandsspezifisch vorgetragen wurde[392].

Zu den flankierenden Maßnahmen der Vorschrift des § 298, insbesondere zur umstrittenen Regelung des § 81 a GWB, die eine ausschließliche Zuständigkeit der Kartellbehörden für die Festsetzung von Unternehmensgeldbußen schafft, wird auf die Ausführungen von König[393] verwiesen.

---

386 BT-Drs. 13/3353, S. 10.

387 Gleichlautend der Koalitions-Entwurf, BT-Drs. 13/5584, S. 13.

388 Vgl. BR-Entwurf, BT-Drs. 13/3353, S. 10; ferner Dölling, Gutachten C, C 93 ff.

389 Verneinend Lüderssen, BB 1996, Beilage 11 zu Heft 25, S. 1 ff. (18); Lüderssen sieht im „Wettbewerb" keine Institution, die in den Rang eines strafrechtlich geschützten Rechtsguts gehoben werden könnte, auch als „Zwischenrechtsgut" fehlten verlässliche Konturen, andererseits sei die Konstruktion eines abstrakten Gefährdungsdelikts verfehlt, da Absprachen das Vermögen des einzelnen nicht gefährden könnten, weil die Bezugsgröße - der erwartbare Schaden - kein realer Faktor, sondern eine normative Fiktion sei.

390 König, JR 1997, S. 397 (402).

391 BT-Drs. II (1955), 1158, S. 28.

392 S. o. S. 74 f.

393 König, JR 1997, S. 397 (402 f.).

7. Keine Kronzeugenregelung für die Bestechungsdelikte[394]

Eine Kronzeugenregelung hat der Gesetzgeber nicht geschaffen[395]. Zwar wird von den Befürwortern ins Feld geführt, dem Geständnis von Beteiligten und dem Beitrag zur Aufklärung komme beim schwer aufzuklärenden Bereich der Korruptionsdelikte erhebliche Bedeutung zu; außerdem solle den Tätern durch eine solche Regelung ein Signal zum Ausstieg aus der Illegalität gegeben werden[396]. Andererseits machen die Gegner der bereits bestehenden Kronzeugenregelungen gewichtige Einwände geltend, wie den Verstoß gegen das Legalitätsprinzip[397]. Auch kriminalpolitische Bedenken sind nur schwer auszuräumen, denn Zweifel an der Glaubhaftigkeit der Angaben eines Kronzeugen können kaum vollständig ausgeschlossen werden.

II. Die näher zu prüfenden materiell-strafrechtlichen Änderungen des KorrBekG

Die beiden mit der Neufassung der Bestechungstatbestände geänderten Tatbestandsmerkmale „Vorteil" und „Unrechtsvereinbarung" bedürfen einer genaueren Untersuchung, weil diese beiden Merkmale in ihrem Zusammenwirken die in Teil B der Untersuchung zu beantwortende Kernfrage berühren, ob der jetzt geschaffene Tatbestand der Vorteilsannahme noch geeignet ist, strafwürdiges von nicht strafwürdigem Verhalten abzugrenzen und damit einerseits dem Bestimmtheitsgebot, andererseits dem ultima ratio-Gedanken des Strafrechts[398] im Hinblick auf bestehende beamtenrechtliche Sanktionsmöglichkeiten genügen kann.

1. Drittvorteile

Die bis zum Inkrafttreten des KorrBekG geltende Rechtslage setzte voraus, dass der Amtsträger einen Vorteil erhält oder erhalten soll. Die Rspr. definiert einen solchen Vorteil als Leistung, „auf die der Amtsträger keinen Anspruch

---

394 S. dagegen den neu geschaffenen § 11 a BDO im Disziplinarrecht, der mit dem Inkrafttreten des BDG zum 1.1.2002 (BGBl. I S. 1510) in § 80 BDG übernommen wurde.

395 So aber Vorschlag des BR-Entwurfs, BT-Drs. 13/3353, S. 12, der die Ausgestaltung des Tatbestandes an § 31 BtMG und § 261 Abs. 10 anlehnen wollte und zur Begründung anführt, Bestechungstaten seien kaum aufzuklären, weil es bei Korruption nur Täter und keine Opfer gäbe und daher ein Anreiz zum Ausstieg gegeben werden müsse; für eine Kronzeugenregelung auch Dölling, Gutachten C, C 74 und Schaupensteiner, Kriminalistik 1994, S. 514 (523); andere Auffassung die BReg, BT-Drs. 13/1020, S.9.

396 Dölling, Gutachten C, C 74.

397 Volk, NJW 1996, S. 881; weitere Nachweise bei Dölling, Gutachten C, C 74.

398 Hierzu Teil C der Untersuchung.

hat und die seine wirtschaftliche, rechtliche oder auch nur persönliche Lage objektiv verbessert"[399]. Die Rspr. hat auch immaterielle Leistungen[400] und Zuwendungen an Dritte, die dem Amtsträger mittelbar zugute kommen, unter den Vorteilsbegriff subsumiert[401].

Warum nun eine Einbeziehung der sog. Drittvorteile?

a) Begründung des Gesetzgebers

Was die Frage der Erforderlichkeit der Erweiterung des Tatbestandsmerkmals des Vorteils auf Drittzuwendungen betrifft, fallen die Begründungen in den Entwürfen der Bundesregierung, des Koalitions-Entwurfs und des Bundesrates eher dürftig aus. Der Entwurf der Bundesregierung verweist darauf, dass auch bei einer Vorteilsannahme der Amtsperson zugunsten Dritter das geschützte Rechtsgut der Lauterkeit des öffentlichen Dienstes verletzt und das Vertrauen der Öffentlichkeit in diese Lauterkeit nachhaltig erschüttert werde[402]. Ergänzt wird diese knappe Feststellung um den Hinweis auf die Klarstellungsfunktion, den die neue Fassung gegenüber der bisherigen Regelung im Hinblick auf Zuwendungen an Personenvereinigungen genießt, deren Mitglied der Amtsträger ist[403]. Auslegungsprobleme bei der Frage einer zumindest mittelbaren Besserstellung des Amtsträgers seien damit beseitigt.

Auch der Entwurf des Bundesrates bringt keine neuen Gesichtspunkte, sondern beschränkt sich auf den Hinweis, dass tatrichterliche Nachweisschwierigkeiten bei Zuwendungen, die vielfach zur Verschleierung der Rolle des Amtsträgers an Dritte vorgenommen würden, nunmehr entfielen, weil diese Zuwendungen vom Vorteilsbegriff umfasst würden[404]. Der Bericht des Rechtsausschusses schließlich enthält überhaupt keine Stellungnahme zu dieser Frage[405], woraus insgesamt resümiert werden kann, dass zur Frage der Erweiterung der §§ 331 ff. um den Vorteil „für einen Dritten" von Politikseite allgemeine Übereinstimmung bestand.

---

399 BGHSt 35, 128 (133).

400 BGH NStZ 1985, S. 497 (499); Voraussetzung ist ein objektiv messbarer Inhalt und die tatsächliche Besserstellung des Amtsträgers in irgendeiner Form; für die Begrenzung auf materielle Vorteile noch E. Schmidt (Fn. 61), S. 9/20 und Geerds (Fn. 42), S. 67.

401 BGHSt 35, 128 (135); Voraussetzung ist auch hier eine Besserstellung des Amtsträgers.

402 Gleichlautend mit dem Koalitions-Entwurf, BT-Drs. 13/5584, S. 16.

403 BT-Drs. 13/5584, S. 16; s. zu dieser Fallgestaltung BGHSt 35, 128 (135 f.).

404 BT-Drs. 13/3353, S. 11.

405 Vgl. BT-Drs. 13/8079, S. 12 ff.

b) Begründung des Schrifttums

aa) Dölling

Auch Dölling problematisiert die Nachweisprobleme bei Verschleierungen von Zuwendungen an den Amtsträger bei Zwischenschaltung von Firmen[406]. Erfreulicherweise beschränkt er sich ausdrücklich nicht auf die Rechtfertigung solcher Praktikabilitätsgedanken für die Einbeziehung von Drittvorteilen, sondern stellt auf den spezifischen Unrechtsgehalt der Bestechungsdelikte ab, der seiner Meinung nach einmal in der „Gefährdung der sachlichen Amtsführung gerade durch den Eigennutz des Amtsträgers" liegen könne[407], aber auch dann gegeben sei, wenn die Amtsperson sich bei ihrer dienstlichen Tätigkeit an Interessen Dritter orientiere und damit eine sachgemäße Erledigung amtlicher Tätigkeiten gefährde[408]. Seinen auch von der Strafrechtlichen Abteilung des 61. DJT aufgegriffenen Vorschlag zur Einbeziehung von Drittvorteilen[409] begründet Dölling ferner mit dem Rechtszustand in vielen ausländischen Rechtsordnungen, die Drittzuwendungen bereits einbezögen[410]. Dölling untermauert schließlich seinen Vorschlag der Erweiterung des Vorteilsbegriffs um Drittvorteile mit der vorherrschenden Meinung im Schrifttum, das teilweise schon nach dem Rechtszustand des EGStGB von 1974 Drittzuwendungen für tatbestandsmäßig gehalten hätte[411] oder jedenfalls für deren Einbeziehung votiert hätte[412].

bb) Möhrenschlager

Möhrenschlager verweist zur Rechtfertigung der Aufnahme von Drittzuwendungen ebenso wie Dölling auf internationale Bestrebungen und Regelungen, die – wenn auch nur für Fälle der Bestechlichkeit und Bestechung – Drittvorteile miteinbeziehen würden[413].

---

406 Dölling, Gutachten C, C 67.

407 Vgl. hierzu Geerds (Fn. 42), S. 50.

408 Dölling, Gutachten C, C 67.

409 Vgl. Beschlüsse des 61. DJT, Vh., Bd. II/2, L 190.

410 Dölling, Gutachten C, C 67; vgl. hierzu im Einzelnen das umfassende rechtsvergleichende Gutachten von Eser (Max-Planck-Institut für ausländisches und internationales Strafrecht), Korruptionsbekämpfung durch Strafrecht, 1997, dort speziell zu Drittvorteilen Überhofen, S. 737/738, der die Bestechungsbestimmungen von England und Wales, Österreich, Polen, Portugal und Italien, aber auch das Strafrecht von New York benennt, die allesamt eine Drittzuwendung im Tatbestand verankert haben; Erwähnung der „Drittvorteile" auch im IntBestG in Art. 2 § 1 mit Verweis auf § 334, BGBl. II (1998), 2327.

411 Dölling, Gutachten C, C 67 unter Fußnote 322.

412 Dölling, Gutachten C, C 68 unter Fußnote 324; Ausnahmen insoweit Bauchrowitz (Fn. 265), S. 130 ff. und Graupe (Fn. 63), S. 21 f., die sich gegen eine Einbeziehung von Drittzuwendungen aussprechen.

413 Möhrenschlager, JZ 1996, S. 822 (826).

cc) Schaupensteiner

Schaupensteiner begründet seine Zustimmung zur Einbeziehung von Drittvorteilen mit Fallbeispielen, in denen bei Gewährung des Vorteils ausschließlich an Dritte die Amtsperson ebenso in ihrer Entscheidung beeinflusst sei wie wenn sie den Vorteil selbst erhalten hätte[414]. Er plädiert daher für die Aufnahme von Drittzuwendungen in den Tatbestand, um „Verschleierungen von Zuwendungen durch Zahlung an Strohmänner, Scheinfirmen oder durch Abrechnung tatsächlich nicht erbrachter Leistungen über Fremdfirmen" künftig unter Strafe stellen zu können[415].

c) Eigene Auffassung

Die §§ 331-334 regeln nach der Neufassung durch das KorrBekG nunmehr ausdrücklich, dass Vorteile, die ausschließlich einem Dritten zugute kommen, vom Tatbestand erfasst werden. Insoweit ist eine Korrektur und nicht nur eine Klarstellung[416] der bis 1997 bestehenden Rspr. erfolgt, die zumindest einen mittelbaren Nutzen beim Amtsträger vorausgesetzt hat[417]. Erstaunlich ist, dass sich Politik und Wissenschaft weitgehend in der Erforderlichkeit der Erweiterung der Bestechungstatbestände auf Drittvorteile einig waren und im Schrifttum nur vereinzelt Kritik geäußert wurde[418]. Zwar weisen auch die wenigen kritischen Stimmen darauf hin, dass die eigentliche Problematik der Straftatbestandserweiterung erst im Zusammenwirken mit der in ihren Anforderungen abgeschwächten Unrechtsvereinbarung zum Tragen kommt. Ein erster Schritt zu einer immer schwerer werdenden Abgrenzung von strafwürdigem und nicht strafwürdigem Handeln ist mit der Einbeziehung von Drittvorteilen getan. Natürlich sind altruistische Verhaltensweisen von Amtspersonen vorstellbar, etwa Handeln zugunsten gemeinnütziger Einrichtungen ohne eigene Vorteilserlangung[419], ohne dass dieses Verhalten den „Makel der Strafbarkeit" zwingend verdient hätte[420]. In diesen Fällen ist der vorgeschlagene Ausweg über die Rechtsfolgenseite[421] nicht überzeugend, denn dies hat zur Konsequenz, dekla-

---

414 Schaupensteiner, der kriminalist 1996, S. 7 (10) und Kriminalistik 1996, S. 237 (243).

415 Schaupensteiner, Kriminalistik 1996, S. 237 (243).

416 So Entwurf des BR, BT-Drs. 13/3353, S. 11.

417 BGHSt 14, 123 (128); 33, 336 (339) und 35, 128 (135 f.).

418 Volk mit seinem Referat auf dem 61. DJT, Vh. Bd. II/1, L 35 (L 41 ff.); König in der Rückschau auf das KorrBekG, JR 1997, S. 397 (399); Ransiek zum Gutachten von Dölling, StV 1996, S. 446 (451).

419 Beispiele bei Ransiek, StV 1996, S. 446 (451), z.B. der Bürgermeister, der Geld für kulturelle Zwecke der Stadt erhält und einsetzen will; siehe auch Beispiel von Volk, Referat, Vh. Bd. II/1, L 35 (L 42), der den Intendant benennt, der sich um Sponsorengelder für sein Theater bemüht.

420 König, JR 1997, S. 397 (399).

421 So König, JR 1997, S. 397 (400) und Dölling, Gutachten C, C 68.

riertes „Unrecht“ wegen mangelnder Abgrenzungsschärfe des Tatbestandes über die Strafhöhe zu eliminieren. Die Fragestellung um die Einbeziehung von Drittvorteilen vertieft sich mit der auch auf dem 61. DJT zentral diskutierten und nachfolgend zu begutachtenden Neufassung des Tatbestandsmerkmals der Unrechtsvereinbarung.

2. Unrechtsvereinbarung

a) Die Lösung des Gesetzgebers

Die wohl beachtenswerteste Strafbarkeitserweiterung im Rahmen der Neufassung der §§ 331-334 hat der Gesetzgeber mit der Lockerung des Merkmals der Unrechtsvereinbarung bei den Tatbeständen der Vorteilsannahme und der Vorteilsgewährung vorgenommen. Danach sind schon die Annahme und die Gewährung von Vorteilen strafbar, wenn diese „für die Dienstausübung“ des Amtsträgers getätigt werden. Ein Nachweis für eine hinreichend bestimmte Diensthandlung als „Gegenleistung“ ist nicht mehr erforderlich. Dabei hatte der BGH schon zuvor das bislang geltende Erfordernis der Feststellung einer konkreten Diensthandlung gelockert[422]. Auch weiterhin bedarf es allerdings einer Beziehung zwischen Vorteilsannahme und den Diensthandlungen des Amtsträgers. Es kann mithin nur von einer Lockerung der Voraussetzungen der Unrechtsvereinbarung, nicht aber von deren gänzlicher Abschaffung gesprochen werden[423].

aa) Begründung des Vorschlags „für die Dienstausübung“

Nachdem im Gesetzentwurf der Bundesregierung und im Koalitionsentwurf zunächst keine Veränderung bezüglich des Merkmals „Unrechtsvereinbarung“ vorgesehen war, ist in der Diskussion um dieses Merkmal im Anschluss an den Beschluss des 61. DJT in Karlsruhe[424] der Rechtsausschuss des Deutschen Bundestages zu seiner Beschlussempfehlung einer Formulierung „für die Dienstausübung“ gelangt. Zaghaft ist allerdings seine Begründung, mit der er offen lässt, welche strafwürdigen und strafbedürftigen Fälle er denn jetzt explizit bestraft sehen will[425]. Der Rechtsausschuss beschränkt sich auf die allgemeine Absichtserklärung, diejenigen strafwürdigen Fälle erfassen zu wollen,

---

[422] BGHSt 32, 290 (291) und 39, 45 (46 f.); das zusammenwirkende Einvernehmen musste sich danach nur noch darauf beziehen, „daß der Amtsträger innerhalb eines bestimmten Aufgabenkreises oder Kreises von Lebensbeziehungen nach einer gewissen Richtung hin tätig werden soll ...; die einvernehmlich ins Auge gefaßte Diensthandlung muß dabei nach ihrem sachlichen Gehalt zumindest in groben Umrissen erkennbar und festgelegt sein“.

[423] Beschlussempfehlung des Rechtsausschusses, BT-Drs. 13/8079, S. 15.

[424] Beschlüsse der Abt. Strafrecht, 61. DJT Vh., Bd. II/2, L 189.

[425] BT-Drs. 13/8079, S. 15.

bei denen die Annahme oder Gewährung eines Vorteils „als Gegenleistung für eine Diensthandlung“ nicht nachgewiesen werden kann[426]. Welche Fälle das nun genau sein sollen oder anders formuliert, welche Fallgestaltungen er nicht für strafwürdig ansieht, lässt der Ausschuss offen. Den Vorschlag des Bundesrates[427] wehrt er mit der Begründung ab, dieser erfasse ein breites Spektrum nicht strafwürdiger Handlungen und würde die Schwierigkeiten einer klaren Abgrenzung zu nicht strafwürdigen Zuwendungen geringeren Gewichts vergrößern[428].

Aufmerksamkeit gebührt der Bemerkung des Rechtsausschusses, die Strafverfolgungspraxis und die Strafrechtswissenschaft forderten eine Lockerung der Unrechtsvereinbarung insbesondere in Fällen hoher Zuwendungen[429]. Offensichtlich hat der Rechtsausschuss sein Votum nicht zuletzt unter dem Eindruck dieser Forderung abgegeben. Man vermisst allerdings eine nähere Auseinandersetzung mit dieser Problematik. So besteht beim Merkmal „Vorteil“ durchaus die Möglichkeit einer eingrenzenden tatbestandlichen Bewertung im Hinblick auf dessen Eignung, eine Amtsperson in ihrer Dienstausübung korrumpieren zu können[430].

bb) Begründung des Vorschlags „im Zusammenhang mit dem Amt“

Der Bundesrat begründet seinen Vorschlag der Aufspaltung der Vorteilsannahme in einen Grund- und in einen Qualifikationstatbestand[431] unter gleichzeitigem Ersetzen des Merkmals „als Gegenleistung dafür“ durch das Merkmal „im Zusammenhang mit seinem Amt“ mit dem Erfordernis einer umfassenderen und wirkungsvolleren Bekämpfung der Korruption[432]. Er sieht im Hinblick auf das geschützte Rechtsgut eine Strafbarkeitslücke insbesondere in den Fällen des „Anfütterns“, bei denen der Vorteil zunächst nur das allgemeine Wohlwollen und die Geneigtheit des Amtsträgers sichern soll[433]. Das Merkmal „im Zusammenhang mit dem Amt“ sieht er gegeben, wenn „die zuwendende Person sich davon leiten läßt, daß der Beamte ein bestimmtes Amt bekleidet oder bekleidet hat“[434]. Danach würde auch schon jede Vorteilsannahme und -gewährung in der privaten Sphäre des Beamten strafbar sein, wenn derartige Austauschbeziehungen mit der Erwartung in Bezug auf die dienstliche Tätig-

426 BT-Drs. 13/8079, S. 15.
427 Dazu u. unter bb).
428 BT-Drs. 13/8079, S. 15.
429 BT-Drs. 13/8079, S. 15.
430 Zu diesem Ansatz näher u. unter ee).
431 BT-Drs. 13/3353, S. 5.
432 BT-Drs. 13/3353, S. 11.
433 BT-Drs. 13/3353, S. 11.
434 BT-Drs. 13/3353, S. 11.

keit des Beamten verknüpft wären[435]. Nachdem der 61. DJT diesen Vorschlag mit großer Mehrheit verworfen hatte[436], fand er auch keinen Niederschlag im Gesetz.

b) Die Meinungen im Schrifttum

aa) Dölling

Dölling, auf dessen Vorschlag der Beschluss des 61. DJT in dieser Frage der Lockerung der Unrechtsvereinbarung gefasst wurde[437] und dessen Votum Grundlage für die geltende Gesetzesfassung der §§ 331,333 geworden ist, begründet seine vorgeschlagene Erweiterung der Tatbestände der Vorteilsannahme und Vorteilsgewährung[438] mit der Strafwürdigkeit auch jener Fälle, in denen der Vorteil ohne Beziehung zu einer näher konkretisierten Diensthandlung als Gegenleistung in dem beidseitigen Bewusstsein gewährt wurde, die Amtsperson werde irgendeine dienstliche Tätigkeit vornehmen oder habe eine dienstliche Tätigkeit vorgenommen[439]. Damit wären dann ausdrücklich auch die die Sachlichkeit der Amtsführung erheblich gefährdenden Fälle wie z.B. der des Bauunternehmers erfasst, der einem Bürgermeister mit den Worten „auf gute Zusammenarbeit“ 100.000 DM überreiche, ohne auf ein bestimmtes Vorhaben anzuspielen[440]. Eine darüber hinausgehende Ausdehnung der Tatbestände der §§ 331, 333 lehnt Dölling mit Hinweis auf die Gefahr ab, dann auch nicht strafwürdige Fälle tatbestandlich zu erfassen und damit eine hinreichend sichere Rechtsanwendung zu gefährden[441].

bb) Möhrenschlager

Möhrenschlager argumentiert zum Merkmal der Unrechtsvereinbarung vorsichtig im Sinne der Vorschläge von Dölling, die er im Hinblick auf die bis dahin regelmäßig straffreien Fälle des „Anfütterns“ und der „Klimapflege“ für über-

435 BT-Drs. 13/3353, S. 11.

436 Bei 7:108:4 Stimmen, Vh. Bd. II/2 (Beschlüsse, L 189); zur Kritik an dieser sogenannten Zusammenhangsklausel vgl. vor allem König, JR 1997, S. 397 (399); Möhrenschlager, JZ 1996, S. 822 (825/826); Volk, Referat, Vh. Bd. II/1, L 35 (L 41); Hettinger, NJW 1996, S. 2263 (2268/2269); ferner Möllering, WRP 1997, S. 933 (935).

437 S. Beschlüsse, Vh. Bd. II/2, L 189.

438 Seine Formulierung im Gutachten: "daß der Vorteil als Gegenleistung für ‚die dienstliche Tätigkeit in der Vergangenheit oder Zukunft' oder ‚für die bisherige oder künftige Amtsführung' zugewendet werden muß“, Gutachten C, C 65.

439 Dölling, Gutachten C, C 64.

440 Dölling, Gutachten C, C 65.

441 Dölling, Gutachten C, C 65/66.

legenswert hält[442]. Dabei weist er auf das schwedische Recht hin, das seiner Meinung nach mit den Vorschlägen Döllings korrespondiere[443].

cc) Volk

Die Überlegungen von Volk basieren auf der von ihm gewählten begrifflichen Definition der Korruption, deren Handlungsmerkmal der Tausch von Vorteilen unter Regelverstoß sei. Danach handele korrupt, wer bei einer Entscheidung zu seinem eigenen oder dem Vorteil eines Dritten gegen Regeln verstoße[444]. Auf das „zentrale Merkmal des Regelverstoßes" könne nicht verzichtet werden, ohne den Tatbestand ins Ungewisse ausufern zu lassen[445]. Entweder müsse der Regelverstoß bei der Diensthandlung durch das Zusammenhangsverhältnis oder beim Merkmal des Vorteils selbst durch Eingrenzung auf unangemessene oder rechtswidrige Vorteile zum Ausdruck kommen[446].

dd) Schaupensteiner und Schaefer

Schaupensteiner vertritt den Standpunkt, bei allen Verhaltensweisen, bei denen ein Nähe- oder Abhängigkeitsverhältnis mit der Absicht aufgebaut werde, „sich die amtliche Funktion des Empfängers früher oder später auf sachwidrige Weise nutzbar zu machen", werde das durch die Amtsdelikte geschützte Rechtsgut der Lauterkeit des öffentlichen Dienstes und das Vertrauen der Allgemeinheit in die Objektivität der Amtsführung verletzt[447]. Nach der von ihm und Schaefer[448] befürworteten Gesetzesformulierung „im Zusammenhang mit seinem Amt" liege eine Vorteilsgewährung vor, wenn der „Zuwendende sich davon leiten läßt, daß der Beamte ein bestimmtes Amt bekleidet oder bekleidet hat und der Empfänger den Vorteil in Kenntnis dessen annimmt"[449]. Mit dem von ihm als Strafbarkeitsvoraussetzung geforderten Zusammenhangsverhältnis zwischen dem Vorteil und der amtlichen Tätigkeit des Empfängers verzichtet auch Schaupensteiner nicht gänzlich auf das Tatbestandsmerkmal der Unrechtsvereinbarung. Allerdings will er sozialadäquate, nicht strafwürdige Verhaltensweisen nur dann anerkennen, wenn die „Amtsstellung des Begünstigten hinwegge-

---

442 Möhrenschlager, JZ 1996, S. 822 (825/826).

443 Möhrenschlager, JZ 1996, S. 822 (826).

444 Volk, Referat, Vh. Bd. II/1, L 35 (L 51).

445 Volk, Referat, Vh. Bd. II/1, L 35 (L 41); bei der Formulierung „im Zusammenhang mit dem Amt" sei ein solcher Regelverstoß nicht mehr erkennbar, L 41 und L 51.

446 Volk, Referat, Vh. Bd. II/1, L 35 (L 41 und L 43).

447 Er nennt das „Anfüttern" von Beamten, die Zahlungen zur „Klimapflege" oder sogenannte „Aufmerksamkeiten" zur Sicherung des allgemeinen „Wohlwollens" in der Erwartung, diese würden künftig honoriert, Kriminalistik 1996, S. 237 (241).

448 S. sein Referat zum 61. DJT, Vh. Bd. II/1, L9 (L 22/23).

449 Schaupensteiner, Kriminalistik 1996, S. 237 (242).

dacht werden kann, ohne daß der Grund für die gewährte Aufmerksamkeit entfiele“[450].

ee) Schlicht, Lüderssen und König

Einen anderen Ansatzpunkt sehen einige Verfasser in einer gegenüber dem Gedanken einer Lockerung der Unrechtsvereinbarung verstärkten Objektivierung der Tatbestandsfassung, indem sie die Eignung des Vorteils, den Empfänger in seiner Amtsführung beeinflussen zu können, als maßgebenden Faktor und strafbarkeitseingrenzendes Korrektiv anführen[451]. Mit dem Hinweis auf den materiellen Wert der Zuwendung, dem eine Schlüsselposition bei der Prüfung der Geeignetheit zukommen würde, schlagen die Verfasser unterschiedliche Begrifflichkeiten zur Umschreibung und Eingrenzung des Vorteils vor[452]. Anhand welcher Kriterien diese den Vorteil umschreibenden Begriffe auszufüllen wären, lassen die Verfasser allerdings offen. Sie betonen die Schwierigkeit, ein trennscharfes Korrektiv zu finden für die Unterscheidung zwischen angemessenem und unangemessenem Vorteil und damit zwischen Nichteignung und Eignung des Vorteils, den Vorteilsnehmer korrumpieren zu können[453].

ff) Hettinger und Ransiek

Hettinger und Ransiek stehen der jetzigen Gesetzesfassung der §§ 331-334 wie auch jeder anderen Ausweitung der Bestechungstatbestände ablehnend gegenüber.

Hettinger begründet dies mit den bestehenden dienstrechtlichen Möglichkeiten. Die Unrechtsvereinbarung i.S.d. vor 1997 geltenden Fassung sei schon nur akzeptabel und die Vorteilsannahme als „abstraktes Vorfeldgefährlichkeitsdelikt“ legitimierbar gewesen, weil das Merkmal des Zusammenhangsverhältnisses zwischen Vorteil und konkret bestimmter Diensthandlung für die Grenzziehung

---

450 Schaupensteiner, Kriminalistik 1996, S. 237 (242).

451 Schlicht , Vh. zum 61. DJT, Bd. II/2, L 116 f.; Lüderssen, JZ 1997, S. 112 (116); König, JR 1997, S. 397 (399).

452 König nennt unter Hinweis auf das schwedische Recht das Auslegungsmerkmal „Ungebührlichkeit“, JR 1997, S. 397 (399); Lüderssen spricht von einem „unangemessenen“ Vorteil und weist in diesem Zusammenhang auf die Einschränkung beim inzwischen neu gefassten § 299 auf die Fälle „unlauteren“ Verhaltens hin, womit zumindest im Bereich der Privatwirtschaft das Strafbarkeitsrisiko begrenzt werde, JZ 1997, S. 112 (116/117); siehe auch Volk, der eine Eingrenzung des Vorteilsbegriffs auf „unangemessene“ oder „rechtswidrige“ Zuwendungen vorschlägt, Vh. Bd. II/1, L 35 (L 41).

453 König, JR 1997, S. 397 (399); zu diesem Ansatz einer Eignungsregelung s. die Erörterungen in Teil B der Untersuchung.

zwischen Straftat und bloßem Dienstvergehen noch hinreichende Trennschärfe gewährleistet habe. Die Hochstufung der disziplinarwidrigen Geschenkannahme zur Straftat sei nur mit der Hereinnahme der Unrechtsvereinbarung alter Fassung in den Tatbestand der §§ 331,333 zu rechtfertigen gewesen[454].

Ransiek vertritt die Auffassung, dass das vor 1997 geltende Recht bereits die Sachlichkeit von Diensthandlungen[455] sehr weitreichend geschützt habe. Es sei nicht zu verstehen, warum tatbestandsspezifische Gefahren noch weitergehend erfasst werden sollten[456]. Die pönalisierte Gefahr des Eintritts des eigentlichen Bestechungsunrechts, pflichtwidriges Handeln für eine Gegenleistung, degeneriere letztlich zur bloßen Vermutung. Auch Ransiek weist auf das beamtenrechtliche Geschenkannahmeverbot mit seinen disziplinarrechtlichen Folgen hin, das solche Gefahren angemessen sanktioniere[457].

c) Eigene Auffassung

Die in der Strafrechtswissenschaft diskutierten Ansatzpunkte für eine materielle Neufassung der Bestechungstatbestände betreffen zwei straftaterweiternde Gesichtspunkte, die Lockerung der Unrechtsvereinbarung und die Hereinnahme von Drittzuwendungen in den Tatbestand. Andererseits wird die Diskussion von einem tatbestandseingrenzenden Gedanken getragen, nämlich der Untersuchung und Begrenzung des Vorteilsbegriffs auf seine Eignung hin, jemanden korrumpieren zu können. Bei den vorgeschlagenen Formulierungen zur Unrechtsvereinbarung gibt es eine Variante mit einer stärkeren Lockerung („im Zusammenhang mit dem Amt") und die Formulierung einer abgeschwächten Lockerung („für die Dienstausübung"), die ins Gesetz aufgenommen wurde.

Die im Mittelpunkt der Diskussion stehende Frage, in welchem Ausmaß man die Tatbestände der §§ 331, 333 auf bislang straffreie Verhaltensweisen erstrecken sollte, setzt eine Begutachtung einzelner Lebenssachverhalte voraus, die Aufschluss und Anhaltspunkte für eine tatbestandliche Grenzziehung liefert. In diesem Kontext spielen Schutzzweckerwägungen und Bestimmtheitsgebot eine ebenso tragende Rolle wie die Individualisierung der Anforderungen an den Verständigungsinhalt der Unrechtsvereinbarung. Dabei darf die ultima ratio-Frage im Hinblick auf eine rechtliche Alternative zum Strafrecht, die von

---

454 Hettinger, NJW 1996, S. 2263 (2272).

455 In der Frage des Rechtsguts schließt er sich Dölling an, Ransiek, StV 1996, S. 446 (450).

456 Bei fehlendem Nachweis eines Bezugs der Vorteilsannahme zu einem der Sache nach konkretisierbaren Kreis von Diensthandlungen „... wird die Gefahr immer weniger greifbar.", Ransiek, StV 1996, S. 446 (451).

457 Ransiek, StV 1996, S. 446 (451).

einigen Verfassern im dienstrechtlichen Beamtenrecht gesehen wird[458], nicht aus den Augen verloren werden. Die Teile B und C dieser Arbeit beschäftigen sich mit diesen Fragen. Auch die weitergehenden Überlegungen, ob bei Drittzuwendungen in allen Fällen noch der spezifische Unrechtscharakter der Bestechungstatbestände[459] gewahrt bleibt oder ob vorzugsweise am Tatmerkmal des Vorteils eine straftatbestandseinschränkende Begriffsbestimmung erfolgen sollte, können erst im Anschluss an die in Teil B der Untersuchung vorzunehmenden Fallanalysen wieder aufgenommen werden. An dieser Stelle bedürfen einer genaueren Analyse die Fragen nach der Definition, der inhaltlichen Ausgestaltung und der Nachweisseite der beiden Reformvorschläge zur Lockerung des Merkmals der Unrechtsvereinbarung. Nur so kann die unterschiedliche Reichweite der beiden Ansätze exakt bestimmt werden.

aa) „Im Zusammenhang mit dem Amt“

Nach Auffassung des Bundesrates liegt dieses Merkmal vor, „wenn die zuwendende Person sich davon leiten läßt, daß der Beamte ein bestimmtes Amt bekleidet oder bekleidet hat“[460]. Damit enden aber auch schon die begrifflichen Erläuterungen. Auch die Befürworter dieser sogenannten Zusammenhangsklausel beschränken sich auf diese Definition mit dem Hinweis, dass der Bezug zu einer bestimmten Amtshandlung nicht erforderlich sei[461]. Nach der Kommentierung ist für dieses Merkmal eine sachliche und zeitliche Beziehung erforderlich[462].

Dabei will Schaupensteiner unter Zuhilfenahme des Gedankens der Sozialadäquanz der Gefahr einer uferlosen Ausweitung des Tatbestandes begegnen. Immer dann, „wenn die Amtsstellung des Begünstigten hinweggedacht werden kann, ohne daß der Grund für die gewährte Aufmerksamkeit entfiele“ (sachliche Beziehung) handele es sich um sozialadäquates und nicht tatbestandsgemäßes Verhalten[463]. Die in der Kommentierung geforderte zeitliche Komponente besitzt hierbei keine erkennbare Relevanz.

Hält man sich streng an diese Definition und Begriffsbestimmung der Zusammenhangsklausel, wird schnell deutlich, warum der Gesetzgeber sie verworfen hat. Sie greift eindeutig zu weit, ohne dass ihr ein handhabbares Korrektiv zur Seite stünde, um eine Abgrenzung zu Schenkungen im privaten Bereich zu er-

---

458 Hettinger, NJW 1996, S. 2263 (2269 ff.); ferner Ransiek, StV 1996, S. 446 (451); Wagner, Vh. 61. DJT, II/2, L 118.

459 Allgemein wird er mit dem Kauf von Diensthandlungen interpretiert, BT-Drs. 7/550, S. 269; Dölling, Gutachten C, C 62; vgl. ferner BGHSt 18, 59 (62).

460 BT-Drs. 13/3353, S. 11.

461 Schaupensteiner, Kriminalistik 1996, S. 237 (242).

462 Tröndle/Fischer zum Zusammenhangsbegriff des § 264 a, dort Rn. 8.

463 Schaupensteiner, Kriminalistik 1996, S. 237 (242).

möglichen. Denkt man die Amtsstellung des Briefträgers und damit seine amtliche Funktion hinweg, entfiele auch das ansonsten übliche Neujahrsgeschenk, das natürlich im Zusammenhang mit seinem Amt und seiner diesbezüglichen Tätigkeit hingegeben wird. Dennoch wird die Straflosigkeit des bedachten Briefträgers im Rahmen sozialadäquater Maßstäbe nicht bezweifelt. Die Abgrenzungsschwierigkeiten werden bei privaten Verbindungen zwischen Amtsträger und Privatem noch sichtbarer. Welche Plausibilitätsgesichtspunkte könnten dem Tatrichter bei seiner Abwägung darüber wirklich helfen, ob ein zum 50. Geburtstag privat dargereichtes Geschenk für den Bürgermeister vom eng mit ihm befreundeten Architekten ohne „falsche" Gedanken an das Amt des Freundes übergeben wurde? Derart verwerfliche Gedanken sind möglich und nie ganz auszuschließen, können aber als Vermutungen eventueller ursächlicher Zusammenhänge strafprozessual selten der Entscheidungsfindung dienen. Eine Anwendung der Grundsätze der Sozialadäquanz hilft hier zur Fixierung einer tatbestandlichen Grenzlinie nicht weiter.

bb) „Für die Dienstausübung"

aaa) Erster Schritt: Definition und Begriffsbestimmung durch Gesetzgeber

Der Rechtsausschuss des Bundestages spricht in seiner Beschlussempfehlung einmal von einer Klarstellung, dass weiterhin eine Beziehung zwischen der Vorteilsannahme und den Diensthandlungen des Amtsträgers bestehen müsse, und zum anderen grenzt er zum bestehenden Rechtszustand ab, dass eine hinreichend bestimmte Diensthandlung als Gegenleistung nicht mehr nachgewiesen werden müsse[464]. Ohne weitere Auseinandersetzung mit der neu definierten Grenzziehung der Strafbarkeit stellt der Rechtsausschuss einseitig auf das positive Erfassen der für strafwürdig befundenen Verhaltensweisen ab. So enthält die Beschlussempfehlung allein die Feststellung, dass von der Strafverfolgungspraxis und der Strafrechtswissenschaft die Forderung nach Lockerung der Unrechtsvereinbarung besonders für Fälle hoher Zuwendungen erhoben werde, die keinen Diensthandlungen zugerechnet werden könnten[465]. Aufgrund dieser spärlichen Ausführungen ist ein kurzer Rückblick auf die Rechtslage vor 1997 erforderlich.

bbb) Zweiter Schritt: Bisherige BGH-Rspr.

Der BGH wollte auf der Grundlage der Rechtslage vor Inkrafttreten des KorrBekG mit einer Lockerung der Anforderungen an die Bestimmtheit der Diensthandlung insbesondere solche Täter nicht straflos stellen, „die sich nicht nur im Hinblick auf eine einzelne, konkrete Diensthandlung, sondern für weite Berei-

464 BT-Drs. 13/8079, S. 15.
465 BT-Drs. 13/8079, S. 15.

che ihres Wirkens als käuflich erweisen"[466]. Daher ließ der BGH das zwischen den Beteiligten bestehende Einverständnis genügen, dass der Vorteilsnehmer innerhalb eines bestimmten Aufgabenbereichs nach einer gewissen Richtung hin tätig werden soll, wobei zwischen den Beteiligten keine genauen Vorstellungen über das „Wann", den „Zeitpunkt der Gelegenheit" und die „Art und Weise der Einlösung der Unrechtsvereinbarung" bestehen müssen, nur muss die ins Auge gefasste Diensthandlung mindestens in groben Umrissen erkennbar und festgelegt sein[467].

ccc) Dritter Schritt: Nur ein gradueller Unterschied zwischen alter und neuer Gesetzesfassung?

Im Beispielsfall der Freundschaft zwischen Bürgermeister und Architekt, der seinem Freund zum 50. Geburtstag ein ansehnliches Geschenk überreicht, stellt sich die Frage nach der Tatbestandsverwirklichung nach altem wie nach neuem Recht. Für die alte Gesetzesfassung des § 331 wird man die Frage verneinen, weil die vom BGH genannten Voraussetzungen an die Konkretisierung einer Diensthandlung ohne weitere Sachverhaltsaufklärung nicht erfüllt sind. Wie sieht das Ergebnis bei der aktuellen Gesetzesfassung des § 331 aus? Keinesfalls reicht für eine Bestrafung die übereilte Schlussfolgerung aus, der Architekt habe das kostspielige Präsent dem befreundeten Bürgermeister sicherlich (auch) in der Erwartung übergeben, dieser solle ihn bei der künftigen Amtsführung begünstigen, d.h. ihn z.B. bei der etwaigen Vergabe von Bauaufträgen bevorzugt berücksichtigen. Zum einen setzt auch die neue Gesetzesfassung ein Beziehungsverhältnis in der Art voraus, dass die Beteiligten im Sinne eines echten Korrespondenzverhältnisses[468] im gegenseitigen Wissen um den zugrunde liegenden verwerflichen Sinngehalt des teuren Geschenks gehandelt haben, zum anderen vermittelt der geschilderte Sachverhalt zunächst nachweisbar nur den Verständigungsinhalt einer Geschenkübergabe von Freund zu Freund.

Welche Fragen müsste der Tatrichter demnach aufklären, um zur Überzeugung einer Vorteilsannahme bzw. Vorteilsgewährung zu gelangen? In jedem Fall müsste er nach den Grundsätzen des Beweisrechts der StPO[469] davon sicher überzeugt sein, dass das Geschenk zumindest auch dem Zweck der Bevorzugung des Architekten bei der künftigen Amtsführung diente und dies beiden Beteiligten bewusst war.

---

466 BGHSt 32, 290 (291).

467 BGHSt 32, 290 (291); 39, 45 (46/47).

468 So die hier vertretene Auffassung der subjektiven Voraussetzungen der Unrechtsvereinbarung, oben S. 58 ff.

469 Der Grad der tatrichterlichen Überzeugung besteht in einem „nach der Lebenserfahrung ausreichende(n) Maß an Sicherheit, demgegenüber vernünftige Zweifel nicht mehr aufkommen", BGH StV 1996, S.418.

Welche nachzuweisenden Tatsachen könnten dem Tatrichter helfen, diese hohe beweisrechtliche Hürde zu überspringen? Er müsste bei der Sachaufklärung zunächst herausfinden, ob sich die beruflichen Interessen des Architekten dem Aufgaben- und Zuständigkeitsbereich des Bürgermeisters zuordnen lassen. Weiter wäre von Bedeutung, ob in der Vergangenheit bereits geschäftsmäßige Berührungspunkte bestanden, ob der Architekt Aufträge von der Stadt bekam, die auf den Bürgermeister als Veranlasser dieser Auftragsvergaben zurückgingen. Ferner käme der Tatsache Indizwirkung zu, wenn in naher Zukunft für den Geschäftsbereich des Architekten finanziell interessante Auftragsvergaben bevorstanden. Und nicht zuletzt dürfte die Art des Geschenks und dessen Geldwert für die tatrichterliche Überzeugung wesentlich sein. Ein neues Auto (Höhe des Geschenks) oder die Komplettrenovierung des Hauses (Art des Geschenks) dürften als Geburtstagsgeschenk unter Freunden eher selten und unüblich sein. Der Tatrichter müsste zudem bei lebensnaher Betrachtung die Überzeugung begründen, warum es dem Architekten neben dem Freundesdienst nicht nur um „allgemeine Klimapflege" ging, sondern die Geschenkübergabe mit Bezug zur Amtsführung des Bürgermeisters „für die Dienstausübung" erfolgte. Ob er dies mit der erforderlichen Sicherheit zu Ungunsten der Beteiligten annehmen kann, hängt im Einzelfall von dem geschäftlichen Näheverhältnis beider Seiten ab, inwieweit in welcher Häufigkeit und in welchen zeitlichen Abständen Aufträge für die Kommune bereits durchgeführt wurden und weitere Vergaben unmittelbar in Aussicht standen.

Auch mit der richterlichen Feststellung einer regen Geschäftsbeziehung ist der Nachweis einer beabsichtigten Beeinflussung der Amtsführung aufgrund der denkbaren Interpretationsalternativen nicht zwingend erbracht. Allerdings liefert die im Kontext zu teuren Geschenken stehende Tatsache einer für die Kommune erfolgten oder in Aussicht stehenden Geschäftstätigkeit ein starkes Tatindiz, wenn diese durch konkrete Diensthandlungen des Bürgermeisters mitveranlasst wurde. Dies zeigt, dass es im Rahmen der Beweisführung – nicht mehr dagegen bei der Erfüllung der Tatbestandsvoraussetzungen – in vielen Fällen immer noch auf die Feststellung einer erfolgten oder künftig in Betracht gezogenen konkreten Diensthandlung zu Gunsten des Vorteilsgebers ankommen wird. Häufig wird nur mit einer solchen Feststellung die Beweisführung im Hinblick auf eine von den Betroffenen ins Kalkül gezogene Beeinflussung der Dienstausübung des Amtsträgers gelingen.

Faktisch hat eine Verschiebung eines Elements der Unrechtsvereinbarung vom materiellen Strafrecht ins Strafprozessrecht stattgefunden. Im geschilderten Fall könnte selbst bei einem außergewöhnlich großzügigen Geschenk der Nachweis des Leistungsverhältnisses „Vorteil für die Dienstausübung" kaum geführt werden, wenn sich nicht ein in der Vergangenheit liegendes oder in Aussicht stehendes geschäftliches Interesse beim Vorteilsgeber in der Verknüpfung mit konkretisierbaren Diensthandlungen des Vorteilsnehmers als korruptive Verflechtung verifizieren lässt.

Der Unterschied zwischen alter und neuer Gesetzesfassung reduziert sich somit auf einen „Standortwechsel“ des Elements „konkrete Diensthandlung“. Während nach altem Recht dieses Element Teil des Tatbestandmerkmals der Unrechtsvereinbarung war, tritt es nun auf der prozessualen Nachweisseite in den Mittelpunkt beweiserheblicher Tatsachenfeststellung.

ddd) Lockerung der Unrechtsvereinbarung ein richtiger Schritt?

Die Erörterungen zuvor haben gezeigt, dass die Problematik des Nachweises einer konkreten Diensthandlung mit der Lockerung des Merkmals der Unrechtsvereinbarung nicht gänzlich beseitigt werden konnte. Warum dann überhaupt eine Lockerung?[470] Der jetzt Gesetz gewordene Inhalt der Unrechtsvereinbarung ist in seinen Konturen und Grenzbereichen indifferenter geworden. Inwieweit dadurch eine Überdehnung des Tatbestandes mit ihren ungewollten Folgen einer Erfassung auch nicht strafwürdiger Verhaltensweisen eingetreten ist, wird in Teil B dieser Arbeit untersucht. An dieser Stelle ist festzuhalten, dass das nachzuweisende Austauschverhältnis „Vorteil für die Dienstausübung“ in der jetzigen Gesetzesfassung dem Tatrichter keineswegs in allen Fällen eine dieses Beziehungsverhältnis näher zu konkretisierende Indizienbeweisführung erspart.

Nachfolgend soll im Rahmen einer Darstellung des Standes der Rechtsentwicklung der Korruptionsbekämpfung auf internationaler Ebene der Frage nachgegangen werden, ob die deutlich erkennbaren Tendenzen einer Europäisierung des Strafrechts Kompatibilität zur nationalen, mit dem KorrBekG zunächst zum Abschluss gekommenen Rechtsetzung aufweisen und in dieselbe strafrechtsdogmatische Richtung zeigen.

Im Hinblick auf die in dieser Arbeit problematisierten Bezugspunkte „Rechtsgüterschutz“ und „Unrechtsvereinbarung“ soll mit einem rechtsvergleichenden Blick auf korrespondierende Lösungen in anderen nationalen Rechtsordnungen untersucht werden, ob die mit dem KorrBekG getroffene Entscheidung für eine Ausweitung des Strafrechtsschutzes bei Vorteilsannahme und Vorteilsgewährung mit der Entwicklung in anderen Staaten kongruent verläuft.

---

470 Zum Teil wurde bereits die bis 1997 geltende Fassung der §§ 331, 333 i.S. der jetzt geltenden Regelung ausgelegt, Schönke/Schröder/Cramer, 25. Aufl., § 331, Rn. 29.

III. Strafrechtliche Regelungen zur internationalen Korruptionsbekämpfung und Rechtsvergleich nationaler Rechtsordnungen im Hinblick auf die Rechtsgutsfrage und die Unrechtsvereinbarung

1. Strafrechtliche Regelungen zur internationalen Korruptionsbekämpfung

Internationale Übereinkommen zur Bekämpfung korruptiver Verhaltensweisen haben den deutschen Gesetzgeber zur Verabschiedung zweier Gesetze veranlasst, mit denen die bereits bestehenden Strafvorschriften für inländische Amtsträger auf Ausländer mit vergleichbarer Amtsträgerstellung erstreckt werden. Interessant erscheint die Untersuchung, inwieweit der nationale Gesetzgeber den in den internationalen Übereinkommen zum Ausdruck kommenden Grundkonsens über Rechtsangleichungen bei der grenzüberschreitenden Korruptionsbekämpfung bei der innerstaatlichen Umsetzung realisiert hat.

a) EUBestG[471]

Mit dem EUBestG hat die Bundesregierung einmal das Protokoll vom 27.9. 1996[472] zum Übereinkommen über den Schutz der finanziellen Interessen der Europäischen Gemeinschaften vom 26.7.1995[473] in das deutsche Recht umgesetzt, zum anderen ihre Verpflichtungen aus dem Übereinkommen über die Bekämpfung der Bestechung, an der Beamte der EG oder der Mitgliedstaaten der EU beteiligt sind[474], erfüllt.

Nach Art. 2 § 1 EUBestG werden die §§ 332, 334-336, 338 u. a. auf Amtsträger eines anderen Mitgliedstaats der EU, soweit deren Stellung einem Amtsträger i.S. von § 11 Abs. 1 Nr. 2 entspricht, angewendet und nach Art. 2 § 2 EUBestG bei Taten im Ausland u. a. auf Täter erstreckt, die zum Tatzeitpunkt Deutsche sind oder Ausländer mit Amtsträgereigenschaft i.S. von § 11 Abs. 1 Nr. 2 oder als Gemeinschaftsbeamte i.S.d. Art. 2 § 1 Abs. 1 Nr. 2b EUBestG einer Einrichtung mit Sitz in Deutschland handeln.

Allerdings werden nur die auf künftige pflichtwidrige Diensthandlungen abzielende Tathandlungen erfasst. Die Beschränkung auf pflichtwidrige Diensthandlungen entspricht zwar dem Wortlaut des Protokolls, der die nach den §§ 331, 333 strafbaren Tathandlungen nicht einbezieht. Der deutsche Gesetzgeber hätte aber aus eigener rechtspolitischer Überzeugung die Erweiterung auf pflichtgemäße Diensthandlungen vornehmen können. Er hat damit die straflose

---

471 Vom 10.9.1998, BGBl. II S. 2340.

472 BT-Drs. 13/10424, S. 8 ff.

473 ABl.EG Nr. C 316 vom 27.11.1995, S. 49 ff.

474 Vom 26.5.1997, ABl.EG Nr. C 195 vom 25.6.1997, S. 1.

Vorteilsannahme des gebundenen EU-Beamten, der seine Aufgaben pflichtgemäß erfüllt, für (zumindest vorerst) nicht sanktionsbedürftig erklärt.

Andererseits hat der deutsche Gesetzgeber im EUBestG eine über die Verpflichtung im Protokoll hinausreichende Ausdehnung der Strafbarkeit auf den genannten Personenkreis vorgenommen, indem er die in Art. 2 und 3 des Protokolls enthaltene Voraussetzung, dass die Bestechungshandlung auf die Schädigung der finanziellen Interessen der EU gerichtet sein muss, nicht übernommen hat. Er hat damit die Transformation des Protokolls mehr als gefordert vollzogen. Dies wäre verständlich und auch zu befürworten, wenn der gesetzgeberische Beweggrund in der Absicht einer weit reichenden Erfassung der Strafbarkeit von Bestechungshandlungen von und gegenüber Gemeinschaftsbeamten und Amtsträgern von Mitgliedsstaaten der EU gelegen hat[475]. Dann hätte er aber auch in Kongruenz und systemgerecht zum KorrBekG pflichtgemäße Diensthandlungen in den Strafbarkeitsbereich miteinbeziehen müssen, um dem Anliegen umfassender Pönalisierung gerecht zu werden.

b) IntBestG[476]

Dem IntBestG liegt das OECD-Übereinkommen über die Bekämpfung der Bestechung ausländischer Amtsträger im internationalen Geschäftsverkehr zugrunde[477], das von Deutschland als einem von 33 Staaten am 17.12.1997 unterzeichnet wurde. Art. 2 § 1 IntBestG erweitert den Anwendungsbereich des § 334 auf Richter, Amtsträger und Soldaten ausländischer Staaten sowie auf Amtsträger und sonstige Bedienstete internationaler Organisationen. Der Anwendungsbereich des IntBestG ist somit enger als der des EUBestG, da es nur die Gewährung von Zuwendungen unter Strafe stellt, allerdings auch gegenüber Amtsträgern supranationaler Staaten[478].

Nach Art. 2 § 1 IntBestG muss sich die Tathandlung wie beim EUBestG auf eine künftige pflichtwidrige Diensthandlung beziehen und begangen werden, um sich oder einem Dritten einen Auftrag oder einen unbilligen Vorteil im internationalen Geschäftsverkehr zu verschaffen. Anders als das insoweit eindeutige, dem EUBestG zugrundeliegende Protokoll, enthält hier der Wortlaut der Formulierung in Art. 1 des OECD-Übereinkommens „...in Zusammenhang mit der Ausübung von Dienstpflichten eine Handlung vornimmt oder unterläßt“ keine Begrenzung auf pflichtwidrige Diensthandlungen. Wenn auch in der Gesetzesbegründung zum IntBestG ein diesbezüglicher Eindruck erweckt

475 So Zieschang, NJW 1999, S. 105 (106).
476 Vom 10.9.1998, BGBl. II S. 2327.
477 BT-Drs. 13/10428, S. 9 ff.
478 Vgl. Korte, wistra 1999, S. 81 (86).

wird[479], so ist der Ausschluss der Vorteilsgewährung für pflichtgemäße Diensthandlungen kaum verständlich, wie ein Blick auf die Erläuterungen zum OECD-Übereinkommen beweist[480]. Dort heißt es, dass „kleinere Zahlungen" zur „Erleichterung" keine Zahlungen seien, die geleistet werden, um einen Auftrag oder einen sonstigen unbilligen Vorteil zu erlangen oder zu behalten, und somit nicht strafbar seien. Diese Regelung kann aber nur Bedeutung erlangen, wenn auch rechtmäßige Diensthandlungen des Amtsträgers in den strafgesetzlichen Anwendungsbereich einbezogen werden sollen[481]. Keinesfalls können die Erläuterungen zum OECD-Übereinkommen im Sinne eines straflosen Freiraums sozialadäquater Bestechungen nach § 334 interpretiert werden[482]. Der mit dem Institut der Sozialadäquanz in enger Verwandtschaft stehende Gedanke der Geeignetheit des Vorteils, einen Amtsträger zu einer rechtmäßigen Diensthandlung veranlassen zu können, lässt sich nur bei den Delikten der Vorteilsannahme und -gewährung nach §§ 331, 333 als mögliches tatbestandliches Abgrenzungskriterium der strafbaren von straflosen Handlungsalternativen anführen. Der deutsche Gesetzgeber hat sich demnach entgegen entsprechender internationaler Vorgaben und in nicht nachvollziehbarer Auslegung der Erläuterungen zum OECD-Übereinkommen für die Ausgrenzung pflichtgemäßer Amtshandlungen im IntBestG entschieden.

c) Stellungnahme

Die internationale Angleichung des Strafrechts bei der länderübergreifenden Korruptionsbekämpfung schreitet erkennbar voran[483] und hat Mindeststandards gesetzt, welche in die nationalen Strafbestimmungen aufgenommen werden. Ob mit der Beschränkung des Anwendungsbereichs des EUBestG und des IntBestG auf künftige pflichtwidrige Diensthandlungen nur ein Zwischenschritt hin zu einer umfassenden, rechtmäßige Diensthandlungen einschließenden internationalen Bekämpfungsstrategie erfolgt ist oder aber darin eher ein Wandel in der Auffassung über die Sanktionierung von Bestechungshandlungen gesehen werden kann, wird erst mit der weiteren internationalen Strafrechtsangleichung zuverlässig bewertet werden können. Jedenfalls dürfte angesichts der nationalen gesetzgeberischen Möglichkeiten und deren tatsächlicher Inanspruchnahme in den beiden Gesetzen, die mit dem KorrBekG nach außen dokumentierte Überzeugungskraft von der Bedeutung der strafrechtlichen Sanktionierung auch vorteilsbehafteter pflichtgemäßer Diensthandlungen deutlich gelitten haben, zumal sich mit der Lockerung der Unrechtsvereinbarung

479 BT-Drs. 13/10428, S. 6.

480 S. Nr. 9 der Erläuterungen, BT-Drs. 13/10428, S. 23.

481 Vgl. Korte, wistra 1999, S. 81 (87); Pelz, StrafFo 2000, S. 300 (304).

482 Vgl. aber Gänßle, NStZ 1999, S. 543 (545).

483 Zu den Möglichkeiten s. Pieth, ZStW 109 (1997), S. 756 (761 ff.).

die im Hinblick auf eine Angleichung an europäische Standards konträre Entwicklung eher vertieft hat, wie der folgende Vergleich zeigen wird.

2. Rechtsvergleich nationaler Rechtsordnungen im Hinblick auf die Rechtsgutsfrage und die Unrechtsvereinbarung

Eingangs der vergleichenden Betrachtung der Strafbestimmungen zur Korruptionsbekämpfung anderer Staaten ist trotz der sich häufig ähnelnden Tatbestandsformulierungen vorweg zu schicken, dass mit dem Herausgreifen einzelner Tatbestandsmerkmale aus dem Kontext der Strafbestimmungen keine Grundlage für umfassende systematische Bewertungen geschaffen ist[484]. Dies ist auch nicht das Ziel dieser Arbeit. Vielmehr sollen zum einen Belege und Ansatzpunkte zu Schutzzweckerwägungen anderer Staaten herausgestellt werden, um Abweichungen oder Parallelitäten zu den deutschen Strafvorschriften sichtbar zu machen. Darüber hinaus sollen mit der Erkundung des zentralen Tatelements der tatbestandlichen Verknüpfung von Vorteil und Amtshandlung in den Strafvorschriften der einzelnen Nationalstaaten Hinweise erlangt werden, welcher dogmatische Ansatz zur Begründung der Strafbarkeit von Vorteilsannahme und -gewährung im Rahmen pflichtgemäßer Amtshandlungen gewählt wurde.

a) Ansatzpunkte für einen Rechtsgüterschutz

aa) Verallgemeinerungsfähiger Grundgedanke?

Ausgehend vom Meinungsstreit in Deutschland, der in seinen Eckpositionen auf der einen Seite mit dem „Vertrauensschutz" und andererseits mit der „Funktionsfähigkeit der staatlichen Verwaltung" unterschiedlich ausgerichtete Schutzzweckerwägungen beinhaltet, stellt sich die Frage nach dem Standort eines gemeinsamen Nenners im Vergleich zu den in anderen Staaten vertretenen Auffassungen. Eine Vergleichsgrundlage ergibt sich aus den im Kernstrafrecht enthaltenen, den §§ 331, 333 nachgebildeten Strafvorschriften der einzelnen Länder.

aaa) Italien

In Italien ist die Rechtsgutsfrage in Rspr. und Schrifttum umstritten. Während die Rspr. generell das einwandfreie Funktionieren und die Unparteilichkeit sowie Korrektheit der öffentlichen Verwaltung geschützt sieht, unterscheidet das überwiegende Schrifttum zwischen dem Rechtsgüterschutz bei der einfachen Bestechung i.S. rechtmäßiger Amtshandlungen (Unparteilichkeit der öffent-

---

[484] Umfassend die Arbeit von Überhofen, Korruption und Bestechungsdelikte im staatlichen Bereich, 1999, S. 239 ff. und insbesondere S. 455 ff.

lichen Verwaltung) und dem bei der schweren Bestechung (Unparteilichkeit als auch einwandfreies Funktionieren der öffentlichen Verwaltung)[485].

bbb) Österreich

Nach der in Österreich geführten Diskussion soll zum einen allgemein die Verletzung der Amtspflichten vermieden und zum anderen die Ordnungsgemäßheit der Verwaltung sichergestellt werden[486].

ccc) Frankreich

Bei der passiven Bestechung steht die Rechtschaffenheit des Beamten und damit die Integrität der Verwaltung insgesamt als geschütztes Rechtsgut im Vordergrund, bei der aktiven Bestechung liegt der Schwerpunkt mehr in der Funktionsfähigkeit der öffentlichen Verwaltung wegen deren befürchteter Beeinträchtigung[487].

ddd) Spanien

Das spanische Schrifttum unterscheidet zwischen aktiver und passiver Bestechung. Das Rechtsgut der aktiven Bestechung besteht in dem Respekt gegenüber dem normalen und ordnungsgemäßen Gang der staatlichen Organe, während das Rechtsgut der passiven Bestechung in der wissenschaftlichen Literatur einerseits mit der Integrität der öffentlichen Verwaltung, andererseits mit deren Unparteilichkeit begründet wird[488].

eee) Griechenland

Nach allgemeiner Übereinstimmung in Literatur und Rspr. besteht der Schutzzweck der Bestechungstatbestände in der Integrität des Amtes und seiner Funktionstüchtigkeit, nach vereinzelt vertretener Ansicht in der unverfälschten Willensbildung des Staates[489].

fff) Portugal

Einer entsprechenden portugiesischen Tradition folgend wird das Rechtsgut in der Gesetzlichkeit der Verwaltung gesehen[490].

---

485 Hein in Eser (Fn. 410), S. 225.
486 Überhofen in Eser (Fn. 410), S. 389.
487 Barth in Eser (Fn. 410), S. 116/117.
488 Hoffmann in Eser (Fn. 410), S. 580/581.
489 Papacharalambous in Eser (Fn. 410), S. 178/179.
490 Hünerfeld in Eser (Fn. 410), S. 448.

ggg) Türkei

Nach türkischem Recht wird das Vertrauen des Bürgers in einen korrekten Ablauf der Verwaltung geschützt. Daneben besteht Rechtsgüterschutz im Hinblick auf ein korrektes Handeln in der Verwaltung und dem damit korrespondierenden Ansehen der Verwaltung sowie hinsichtlich der Bewahrung des Bürgers vor Schaden durch Amtsmissbrauch[491].

hhh) Niederlande

Das niederländische Recht unterscheidet bei der Rechtsgutsbestimmung sehr differenziert nach aktiver und passiver sowie einfacher und schwerer Bestechung. Bei der einfachen passiven Bestechung, bei der der Beamte keine Dienstpflichten verletzt, steht der Schutz des Vertrauens der Bürger in die Objektivität der staatlichen Entscheidung im Vordergrund, bei der schweren passiven Bestechung der Schutz dieser Objektivität selbst bzw. der Schutz vor Verleitung zu amtswidrigem Handeln[492]. Das geschützte Rechtsgut bei der aktiven Bestechung besteht im ordentlichen Funktionieren behördlicher Organe[493].

iii) Japan

Nach Auffassung der obersten Gerichte Japans und der herrschenden Meinung setzt sich das Rechtsgut aus einem objektiven und einem subjektiven Element zusammen. Danach ist die Unparteilichkeit des Amtsträgers bei der Ausübung seiner Dienstpflichten einerseits als objektiver Aspekt und das Vertrauen der Gesellschaft allgemein in diese Unparteilichkeit andererseits als subjektives Kriterium geschützt[494].

jjj) USA

Die Bestrafung der Bestechung von Staatsbediensteten erfolgt in der Regel nach Bundesrecht, obwohl die Gesetzgebungskompetenz für das materielle Strafrecht bei den Einzelstaaten liegt[495]. Schutzzweck der Bestechungsdelikte ist die Integrität der öffentlichen Verwaltung, der Gerichte und der Gesetzgebung[496].

---

491 Tellenbach in Eser (Fn. 410), S. 627.
492 Van de Reyt in Eser (Fn. 410), S. 362.
493 Van de Reyt in Eser (Fn. 410), S. 363.
494 Lenz in Eser (Fn. 410), S. 288.
495 Benseler in Eser (Fn. 410), S. 665.
496 Benseler in Eser (Fn. 410), S. 666.

kkk) China, Rußland und Polen

In China wird mit der Bestrafung der Vorteilsannahme nach herrschender Meinung das ordnungsgemäße Handeln des Staatsapparats und dessen guter Ruf geschützt[497].

In Rußland schützen die Bestechungstatbestände die Autorität des Staatsapparats und die Rechtsordnung im Allgemeinen[498].

Die polnischen Strafvorschriften bei Amtsträgerbestechung schützen das rechtmäßige Funktionieren der staatlichen, gesellschaftlichen und sonstigen Institutionen[499].

lll) Schweden

Die Reformgesetzgebung in Schweden hat in den siebziger Jahren einen interessanten Weg beschritten, indem sie der Überlegung einer gemeinsamen Strafvorschrift für Korruption im öffentlichen und privatwirtschaftlichen Bereich in der Erkenntnis gefolgt ist, dass die gesamtgesellschaftlichen schädlichen Auswirkungen in beiden Bereichen annähernd gleich seien und eine zunehmende Einebnung der Unterschiede sowohl beim Aufgabenspektrum als auch bei der Ausgestaltung der Anstellungsverhältnisse im Vergleich der Privatwirtschaft zum öffentlichen Dienst zu beobachten wäre[500]. Danach ist gemeinsam geschütztes Rechtsgut der Bestechungstatbestände das Interesse des (öffentlichen wie privaten) Arbeit- oder Auftraggebers an einer loyalen und von dritter Seite unbeeinflussten Aufgabenerfüllung durch seine Arbeitnehmer oder Beauftragten[501]. Eingebunden ist auch der Schutz der Integrität des öffentlichen Dienstes und der Allgemeinheit als sein eigentlicher Auftraggeber sowie der Schutz des gesellschaftlichen Interesses an einem freien Wettbewerb im Wirtschaftsleben[502]. Dieser Weg einheitlicher Strafbestimmungen für den privaten und öffentlichen Bereich hat sich offenkundig bewährt[503].

bb) Ergebnis

Auffällig ist zunächst die im Vergleich zu Deutschland in den meisten genannten Ländern sehr zurückhaltend geführte Diskussion um das geschützte Rechts-

---

497 Richter in Eser (Fn. 410), S. 32.
498 Lammich in Eser (Fn. 410), S. 478.
499 Weigend in Eser (Fn. 410), S. 434.
500 Cornils in Eser (Fn. 410), S. 505/506.
501 Cornils in Eser (Fn. 410), S. 510.
502 Cornils in Eser (Fn. 410), S. 510.
503 Cornils in Eser (Fn. 410), S. 506.

gut. Wenn überhaupt dann nur nachrangige Bedeutung hat die Frage offensichtlich in England[504]. Andererseits lässt sich ein Konsens im Hinblick auf den bei fast allen Ländern[505] vorzufindenden Grundgedanken feststellen, der in der tragenden Bedeutung der Objektivität und der Ordnungsgemäßheit staatlichen Verwaltens zum Ausdruck kommt[506]. Wesentlich ist demnach das objektive Moment dieser im Grundtenor vergleichbaren Schutzzweckerwägungen. Nur ganz vereinzelt steht der Vertrauensgedanke im Vordergrund[507], teilweise wird er als zusätzlicher oder mittelbarer Schutzzweck angeführt[508]. Darüber hinaus gibt es wie dargestellt Differenzierungen im Detail, wobei sich hier vor allem der schwedische Ansatz abgrenzt, der insoweit von dem in anderen Ländern geteilten Grundgedanken der Trennung der Schutzrichtungen bei Delikten im Privatbereich von denen im öffentlichen Sektor abweicht. Die in Deutschland bereits seit Jahren intensiv betriebene Privatisierung von staatlichen Aufgabenbereichen wird auch in Zukunft kaum rückläufig tendieren und dem schwedischen Ansatz insoweit Argumentationshilfe liefern, als die Grenzlinien unterschiedlich schützenswerter Teilbereiche, der freie Wettbewerb im Privatbereich und die Integrität des staatlichen Bereichs, weiter zusammenwachsen werden. Im Ergebnis ist festzuhalten, dass im internationalen Vergleich ein primär funktionsbezogener Ansatz zum geschützten Rechtsgut der Bestechungsdelikte vertreten wird, der auch der hier vertretenen Ansicht nahe kommt.

b) Konzeptioneller Ansatz bezüglich des Tatmerkmals der Unrechtsvereinbarung

aa) Fragestellung

Es geht um die Frage nach den tatbestandsinternen Mechanismen, die bei pflichtgemäßen Amtshandlungen zur Annahme strafbaren Verhaltens führen. Die diesbezügliche Schlüsselrolle kommt der tatbestandlichen Verknüpfung von Vorteil und Amtshandlung zu, die in Deutschland mit dem Begriff der Unrechtsvereinbarung umschrieben wird. Nachdem bei der Neufassung der Bestechungsdelikte eine lebhafte Diskussion zu diesem Tatmerkmal geführt worden ist, stellt sich die Frage nach der Rechtskonstruktion im internationalen Vergleich. Wie streng sind die Anforderungen an das Beziehungsverhältnis ausgestaltet und findet die deutsche Lösung einer Lockerung dieser Unrechtsvereinbarung Entsprechung in anderen Strafrechtsordnungen?

---

504 Huber in Eser (Fn. 410), S. 76, die allenfalls noch die „Reinheit der öffentlichen Amtsmoral" als Schutzzweck ausmachen kann.

505 Eine Ausnahme bilden die sozialistisch geprägten Strafrechtsordnungen mit dem primär geschützten Staatsapparat als solchem.

506 Ähnlich Überhofen in Eser (Fn. 410), S. 729.

507 So im türkischen und im niederländischen Strafrecht.

508 So in Griechenland, Papacharalambous in Eser (Fn. 410), S. 178; in Japan, Lenz in Eser (Fn. 410), S. 288; auch in Frankreich, Barth in Eser (Fn. 410), S. 117.

aaa) Italien

Rspr. und Lehre halten für den Fall pflichtgemäßer Amtshandlungen (einfache Bestechung) eine Unrechtsvereinbarung mit einem synallagmatischen Verhältnis zwischen Vorteil und Amtshandlung für erforderlich[509]. Zur Korrektur des weiten Vorteilsbegriffs wird eine „retribuzione" verlangt, d.h. eine Vergütung oder ein Entgelt und damit ein Angemessenheitsverhältnis zwischen Amtshandlung und Vorteil[510]. Um diese Vergütungsbeziehung überhaupt prüfen zu können, muss die betroffene Amtshandlung vom Inhalt her mindestens konkretisierbar feststehen, wenn auch ihre Ausgestaltung im Einzelnen noch nicht konkret geplant ist[511]. Nicht strafbar ist daher eine Vorteilsgewährung im Hinblick auf eine in keiner Weise konkretisierbare Amtshandlung. Reformbestrebungen mit dem Ziel des Verzichts auf diese Voraussetzung sind wohl nicht zuletzt an der massiven Kritik aus der Wissenschaft zunächst gescheitert[512].

bbb) Österreich

Das österreichische Strafgesetzbuch erfordert das Kriterium einer Beziehung zwischen Zuwendung und Amtshandlung, ohne aber eine Unrechtsvereinbarung im Sinne des deutschen Strafrechts vorauszusetzen[513]. Dabei muss nach herrschender Meinung die erstrebte Amtshandlung zwischen den Parteien in groben Umrissen feststehen[514]. Auch in Österreich wird somit auf die Konkretisierbarkeit der Amtshandlung abgestellt, wobei der erforderliche Konkretisierungsgrad nicht näher thematisiert wird. Aus dieser verbleibenden Unbestimmtheit der Abgrenzungskriterien und aus prozessrechtlichen Gesichtspunkten schließt Überhofen auf eine „tendenzielle Lockerung" der tatbestandlichen Anforderungen insbesondere bei der einfachen Bestechung[515].

ccc) Frankreich

Die französischen Strafvorschriften erfordern für die passive und aktive Handlungsform ein zeitliches Vorausgehen der Vorteilsannahme bzw. -gewährung

---

509 Hein in Eser (Fn. 410), S. 236.
510 Hein in Eser (Fn. 410), S. 231 f.
511 Hein in Eser (Fn. 410), S. 236.
512 Hein in Eser (Fn. 410), S. 247.
513 Überhofen in Eser (Fn. 410), S. 396 ff.: in der Terminologie ist von „Motivationszusammenhang" oder einem „Konnex" die Rede.
514 Überhofen in Eser (Fn. 410), S. 397/398; Ähnliches gilt für die Schweiz und für Liechtenstein, Überhofen (Fn. 272), S. 347.
515 Die Indizienbeweisführung geht so weit, dass ein Zusammenhang zwischen Vorteil und Amtshandlung bereits angenommen wird, wenn sich vernünftigerweise keine anderen Gründe für die Zuwendung finden lassen als der bestehende dienstliche Kontakt, Überhofen in Eser (Fn. 410), S. 399.

vor der mit ihr in Beziehung stehenden Amtshandlung, was zur Straflosigkeit der nachträglichen Belohnung für eine vorgenommene oder unterlassene Amtshandlung führt[516]. Aus dieser zeitlichen Reihenfolge wird die Notwendigkeit einer kausalen Verknüpfung zwischen Vorteil und Amtshandlung gefolgert, darüber hinaus werden aber neben dem allgemeinen Tatvorsatz keine weiteren (subjektiven) Anforderungen an die Unrechtsvereinbarung oder die Konkretisierbarkeit der Amtshandlung gestellt[517].

ddd) Spanien

Die spanische Rspr. und Lehre unterscheidet wie bei der Rechtsgutsfrage zwischen aktiver und passiver Bestechung, beurteilt die Deliktsstrukturen insgesamt aber uneinheitlich und zum Teil widersprüchlich[518]. Der Begriff der Amtshandlung als objektives Tatbestandsmerkmal wird nicht näher definiert, so dass die Frage nach dem Erfordernis der Individualisierung unbeantwortet bleibt. Allein die Kausalität zwischen Zuwendung und Amtshandlung wird für erforderlich gehalten, eine Übereinkunft i.S. einer Unrechtsvereinbarung dagegen nicht[519].

eee) Griechenland

Die Rechtslage in Griechenland ähnelt sehr der deutschen vor Inkrafttreten des KorrBekG. Für die Unrechtsvereinbarung wird keine vertragsmäßige Willensbekundung beider Seiten vorausgesetzt, sondern es genügt ein Äquivalenzverhältnis zwischen Vorteil und Amtshandlung i.S. einer Übereinkunft bzw. Wissensgemeinschaft über den Zweck der Absprache[520]. Der Beamte muss ferner die Vorgehensweise des ihm gegenüber Stehenden zumindest stillschweigend akzeptieren, was bereits dann der Fall sein dürfte, wenn er den Vorteil im Wissen um die erstrebte oder vollzogene Amtshandlung annimmt[521]. Auch muss die Amtshandlung in der Weise konkretisierbar sein, dass die inhaltliche Bestimmung der ins Auge gefassten Tätigkeit ohne genaue Fixierung auf Zeitpunkt und Vorgehensweise die Amtshandlung in ihren Merkmalen hervorhebt[522].

---

516 Barth in Eser (Fn. 410), S. 122/123.
517 Barth in Eser (Fn. 410), S. 122/123.
518 Vgl. Hoffmann in Eser (Fn. 410), S. 599/600.
519 Hoffmann in Eser (Fn. 410), S. 599/600.
520 Papacharalambous in Eser (Fn. 410), S. 184; in diesem Grundverständnis auch die hier vertretene Auffassung der Rechtslage in Deutschland vor dem KorrBekG.
521 Papacharalambous in Eser (Fn. 410), S. 184.
522 Papacharalambous in Eser (Fn. 410), S. 185.

fff) Portugal

Auch das portugiesische Strafrecht erfordert ein Gegenleistungsverhältnis zwischen Vorteil und anvisierter Amtshandlung, wobei die subjektiven Anforderungen an die Unrechtsvereinbarung weniger streng als im deutschen Recht interpretiert werden[523]. Die Amtshandlung muss konkretisierbar sein, ohne dass sie in allen Einzelheiten vorher festgelegt sein muss[524].

ggg) Türkei

Das türkische Strafrecht hält bei der passiven Bestechung eine Unrechtsvereinbarung für erforderlich, nicht dagegen bei der aktiven Bestechung, bei der ausreicht, dass die Vorteilsgewährung nur angeboten, vom Beamten aber abgelehnt wurde[525]. Eine nach Ort und Zeit konkretisierte Amtshandlung wird aber in jedem Fall vorausgesetzt[526].

hhh) Niederlande

Das niederländische Strafrecht umschreibt das Beziehungsverhältnis zwischen Vorteil und Amtshandlung in Art. 362 nlStGB[527] sehr genau, in dem es das Bewusstsein um das Zusammenhangsverhältnis voraussetzt. Zur Verwirklichung des Tatbestandes reicht die Annahme von Vorteilen für schon vorgenommene Handlungen nicht aus[528]. Die Anforderungen an die Konkretisierbarkeit der Amtshandlung dürften dagegen nach der Tatbestandsformulierung „... in seinem Amt etwas zu tun oder zu unterlassen ...“ nicht allzu hoch gesetzt sein.

iii) Japan

Unterhalb der schwerer wiegenden sog. Auftragsbestechung, bei der die konkrete Bitte an den Amtsträger gerichtet wird, in Bezug auf seine Amtspflichten eine bestimmte Handlung vorzunehmen[529], verlangt der Grundtatbestand der Bestechung nur ein Beziehungsverhältnis zwischen Vorteilsgewährung und Amtshandlung, ohne dass die Amtshandlung konkretisiert zu sein braucht[530]. Bei dieser gelockerten Form der geforderten Unrechtsvereinbarung darf die japanische Besonderheit nicht übersehen werden, nach der der Rahmen sozial

---

523 Hünerfeld spricht daher von einer „pseudosynallagmatischen“ Beziehung, in Eser (Fn. 410), S. 453.

524 Hünerfeld in Eser (Fn. 410), S. 453.

525 Tellenbach in Eser (Fn. 410), S. 632/633.

526 Tellenbach in Eser (Fn. 410), S. 633.

527 Gesetzestext siehe van de Reyt in Eser (Fn. 410), S. 376.

528 Van de Reyt in Eser (Fn. 410), S. 365.

529 Lenz in Eser (Fn. 410), S. 295.

530 Lenz in Eser (Fn. 410), S. 297/298.

üblicher Geschenke aus Dankbarkeit und vor allem Verehrung zu bestimmten Jahreszeiten und Anlässen sehr weit gesteckt ist und in diesen Fällen ein Gegenleistungsverhältnis verneint wird[531].

jjj) USA

Zwei tatbestandliche Abstufungen kennt das amerikanische Bundesrecht am unteren strafbaren Rand der Bestechungsdelikte[532]. Die schwächste Form der Bestechung ist die unerlaubte Beschenkung, die kein Kausalverhältnis zwischen Zuwendung und Amtshandlung erfordert, sondern allein auf die mögliche Beeinflussbarkeit des Amtsträgers abhebt[533]. Die an engere Voraussetzungen anknüpfende eigentliche Bestechung verlangt zwar keine Unrechtsvereinbarung im Wortsinn, immerhin aber eine auf ein Austauschverhältnis („quid pro quo") gerichtete Bestechungsabsicht auf Seiten des Gebenden und das Wissen auf Seiten des Amtsträgers, dass ihm die Zuwendung nicht zustand[534].

kkk) China, Rußland und Polen

In China wird in Bezug auf die Art der Beziehung zwischen Vorteil und Amtshandlung weder die Frage der Kausalität noch die der Anforderungen an die Konkretisierbarkeit der Amtshandlung problematisiert. Bei den einzelnen Tathandlungsalternativen wird die kausale Verknüpfung zwischen Zuwendung und Amtshandlung tatbezogen vorausgesetzt[535].

In Rußland wird wesentlich auf die Konkretisierbarkeit der Amtshandlung abgestellt, nicht dagegen eine auf ein Austauschverhältnis gerichtete Unrechtsvereinbarung vorausgesetzt[536]. Im Rahmen des Tatvorsatzes muss dem Amtsträger allerdings bewusst sein, dass der Geber ihm den Vorteil für die Vornahme oder Unterlassung einer konkretisierbaren Amtshandlung hat zukommen lassen[537].

In Polen schließlich wird für den Grundtatbestand der Vorteilsannahme (Art. 239 § 1 polnStGB) weder eine Unrechtsvereinbarung noch eine Kausalbeziehung zwischen Vorteil und konkretisierter Amtshandlung vorausgesetzt[538].

---

531 Lenz in Eser (Fn. 410), S. 293/297.

532 S. die Generalnorm des § 201 des United States Code – Title 18 Crimes und Criminal Procedure, Benseler in Eser (Fn. 410), S. 689/690.

533 Benseler in Eser (Fn. 410), S. 669.

534 Benseler in Eser (Fn. 410), S. 668/669.

535 Richter in Eser (Fn. 410), S. 40.

536 Lammich in Eser (Fn. 410), S. 482.

537 Lammich in Eser (Fn. 410), S. 481.

538 Weigend in Eser (Fn. 410), S. 436/437.

Maßgeblich wird darauf abgestellt, ob die Vorteilsannahme „im Zusammenhang mit der Erfüllung einer öffentlichen Funktion“ steht, was schon dann anzunehmen ist, wenn die Zuwendung mit dem Ziel der allgemeinen „Klimapflege“ erfolgt[539].

lll) Schweden

In Schweden sind die Anforderungen an das Beziehungsverhältnis zwischen Vorteil und Amtshandlung stark gelockert, da weder eine Unrechtsvereinbarung noch ein Kausalitätszusammenhang zwischen Vorteil und einer konkretisierbaren Amtshandlung vorliegen muss[540]. Der Gesetzgeber stellt auf die Dienstausübung als solche ab und lässt einen äußeren Zusammenhang zwischen Zuwendung und Amtshandlung im Sinne eines dienstlich bestehenden Kontakts ausreichen[541]. Einen Ausgleich für dieses stark gelockerte Unrechtsverhältnis hält das schwedische Korruptionsstrafrecht mit dem Erfordernis der „Ungebührlichkeit“ der Belohnung bereit. Danach kommt es im Rahmen einer Gesamtwürdigung der Tatgeschehnisse darauf an, ob der Vorteil objektiv geeignet ist, den Empfänger in seiner Dienstausübung zu beeinflussen[542]. Prüfungskriterium bildet aber nicht eine festgelegte materielle Wertgrenze, bis zu deren Höhe mögliche Unrechtsabsprachen legalisiert würden, sondern der wirtschaftliche Wert des Vorteils in Abhängigkeit zur Funktion und Stellung des Empfängers. Diese Wertgrenze zur Ungebührlichkeit ist variabel und kann sehr niedrig liegen bei hohen Integritätsanforderungen an die Stellung des Empfängers[543].

bb) Ergebnis

Bei einer – wie hier – an einem Einzelmerkmal orientierten Betrachtung steht nicht die rechtliche Würdigung der Gesamtsystematik der im Kontext zueinander stehenden Einzelvorschriften der ausländischen Rechtsordnungen im Mittelpunkt. Dies würde erfordern, auch alle anderen, der Korruptionsbekämpfung im weiteren Sinne dienenden Strafvorschriften, die in Deutschland keine Entsprechung finden, einzubeziehen. Die daher nicht auszuschließende „Verzerrung“ einer punktuellen Betrachtung hält sich aber in engen Grenzen, da sich der Untersuchungsgegenstand dieser Arbeit auf den äußeren Rand strafbarer Vorteilsannahme in Abgrenzung zu straflosem Verhalten beschränkt und an dieser Stelle durchaus Aussagekraft besitzt.

---

539 Weigend in Eser (Fn. 410), S. 437.
540 Cornils in Eser (Fn. 410), S. 517.
541 Cornils in Eser (Fn. 410), S. 517.
542 Cornils in Eser (Fn. 410), S. 515.
543 Cornils in Eser (Fn. 410), S. 516; ist die Zuwendung dagegen mit der Dienstausübung selbst unmittelbar verbunden, wie bei Arbeitsessen, liegt keine Ungebührlichkeit vor.

Die Betrachtung von mit nationalen Strafbestimmungen vergleichbaren Vorschriften in anderen Ländern zeigt insgesamt ein uneinheitliches Bild. Gemeinsam scheint aber den Strafvorschriften der genannten Länder zu sein, dass die dogmatische Verwurzelung des Tatmerkmals der Unrechtsvereinbarung nicht in dem Maße vertieft ist und dem Bedeutungsgehalt entspricht wie dies im deutschen Strafrecht der Fall ist[544].

Von den untersuchten Ländern enthalten das amerikanische Bundesrecht und das polnische Strafrecht einen gegenüber der deutschen Rechtslage erweiterten Strafbarkeitsbereich[545]. Dies ist Folge des Verzichts auf die Anforderung eines Beziehungsverhältnisses zwischen Vorteil und Amtshandlung als auch auf die Konkretisierbarkeit der Amtshandlung selbst. Kernaussage dieser Strafvorschriften ist somit die strafrechtliche Sanktionierung der verbotenen Geschenkannahme, die in ursächlichem äußeren Zusammenhang mit der Amtsstellung des Vorteilsempfängers steht.

Andere Länder, die eine gegenüber deutschem Recht vergleichbare Absenkung der Anforderungen an die Bestimmtheit oder Konkretisierbarkeit der Amtshandlung vorsehen, fangen diese Lockerung an anderer Stelle mit der Beschränkung der Strafbarkeit auf zukünftige Amtshandlungen[546] oder mit einem normativen Korrektiv wie der „Ungebührlichkeit" im schwedischen Recht[547] wieder auf[548]. Die vom deutschen Recht sich unterscheidende italienische Lösung stellt als Korrektiv auf eine Prüfung der Angemessenheit des Vorteils in Bezug auf die Amtshandlung ab[549].

In der überwiegenden Anzahl der hier genannten Rechtsordnungen wird eine kausale Beziehung zwischen Vorteil und Amtshandlung vorausgesetzt, bei der der Bezugspunkt eine hinreichend konkretisierbare Amtshandlung erfordert. Die Unterschiedlichkeit der tatbestandlichen Ausprägung im Einzelnen erlaubt aber keine isolierte Wertung und Einstufung zur deutschen Regelmaterie. Ein tendenzielles Übergewicht in den dogmatischen Ansätzen hin zu einer ersatzlosen allgemeinen Lockerung der Anforderungen an das tatbestandliche Unrechtsverhältnis lässt sich aber nicht feststellen.

---

544 Ähnlich Überhofen in Eser (Fn. 410), S. 745.

545 Unklar insoweit die spanischen Regelungen, s. o. S. 103.

546 So die französischen Strafvorschriften, s. o. S. 102.

547 Oben S. 106.

548 Im japanischen Recht sind die Grenzen sozial üblicher Zuwendungen aufgrund der landesweiten Sitten und Gebräuche weit gesteckt und begrenzen auf diese Weise die Strafbarkeit.

549 Oben S. 102.

IV. Ergebnis Teil A

Die Untersuchung der subjektiven Tatumstände in der Rechtsentwicklung vom RStGB über das EGStGB von 1974 bis zum KorrBekG von 1997 hat gezeigt, dass durch die höchstrichterliche Rspr. des RG und des BGH und nachfolgend durch Eingriffe des Gesetzgebers eine sukzessive Ausweitung der Strafbarkeitsgrenzen bei den Bestechungsdelikten an zwei Einbruchstellen vorgenommen wurde. Die erste Einbruchstelle besteht in der materiell-rechtlichen Vorverlegung der Strafbarkeit in das Gefährdungsvorfeld des eigentlichen Unrechtsbereichs. Ein Beispiel liefern die mit dem EGStGB neu geschaffenen Absätze 3 der §§ 332, 334. Die zweite noch bedeutendere normative Einbruchstelle besteht in einer nach und nach vollzogenen Entkernung der tatbestandlichen Voraussetzungen der Bestechungsdelikte seit den Entscheidungen RGSt 74, 251 und 77, 75. Zusammenfassend sind zu nennen:

Das von der herrschenden Meinung herangezogene Schutzgut des „Vertrauens der Allgemeinheit in die Lauterkeit des öffentlichen Dienstes“[550] bildet mit seinem subjektiven Einschlag die Grundlage für alle Bestrebungen nach Ausweitung der Tatbestände. Vertrauen geht allzu schnell verloren und ist nur schwer wieder zurückzugewinnen. So kann jeder Vertrauensdefizite auslösende Verstoß gegen beamtenrechtliche Regelungen als Anlass für die Forderung nach schärferen Strafgesetzen dienen. Dies kann nur vermieden werden, wenn man das Rechtsgut der Bestechungsdelikte in der Weise objektiviert wie es hier vorgeschlagen wird[551].

Mit der gesetzlichen Festschreibung der vom BGH entwickelten Grundsätze zur Vollendung der Tat beim Ermessensbeamten[552] wurde die Vorverlegung der Strafbarkeit in den §§ 332 Abs. 3 und 334 Abs. 3 mit subjektiven Tatelementen wie dem „Sichbereiterklären“ und dem „Bestimmungsversuch“ konzipiert, die in der tatrichterlichen Subsumtion zu erheblichen Schwierigkeiten auf der Nachweisseite und zu dogmatischen Unschlüssigkeiten bei den subjektiven Vorbehalten oder bei Fehlvorstellungen beim Tatverdächtigen führen[553].

Bei der Unrechtsvereinbarung erfolgte der erste Schritt einer Entkernung ihrer ursprünglichen Bestandteile durch die oben genannten Entscheidungen des RG. In diesen wurde beim Ermessensbeamten auf die konkrete Feststellung des inneren Willensbildungsprozesses im Hinblick auf eine denkbare, auf Bevorzugung des Vorteilgebers gerichtete Beeinflussung durch die Vorteilsannahme verzichtet. Die Annahme des Vorteils sollte ausreichen, um die Beeinflussung

550 Vgl. BGHSt 30, 46 (48).
551 S. o. S. 53 ff.
552 BGHSt 15, 239.
553 S. o. S. 62 ff.

der Amtsperson regelmäßig für gegeben ansehen zu können. Auch der BGH hat sich an einem Abbau subjektiver Prüfkriterien beim Gegenleistungsverhältnis beteiligt. In BGHSt 10, 237 hat er sich bei der Handlungsalternative des „Forderns" darauf festgelegt, dass die Erkennbarkeit des Forderungsinhalts beim Adressaten nicht gegeben sein müsse. Den letzten gewichtigen Schritt hat nun der Gesetzgeber mit einer Lockerung der Anforderungen an den Verständigungsinhalt innerhalb des Beziehungsverhältnisses getan. Die Unrechtsvereinbarung setzt nur noch voraus, dass die Beteiligten den Vorteil als für die Dienstausübung hingegeben ansehen. Auch hier ist eine Rückführung subjektiver Tatelemente bezogen auf das Merkmal der bis dahin erforderlichen Konkretisierung bzw. Konkretisierbarkeit der Amtshandlung erfolgt.

Neben dieser Zurückdrängung tatbestandlicher Voraussetzungen sind aber auch Unstimmigkeiten bei der Rechtsauslegung auszumachen.

Die Handlungsalternative der „Annahme" eines Vorteils sowohl als materiellrechtlicher Bezugspunkt für die ihr zugrunde liegende Unrechtsvereinbarung als auch als prozessuales Beweisindiz für Rückschlüsse auf Vorstellungen und Motive der Tatverdächtigen kollidiert mit der unterschiedlichen Bewertung geheimer Vorbehalte beim Vorteilsnehmer und mit dem Rechtsgutsansatz der h.M. vom „Vertrauensschutz". Die von der Rspr. beim Merkmal des „Sichbereiterklärens" in § 332 Abs. 3 grundsätzlich für unbeachtlich gehaltenen geheimen Vorbehalte beim Tatverdächtigen sollen andererseits beachtlich sein, wenn es beim Merkmal der „Annahme" eines Vorteils um die Frage des endgültigen Behaltenwollens des Vorteils geht, obwohl die Gefahr eines handlungsbedingten Vertrauensverlustes beim neutralen Beobachter in beiden Fällen gleich besteht[554].

Die normative Schwachstelle der Bestechungsdelikte liegt im Wirkbereich der subjektiven Tatumstände, deren Beweisschwierigkeiten den Gesetzgeber im Jahre 1997 erneut zu Gesetzesänderungen veranlasst haben, um die strafprozessuale Beweisproblematik zu entschärfen. In Teil B dieser Arbeit werden die Konsequenzen der gesetzgeberischen Änderungen näher untersucht. Im Mittelpunkt steht dabei die Frage, ob das berechtigte Anliegen einer umfassenden Bekämpfung der Korruption inzwischen zu einer Überdehnung der Straftatbestände geführt hat, die auch vom ultima ratio-Gedanken des Strafrechts nicht mehr getragen wird.

Aus einer Betrachtung der nationalen Gesetzgebung zur Bekämpfung der internationalen Korruption und einer vergleichenden Untersuchung ausländischer Strafvorschriften sind zwei kriminalpolitisch interessante Erkenntnisse herauszulesen: Einmal die gesetzgeberische Überlegung, beim EUBestG und beim

554 S. o. S. 59 ff.

IntBestG die Vorteilsannahme oder -gewährung für pflichtgemäße Amtshandlungen nicht unter Strafe zu stellen. Die von dieser Entscheidung ausgehende Signalwirkung für die Gewichtung einer Pönalisierung derartiger Handlungen dürfte erheblich sein. Zum anderen ist die in nationalen Strafvorschriften einiger Länder mit einer etwaigen Lockerung des Beziehungsverhältnisses zwischen Vorteil und pflichtgemäßer Amtshandlung verbundene „Auffanglösung" zu erwähnen. Diese beinhaltet, als Ausgleich für tatbestandliche Erweiterungen an anderer Stelle innerhalb oder außerhalb des Tatbestands ein Korrektiv bereitzuhalten bzw. festzuschreiben.

Teil B: Die Auswirkungen des KorrBekG

Dieser Teil der Arbeit setzt sich zum Ziel, Überschneidungen im Grenzbereich zwischen in der strafrechtlichen Bewertung unbedenklichen Zuwendungen[555] und den nach dem KorrBekG strafbewehrten Verhaltensweisen offen zu legen. Es ist der Frage nachzugehen, ob ein Grauzonenbereich besteht, in dem das Ergebnis einer materiell-rechtlichen Prüfung nicht deckungsgleich ist mit der Antwort auf die Frage nach der Strafwürdigkeit derartiger Verhaltensweisen[556]. Sollte demnach die akute Gefahr einer Kriminalisierung nicht strafwürdiger Verhaltensweisen verifiziert werden können, sind strafrechtsinterne oder externe Ausgleichsmechanismen zu erwägen. Die Lebenssachverhalte, die hier untersucht werden, erscheinen besonders geeignet, nicht nur weil sie sich in der wissenschaftlichen Diskussion befinden, sondern weil die strafrechtsdogmatischen Unsicherheiten in diesen Bereichen am größten erscheinen. Es handelt sich im Kern um die Privatfinanzierung staatlicher Aufgaben[557], die die Gefahr unerwünschter Einflussnahmen der Mittelgeber auf staatliche Entscheidungen auslösen kann. Drei Sachverhalte aus den Förderbereichen der Drittmittelforschung und des Sponsoring bilden die Prüfungsgrundlage.

Erster Abschnitt: Die strafrechtliche Subsumtion

I. Die Fälle

1. Fall A

Das Pharma-Unternehmen U übergibt dem städtischen Universitätsklink-Professor P ein modernes Elektronenmikroskop für dessen, U nicht interessierende allgemeine universitäre Forschungsarbeiten in der von beiden Seiten erkannten Hoffnung, die mangelhafte Geräteausstattung des P derart zu verbessern, dass dieser durch den technikbedingten schnelleren Abschluss seiner eigenen Forschungsarbeiten mehr Zeit für die Grundlagenforschung erwirtschaften kann, für die U der Uniklinik Geld zur Verfügung gestellt hat. P vergisst, der Universitätsverwaltung den Erhalt des Mikroskops anzuzeigen.

---

555 Grundsätzlich ist hier das Prüfungskriterium die Sozialadäquanz, Beispiele bei König, JR 1997, S. 397 (398/399); grundsätzlich dazu Geerds (Fn. 42), S. 73 ff.; Gribl (Fn. 265), S. 97 ff.

556 Kerner/Rixen, GA 96, S. 355 (362), spricht von „Gemengelage“, aus der das Strafrecht das Strafwürdige herausfiltern müsse.

557 Vgl. Lüderssen, JZ 1997, S. 112.

2. Fall B

Das Pharma-Unternehmen U überlässt der Uniklinik einen größeren Geldbetrag für die Grundlagenforschung des Klinikprofessors P in der Erwartung, neue Erkenntnisse im Hinblick auf eine Verbesserung ihrer am Markt befindlichen Produkte (Medikamente) zu erlangen. Darüber hinaus erhofft sich U auch einen engen wissenschaftlichen Kontakt zur Uniklinik und zu P und mittelfristig eine bevorzugte Abnahme ihrer vorhandenen oder künftig mit Hilfe der Grundlagenforschung verbesserten Medikamente durch die Uniklinik zu dann gegenüber dem Marktpreis vergünstigten Abnahmepreisen. Alle Beteiligten kennen diese „Geschäftsgrundlage". Der zwischen den Parteien geschlossene Vertrag beschreibt nur den Forschungsauftrag und die dafür vorgesehene Drittfinanzierung. P möchte verständlicherweise sein berufliches Renommee mit der Grundlagenforschung über die Klinikgrenzen hinaus ausbauen.

3. Fall C

Der örtliche Bauunternehmer B will das kommunale Theater mit einem höheren Geldbetrag unterstützen, damit es eine geplante Inszenierung zu niedrigeren Eintrittspreisen durchführen kann. B übergibt dem Bürgermeister M, der Vorsitzender des Theatervereins in seiner Funktion als Bürgermeister ist, das Geld in der beiderseitigen Übereinkunft, dass M nun mit dem Geld die Organisation und Durchführung des Theaterstücks in die Wege leiten und das Geld für diese Kosten verbraucht werden soll. Dies geschieht auch. Im Gegenzug vereinbaren beide, dass in den Programmheften und auf den Eintrittskarten B als Sponsor mit seinem Namen aufgeführt wird. B und M sind privat eng befreundet. B hat auch schon einige Bauvorhaben für die Kommune nach ordnungsgemäßer Ausschreibung des Bauvorhabens und Zuschlagserteilung abgewickelt.

II. Bewertung

1. Bewertung außerhalb der Strafrechtsordnung

Auf den ersten Blick mag man bei den genannten Fällen kaum glauben, dass hier mit der Einleitung von Ermittlungsverfahren durch die Strafverfolgungsbehörden wegen des Verdachts der Vorteilsannahme und Vorteilsgewährung gerechnet werden muss. Der Eindruck von Käuflichkeit oder einer ernsthaften Gefährdung objektiver Amtsführung stellt sich insbesondere vor dem Hintergrund zunehmender gesellschaftlicher Billigung nicht ein. Denn überall dort, wo der Staatshaushalt in seinen Mittelansätzen notleidend geworden ist oder der Staat sich aus privatisierungsfähigen Aufgabenbereichen zurückzieht und auf die Wahrnehmung staatlicher Kernaufgaben besinnt, springen ersatzweise Private zur Finanzierung allgemein anerkennenswerter Förderzwecke ein. Unzweifelhaft besteht ein allgemeiner gesellschaftspolitischer Konsens darüber, dass sowohl die durch Drittmittel finanzierten Forschungsvorhaben als auch das von privater Seite angebotene Sponsoring von Kulturvorhaben förderungswürdigen Aufgabenbereichen zuzurechnen sind. Diese Erkenntnis beseitigt aber nicht die Verunsicherung darüber, was im Hinblick auf die normative Unschärfe der Bestechungstatbestände im Rahmen der förderungswürdigen Zusammenarbeit zwischen Privatwirtschaft und staatlichen Einrichtungen erlaubt ist und was nicht[558]. Ein ebenso unsicheres Rechtsgefühl irritiert den Betrachter in seiner Wertung der weitergehenden Motive der an den Austauschbeziehungen Beteiligten. Es fällt ihm schwer, die Verfolgung weitergehender Interessen der Beteiligten rechtlich einzuordnen.

a) Definitionen und Abgrenzungen

aa) Sponsoring

Unter dem Begriff des Sponsoring werden Geldzuwendungen oder geldwerte Leistungen verstanden, die in aller Regel von Unternehmen zur Förderung von Personen oder Einrichtungen u.a. auf den Gebieten der Wissenschaft, des Sports und der Kultur mit der Zielrichtung erbracht werden, eigene unternehmensbezogene Werbung oder Öffentlichkeitsarbeit zu betreiben[559]. Beim Sponsoring besteht ein wechselseitig verpflichtender Vertrag[560], nach dem sich Sponsor und Gesponserter zu einem Tun oder Unterlassen verpflichten, um die Gegenleistung der jeweils anderen Seite zur Verfolgung des eigenen Interesses zu erlangen.

bb) Drittmittelforschung

Unter der sog. Drittmittelforschung sind alle Forschungsvorhaben einer staatlichen Einrichtung zu verstehen, die ganz oder zumindest teilweise von privater Seite, vornehmlich der Industrie, vor allem durch Geldleistungen oder Sachmittelbereitstellung finanziert werden, weil der zuständige staatliche Haushaltsträger mit seinem Forschungsetat die projektgebundene Förderung dieser Forschungsvorhaben jedenfalls nicht in vollem Umfang gewährleisten kann[561]. Die Forschungstätigkeit selbst ist dann die mit dem privaten Geldgeber vereinbarte Gegenleistung für die bereitgestellten Mittel.

558 Vgl. Göben, MedR 1999, S. 345; Lüderssen, JZ 1997, S. 112 (116), der Fälle aus dem „Grauzonen“-Bereich benennt; natürlich kommt den Beweggründen der Handelnden wesentliche Bedeutung für die Beurteilung strafbaren Verhaltens zu: Unterstellt man dem Bürgermeister im Fall C die „böse Absicht“, beim nächsten Bauvorhaben der Kommune den Bauunternehmer als Dank für das Sponsoring bei der Vergabe bevorzugt zu berücksichtigen, steht man inmitten korrupter Verhaltensmuster.

559 Bruhn / Mehlinger, Rechtliche Gestaltung des Sponsorings, S.4.

560 Bruhn / Mehlinger (Fn. 559), S. 54.

561 Vgl. Göben, MedR 1999, S. 345.

cc) Spenden und Schenkungen

Sowohl vom Sponsoring als auch von der Drittmittelforschung zu unterscheiden sind die Begriffe der Schenkung, bei der der Schenkende mit der Absicht einer unentgeltlichen Zuwendung einen anderen aus seinem Vermögen bereichert, und der Spende, die unentgeltlich von privater Seite mit dem Motiv der Unterstützung einer Sache oder einer Partei erbracht wird. Im Unterschied zur Schenkung wird bei der Spende in der Regel eine Spendenbescheinigung ausgestellt.

dd) Fallzuordnung

Nach der Definition liegt beim Sachverhalt B ein Fall der Drittmittelforschung vor, im Sachverhalt C dagegen ein Fall des Sponsorings. Im Fall A ist zwar eine äußere Verknüpfung zwischen der Bereitstellung des Mikroskops und der Finanzierungsbeteiligung von U an der Grundlagenforschung der Uniklinik gegeben, ein vertraglicher Zusammenhang besteht aber nicht. Genauso wenig liegt ein Fall des Sponsorings vor, da mit der Bereitstellung des Mikroskops keine unternehmensbezogene Werbung verfolgt wird. Letztlich liegt aber auch keine eindeutige Schenkung oder Spende vor, da der Überlassung des Mikroskops immerhin eine Erwartung der Parteien gegenübersteht, nämlich die beschleunigte Abwicklung eigener, universitärer Forschungsarbeiten des P mit dem Ziel vorzeitiger Verfügbarkeit für die von U mitfinanzierte Grundlagenforschung. Fall A entzieht sich daher einer klaren Zuordnung. Der Schwerpunkt der Handlungsintention liegt aber auf einer schenkweisen Überlassung des Mikroskops zu Forschungszwecken. Den Charakter einer Schenkung verliert das Verhalten des U nicht dadurch, dass mit ihm eine gewisse „Hoffnung" auf Zeitgewinn für andere Forschungsarbeiten verbunden wird.

b) Billigung durch den Gesetzgeber

Die Frage, ob die verstärkte Heranziehung der Kooperationsformen des Sponsoring und der Drittmittelbereitstellung zur Finanzierung öffentlicher Aufgaben staatspolitisch opportun ist, ist primär von den politisch Verantwortlichen zu entscheiden. Hier ist nach den Rechtsquellen zu fragen, mit denen die Legitimität der genannten Finanzierungsmodelle belegt werden kann.

aa) Sponsoring

Ein der Befürwortung von Sponsoring eher restriktiv gegenüberstehender Beschluss der Konferenz der Präsidentinnen und Präsidenten der Rechnungshöfe des Bundes und der Länder verdeutlicht das mit dieser Förderart verbundene

Gefährdungspotenzial im Hinblick auf eine Einflussnahme Dritter auf die Ausübung der Tätigkeit der öffentlichen Verwaltung[562]. In dem Beschluss werden daher Anforderungen an die Verwaltungen zur Begrenzung des Risikos gestellt: „Die Rechnungshöfe betrachten die Entwicklung des Sponsoring im Bereich der öffentlichen Hände mit Sorge. Sie sind der Auffassung, daß die Verwaltungen sich Richtlinien für die Behandlung des Sponsoring geben müssen, in denen für eine Transparenz des Einsatzes des Sponsoring gesorgt wird. Es ist sicherzustellen, daß die Verwaltung durch den Einsatz dieser Finanzierungsmittel nicht in ein Abhängigkeitsverhältnis gerät und Sponsoring nicht als Einfallstor in die Korruption dienen kann. Die Entgegennahme von Sponsoringmitteln darf nicht den Budgetzielen des Parlaments entgegenstehen und sie muß insgesamt wirtschaftlich sein." Auch die Rechnungshöfe verschließen sich damit letztlich nicht der Rechtswirklichkeit notleidender Staatshaushalte, die das Finanzierungsmodell des Sponsorings zu einem ergänzenden Instrument der Wahrnehmung gesellschaftspolitischer Zielsetzungen haben werden lassen.

Im Bund ist am 14.7.1998 die „Richtlinie der Bundesregierung zur Korruptionsprävention in der Bundesverwaltung" vom 17.6.1998 in Kraft getreten[563]. In dieser Richtlinie ist unter Nr. 18 festgelegt, dass „für die Annahme von Zuwendungen von außerhalb der Dienststelle stehenden Dritten zu Gemeinschaftsveranstaltungen und Gemeinschaftseinrichtungen der Beschäftigten ... die vorherige Zustimmung der obersten Dienstbehörde einzuholen" ist. „Das gleiche gilt für jede Art von freiwilliger materieller Förderung (Sponsoring) zugunsten von Tätigkeiten, Veranstaltungen und Einrichtungen der Dienststelle."

Aus diesem Richtlinieninhalt und einer ergänzenden Empfehlung des Bundesministeriums des Innern zu Nr. 18 dieser Richtlinie kann die grundsätzliche Zulässigkeit dieser Form der Mittelbereitstellung für die Finanzierung staatlicher Aufgaben hergeleitet werden[564].

In einem ressortinternen Entwurf einer „Allgemeinen Verwaltungsvorschrift der Bundesregierung zur Förderung von Tätigkeiten des Bundes durch Leistungen Privater (Sponsoring)"[565] werden bestimmte Voraussetzungen zur Vermeidung jeden Anscheins fremder Einflussnahme auf die öffentliche Verwaltung aufgestellt. Auch die Empfehlung des Bundesministeriums des Innern zu Nr.

---

562 Niederschrift der Konferenz vom 28. bis 30.9.1998 in Mainz.

563 BAnz. S. 9665.

564 Dort heißt es: „Die öffentliche Verwaltung darf sich nicht unbeschränkt dem Sponsoring öffnen, andererseits kann Sponsoring in geeigneten Fällen zur Erreichung von Verwaltungszielen beitragen. Allgemein gültige Regelungen hierfür sind noch nicht aufgestellt."

565 Diese gegenwärtig noch nicht in Kraft getretene Verwaltungsvorschrift soll Nr. 18 der Richtlinie ersetzen.

18 der Richtlinie enthält bestimmte Vorgaben, vor allem im Hinblick auf eine vollständige Transparenz des Umfangs, der Art von Sponsoring und der Sponsoren. Selbstverständlich dürfen daher an die Annahme von Sponsorenleistungen über den Inhalt der Vereinbarung hinaus keine weiteren Pflichten für oder Erwartungen an den Gesponserten entstehen oder darüber hinausgehende Erwartungshaltungen begründet werden.

Diese verständlicherweise zurückhaltende Befürwortung des Sponsorings ändert jedoch nach gegenwärtiger Rechtslage nichts an der grundsätzlich für rechtens erklärten Unterstützungsform dieses Instituts zur Erfüllung öffentlicher Aufgaben.

bb) Drittmittelforschung

Die Zulässigkeit der Gewährung finanzieller Hilfe von dritter Seite für die staatlicherseits regelmäßig unterfinanzierte Forschung und Lehre steht grundsätzlich außer Frage[566]. Den Rahmen für die durch Drittmittel finanzierten Forschungsvorhaben an Universitäten und Unikliniken gibt § 25 HRG vor, flankiert durch die Hochschulgesetze der Länder[567]. Nach § 25 Abs. 1 HRG sind die in der Forschung tätigen Hochschulmitglieder befugt, als Dienstaufgabe auch solche Forschungsvorhaben durchzuführen, die aus Mitteln Dritter finanziert werden. Soweit die Erfüllung anderer Aufgaben der Hochschule dadurch nicht beeinträchtigt wird, besteht sogar ein Rechtsanspruch auf Durchführung entsprechender Drittmittelprojekte[568]. Um Transparenz über den Umfang der eingeworbenen Drittmittel zu schaffen und die einzelnen Hochschulmitglieder von administrativen Aufgaben zu entlasten, sieht § 25 Abs. 4 HRG eine Mittelbewirtschaftung durch die Universität selbst vor[569].

---

566 Ausgehend von der Garantie der Forschungsfreiheit des Art. 5 Abs. 3 Satz 1 GG, die die wissenschaftliche Betätigung gegen staatliche Eingriffe schützt und jedem zusteht, der wissenschaftlich tätig ist oder sein will, vgl. BVerfGE 15, 256 (263 ff.) und 35, 79 (112 ff.); vgl. ferner Ratzel, MedR 1998, S. 98 (99); Dieners, JZ 1998, S. 181 (183/184); Pfeiffer, NJW 1997, S. 782 (783); Göben, MedR 1999, S. 345/346; aus den Spezialgesetzen „Arzneimittelgesetz" von 1976 (BGBl. I, S. 2445) und „Medizinproduktegesetz" von 1994 (BGBl. I, S. 1963), nach denen Hersteller von Arzneimitteln und Medizinprodukten vor dem Inverkehrbringen der Produkte diese regelmäßig an Universitätskliniken einer klinischen Prüfung zu unterziehen haben, lässt sich das Gebot enger Zusammenarbeit zwischen Kliniken, Ärzten und Industrie entnehmen, vgl. Pfeiffer, NJW 1997, S. 782 (783); Dieners, JZ 1998, S. 181 (184).

567 Vgl. z.B. § 36 Hess. Hochschulgesetz in der Fassung vom 31. Juli 2000, Gesetz- und Verordnungsblatt des Landes Hessen Teil I, S. 374 (385).

568 Hailbronner, Kommentar zum HRG, § 25 Rn. 6.

569 Hailbronner (Fn. 568), § 25 Rn. 17.

Die sich häufig über einen langen Zeitraum erstreckende enge Zusammenarbeit zwischen Industrie und vor allem Unikliniken führt zwangsläufig zu einem systembedingten Näheverhältnis, das sich einem wechselseitigen Austauschverhältnis mit seinen Risiken gegenseitiger Abhängigkeiten annähern kann. In den Fällen A und B ist eine derartige Wechselseitigkeit in unterschiedlicher Intensität auszumachen. So beabsichtigt das Pharma-Unternehmen im Fall A, mit der schenkweisen Verbesserung der Geräteausstattung des Klinik-Professors zunächst dessen technisches Leistungspotenzial zu erhöhen in der nicht ganz uneigennützigen Hoffnung, damit dessen erhöhte Aufmerksamkeit und zeitliche Einsatzbereitschaft für die mitfinanzierte Grundlagenforschung zu erwirken. § 25 Abs. 3 HRG will bei all diesen Unterstützungsleistungen Dritter durch entsprechende Anzeige- und Genehmigungspflichten Transparenz schaffen. Dem einzelnen Forschungsträger bleibt damit aber nicht erspart, mit der Einflussnahme auf die Intensität und Ausgestaltung des Beziehungsverhältnisses zum Drittmittelgeber die aus einem solchen Näheverhältnis erwachsenden rechtlichen Risiken für die sachgemäße Abwicklung der Forschungsvorhaben gering zu halten.

c) Zwischenergebnis

Nicht nur aus einem allgemeinen staatlichen Interesse an einer Beteiligung der Privatwirtschaft bei der Bewältigung gesellschaftspolitischer Aufgaben wie Kultur- und Wissenschaftsförderung, sondern explizit durch die Rechtsordnung werden gebräuchliche Förderinstrumente wie Sponsoring und Drittmittelfinanzierung legitimiert. Gegen die den Fällen A, B und C zugrunde liegenden Gestaltungselemente bestehen damit keine grundlegenden Rechtsbedenken. Weder die Bereitstellung eines Elektronenmikroskops zu Forschungszwecken an einen Professor einer mit Grundlagenforschung betrauten Uniklinik, noch die finanzielle Förderung dieser Grundlagenforschung selbst oder die Mittelbereitstellung von privater Seite für eine kommunale Theaterinszenierung weisen für sich betrachtet rechtsfeindlichen Charakter auf. Diese in der Außenwahrnehmung unbedenklich erscheinenden Verhaltensweisen können als objektiver Handlungsbestandteil daher erst im Zusammenwirken mit subjektiven Absichten, Beweggründen und Motiven der handelnden Personen ein Unwerturteil begründen.

2. Prüfung der Strafbarkeit nach § 331

Die drei Fallbeispiele wurden mit dem Versuch einer realitätsnahen Ausgestaltung ausgewählt. Anhand der die Motivationslage der Beteiligten widerspiegelnden Lebenswirklichkeit soll das problematische Näheverhältnis zum Deliktsbereich des § 331 aufgezeigt werden. Die strafrechtliche Prüfung ist auf die Schnittstellen zu konzentrieren, an denen das Risiko einer Straftatbegehung für die handelnden Personen unüberschaubar wird[570]. Der näheren Prüfung werden daher nur diejenigen Subsumtionsbestandteile unterzogen, die im Kontext der tatbestandlichen Unrechtsbeziehung zwischen (Dritt-)Vorteil und Dienstausübung stehen.

Es ließen sich zahlreiche weitere lebensnahe Fallvariationen mit ähnlicher Intention in gänzlich unterschiedlichen Firmenproduktbereichen bilden, die der Gefahr des in § 331 enthaltenen Unwerturteils ausgesetzt wären. Man denke an die notwendigerweise enge Zusammenarbeit zwischen Industrie und Verwaltung beim Aufbau interner Informationstechniksysteme. Auch dort entspricht es allgemeiner Übung, firmeneigene Hilfsmittel zur Erprobung und zum Nachweis der Leistungsfähigkeit der Firmenprodukte der Verwaltung zur Verfügung zu stellen[571]. Das Firmeninteresse besteht dabei einmal in der Verbesserung eigener Marktchancen bei der Auswahlentscheidung der Verwaltung, aber auch in der Produkterprobung im sogenannten Echtbetrieb bei potenziellen Kunden. Andererseits können Kaufentscheidungen der Verwaltung bei Softwareprodukten nur nach langwierigen Erprobungs- und Testvorläufen sinnvoll getroffen werden, so dass auch ein verwaltungsseitiges Interesse an einer Benutzung firmeneigener Arbeits- und Hilfsmittel besteht. Vielfach stehen diese Firmendienstleistungen als vorweggenommene oder zusätzlich gewährte „Arbeitserleichterungen" außerhalb der eigentlichen Vertragsvereinbarungen. Es entspricht dabei der Lebenserfahrung, dass überlassene Hilfsmittel, wie z.B. Laptops, bei Gelegenheit auch für die Erledigung verwaltungsinterner Aufgaben im gegenseitigen Einverständnis eingesetzt werden und derartige „stille" Übereinkünfte die Gefahr eines gegenseitigen Abhängigkeitsverhältnisses bei künftigen Kaufentscheidungen begründen können. Auch hier – wie in anderen gleichgelagerten Fällen – geht es um die grundsätzliche Frage, ob ökonomisch oder gesellschaftspolitisch sinnvolle Gestaltungsprozesse zwischen Staat und Wirtschaft schon aufgrund bestehender Missbrauchsgefahren die Androhung strafrechtlicher Sanktion verdienen. Die Antwort kann nicht ohne Einbeziehung der gewandelten Anforderungen an die Verwaltung wie höhere Effizienz und nachhaltige Wirtschaftlichkeit erfolgen[572].

---

570 Aufgrund der Spiegelbildlichkeit des § 333 zu § 331 gilt dies für alle an der Austauschbeziehung Beteiligten.

571 Z.B. der Laptop, mit dem die Firmensoftware getestet werden kann.

572 Vgl. die Synonyme „Schlanker Staat", „Moderner Staat" und zuletzt „Aktivierender Staat".

a) Sanktionsbedürftigkeit?

aa) Gewandeltes Staatsverständnis

In einer Erklärung des Bundesministeriums des Innern vom März 2000 heißt es: „Die Bundesregierung hat am 1. Dezember 1999 im Kabinett das Leitbild und Programm >Moderner Staat – Moderne Verwaltung< beschlossen. Mit diesem Programm will die Bundesregierung Staat und Verwaltung dem gewandelten Staatsverständnis und den sich veränderten Aufgaben von Regierung und Verwaltung anpassen. Auf der Grundlage der Koalitionsvereinbarung vom 20. Oktober 1998 >Aufbruch und Erneuerung – Deutschlands Weg ins 21. Jahrhundert< wird damit eine neue Ausrichtung für die Modernisierung von Staat und Verwaltung festgelegt. Das Programm enthält vier Prinzipien, die sich aus dem Leitbild des aktivierenden Staates ergeben:

- neue Verantwortungsteilung zwischen Staat und Gesellschaft,
- mehr Bürgerorientierung,
- staatliche Vielfalt,
- effiziente Verwaltung.“[573]

Unter effizienter Verwaltung versteht das BMI eine leistungsstärkere und kostengünstigere staatliche Verwaltung, deren bürokratische Hürden abzubauen seien durch Einführung betriebswirtschaftlicher Instrumente wie Kosten- und Leistungsrechnung und Controlling sowie neuer Informationstechnologien, die wiederum eine schnellere Abwicklung der Verwaltungsarbeit gewährleisten sollen. Hinzu kommen sollen innerbetriebliche Zielvereinbarungen, Budgetierung und Verfahren zu kontinuierlichen Verbesserungsprozessen, die allesamt im Ergebnis zu einer Veränderung der Verwaltungskultur in der Bundesverwaltung führen sollen[574].

Wenn die Bundesregierung – wie geschildert – von einer Anpassung von Staat und Verwaltung an ein gewandeltes Staatsverständnis und von veränderten Aufgabenprofilen der Verwaltung spricht, bedarf dies näherer Erläuterung. Vier Reformbereiche werden benannt, von denen ein Bereich die „bessere Kooperation zwischen Bund, Ländern und Kommunen sowie zwischen Staat und Privaten“ betrifft[575]. Flankierend beabsichtigt die Bundesregierung die Einführung

---

573 So die Veröffentlichung des BMI unter der Internet-Adresse (April 2001) >www.staat-modern.de<.

574 S. Fn. 573.

575 Durch das BMI veröffentlicht unter der Internet-Adresse (Oktober 2001) >www.staat-modern.de<; die drei anderen Reformbereiche betreffen die „höhere Akzeptanz und Wirksamkeit von Recht“, eine „leistungsstarke, kostengünstige und transparente Verwaltung“ und nicht zuletzt „motivierte Beschäftigte“.

von modernem Management in der Bundesverwaltung u.a. durch Implementierung eines umfassenden Qualitätsmanagements zur Steigerung der Wirtschaftlichkeit staatlichen Handelns. Die in diesem staatlichen Veränderungsprozess enthaltenen Flexibilisierungselemente müssen dann aber auch konsequent bis auf die Arbeitsebene des einzelnen Bediensteten herunterreichen. Daraus kann gefolgert werden, dass zu den bislang geltenden beamtenrechtlichen Grundsätzen der gesetz- und ordnungsgemäßen Pflichtenerfüllung sowie der ermessensfehlerfreien Entscheidungsfindung der neue betriebswirtschaftliche Grundsatz des erfolgsbezogenen Tätigwerdens hinzutritt. Unter solchen Kosten-/Leistungs-Gesichtspunkten wird sich das Verwaltungshandeln insgesamt verändern und sich den Parametern der Privatwirtschaft sichtbar annähern.

An dieser Stelle setzt dann ein weiterer gesellschaftspolitischer Veränderungsprozess ein, in dessen Mittelpunkt die neu zu bestimmende Erwartungshaltung und Vertrauensbildung innerhalb der Bevölkerung gegenüber einer transparenten, kunden- und ergebnisorientierten Verwaltung einschließlich dem Handeln ihrer Bediensteten steht.

Kosten- und Nutzengegenüberstellung entstammen dem Sprachgebrauch der Betriebswirtschaftslehre, sie sind aber auch in der Verwaltungspraxis gebräuchliche Vokabeln geworden. Die Bundesverwaltung bedient sich zunehmend projektbezogener Aufgabenbewältigung[576], was darauf hindeutet, dass sie in geeigneten Bereichen inzwischen einer auf internen Zielvereinbarungen beruhenden, zeitlich befristeten und erfolgsorientierten Aufgabenerledigung gegenüber der bisherigen Arbeitsweise den Vorzug gibt, die alle Aufgaben festgelegten Zuständigkeitsbereichen auf Dauer zuweist.

Welche berechtigte Erwartungshaltung der Bevölkerung sich nun aus dieser Entwicklung zukünftig konkret ableiten lässt, hängt nicht unwesentlich mit dem Einsatz und der Reichweite betriebswirtschaftlicher Instrumente im Verwaltungsalltag zusammen. Privatisierte Staatsunternehmen wie Post und Telekom konfrontieren den einzelnen Bürger mit dem Leitbild der kooperativen Kundenorientierung, aber auch mit dem für den Bürger häufig nachteilig empfundenen Kosten-/Nutzen-Aspekt der Marktwirtschaft. Bedienstete dieser ehemaligen Staatsunternehmen werden nicht mehr als Staatsdiener mit dem ihnen abverlangten Amtsethos wahrgenommen, obwohl auch in diesen Unternehmen Amtsträger noch zahlreich vertreten sind. Die Erwartungshaltung des Einzelnen ist danach eng verbunden mit der Frage der Organisationsform, der Aufgabenstellung und der Art der Aufgabenerledigung.

---

[576] Nach einer Erklärung des BMI vom 10.3.2000 plant die Bundesregierung die Umsetzung ihres Modernisierungsprogramms mit insgesamt 38 begleitenden Leit- und Ergänzungsprojekten.

Parallel hierzu wird sich der bei der Rechtsgutsdiskussion bei den Bestechungsdelikten stets bemühte Vertrauensschutzgedanke einer Wandlung jedenfalls in der Rechtswirklichkeit jener Verwaltungsbereiche unterziehen, die nicht dem engeren Kreis hoheitlicher Tätigkeiten angehören[577] und daher den Einsatz wirtschaftsnaher Förderinstrumente wie Drittmittelfinanzierung und Sponsoring erlauben. Die Fälle A, B und C sind daher zunächst im Hinblick auf diesen Schutzzweckgedanken des Vertrauens der Bevölkerung in die Integrität der Verwaltung zu untersuchen, um festzustellen, ob diese normbezogenen Schutzguterwägungen dem heutigen Anforderungsprofil an die Verwaltungspraxis noch standhalten und dementsprechend mit der Erwartungshaltung der Bürger korrespondieren.

bb) Schutzgut des Vertrauens der Bevölkerung in die Integrität der Verwaltung ein verlässliches Kriterium zur Erfassung korruptiven Unrechts?

aaa) Fall A

aaaa) Geschehensablauf (Was passiert wirklich?)

Im Rahmen bestehender vertraglicher Vereinbarungen zwischen der Firma U und der Uniklinik über Grundlagenforschung überlässt die Firma U dem P ein Elektronenmikroskop für dessen allgemeine dienstliche Forschungsarbeiten. In der Praxis hat P immer wieder über die schlechte universitäre Geräteausstattung gegenüber U geklagt und auf den Zusammenhang zwischen verbesserten Arbeitshilfsmitteln und vorzeitiger Verfügbarkeit für die im Interesse der U stehenden Forschungsarbeiten hingewiesen. Natürlich hat U ein Interesse an baldigen Forschungsergebnissen, soweit sie die Arbeiten daran mitfinanziert und auf deren Grundlage sie ihre Produktpalette erneuern will. In einer Kosten- und Nutzen-Abwägung stellt ein einzelnes Mikroskop einen unbedeutenden Kostenfaktor dar. P dagegen hat ein nennenswertes dienstliches Interesse an bestmöglicher Geräteausstattung, die die Effizienz seiner Arbeit insgesamt steigern kann. Was könnte an diesem Geschehensbild verwerflich sein, wenn man berücksichtigt, dass der Staat über benötigte Haushaltsmittel nicht verfügt, die Leistungsanforderungen in der Verwaltung aber betriebswirtschaftlichen Maßstäben unterworfen werden? Mit dem Einsatz des Mikroskops zu dienstlichen Forschungszwecken folgt P dem Gebot verwaltungsökonomischen Verhaltens.

bbbb) Betrachtung von außen

Kann aus diesem Sachverhaltszusammenhang ein verständiger außenstehender Beobachter einen Anfangsverdacht korrupter Verhaltensweise herleiten? Dies erscheint jedenfalls vor dem Eindruck einer sich den Funktionsbedingungen der

---

577 Wie das Justizwesen und die Steuer- und Abgabenverwaltung.

freien Wirtschaft bewusst annähernden Verwaltung höchst zweifelhaft. Der objektivierende Maßstab der Vorstellung des unvoreingenommenen Beobachters für die Begründung eines derartigen „bösen Anscheins“ kann jedenfalls nicht allein auf die Feststellung der Zuwendung eines Forschungshilfsmittels an einen Bediensteten im staatlichen Forschungsbereich reduziert werden. Der Sachzusammenhang vermittelt die Umsetzung betriebswirtschaftlichen Denkens auf der Empfänger- wie auf der Geberseite, weil das zugewendete Hilfsmittel der schnelleren Erledigung anderweitiger dienstlicher Tätigkeiten dienen soll, um Zeitgewinn für die Grundlagenforschung zu erwirtschaften. Einem betriebswirtschaftlichen Prinzipien folgenden Hochschulbetrieb kann nicht der Verdacht unrechtsbegründender Austauschbeziehungen schon dann anhaften, wenn ökonomische und effizienzorientierte Verhaltensmuster tatsächlich praktiziert werden. Das bedeutet aber auch, dass ein Vertrauensverlust in der Bevölkerung in die Integrität der Verwaltung bei der Wahrnehmung derartiger Geschehensabläufe nicht ernsthaft befürchtet werden kann. Diese Bewertung verfestigt sich mit zunehmender Angleichung der bestehenden Vertrauensmaßstäbe in der Bevölkerung mit dem Flexibilisierungsprozess in der öffentlichen Verwaltung. Vertrauensbildung in diesem Sinne ist ein fließender Prozess, der deshalb aber auch die Tauglichkeit und Verlässlichkeit des objektivierten Vertrauensgedankens für die Bestimmung des Umfangs strafbedürftiger Verhaltensweisen in Zweifel zieht[578].

cccc) Ergebnis

Unabhängig von einer streng strafrechtsdogmatisch orientierten Prüfung lässt sich im Fall A, abgesehen von etwaigen dienstrechtlichen Verstößen gegen Anzeigepflichten, kein verwerfliches Tun erkennen, auch dann nicht, wenn man den Vertrauensschutz-Gedanken als maßgebliches Prüfkriterium heranzieht.

bbb) Fall B

aaaa) Geschehensablauf

Im Sachverhalt B liegt ein typischer und von der Rechtsordnung grundsätzlich gebilligter[579] Fall der Drittmittelforschung vor. Die Parteien haben die gegenseitigen Leistungen vertraglich vereinbart. Von den Forschungsergebnissen erwartet der Drittmittelgeber Erkenntnisse für seine Produktverbesserung, mit der er seine Marktfähigkeit auf Dauer sichern will. Die Forschungseinrichtung erbringt im Gegenzug für die Finanzierung die Forschungsleistung. Sollten darüber hinaus weitergehende Interessen der Parteien bestehen, so folgen diese

---

578 Zur Kritik an dem Schutzgut des „Vertrauens“ s. o. S. 53 ff.

579 Dazu o. S. 116 f.

regelmäßig ökonomischen Prinzipien. Da steht auf der Seite des Geldgebers das verständliche wirtschaftliche Interesse an einem hohen Produktabsatz und auf der Seite der solche Produkte einsetzenden Forschungseinrichtung das ebenso marktwirtschaftlichen Regeln folgende Interesse an einem Einkauf selbst mitentwickelter oder überprüfter Produkte zu marktgünstigen Preisen. Wenn im Sachverhalt von einer „bevorzugten" Abnahme die Rede ist, dann ist dieses ökonomisch nachvollziehbare Interesse beider Vertragspartner gemeint.

bbbb) Betrachtung von außen

Der Vereinbarung einer bevorzugten Produktabnahme könnte für einen außen stehenden Betrachter der Makel einer unseriösen einseitig begünstigenden Leistungsabsprache anhaften[580] i.S. einer Abhängigkeit der Forschungsgelder von der Zusage späterer Produktabnahme. Eine solche Sachverhaltsbewertung liegt nicht außerhalb jeder Vorstellung, auch wenn hier günstig in Aussicht gestellte Einkaufspreise eher ein ausgewogenes Austauschverhältnis indizieren. Eine Vertrauensgefährdung, deren Bezugspunkt in der Befangenheit bei der Entscheidung über die spätere Produktabnahme durch das Versprechen von Forschungsgeldern zu suchen wäre, kann im Hinblick auf eine ordnungsgemäße Amtsführung nicht gänzlich ausgeschlossen werden. An dieser Stelle drängt sich die Frage nach der Tauglichkeit des Vertrauensschutzgedankens zur Eingrenzung strafbaren Unrechts erneut auf[581]. Aufgrund der oftmals unterschiedlich interpretierbaren Vertragsbestandteile in ihrer gegenseitigen Bedeutungswirkung kann bei komplexen Vertragsgestaltungen trotz völlig korrekter Amtsführung dennoch der Verdacht einseitiger Einflussnahme und die daran unmittelbar anknüpfende Vertrauensgefährdung aufgrund der Behauptung fehlender Eindeutigkeit der Handlungsmotive der Vertragspartner erzeugt werden, ohne dass der Anschein von Käuflichkeit nach der objektiven und subjektiven Tatsachenerhebung gerechtfertigt wäre. Eine Objektivierung und Differenzierung zwischen gerechtfertigten und ungerechtfertigten Vertrauensdefiziten im Hinblick auf eine redliche Amtsführung ist in den Fällen der Drittmittelforschung mit ihren vielerlei Wertungen zulassenden Vertragsgestaltungen kaum möglich. Die Schwierigkeit liegt in der Bestimmung und Messbarkeit des Grades an objektivierbaren Verdachtsmomenten, die in ihrem Substrat ein Maß an Gewichtigkeit erlangen, dass man eine strafbarkeitsbegründende Vertrauenseinbuße annehmen könnte. Hier bestätigt sich die Auffassung von Dölling, der zu Recht zur Vorsicht mahnt, den Aspekt des Vertrauensschutzes zur Begründung der Strafbarkeit heranzuziehen[582].

---

580 Vgl. Lüderssen, JZ 1997, 112 (116).

581 S. o. unter Fn. 578.

582 Dölling, Gutachten C, C 51.

cccc) Ergebnis

Ohne Hinzutreten weiterer Anhaltspunkte verdienen die Fälle der Drittmittelforschung grundsätzlich nicht das Unwerturteil des Strafrechts. Dabei bildet die weitgehende Gleichgewichtigkeit der sich gegenüberstehenden Leistungen ein starkes Indiz für das Fehlen rechtswidriger Einflussnahme. Soweit diese Leistungen sich gegenseitig kompensieren, bedarf ein dennoch erzeugter „böser Schein“ unkorrekter Amtsführung einer durch Tatsachen zu konkretisierenden Bekräftigung, um eine Sanktionsbedürftigkeit begründen zu können. Dem Vertrauensschutzgedanken kann dabei wegen der genannten Schwierigkeiten wenn überhaupt nur eine untergeordnete Rolle zukommen.

ccc) Fall C

aaaa) Geschehensablauf

Der Sachverhalt C enthält einen exemplarischen Fall des Sponsorings, bei dem die eine Seite (Unternehmer B) Geldbeträge zur Förderung eines gesellschaftspolitischen Zwecks, wie hier der Kultur, gewährt und von der anderen Vertragspartei (Kommune, vertreten durch den Bürgermeister M) für die Bezuschussung der jeweiligen Einrichtung (Theater) die Möglichkeit der öffentlichkeitswirksamen Eigenwerbung eingeräumt bekommt. Es geht um einen wechselseitigen Leistungsaustausch zur Verfolgung der jeweiligen Interessen der Vertragsparteien. Gegen diese Form des Sponsorings kulturell förderungswürdiger Ziele ist im Grundsatz nichts einzuwenden. Im Fall C sind die Sponsorengelder auch wie zugesagt für die Kosten der Theateraufführung eingesetzt worden. Die vertragliche Vereinbarung der Kulturförderung ist damit ebenso eingehalten wie die ökonomisch werthaltige Eigenwerbung des B für sein Unternehmen.

bbbb) Betrachtung von außen

Die Problematik im Fall C, wie überhaupt beim Sponsoring, liegt in der nicht zu leugnenden Gefahr einer unzulässigen Einflussnahme des Sponsors auf staatliche Entscheidungen. Je höher der Förderbetrag und je geringer die Einschätzung der wirtschaftlichen Wertigkeit der behördlichen Gegenleistung (hier Einräumung der Eigenwerbung für das Bauunternehmen) ausfällt, wird ein Missverhältnis zwischen den Vertragsleistungen zu Lasten des Sponsors anzunehmen sein. Treten dann weitere Geschehensmerkmale hinzu, wie im Fall C die enge Freundschaft zwischen den Vertragspartnern und die für den Sponsor profitable Abwicklung zurückliegender Aufträge für die jetzt sponsorenweise geförderte Kommune, ergibt sich leicht ein erster Anschein, der Sponsor verfolge mit seiner lobenswerten finanziellen Förderung des Theaters ganz andere „versteckte“ Ziele. Natürlich kann ein solcher Anschein mit der Feststellung ausgeräumt werden, dass diese Bauaufträge gerade wegen der privaten Freundschaft besonders sorgfältig und ordnungsgemäß ausgeschrieben und im Rahmen einer „Bestenauswahl“ vergeben wurden. Dennoch vermittelt der Sachverhalt dem objektiven Betrachter zunächst das ungute Gefühl, hier gehe etwas nicht mit rechten Dingen zu. Nur die Unterbindung der Sponsoringaktivitäten insgesamt könnte diese Verdachtsmomente ausräumen[583].

Für die Frage der Sanktionsbedürftigkeit ist aber in erster Linie die Motivation des Sponsors und das entsprechende Wissen seines Gegenübers um diese Beweggründe entscheidend. Hier helfen die objektiven Sachverhaltskriterien allein nicht weiter. Die durch ihre Wahrnehmung bedingte Vertrauenseinbuße bei einem außen stehenden Dritten korrespondiert nicht regelmäßig mit der Rechtswirklichkeit.

Es besteht zudem ein Zielkonflikt zwischen dem – wie beim Sponsoring zwangsläufig aufgebauten – Näheverhältnis des Staates zur Wirtschaft einerseits und andererseits der kriminalpolitischen Forderung nach Kriminalisierung jedweden amtlichen Verhaltens, dem aufgrund seines Wirkbereichs innerhalb gesellschaftspolitisch und ökonomisch befürworteter Austauschbeziehungen sehr schnell ein dienstrechtlich fragwürdiger Ruf anlastet. Die Gefahr, sich bei der Auflösung dieses Konflikts „ins eigene Fleisch zu schneiden“ besteht durchaus, zöge man die Konsequenz des generellen Verzichts auf den Einsatz von Förderinstrumenten wie Drittmitteleinsatz und Sponsoring. Dies würde vor allem dem Staat zum Nachteil gereichen, da gerade er in den betroffenen Förderbereichen auf die Hilfe Privater angewiesen ist[584].

Der Vertrauensschutzgedanke verschärft den genannten Zielkonflikt, weil der ihm eigene, unpräzise Prüfungsmaßstab die Befürwortung einer Kriminalisierung zusätzlich stützt. Aus dem bloßen Näheverhältnis zwischen Staat und Wirtschaft schöpft er bereits Verdachtsmomente, ohne ein handhabbares Regulativ zur Entkräftung dieses ersten Anscheins anzubieten. Er kann daher auch im Fall C für die Beurteilung strafbegründenden Verhaltens nicht hilfreich sein. Auf objektiver Geschehensgrundlage muss der Schutzzweck der sachlich-korrekten Amtsführung zur Gewährleistung der Funktionsfähigkeit staatlicher Einrichtungen zum Gegenstand der Prüfung werden, die die Motive der handelnden Personen mit einzubeziehen hat.

---

583 Ein striktes und generelles Sponsoring-Verbot existiert auf Bundesebene gegenwärtig aber nicht, vgl. o. S. 114 ff.

584 So völlig zu Recht Lüderssen, der das Dilemma solcher „komplizierten Geflecht(e) zwischen Markt und Staat“ beschreibt und strafgesetzliche Entscheidungen infrage stellt, „die der Vermutung Raum geben könnten, daß die eine Hand des Gesetzgebers nicht weiß, was die andere tut, indem der Staat gerade dort mit Strafen umfassender, schärfer und intensiver einzugreifen sich anschickt, wo man dabei ist, ihm aus anderen Nöten heraus zu helfen“, JZ 1997, S.112 (113).

cccc) Ergebnis

Die Sponsoring-Absprache zwischen B und M begründet kein Unwerturteil. In der Sachverhaltsschilderung ist auch kein konkreter Verdacht einer Unrechtsübereinkunft mit dem Verständigungsinhalt der Bevorzugung des Sponsors bei künftigen Bauausschreibungen der Kommune enthalten, der eine sachgemäße Amtsführung des M infrage stellen würde.

b) Tatbestandliche Begutachtung

Wenn in allen drei Sachverhalten ein strafrechtliches Unwerturteil nicht indiziert erscheint, warum besteht dann überhaupt die Befürchtung staatsanwaltlicher Ermittlungen? Die Antwort liegt in der Entwicklung der Straftatbestände der Bestechungsdelikte[585] und in der Motivation des Gesetzgebers begründet, in erster Linie die Sanktionierung strafwürdiger Verhaltensweisen mit einer in ihrem Wirkbereich weit gefassten Strafnorm sicherstellen zu wollen und dabei in Kauf nehmen zu müssen, auch eindeutig nicht strafwürdige Sachverhalte zu erfassen[586].

Die nachfolgende strafrechtliche Begutachtung der Fälle A, B und C beschränkt sich auf das durch die Neufassung des § 331 geschaffene Spannungsverhältnis zwischen der gelockerten Unrechtsvereinbarung und der Einbeziehung der „Drittvorteile“[587]. Mit der Untersuchung soll anhand des einzelnen Sachverhalts die straftatbestandliche Schnittstelle offen gelegt werden, an der das Risiko einer strafprozessualen Verurteilung unüberschaubar wird.

aa) Fall A

aaa) Tatbestandliche Fragestellung

Problematisch erscheint im Fall A die Frage, ob P <u>für die Dienstausübung</u> einen <u>Vorteil</u> für sich oder einen Dritten angenommen hat. P hat als Universitätsprofessor und damit als „Amtsträger“ i.S.d. § 331[588] das Elektronenmikroskop entgegengenommen. Es ist dabei gleichgültig, ob P das Mikroskop für sich selbst oder für die Universitätsklinik erstanden hat, da beide Fallkonstellationen

---

585 Vgl. o. Teil A der Untersuchung.

586 Vgl. Schönke/Schröder/Cramer, § 331 Rn. 53a und b, der u.a. den auf Volk beim 61. DJT (Bd. II/1, L 42) zurückgehenden Fall des Staatsanwalts bildet, der für eine (endgültige) Einstellung nach § 153a StPO (= Dienstausübung) eine Geldbuße an einen gemeinnützigen Verein (= einen Dritten) fordert und der damit den Tatbestand des § 331 erfüllt.

587 Der mit dem KorrBekG zu § 331 spiegelbildlich abgefasste § 333 enthält auf der Aktivseite die gleiche Problematik.

588 Vgl. Göben, MedR 1999, S. 345 (346).

unter den Tatbestand des § 331 fallen. Die Überlegung von Dauster[589], ob Dritter i.S.d. § 331 auch die Anstellungskörperschaft des Amtsträgers selbst sein könne, bezeichnet er zunächst als offene grammatische Auslegungsfrage, die er dann aber im Hinblick auf den Schutzzweck der Norm – Bekämpfung der von Korruption ausgehenden Gefährdung des Staates an sich und im Besonderen der Gefährdung des rechtsstaatlichen und an objektiven Sachkriterien orientierten Staatshandelns – dahingehend beantwortet, dass es keinen Unterschied mache, ob Dritter eine private Personenvereinigung oder die mit der Zuwendung an den Amtsträger eigentlich bedachte Anstellungskörperschaft sei. Dieser Auffassung ist zuzustimmen.

Fraglich ist zunächst, ob es sich bei dem Mikroskop als Forschungshilfsmittel um einen Vorteil i.S.d. § 331 handelt.

aaaa) Der Vorteilsbegriff des § 331

Nach der Definition der Rspr. und des Schrifttums ist Vorteil jede unentgeltliche Leistung materieller oder immaterieller Art, die zu einer objektiven Besserstellung führt und auf die der Täter keinen rechtlich begründeten Anspruch besitzt[590]. Der in dem Mikroskop liegende wirtschaftliche Vermögenswert verbessert die Vermögenslage von P bzw. der Uniklinik. Ein Vertragsverhältnis i.S. eines gegenseitig verpflichtenden Vertrages liegt der Bereitstellung des Mikroskops nicht zugrunde, so dass P auch keinen Rechtsanspruch auf das Mikroskop besaß. Damit wäre ein „Vorteil" zu bejahen. Man könnte allenfalls einwenden, das Mikroskop sei als Hilfsmittel ein Teil der vertraglichen Vereinbarung zwischen U und der Uniklinik zur Grundlagenforschung. Es wäre dann ein Austauschverhältnis mit gegenseitigen Leistungspflichten (Forschungsarbeiten gegen Finanzierung <u>und</u> Hilfsmittel) anzunehmen. Der Sachverhalt schließt hingegen eine derartige Auslegung aus, da die Überlassung des Mikroskops schenkweise und ohne vertraglich verpflichtenden Bezug zur Grundlagenforschung erfolgte.

Auch der von den dienstlichen Arbeiten getrennt zu bewertende Zeitgewinn für die Grundlagenforschung als Folge des Einsatzes des Mikroskops ist nicht gesondert vereinbart worden. Der in seiner Entstehung und in seinem Umfang nicht näher quantifizierte Zeitgewinn kann nicht als von U gefordert oder sogar stillschweigend vereinbart gelten, sondern ist nur allgemeiner Ausdruck einer von den Parteien mit der Überlassung des Mikroskops verbundenen Erwartungshaltung ohne verpflichtenden Charakter.

---

589 Dauster, NStZ 1999, S. 63 (65/66).

590 BGHSt 31, 264 (279) und 35, 128 (133); OLG Zweibrücken, JR 1982, S. 381 (382); Schönke/Schröder/ Cramer, § 331 Rn. 17; Jescheck, LK § 331 Rn. 7; Tröndle/Fischer, § 331 Rn. 11.

P hat somit einen Vorteil für sich oder einen Dritten angenommen.

bbbb) „Für die Dienstausübung“

In Ausfüllung der in Teil A hergeleiteten Begriffsdefinition ist hier danach zu fragen, ob zwischen P und U eine Unrechtsübereinkunft in der Weise bestand, dass das Mikroskop für irgendeine dienstliche Tätigkeit des P gewährt werden sollte.

Durch die Lockerung der Unrechtsvereinbarung im Hinblick auf die nun nicht mehr erforderliche Konkretisierung der Diensthandlung entfällt das Erfordernis einer hinreichend bestimmbaren Diensthandlung[591]. Unter dieser Prämisse könnte man schnell geneigt sein, die Zuwendung des Elektronenmikroskops als „für die Dienstausübung“ hingegeben anzusehen, denn der Sachverhalt einer schenkweisen Überlassung von technischem Gerät zur Unterstützung klinischer Forschungsarbeiten entspricht der Tatbestandsformulierung des § 331.

Ausreichend ist danach die Verknüpfung einer uneigennützigen Entgegennahme einer Zuwendung in dem beiderseitigen Bewusstsein, dass der Amtsträger im Gegenzug der Zuwendung dafür eine nicht näher ins Auge gefasste Diensthandlung vornehmen wird oder bereits vorgenommen hat[592].

Nach der alten Fassung des § 331 in der Formulierung „als Gegenleistung dafür“ war umstritten, ob Vorteile, die nur zur Ermöglichung der Durchführung der Diensthandlung bereitgestellt wurden und damit dem Wortsinn einer Gegenleistung nicht entsprachen, unter den Tatbestand zu subsumieren waren[593]. Das OLG Zweibrücken hat den Tatbestand des § 331 a.F. in dem Fall des Polizeibeamten verneint, der sich für die Durchführung zugesagter privater Ermittlungen das für die Ermittlungsfahrten benötigte Benzin unentgeltlich bereitstellen ließ[594]. Dieser Auffassung ist zuzustimmen, da sie dem vom Normtext des § 331 a.F. geforderten Gegenleistungsverhältnis und damit dem Verbotsinhalt gerecht wird.

---

591 Schönke/Schröder/Cramer, § 331 Rn. 28 m.w.N.

592 Schönke/Schröder/Cramer, § 331 Rn. 7/8 und 28-29a.

593 Verneinend Kuhlen, der in den sogenannten Weiterleitungsfällen von einer Mittel-Zweck-Relation spricht, die das nach dem Normtext geforderte Gegenleistungsverhältnis innerhalb der Unrechtsvereinbarung ausschließe, NStZ 1988, S. 433 (439).

594 OLG Zweibrücken, JR 1982, S. 381 (382), es heißt dort: „... (war) der in der Benzinüberlassung liegende momentane Vermögenszuwachs auf seiten des Angeklagten kein Äquivalent für die zusätzlichen Ermittlungen, mithin nicht deren Preis, sondern deren Existenzbedingung, die objektive Bedingung ihrer Durchführbarkeit“; zur Zustimmung des Schrifttums siehe Geerds, JR 1982, S. 384 (385).

Unentschieden bleibt aber bei der aktuellen Gesetzesfassung des § 331 die Frage, ob nach dem Verzicht des Gesetzgebers auf die Formulierung „als Gegenleistung" die bisherige Auffassung noch beibehalten werden kann[595]. Das synallagmatische Verhältnis zwischen Diensthandlung und Vorteil besteht nach dem Wortlaut jetzt nicht mehr, mithin ist der Bejahung eines solchen Erfordernisses der tatbestandliche Boden entzogen. Daher ist in den Fällen, in denen nur die Mittel für die Durchführung der dienstlichen Tätigkeit bereitgestellt werden, nach den erforderlichen, aber auch ausreichenden Voraussetzungen für die Bejahung einer Vorteilsannahme gemäß § 331 zu fragen.

Der Rechtsausschuss des Deutschen Bundestages stellt in seiner Begründung einer Beschlussempfehlung zum Entwurf eines KorrBekG zum Tatmerkmal „für die Dienstausübung" fest, mit dieser Formulierung werde klargestellt, „daß weiterhin eine Beziehung zwischen der Vorteilsannahme und den Diensthandlungen des Amtsträgers bestehen muß. Lediglich eine hinreichend bestimmte Diensthandlung als ‚Gegenleistung' muß nicht mehr nachgewiesen werden."[596] Welche konkrete inhaltliche Ausprägung dieses Beziehungsverhältnis aufweisen muss, wird offen gelassen.

Nach der neuen Rechtslage entfällt das Erfordernis des Nachweises eines tatsächlich bestehenden Gegenleistungsverhältnisses zwischen Vorteil und Dienstausübung insofern, als die Individualisierung einer bestimmten Diensthandlung nicht mehr erforderlich ist. Sowohl nach dem Wortlaut des § 331 als auch nach dem gesetzestechnisch interpretierbaren Sinnzusammenhang muss danach jedes Zusammenhangsverhältnis zwischen Vorteil und Dienstausübung für die Unrechtsübereinkunft ausreichend sein[597]. Die hier betroffenen Fälle wären demnach von diesem Beziehungszusammenhang bereits dann erfasst, wenn außerhalb vertraglicher Absprachen der Vorteil „für die" und nicht weitergehend „wegen der" oder „aufgrund der" oder sogar „als Gegenleistung für die" Durchführung dienstlicher Tätigkeiten hingegeben wird. Selbst wenn also wie im Fall des OLG Zweibrücken die Durchführung der Diensthandlung (Ermittlungsfahrten mit PKW) den Vorteil vollständig aufzehrt, wäre er nach diesem Verständnis „für die Dienstausübung" hingegeben worden. Ein Zusammenhangsverhältnis zwischen Vorteil und Dienstausübung lässt sich kaum verneinen. Eine grammatische Auslegung des § 331 führt daher zum Ergebnis, dass auch diejenigen Fälle tatbestandsmäßig sind, in denen ein Leistungstransfer aus der Sphäre des privat Handelnden in die Sphäre des Amtsträgers mit dem Zweck erfolgt, diesem die Durchführung einer Diensthandlung zu ermöglichen bzw. zu finanzieren.

---

595 Dafür Zieschang, WissR 1999, S. 111 (125).

596 BT-Drs. 13/8079, S. 15.

597 Vgl. Schönke/Schröder/Cramer, § 331 Rn. 7.

Wie ist nun im Fall A bezüglich des Tatmerkmals „für die Dienstausübung" zu entscheiden? Beide Parteien waren sich nicht nur darüber einig, dass das Mikroskop der besseren und schnelleren Bewältigung dienstlicher Aufgaben dienen sollte, sondern hatten damit auch die Erwartungshaltung verbunden, dass durch die Verbesserung der Arbeitsbedingungen dem P mehr Zeit für die zwischen U und der Klinik vertraglich vereinbarte Grundlagenforschung verbliebe. Gegenstand des Verständigungsinhalts war somit nicht nur die schenkweise Bereitstellung eines Arbeitsgeräts für die dienstliche Tätigkeit, sondern es wurde von beiden Seiten ein Äquivalent für diese Bereitstellung in Form – wenn auch nicht näher konkretisierter – vorzeitiger dienstlicher Verfügbarkeit des P für die Grundlagenforschung in Aussicht genommen. Die in diesem Kontext stehende Geräteüberlassung indiziert somit ein Gegenleistungsverhältnis, das über ein beidseitig bedachtes Zusammenhangsverhältnis zwischen Vorteil und Dienstausübung hinausgeht. Das Tatmerkmal „für die Dienstausübung" ist daher erfüllt.

Wie wäre der Fall aber einzuordnen, wenn das ein Gegenleistungsverhältnis begründende Motiv entfiele? Zieschang verneint im Fall der Überlassung eines Mikroskops in Form einer Spende den Tatbestand der Vorteilsannahme[598]. Zieschang ist zunächst darin zuzustimmen, dass auch die Neufassung des § 331 eine Unrechtsvereinbarung voraussetzt wenn auch in abgeschwächter Form. Die weiteren Schlüsse, mit denen er das Erfordernis eines Gegenleistungsverhältnisses nach neuem Recht herleitet, überzeugen nicht.

Einmal beruft er sich auf Dölling, der mit der zur Neufassung des § 331 vorgeschlagenen Formulierung „für die dienstliche Tätigkeit" Zuwendungen gemeint habe, die „in dem Bewußtsein vorgenommen werden, daß der Amtsträger hierfür irgendeine dienstliche Tätigkeit vorgenommen hat oder künftig vornehmen werde"[599]. Aus dem Begriff „hierfür" folgert Zieschang die Notwendigkeit der Vereinbarung einer „Dienstausübung als Gegenleistung"[600].

Zum anderen verweist Zieschang auf die Rechtslage vor dem EGStGB 1974, nach der die im RStGB vorhandene Formulierung „für eine in sein Amt einschlagende Handlung" nach Meinung der Rspr. und des Schrifttums bereits die Annahme des Erfordernisses einer Unrechtsvereinbarung in der Ausformung eines Gegenleistungsverhältnisses begründet habe, ohne den erst mit dem EGStGB gewählten Begriff „als Gegenleistung dafür" im Gesetzestext verwandt zu haben[601].

---

598 Zieschang, WissR 1999, S. 111 (125).
599 Zitat bei Zieschang, WissR 1999, S. 111 (125), Fundstelle bei Dölling, Gutachten C, C 64.
600 Zieschang, WissR 1999, S. 111 (125).
601 Zieschang, WissR 1999, S. 111 (125).

Soweit Zieschang auf Aussagen Döllings zurückgreift, sind seine daraus gezogenen Schlussfolgerungen nicht überzeugend. Dölling bejaht in seinem Beispiel des Bauunternehmers, der dem Bürgermeister mit den Worten „auf gute Zusammenarbeit“ 100.000 DM überreicht, ohne auf ein bestimmtes Verhalten anzuspielen, auf der Grundlage seines Formulierungsvorschlags zur Gesetzesneufassung den Tatbestand des § 331[602]. Dies ist in der Sache berechtigt und zwar auch dann, wenn man unter Zurückstellung überspannter Anforderungen an die Intensität einer zur konkreten Gegenleistung verpflichtenden Motivlage verstärkt auf das beiderseitige Bewusstsein um den Beziehungszusammenhang „Geld für irgendeine Amtshandlung“ abstellt. Der Charakter des Vorteils i.S. eines synallagmatischen Gegenwerts kann hierbei nicht die beherrschende Rolle spielen, weil die „Leistung“ in Form der Diensthandlung im Einzelnen überhaupt noch nicht konkretisiert ist und daher auch nicht synallagmatisch mit einer individualisierten Gegenleistung verknüpft sein kann. Es soll eben im Hinblick auf die nicht mehr notwendig zu konkretisierende Diensthandlung das von den Parteien in ihr Bewusstsein aufgenommene Zusammenhangsverhältnis zwischen Vorteil und irgendeiner, den dienstlichen Tätigkeiten zurechenbaren Amtshandlung ausreichen[603]. Ein Beziehungs- oder Zusammenhangsverhältnis ist aber ein Minus gegenüber einem Gegenleistungsverhältnis.

Auch das zweite Argument von Zieschang überzeugt nicht, weil der Gesetzgeber ohne Not an der Formulierung „als Gegenleistung“ hätte festhalten können, nachdem er mit dem EGStGB von 1974 gerade mit diesem Begriff die Gegenleistungsqualität von Vorteil und Diensthandlung im Sinne eines „do ut des“ zur Verdeutlichung der sich bis dahin in der Rspr. gebildeten Rechtsansicht herausgestellt hat[604]. Dass der Gesetzgeber auf die Beibehaltung dieser Formulierung verzichtet hat, spricht eindeutig für die These einer auch insoweit bewusst vertretenen Lockerung der Unrechtsvereinbarung im Hinblick auf eine synallagmatische Verknüpfung.

Die Diskussion auf dem 61. DJT um das Tatmerkmal der „Unrechtsvereinbarung“ im Vorfeld der gesetzgeberischen Entscheidung verlief denn auch im

---

602 Dölling, Gutachten C, C 65; Dölling schlägt eine Fassung des Gesetzestextes vor, nach der „der Vorteil als Gegenleistung für ‚die dienstliche Tätigkeit in der Vergangenheit oder Zukunft' ... zugewendet werden muß“. Zieschang ist daher insoweit zu folgen, als Dölling in seinem Gutachten zum 61. DJT noch von einer Gegenleistungsbeziehung ausgeht, die aber auf dem Juristentag bei der Beschlussfassung in der vorgeschlagenen Formulierung „als Gegenleistung“ unberücksichtigt blieb.

603 So wie dies bei Anbahnungszuwendungen der Fall sein wird, wenn sie sich auf noch nicht näher konkretisierte Diensthandlungen beziehen, vgl. Schönke/Schröder/Cramer, § 331 Rn. 29.

604 Vgl. BT-Drs. 7/550, S. 271.

Spannungsfeld zweier vorgeschlagener Gesetzesformulierungen[605], deren gemeinsames Bestreben in der Lockerung des Gegenleistungsverhältnisses zwischen Vorteil und zu konkretisierender Amtshandlung bestand[606]. Im Mittelpunkt der Diskussion stand die Frage, ob ein bloßes Zusammenhangsverhältnis zwischen Vorteil und Amt einem effektiven Rechtsgüterschutz nicht am besten gerecht werde[607]. Durchgesetzt hat sich schließlich die Grundposition von Dölling, der unter Hinweis auf die nach anderer Meinung dann vom Tatbestand auch erfassten nicht strafwürdigen Fälle die Herstellung eines Beziehungsverhältnisses zur dienstlichen Tätigkeit für erforderlich erachtete[608]. Dass sowohl der 61. DJT in seiner Beschlussempfehlung zur Neubestimmung der Unrechtsvereinbarung als auch der Gesetzgeber auf die von Dölling in seinem Gutachten noch gebrauchte Formulierung „... als Gegenleistung für ‚die dienstliche Tätigkeit in der Vergangenheit oder Zukunft'..."[609] nicht zurückgegriffen haben, spricht für die Absicht einer starken Annäherung an die Position der Vertreter einer „Zusammenhangsklausel", bei deren Zugrundelegung sich der Wegfall einer Gegenleistungsbeziehung selbsterklärend ergeben hätte.

Der Auffassung von Zieschang ist aber auch noch in einem weiteren Punkt zu widersprechen. Auf der Grundlage, dass er weiterhin auf ein Gegenleistungsverhältnis im Sinne eines „do-ut-des" abstellt, verkennt er den richtigen Bezugspunkt, indem er vorträgt, die Diensthandlung müsse als Äquivalent für den Vorteil vereinbart sein[610]. Der spezifische Unwertgehalt des § 331 a.F., nämlich die Gefährdung der sachgemäßen staatlichen Aufgabenerledigung durch unsachgemäß handelnde Amtsträger, ergibt sich aus der den Parteien bewussten

605 Alternative 1: Die §§ 331,333 sollten bereits dann eingreifen, wenn die Zuwendung im Zusammenhang mit dem Amt steht; diese Alternative wurde mit 7:108:4 Stimmen abgelehnt; Alternative 3: Die §§ 331,333 sollten dann eingreifen, wenn der Vorteil für die dienstliche Tätigkeit gewährt wird oder gewährt werden soll, ohne dass die Vereinbarung einer bestimmten Diensthandlung erforderlich ist; diese Alternative wurde mit 71:39:6 Stimmen angenommen; ganz anders die Alternative 2, die auf die Eignung des Vorteils abstellt, den Amtsträger bei der lauteren Wahrnehmung seiner dienstlichen Aufgaben zu beeinflussen; diese Alternative wurde mit 45:60:10 Stimmen abgelehnt, 61. DJT, Bd. II/2 Beschlüsse, L 189.

606 Vgl. Eser, 61. DJT, Vh. Bd. II/2, L 72 (74), der dies durch seine Feststellung untermauert, der Begriff der Unrechtsvereinbarung existiere in keinem anderem Land und daher müsse das Petitum lauten, „von diesem Begriff wieder herunterzukommen und das zu finden, was letztlich eigentlich erfaßt werden soll, nämlich einen gewissen – das sage ich jetzt im untechnischen Sinne – Zusammenhang zwischen Vorteil und Amt".

607 Vgl. Schaupensteiner, 61. DJT, Vh. Bd. II/2, L 111 ff.

608 Dölling, Gutachten C, C 64/65.

609 Dölling, Gutachten C, C 65, Unterstreichung vom Verfasser.

610 Vgl. Zieschang, WissR 1999, S. 111 (125), wo es heißt: „..., so ist festzustellen, daß die Zuwendung seitens des Industrie-Unternehmens U nicht erfolgt, damit A nun dafür in irgendeiner Weise dienstlich tätig wird. Eine – wenn auch nicht konkretisierte – Dienstausübung als Gegenleistung ist nicht vereinbart".

Verknüpfung einer rechtmäßigen Diensthandlung (= Leistung) mit einer nicht zustehenden Vorteilsgewährung (= Gegenleistung), nicht auch umgekehrt aus einem Vorteil (= Leistung), der mit einer Diensthandlung als Gegenleistung verknüpft wird[611]. Die rechtmäßige Dienstausübung bildet das Anforderungsprofil an eine sachgemäße staatliche Aufgabenerledigung ab, die erst durch den Aufbau eines Beziehungszusammenhangs zu einem unrechtmäßigen Vorteil in Gefahr gerät, gleichsam ihre Reputation zu verlieren. Der Gefährdungszusammenhang richtet sich somit an der Dienstausübung aus, nicht an einem Vorteil, der immer nur die Gegenleistung abbilden kann. Zieschang hätte seine Frage demnach umgekehrt formulieren müssen, ob nämlich der Tatbestandsbereich des § 331 dadurch betreten wird, dass eine rechtmäßige Dienstausübung (= allgemeine Forschungstätigkeit) mit einer dem Amtsträger nicht zustehenden Zuwendung (= spendenweise überlassenes Mikroskop) in ein Zusammenhangsverhältnis – oder wie Zieschang meint in ein Gegenleistungsverhältnis – gebracht wird. In dieser Fragekonstellation wäre Zieschang die Antwort nicht so leicht gefallen. Nur bei völlig selbstloser, karitativer Einstellung des Pharmaunternehmens wird man ein schenkweise übergebenes Mikroskop zwar als in einem Zusammenhangsverhältnis, nicht aber als in einem Gegenleistungsbezug zur Dienstausübung stehend interpretieren können. Derartige Fälle dürften an der Lebenswirklichkeit regelmäßig vorbeigehen[612]. Denn wie im hier geschilderten Fall A stehen häufig unmittelbare oder mittelbare ökonomische Interessen der Unternehmen hinter vordergründigen „Spendenaktionen“, mäzenatische Verhaltensweisen wird man in diesem Bereich selten antreffen.

Im Ergebnis ist auch in der abgewandelten Fallvariante A einer schenkweisen Überlassung des Mikroskops das Tatmerkmal der Unrechtsvereinbarung zu bejahen, da das Erfordernis einer Gegenleistungsbeziehung zwischen Vorteil und Dienstausübung aus der Entstehungsgeschichte und der gesetzestechnischen Formulierung des Tatbestands des § 331 nicht gefolgert werden kann.

cccc) Tatbestandliche Einbruchstelle

Die Schwierigkeit, einzelne Lebenssachverhalte unter die gelockerten rechtlichen Anforderungen der Unrechtsvereinbarung zu subsumieren, zeigt die vorangestellte Diskussion. Die unterschiedlichen Ergebnisse sind Folge graduell voneinander abweichender Gewichtungen innerhalb der Einzelelemente der Unrechtsübereinkunft, die der Gesetzgeber mit der Neufassung der §§ 331 ff.

611 Ebenso Kuhlen, NStZ 1988, S. 433 (438 ff.), der darauf abstellt, dass durch die §§ 331 ff. a.F. verhindert werden soll, „daß die Diensthandlung in eine Äquivalenz- und damit Abhängigkeitsbeziehung zu Tauschmitteln Privater gestellt wird, nicht dagegen, daß diese Mittel in Abhängigkeit von dienstlichem Handeln gebracht werden“.

612 Vgl. Dauster, NStZ 1999, S. 63 (66).

zwar abgeschwächt, in ihren Grenzwirkungen aber nicht hinreichend exakt bestimmt hat.

Nach dem hier vertretenen Verständnis vom Tatmerkmal der Unrechtsübereinkunft besitzt das ihr zugrundeliegende Beziehungsverhältnis nicht (mehr) die Qualität eines synallagmatischen Gegenleistungsverhältnisses, sondern erfordert nur noch einen vom Bewusstsein der Parteien getragenen Zusammenhangsbezug zwischen Vorteil und dienstlicher Tätigkeit[613]. Damit ist aber auch der schmale Grat zwischen Pönalisierung derartiger Beziehungszusammenhänge und der Begründung ihrer Straflosigkeit beschrieben. Die strafrechtlichen Risiken in nicht strafwürdigen Fällen sind erheblich und können sich je nach strafprozessualer Bewertung des nachweisbaren Verständigungsinhalts leicht verwirklichen, nicht zuletzt auch deshalb, weil altruistische Verhaltensweisen auf Nehmerseite den Tatbestand ebenfalls erfüllen.

bbb) Ergebnis

Da die Annahme des Mikroskops weder i.S.d. § 331 Abs. 3 genehmigt noch von P gegenüber der Universitätsverwaltung angezeigt worden war[614], hat sich P der rechtswidrigen Vorteilsannahme nach § 331 strafbar gemacht.

bb) Fall B

aaa) Tatbestandliche Fragestellung

Fall B enthält mehrere Zweifelsfragen im Zusammenhang mit dem Vorteilsbegriff der §§ 331 ff., der strafrechtliche Risiken außerhalb strafwürdiger Verhaltensweisen birgt.

Die hier vertraglich vereinbarte, durch Finanzierung Dritter geförderte Forschungstätigkeit[615] unterfällt dem Tatbestandsbegriff der „Dienstausübung", mit dem die Wahrnehmung aller übertragenen konkret-funktionalen Dienstaufgaben erfasst wird[616]. Selbst wenn P – wovon der Sachverhalt nicht ausgeht – seine Arbeiten zur Grundlagenforschung in Nebentätigkeit ausführen würde, wäre er damit noch nicht aus dem Schneider. Soweit die Wahrnehmung der Forschungsarbeiten in Nebentätigkeit ausgeführt wird, dürfen keinerlei Über-

---

613 Mit diesem Verständnis wohl auch Schönke/Schröder/Cramer, § 331 Rn. 29.

614 Zum Verhältnis des § 331 Abs. 3 zu § 25 Abs. 3 HRG s. u. S. 154 f.

615 Zur industriell geförderten Forschung, die der durch Art. 5 Abs. 3 GG ohne Gesetzesvorbehalt garantierten Forschungsfreiheit unterfällt, vgl. Pfeiffer, NJW 1997, S. 782 ff.

616 Göben, MedR 1999, S. 345 (346), der auf die Tatbestandserweiterung durch die Gesetzesneufassung hinweist, da „sämtliche im Zusammenhang mit der medizinischen Forschungstätigkeit von Mitgliedern der Hochschule stehenden Zuwendungen privater Wirtschaftsunternehmen erfaßt" würden.

schneidungen zum Hauptamt vorliegen, wie dies z.B. bei Benutzung der klinischen Gerätschaften oder der Mitwirkung bei späteren Beschaffungsentscheidungen im Hauptamt der Fall wäre. Auch diese oftmals nicht scharf voneinander abzugrenzenden Funktionsbereiche können sich insoweit tatbestandserweiternd auswirken[617].

Im Fall B entscheidet sich die Frage tatbestandsmäßigen Tuns bei vertraglich vereinbarter Drittmittelforschung im Rahmen der Begutachtung des Vorteilsbegriffs.

aaaa) Vorteil aus Vertrag

Nach der Definition des Vorteilsbegriffs[618] sind alle Leistungen auszuscheiden, auf die die Uniklinik aufgrund der Vertragsvereinbarung einen rechtlich begründeten Anspruch hat. Dabei ist zu berücksichtigen, dass ein Vorteil auch dann nicht anzunehmen ist, wenn der vertraglich zugesicherte Leistungsbestandteil nur der Durchführung der zugesagten Leistung dient, wie das bei der Bezahlung von Forschungsvorhaben häufig der Fall sein wird[619]. Vor der Aufklärung der Frage des Bestehens eines Äquivalenzverhältnisses steht daher die Prüfung, ob eine unkompensierte Besserstellung erfolgt ist. Dabei sind die sich gegenüberstehenden, vertraglich ausgehandelten Leistungen zu bewerten. Im Meinungsstreit befindet sich die Frage, ob ein wirksam bestehender Rechtsanspruch auf diese Leistungen – selbst wenn diese zum Teil durch die Gegenleistung nicht kompensiert werden – regelmäßig zur Verneinung der Annahme eines Vorteils führen müsse[620]. In dieser Grundsätzlichkeit wird dies zu bezweifeln sein, denn dann könnte, wie Göben zu Recht betont, „der Tatbestand der Vorteilsannahme ... stets durch die Vereinbarung eines Vertragsverhältnisses ... ausgeschlossen werden“[621]. Diese Grundsatzfrage bedarf daher einer genauen Analyse.

aaaaa) BGHSt 31, 264

Die Rspr. vertritt bis in die jüngste Zeit[622] die Ansicht, dass ein Vorteil bereits im Abschluss eines Vertrages liegen könne, welcher Leistungen an den Amtsträger vorsehe, die möglicherweise sogar in einem angemessenen Verhältnis zu

---

617 Göben, MedR 1999, S. 345 (347).
618 Dazu o. unter Fn. 590.
619 Zieschang, WissR 1999, S. 111 (117 f.) unter Hinweis auf OLG Zweibrücken, JR 1982, S. 381 (382); ebenso Lüderssen, JZ 1997, S. 112 (114).
620 Vgl. Lüderssen, der auf das Synallagma abstellt, JZ 1997, S. 112 (114) und Zusammenarbeit, S. 41 ff.
621 Göben, MedR 1999, S. 345 (347).
622 Vgl. OLG Hamburg, MedR 2000, S. 371 (372).

den von diesem geschuldeten Leistungen stünden[623]. In diesem Verständnis argumentiert auch das OLG Hamburg und führt dabei weiter aus: „Soweit Rechtsnormen eine Pflicht des Medizinprodukte-Unternehmens zur Durchführung klinischer Studien als Zulassungsvoraussetzung bestimmen (...), gewähren sie jedoch nicht allen oder einem bestimmten Arzt einen Anspruch darauf, mit der Durchführung solcher Studien beauftragt zu werden"[624]. Das OLG Hamburg bezieht mit diesen Ausführungen die in der Medizinprodukterforschung vorgefundene Situation und Rechtswirklichkeit ausdrücklich mitein, nach der klinische (Vor-)Prüfungen nach dem Medizinproduktegesetz vorgeschrieben sind[625] und diese in enger Zusammenarbeit der Industrie mit den Universitätskliniken und den Ärzten zwingend durchzuführen sind[626].

Verträge über die Durchführung klinischer Studien sind daher geboten, unabhängig von der Auswahl des Vertragspartners. Die bei rein rechtlicher Betrachtung kaum zu bezweifelnde Verneinung eines Kontrahierungszwangs mit der einzelnen Klinik führt nach Auffassung des OLG Hamburg zur Bejahung eines in dem Abschluss des Vertrages liegenden Vorteils.

bbbbb) Kritik des Schrifttums

Die Entscheidung BGHSt 31, 264 ist in der Literatur heftig kritisiert worden[627]. Lüderssen führt an, dass die Vorverlegung der Fixierung eines vertraglichen Austauschverhältnisses vom Inhalt auf den Abschluss des Vertrages nichts an dem nach wie vor bestehenden Synallagma ändere. Die Unterscheidung zwischen Vertragsabschluss und Vertragsabwicklung sei daher nicht nachvollziehbar[628]. Zieschang unterscheidet bei rechtlich wirksamen Vertragsverhältnissen nach der Wertigkeit der sich gegenüberstehenden Leistungsverpflichtungen. Stehen Leistung und Gegenleistung in einem angemessenen und ausgeglichenen Verhältnis zueinander, verneint Zieschang einen Vorteil[629]. Noch grundsätzlicher argumentiert Ratzel, der bei Einhaltung der in § 25 HRG festgelegten Rahmenbedingungen für Drittmittelforschung und insbesondere bei ordnungsgemäßer Verwaltung der von dritter Seite vertraglich zugesicherten Forschungsgelder durch die Klinikverwaltung die Forschungsförderung als von der Rechtsordnung erwünscht ansieht und dementsprechend ungeachtet möglicher

---

623 BGHSt 31, S. 264 (280).
624 OLG Hamburg, MedR 2000, S. 371 (373).
625 Vgl. §§ 19 ff. Medizinproduktegesetz, aber auch §§ 40 ff. Arzneimittelgesetz.
626 Pfeiffer, NJW 1997, S. 782 (783).
627 Vgl. Lüderssen, JZ 1997, S. 112 (114), der von einer „Mischung aus Ungeschicktheit und halber Absicht" spricht; dem BGH zustimmend dagegen Kuhlen, Nomos Kommentar, § 331 Rn. 52 ff.
628 Lüderssen, JZ 1997, S. 112 (114); ebenso Zieschang, WissR 1999, S. 111 (119).
629 Zieschang, WissR 1999, S. 111 (119).

immaterieller Vorteile den Tatbestand des § 331 verneint, weil es hier auf die Frage eines „Vorteils" dann gar nicht ankomme[630].

ccccc) Eigene Auffassung

Lüderssen ist darin zuzustimmen, dass die sich gegenüberstehenden Vertragspflichten in allen Stadien eines gegenseitig verpflichtenden Vertrages nicht durch eine Vorverlegung des Betrachtungszeitpunkts auf den Vertragsabschluss im Ergebnis zur Folge haben können, mit einer rechtlichen Abstrahierung einen „Vorteil" zu begründen. Davon geht jetzt aber wohl auch der BGH in einer neueren Entscheidung aus[631], in der er das Synallagma unabhängig von der zeitlichen Fixierung unmittelbar als Ansatzpunkt für die Beurteilung eines Vorteils i.S. des § 331 ausschliesst[632]. Gleichwohl zieht der BGH – wenn auch nur mittelbar – dieses Synallagma für die Bewertung eines „Vorteils" heran, indem er die sich gegenüberstehenden Vertragspflichten auf Ausgewogenheit hin überprüft und einen Vorteil darin sieht, wenn „eine im Vergleich zum üblichen Werklohn zu niedrige Vergütung vereinbart wird"[633].

Dies erscheint auf den ersten Blick sachgerecht. Aber unabhängig davon, dass auch drittfinanzierte Forschungsvorhaben auf ihre inhaltliche Ausgewogenheit der gegenseitigen Leistungsverpflichtungen zu überprüfen wären und damit ein erhebliches Risiko für die Parteien beinhalten würden[634], drückt sich der BGH mit diesem Versuch einer Objektivierung der Frage nach der Werthaltigkeit der sich gegenüberstehenden Leistungen um die eigentliche Kernfrage herum. Zwar kann die Unausgewogenheit eines vertraglichen Austauschverhältnisses ein prozessuales Indiz für eine objektive Besserstellung des Amtsträgers oder

---

630 Ratzel, MedR 1998, S. 98 (99).

631 BGH-Urteil vom 3.7.1991 – 2 StR 132/91 – in Auszügen veröffentlicht in NStZ 1991, S. 550.

632 Es heißt dort: „..., so könnten nicht die im Garten und Keller ausgeführten Arbeiten selbst als Vorteil im Sinne des § 331 StGB gewertet werden. Denn danach wären zwischen den Beteiligten entgeltliche Werkverträge (§ 631 BGB) zustande gekommen, aus denen sich ... einerseits Vergütungspflichten, andererseits Ansprüche auf Ausführung der vereinbarten Werkleistungen ergeben hätten. Die aufgrund eines Werkvertrags erbrachte Leistung ist aber kein Vorteil, soweit der Empfänger nur das erhält, worauf er nach dem entgeltlichen Vertrag einen Rechtsanspruch hat (...)".

633 BGH-Urteil vom 3.7.1991 – 2 StR 132/91 –; ähnlich Zieschang, WissR 1999, S. 111 (119).

634 Selbst bei dezidierter Auflistung und Zuordnung aller Teilbeträge des Drittmitteletats zu konkreten Teilarbeitsschritten des Gesamtprojekts könnte die Frage immer noch lauten: Warum wurde ein so hoher Kostenbetrag für diesen Arbeitsschritt angesetzt? Eine Antwort wäre nicht schon mit dem ordnungsgemäßen Nachweis des konkreten Verbrauchs der Finanzmittel befriedigend erbracht, sondern es wäre abstrakt nach der Ausgewogenheit der gegenseitigen Leistungsverpflichtungen zu fragen.

des Drittbegünstigten liefern. Diese Besserstellung ist aber durch das Synallagma gleichsam geschützt[635].

Deshalb ist der Blick auf die Motive der Vertragspartner zu richten. Es ist nach einem überschießenden Motiv zu fragen, das unmittelbar auf die Unausgewogenheit der sich gegenüberstehenden Leistungspflichten gerichtet ist. Das Vorhandensein eines solchen Motivs würde sichtbar machen, dass der Vertrag nicht nach kaufmännischen Regeln ausgehandelt, sondern bewusst einseitig begünstigend gestaltet wurde, um anderweitige „versteckte" Vorteile[636] zu realisieren. Eine wesentliche Bedeutung beim Nachweis solcher überschießender Motive kommt der Prüfung zu, ob die gegenseitigen Vertragspflichten in ihrer jeweiligen Wertigkeit von denselben Parteien auch vereinbart worden wären, wenn sich der Amtsträger nicht in der von ihm konkret ausgeübten sachlich-funktionalen Amtsstellung befunden hätte. Diese Frage bleibt dem Tatrichter ebenso wenig erspart wie die Erforschung außerhalb vertraglicher Vereinbarung in Aussicht gestellter Vorteile, die dann nicht mehr vom Synallagma geschützt wären.

Die Beurteilung eines Vorteils i.S.d. § 331 allein nach der objektiven Angemessenheit der sich gegenüberstehenden Vertragspflichten greift daher zu kurz. Damit würden die Anforderungen an die subjektive Tatseite der Bestechungsdelikte unzulässig verkürzt[637]. Es ist auch nicht zu befürchten, dass mit der hier vertretenen Auffassung die Korrespondenz zum Schutzzweck der §§ 331 ff. unterlaufen würde. Von einer Gefährdung der Sachgemäßheit amtlich zu treffender Entscheidungen kann nur gesprochen werden, wenn die Motive der Vertragsparteien nicht kaufmännisch zulässigem Gewinnstreben entspringen, sondern auf die Beeinflussung und Beeinträchtigung der staatlichen Integrität in der Gesamtheit ihrer handelnden Subjekte abzielen. Das hier vertretene Ergebnis führt zu einer sachgemäßen Bewertung innerhalb der Drittmittelforschung. Die von der Rechtsordnung ausdrücklich gebilligte Förderung staatlicher Forschung durch (Mit-)Finanzierung von privater Seite darf nicht schon durch das Ergebnis einer abstrakten rechnerischen Gegenüberstellung der gegenseitigen Vertragspflichten in den Wirkbereich des § 331 gezogen werden, sondern ver-

---

635 Das Aushandeln einseitig vorteilhafter Verträge ist von der Rechtsordnung nicht untersagt.

636 Wie z.B. die verifizierbare Verbesserung der Chance auf den Zuschlag bei der nächsten behördlichen Bauausschreibung oder das Renommee, das sich eine Klinik durch bedeutende Forschungsvorhaben aufbauen kann; im Einzelfall ist hier zu prüfen, ob diese durch den eigentlichen Vertrag ausgelösten Optionen eigenständige Vorteile i.S.d. § 331 darstellen.

637 Dieser Gefahr unterlag bereits die Rechtsprechung des Reichsgerichts in RGSt 74, 251 und 77, 75; auch die Argumentation in BGHSt 31, S. 264 (280) deutet auf eine Zurückdrängung dieser subjektiven Tatkriterien hin.

liert ihre vom Gesetzgeber verliehene Berechtigung erst mit dem Nachweis der sie in ihrer Unbeeinflusstheit aushöhlenden und diskreditierenden Motive[638].

bbbb) Vorteil aus Überkompensation

Nicht zu verwechseln mit der „Vorteils"-Problematik bei Unausgewogenheit zweier sich gegenüberstehender Leistungspflichten innerhalb vertraglicher Vereinbarungen ist die Frage der Kompensation eines Vorteils durch einen anderen. Es handelt sich um Fälle, bei denen aus der eigentlichen Austauschbeziehung weitere unmittelbare oder mittelbare für den Amtsträger als Vorteil zu bewertende Folgewirkungen entstehen. Fall B liefert das Beispiel hierzu: Die eigentliche Austauschbeziehung besteht in der Gewährung von Forschungsgeldern für eine zu erbringende Forschungstätigkeit. Aufgrund dieser vertraglichen Regelung ergeben sich aber auf beiden Vertragsseiten weitere vorteilhafte Auswirkungen. Bei der Uniklinik bzw. P sind zu benennen:

P1 Erhöhung der wissenschaftlichen Reputation der Klinik durch erfolgreiche Abwicklung des Forschungsauftrages
P2 Verbesserung des beruflichen Renommees von P
P3 Gegenüber dem Marktpreis niedrigere Abnahmepreise der durch die Forschungsleistung verbesserten Produkte
P4 Forschungsbedingte Produktverbesserung, die der Klinik eine bessere Patientenversorgung ermöglicht.

Beim Pharma-Unternehmen U sind zu benennen:

U1 Erzielung firmeninternen wissenschaftlichen Know-hows durch enge Kontakte zu P
U2 Höhere Produktabnahme am Markt wegen der forschungsbedingten qualitativen Verbesserung der Produkte
U3 Verbesserung der eigenen Produktpalette
U4 Bevorzugte Abnahme der forschungsbedingt verbesserten Medizinprodukte durch die Klinik.

Dieser Gegenüberstellung kommt deshalb besondere Bedeutung zu, weil sich aus ihr ein Beziehungsverhältnis zwischen den Parteien ergeben könnte, das über den definierten Inhalt des Vertrages hinausreicht und erst in diesem Kontext eine Unrechtsvereinbarung begründen könnte. Dabei besteht die Gefahr voreiliger Rückschlüsse aus objektiver Geschehenswahrnehmung auf subjekti-

[638] Im Sinne von E. Schmidt unter Hinweis auf RGSt 19, 19, nach dem der Inhalt der Unrechtsvereinbarung „ganz der gedanklichen Welt der Bedeutungen und Sinngebungen angehört", (Fn. 61) S. 72.

ve, der Unrechtsübereinkunft zurechenbarer Motivbildungen[639]. Es gilt daher sorgsam aufzuklären und zu unterscheiden zwischen

1. Motiven, deren Vorliegen überhaupt erst die Bereitschaft zum Eingehen einer eigenen Vertragspflicht auslösen kann, weil die vertraglich zugesicherte Gegenleistung noch keinen materiellen Wert an sich darstellt. Dies gilt hier für die „Vorteile“ U2 und U3, die unmittelbar dem erwarteten Ergebnis der geschuldeten Gegenleistungsverpflichtung (Forschungstätigkeit) als materiell messbare Vorteile entsprechen und daher keinen zusätzlichen, nicht bereits durch die Bezahlung der Forschungstätigkeit kompensierten Vorteil beinhalten.
2. Motiven, die auf eine immaterielle Besserstellung abzielen wie bei P1 / P2 und U1[640].
3. Motiven, die nicht der eigentlichen Austauschbeziehung zugerechnet werden können, sondern auf mittelbare, aus dieser Wechselbeziehung resultierende Vorteile gerichtet sind wie bei P4.
4. Motiven, die nicht auf die vertraglich fixierte Vereinbarung, sondern auf davon unabhängige weiterreichende Ziele hinwirken wie bei P3 und U4, deren wechselseitige Verwirklichung in der Erwartungshaltung der Vertragsparteien stand.

Die Motivlage unter Nr. 3 ist in zweifacher Hinsicht problematisch. Einmal besteht die Schwierigkeit des Nachweises, dass solche aus der Erfüllung von Vertragspflichten folgende oder erwartbare mittelbaren Vorteile zumindest stillschweigend zum Gegenstand einer Unrechtsübereinkunft gemacht wurden. Kuhlen wendet sich in diesem Zusammenhang zu Recht gegen eine vom BGH herangezogene Auslegungsregel, nach der derartige mittelbare Vorteile aufgrund ihres erwartbaren sicheren Eintritts als Folge der Erfüllung der eigentlichen Vereinbarung gleichsam mitvereinbart seien mit der rechtlichen Folge fehlender Notwendigkeit des Nachweises des tatsächlich Vereinbarten[641]. Um andererseits das „strategisch geschickte Schweigen“ nicht zur „ungerechtfertigte(n) Privilegierung der Geschickten gegenüber den Ungeschickten“ werden zu lassen, bildet Kuhlen zur Deutung möglicher stillschweigender Vorteilsabsprachen die Prüffrage, ob es noch andere plausible Erklärungsmöglichkeiten für die Vornahme der Diensthandlungen gibt als die des Interesses des Amtsträgers an diesen mittelbaren Vorteilen[642]. Bei mehreren voneinander abweichenden Motiv-Varianten wäre bei fehlender Nachweisbarkeit einer dieser Varianten die für den Betroffenen günstigste anzunehmen. Der Auffassung von

639 Vgl. Kuhlen, NStZ 1988, S. 433 (437), der diese Tendenz in der Entscheidung des 4. Strafsenats - 4 StR 554/87 -, NStZ 1988, S. 458, bei mittelbaren Vorteilen erkennt.

640 Dazu u. unter cccc).

641 Kuhlen, NStZ 1988, S. 433 (437/438).

642 Kuhlen, NStZ 1988, S. 433 (437/438).

Kuhlen ist beizupflichten. Sie entspricht auch der hier vertretenen Auffassung, dass es innerhalb des aufzuklärenden Unrechtsverhältnisses entscheidend auf die Motivlage, deren Zielrichtung und Nachweisbarkeit ankommt.

Zum anderen mutet es befremdlich an, den von der Klinikleitung bei erfolgreicher Forschungstätigkeit zu erwartenden mittelbaren Vorteil einer verbesserten medikamentösen Versorgung der Klinikpatienten als unrechtsauslösende, zumindest stillschweigende Vorteilsabsprache zu bewerten. Aus diesem Dilemma könnte die fehlende Nachweisbarkeit einer diesbezüglich bestehenden Absprache heraushelfen. Ein solches Ergebnis dürfte aber eher die Ausnahme bilden, da das Motiv einer verbesserten Medikamentenversorgung ein plausibles und sogar erwünschtes Ziel darstellt, das im korrespondierenden Bewusstsein der vertragsschließenden Parteien in aller Regel mitmotivierend wirken wird. Eine andere Lösungsoption führt in die Problematik unter Nr. 4.

Dort geht es um die Frage der Kompensation derjenigen Vorteile, die unabhängig von der eigentlichen Vertragsvereinbarung entweder mittelbar aus diesem Vertragsverhältnis faktisch resultieren oder zusätzlich durch ausdrückliche oder stillschweigende Nebenabrede der Parteien Vereinbarungsbestandteil geworden sind. Bei der näheren Untersuchung kommt es allein darauf an, ob ein nicht kompensierter Vorteil als Äquivalent zur Dienstausübung festgestellt werden kann[643].

Im Fall B stehen sich auf Seiten des Unternehmens eine ins gemeinsame Kalkül gezogene bevorzugte und damit garantierte Produktabnahme durch die Klinik (= Vorteil) und auf Seiten der Klinik neben einem gegenüber Marktpreisen vergünstigten Abnahmepreis der Medizinprodukte (= Vorteil) eine verbesserte Patientenversorgung (= weiterer Vorteil) gegenüber.

Spätestens an dieser Stelle wird das strafrechtliche Risiko der Bejahung einer Vorteilsannahme evident, denn je nachdem, welcher Wertmaßstab an den einzelnen Vorteil im Hinblick auf den Nutzwert für den Bestand eines Unternehmens und den Stellenwert innerhalb des Aufgabenprofils einer Uniklinik angelegt wird[644], ist eine Überkompensation auf der einen oder anderen Seite von vornherein nicht auszuschließen[645]. Eine mathematische Aufrechnung wird in derartigen Fällen der Drittmittelforschung kaum durchführbar sein. Wie

---

643 Vgl. Lüderssen, JZ 1997, S. 112 (114/116).

644 Ein marktorientiertes Unternehmen verfolgt weitgehend ökonomische Interessen der Gewinnmaximierung, eine Uniklinik hat neben haushaltsrechtlichen Aspekten auch eine sozialpolitische Verantwortung gegenüber den Patienten zu berücksichtigen und daher quasi eine ethische Pflicht zur bestmöglichen Medizinversorgung.

645 In die gleiche Richtung Lüderssen auf der Grundlage der nicht Gesetz gewordenen „Zusammenhangsklausel“, JZ 1997, S. 112 (116).

sollte z.B. die zunächst nur in einer Erwartungshaltung zum Ausdruck kommende Verbesserung der medikamentösen Patientenversorgung quantifiziert werden? Welcher materielle Wert ihr zukommt, hängt von verschiedenen Faktoren ab, nicht zuletzt aber auch von der immateriellen Werteinschätzung einer positiven Außenwirkung der erfolgreich forschenden Klinik, die dann wiederum zu handfesten materiellen Verbesserungen wie einer erhöhten Bettenbelegungsquote führen kann[646].

Es besteht offenkundig die strafprozessuale Schwierigkeit, innerhalb eines Ermittlungsverfahrens alle denkbaren Vorteile in einen „Kompensationsabgleich" einzustellen und gleichzeitig die Nachweisbarkeit entsprechender Übereinkünfte bezüglich der in die Abwägung einbezogenen Vorteile zu gewährleisten. Die Ursache solcher Schwierigkeiten liegt in der bestehenden Konturenlosigkeit des Tatbestands des § 331 begründet, nach der sich durch den Wegfall der Anforderungen eines synallagmatischen Gegenleistungsverhältnisses im Hinblick auf eine konkrete Amtshandlung die Prüfkriterien für den Nachweis einer Unrechtsbeziehung verstärkt auf die Vorteilserlangung fokussieren. Und das Tatelement des Vorteils kollidiert mit den von der Wertegemeinschaft anerkannten sozialen, ökonomischen, gesellschaftspolitischen, kulturellen und haushalterischen Handlungszwecken in der Abwägung darüber, welcher Verständigungsinhalt vorteilbehaftet ist und in welcher Nutzenausbeute er besteht. Hat die alte Fassung des § 331 die im Vorfeld eigentlichen Bestechungsunrechts liegende Gefährdungssituation im Hinblick auf eine sachgemäße, unparteiische Aufgabenerledigung des Staates noch deutlich zum Ausdruck gebracht, wird die neue Fassung des § 331 diesem Anspruch nicht mehr gerecht. Bestätigt wird diese Auffassung durch die zahlreichen, dogmatisch unterschiedlichen Ansätze, nicht nur den Bereich der Drittmittelforschung aus der Tatbestandsmäßigkeit des § 331 wieder herauszulösen[647].

cccc) Immaterielle Vorteile

Als immaterielle Vorteile im Bereich der Drittmittelforschung kommen vor allem die unter P1, P2 und U1 genannten Interessen in Betracht, im Kern also persönliche Motive wie beruflicher Ehrgeiz im Hinblick auf verbesserte Karrierechancen und unternehmensbezogene Motive wie Verbesserung des klinik- und firmenexternen Ansehens. Auch diese Vorteile können, sofern sie einen objektiv messbaren Inhalt aufweisen[648], Gegenstand staatsanwaltlicher Ermittlungen werden.

---

646 Verbessertes Renommee der Klinik führt zur verstärkten Belegungsnachfrage.

647 Dazu u. S. 158 ff.

648 So die h.M., vgl. Schönke/Schröder/Cramer, § 331 Rn. 19; Rudolphi, SK, § 331 Rn. 21; Tröndle/ Fischer, § 331 Rn. 11; Hardtung (Fn. 265), S. 54; Gribl (Fn. 265), S. 148; Bauchrowitz (Fn. 265), S. 155; weitergehend Schwieger (Fn. 257), S. 175/176, der

Hier vertieft sich das Problem der Bestimmung geeigneter Parameter zur Prüfung einer wirtschaftlich messbaren Wertsteigerung. Ein strafrechtlich bedeutsames Risiko besteht aber allemal bei der Abwägung, ob ein immaterieller Vorteil als nicht kompensierte Besserstellung z.B. auf der Seite des Forschungsleiters verbleibt, der wie hier P mit der Forschungstätigkeit auch berufliche Ambitionen verfolgt. Es sind daher Fallsituationen nicht auszuschließen, in denen innerhalb einer von der Rechtsordnung befürworteten drittfinanzierten Forschungsabsprache ein innerbetrieblich durchaus erwünschter Forschungsehrgeiz des facheigenen Personals aufgrund der Begleitumstände das Forschungsprojekt insgesamt zur Untat werden lässt, weil ein an der vertraglichen Gestaltung Beteiligter sein berufliches Fortkommen auf erfolgreicher Forschungstätigkeit aufzubauen versucht. Es bereitet einige Anstrengung, derartigen Fällen eine unrechtsbegründende Gefährdung der Integrität der Verwaltung zu entnehmen. Der Eindruck von Käuflichkeit stellt sich nicht ohne weiteres ein, nur weil im Rahmen der vertraglichen Fixierung eines Forschungsabkommens sich einzelne Forschungsmitglieder durch ihr erfolgreiches Mitwirken berufliche Fortkommenschancen erhoffen. So abwegig man eine solche Annahme auch halten mag, der Wirkbereich des § 331 erfasst auch derartige Geschehensabläufe.

dddd) Tatbestandliche Einbruchstelle

Die vom Gesetzgeber mit der Lockerung der Unrechtsvereinbarung und der Einbeziehung von Drittvorteilen in § 331 vorgenommenen tatbestandlichen Grenzverschiebungen werden in ihren Konsequenzen im Fall B deutlicher noch als im Fall A offen gelegt. Unabhängig davon, welches Rechtsgutsverständnis vertreten wird[649], kann von einer dieses Rechtsgut beeinträchtigenden Gefährdungslage im Fall B nicht ernsthaft gesprochen werden.

Dies gilt in erster Linie für die Motivlage der an der Durchführung von derartigen Forschungsprojekten Beteiligten. Die Wertegemeinschaft billigt mit Recht einer der verbesserten Patientenversorgung mit Medizinpräparaten dienenden Forschungszusammenarbeit zwischen staatlicher Verwaltung und Industrie einen hohen Stellenwert zu. Wer diesen Grundkonsens nicht in Zweifel ziehen will, der muss auch die marktwirtschaftlichen Rahmenbedingungen akzeptieren, unter denen Industrie und Verwaltung ihre Interessenlagen auszuhandeln

---

unabhängig von der objektiven Messbarkeit immaterielle Besserstellungen generell für geeignet hält, den äußeren Eindruck der Befangenheit zu erzeugen; vgl. auch BGH NJW 1985, S. 2654 (2656) zur Erhaltung von Karrierechancen und BGH in NJW 2002, S. 2801 (2804) zur letztlich offen gelassenen Frage, ob in einer Ansehensmehrung und Steigerung der wissenschaftlichen Reputation ein Vorteil i.S.d. § 331 erblickt werden kann.

649 S. zur Diskussion dazu o. S. 47 ff.

versuchen. Im konkreten Einzelfall bedeutet dies, dass der kostenbewusste und bevorzugte Medikamenteneinkauf von in Forschungszusammenarbeit entwickelten Produkten ökonomisch für beide Seiten sinnvoll ist und weder das Vertrauen in die Amtsführung beeinträchtigt, noch eine sachgemäße staatliche Aufgabenerledigung gefährdet.

Ebenso verhält es sich mit etwaigen persönlichen Motiven der Forschungsmitarbeiter. Wissenschaftlicher Ehrgeiz und leistungsbezogenes Streben nach beruflichen Aufstiegschancen kommen der Forschungstätigkeit unmittelbar zugute; sie im Kontext der Drittmittelforschung mit einem vorteils- und damit unrechtsauslösenden Stigma zu versehen, wäre mit dem von der Politik und der Gesellschaft für die Verwaltung eingeforderten Leistungs- und Effizienzprinzip kaum verträglich. Wenn dessen ungeachtet § 331 in diesen Fällen der Medizinforschung die Strafbarkeitsfrage dennoch aufwirft, entsteht nicht nur Rechtsunsicherheit unter den Betroffenen, sondern die Strafnorm selbst steht in Zweifel, ob sie dem an Straftatbestände zu stellenden Bestimmtheitsgebot noch gerecht wird. Lüderssen ist daher zuzustimmen, wenn er damals noch auf der Grundlage der alten Fassung des § 331 eine tatbestandliche Erweiterung[650] wie folgt in Frage stellt: „... ist nur festzuhalten, daß ein Tatbestand, der die normativen Voraussetzungen der Verletzung des von ihm geschützten Rechtsgutes schließlich doch nicht hinreichend explizit macht, an seine Grenzen stößt und komplexen, vielerlei soziale Wertungen einschließenden Sachverhalten gewissermaßen nicht gewachsen ist.“[651]

bbb) Ergebnis

Nach der hier vertretenen Auffassung von den Anforderungen sowohl an die im Zusammenhang mit dem Vorteilsbegriff des § 331 stehenden Prüfkriterien als auch an die Voraussetzungen des Eintritts einer Rechtsgutsgefährdung besteht im Fall B kein begründeter Tatverdacht einer Vorteilsannahme. Dies bedeutet andererseits nicht, dass staatsanwaltliche Ermittlungen nicht zu befürchten wären, zumal nach Ansicht des BGH ein Vorteil bereits im Abschluss eines Vertrages liegen kann. Auch die Frage der Bejahung eines nicht kompensierten Vorteils auf Seiten der Klinik hängt davon ab, welche Wertbemessungsparameter man zugrunde legt und welche Bedeutung man darüber hinaus der besonderen Motivlage der an solchen Forschungsvereinbarungen Beteiligten zumisst.

---

650 Wie sie der Bundesrat vorgeschlagen hatte, o. S. 84; Ähnliches gilt aber auch für die Gesetz gewordene Fassung.

651 Lüderssen, JZ 1997, S. 112 (116).

cc) Fall C

aaa) Tatbestandliche Fragestellung

Im Fall C haben die Parteien einen gegenseitig verpflichtenden Vertrag abgeschlossen, bei dem die Gewährung von Sponsorengeldern die Gegenleistung für die Ermöglichung von firmenbezogener Eigenwerbung darstellt. Zwischen den Beteiligten besteht auch Übereinstimmung, dass M, der in seiner Funktion als Bürgermeister auch Vorsitzender des kommunalen Theatervereins ist, mit diesen Geldern die Durchführung einer Theaterinszenierung veranlassen soll. Diese dem M zugedachte Tätigkeit steht in Bezug zu dem ihm übertragenen konkret-funktionalen Bereich seiner Dienstaufgaben als Bürgermeister, der qua Amtes auch die Aufgaben des Vorsitzenden des Theatervereins wahrzunehmen hat[652]. Zunächst stellt sich die Frage, ob M einen Vorteil für sich oder Dritte (Theaterverein) angenommen hat.

aaaa) Vorteil aus Vertrag[653]

Der Abschluss von Sponsorenverträgen ist grundsätzlich legitim, unterliegt aber den verwaltungsseitig vorgenommenen Restriktionen[654]. Der berechtigte Grund für einschränkende Rahmenvorgaben dürfte u.a. auch darin bestehen, dass beim Sponsoring aufgrund der Höhe der Sponsorengelder im Verhältnis zu der als wesentlich geringwertiger erscheinenden behördlichen Leistungspflicht (Ermöglichung der Unternehmenswerbung) häufig eine Unausgewogenheit der sich gegenüberstehenden Vertragspflichten feststellbar ist. Der vorschnelle Rückschluss auf eine unzulässige Austauschbeziehung liegt daher nahe. Die verwaltungsinterne Billigung von Sponsoringabsprachen als möglicher Finanzierungsquelle für gesellschaftspolitisch unterstützungswürdige Förderbereiche wie Kultur, Sport und Wissenschaft steht damit aber nicht in Abrede.

Vor dem Hintergrund der Entscheidung des BGH in BGHSt 31, 264[655] könnte im Fall C bereits im Abschluss des Sponsoring-Vertrages ein Vorteil zugunsten des Theatervereins liegen. Unbeschadet der Feststellung eines objektiv messbaren vertraglichen Missverhältnisses zwischen den gegenseitigen Leistungsverpflichtungen zugunsten des Gesponserten kommt es für die Frage einer Unrechtsübereinkunft entscheidend auf die dem Verständigungsinhalt zugrunde liegenden Motive der Vertragsparteien an[656]. Der Tatsache des Vorliegens eines

[652] Zum Begriff der Dienstausübung siehe Schönke/Schröder/Cramer, § 331 Rn. 8.
[653] Vgl. die Auseinandersetzung mit der Rspr. des BGH o. S. 135 ff.
[654] Oben S. 114 ff.
[655] Zur Kritik an dieser Entscheidung s. o. S. 137 ff.
[656] Vgl. zur Drittmittelforschung o. S. 138 f.

Vertrages und vor allem dem Vertragsinhalt selbst kommt bei dieser Prüfung indizielle Bedeutung zu. Da Sponsoring gerade durch die Förderung von Verwaltungszielen ohne entsprechende oder üblicherweise zu erwartende Gegenleistung gekennzeichnet ist, kommt dem vertraglich fixierten Synallagma eine wichtige Nachweisfunktion dafür zu, dass es aufgrund der schriftlichen Dokumentation der Sponsoringabsprache nichts zu verheimlichen gibt und mit der Offenlegung der Vertragsbestandteile dem Transparenzgebot genüge getan wurde. Dem Anschein einer mit der Sponsorenleistung bezweckten Beeinflussung der amtsbezogenen Aufgabenwahrnehmung des Gesponserten kann durch die Gewährleistung öffentlicher Nachvollziehbarkeit derartiger Vereinbarungen entgegengewirkt werden. Im Gegenfall der nicht schriftlich fixierten Absprache über die Aushändigung von Sponsorengeldern wären Zweifel an der Seriosität der Handlungsmotive angezeigt. Dies gilt insbesondere in denjenigen Fällen, in denen die Parteien privat befreundet sind und darüber hinaus dienstlichen Kontakt pflegen, oder der Sponsor an Vergabeverfahren der Dienststelle beteiligt ist.

Aus der Vereinbarung im Fall C ergibt sich zwar nicht ausdrücklich, dass die Verpflichtung von B zur Zahlung der Sponsorengelder in Relation zur vereinbarten Gegenleistung der Zulassung geldwerter Eigenwerbung für B als betriebswirtschaftlich unausgewogen zu bewerten ist und damit einen nicht kompensierten Vorteil in Form des überschießenden Geldbetrages zum Nutzen der Theatereinrichtung enthielt. Im Regelfall des Kultur-Sponsorings wird dies aber zweckbedingt so sein und die der Förderung dieses Zwecks dienende Sponsorenleistung eine Gegenleistung wertmäßig übersteigen. Die Rspr. des BGH könnte auch hier der Verneinung eines strafrechtsrelevanten Vorteils entgegenstehen, denn im Fall eines wirksamen Werkvertrages hat der BGH bei zu niedrig vereinbarter Vergütung der Werkleistungen auf einen Vergleich zum üblichen Werklohn abgestellt und in dem Differenzbetrag einen möglichen Vorteil i.S.d. § 331 ausgemacht[657]. Bei Sponsorenverträgen ist eine derartige Vergleichsbetrachtung ausgeschlossen, da es an einem Vergleichsfaktor fehlt. Sponsoring ist ein Förderinstrument und als solches auf Bevorteilung förderungswürdiger Bereiche angelegt. Sponsoring ist so gesehen immer ein vereinbarter Vorteil für denjenigen, dem die Förderung zugute kommt. Wenn die Rechtsordnung derartige Finanzierungsvereinbarungen nicht gänzlich untersagt, sie u.a. im Kulturbereich sogar ausdrücklich zulässt[658], kann der aus einem wirksamen Vertrag entstehende Anspruch auf die zugesagten Fördermittel nicht postwendend Gegenstand strafrechtlicher Prüfung werden. Dies gilt allerdings mit der Einschränkung, dass der Verständigungsinhalt der Vertragsparteien ausschließlich auf die kulturelle Förderung des Theatervereins gerichtet war

---

[657] BGH-Urteil vom 3.7.1991 – 2 StR 132/91.

[658] Vgl. o. S. 113 und 114 ff.

und keine stillschweigenden Nebenabreden bestanden, die den Anschein möglicher Beeinflussung des Gesponserten bei der Amtsführung erzeugen könnten.

Die vertraglich vereinbarte Förderung des Theatervereins im Rahmen einer Sponsoring-Absprache ist zulässig und stellt somit keinen Drittvorteil i.S.d. § 331 dar.

bbbb) Vorteil aus faktischer Verfügung über die Sponsorengelder

Bürgermeister M hat das Sponsorengeld vereinbarungsgemäß von B entgegengenommen, um damit die Kosten für die Durchführung der Theaterinszenierung zu begleichen. Beide wollten das Geld dem Theaterverein zugute kommen lassen, was auch geschehen ist. Die Sponsoringabsprache enthielt somit die Vereinbarung der Weiterleitung des Geldes für Zwecke des Theatervereins.

Der BGH vertritt zu den sog. Weiterleitungsfällen die Auffassung, dass eine Abrede über die Zuwendung des zunächst dem Amtsträger ausgehändigten Geldes an Dritte eine Vorteilserlangung beim Amtsträger selbst nicht ausschließe. Der BGH führt dazu aus: „Entscheidend ist, daß der Beamte zunächst die Verfügungsmöglichkeit erhält. Möglicherweise wird durch die Erfüllung der Abrede der Vorteil nachträglich wieder beseitigt; damit entfällt aber nicht die bereits eingetretene Strafbarkeit“[659].

Der Auffassung des BGH kann nur zugestimmt werden, wenn sie um die Voraussetzung ergänzt wird, dass die Möglichkeit des faktischen Verfügenkönnens über das Geld zu eigenen Zwecken vom Verständigungsinhalt der Parteien miteingeschlossen war. Die im Fall C für M objektiv vorteilhafte Situation, über das in Gewahrsam genommene Geld anderweitig als abgesprochen verfügen zu können, kann nur dann eine Vorteilsstellung in seiner Person begründen, wenn dieses „Durchgangsstadium“ nicht nur notwendige Folge der Sponsoring-Absprache, sondern deren mitvereinbarter Bestandteil war[660]. Dies ist aber im Fall C erkennbar nicht der Fall, da die Möglichkeit der Eigenverwendung des Geldes weder Bestandteil der Vereinbarung war, noch eine derartige Annahme aus den Geschehensabläufen hergeleitet werden kann. Das Risiko einer abweichenden beweisrechtlichen Interpretation besteht aber durchaus und nicht nur in Fall C, sondern in allen Fällen, in denen die Sponsoring-Absprache einer exakt und ausführlich fixierten, vertraglichen Regelung entbehrt und durch fehlende Darlegung des Geldtransfers und der Verbuchung aller Abläufe den Anschein einer persönlichen Verfügungsgewalt der zwischengeschalteten Person über das Geld erwecken kann. Auch an dieser Stelle

---

[659] BGHSt 15, S. 286 (287).

[660] In diesem Sinn auch Kuhlen, NStZ 1988, S. 433 (436).

wird deutlich, dass eine vollständige und detaillierte schriftliche Offenlegung der von den Parteien abgesprochenen Förderzuwendung unverzichtbar ist.

cccc) Immaterielle Vorteile

Aus den Gesamtumständen im Fall C lassen sich mehrere für M mittelbar vorteilhafte Auswirkungen ableiten. Als Mitveranlasser der den Gemeindemitgliedern letztlich zugute kommenden Kulturförderung dürfte er seine Chancen auf Wiederwahl als Bürgermeister vermutlich erhöht und auf der gemeindeinternen Beliebtheitsskala einen Schritt nach vorn getan haben. Zudem könnte er als Theatervereinsvorsitzender Einfluss auf den theaterinternen Verwendungsmodus der Sponsorengelder nehmen und auch in dieser Funktion dann als einflussreich erscheinen, eben als jemand, dem zugetraut werden kann, dass er Sponsorengelder erfolgreich einwirbt und für das Gemeinwesen zweckgerichtet einsetzt. Dies lässt die Schlussfolgerung zu, dass M bereits mit der Chance auf Abschluss der Sponsorenvereinbarung und damit der Erlangung der Sponsorengelder eine für ihn persönlich vorteilhafte und nicht durch die gegenseitigen Vertragspflichten kompensierte Rechtsposition eingenommen hat.

Die herrschende Meinung fordert zwar zur Eingrenzung solcher immaterieller Vorteile die objektive Messbarkeit der dem Anschein nach vorteilbehafteten Auswirkungen auf die Person des Amtsträgers[661], die Meinungen fallen aber bei der Beurteilung des Einzelfalles häufig unterschiedlich aus. So kann man außerhalb wertmäßig nur schwer einzuschätzender subjektiver Gefühlsempfindungen, wie etwa bei befriedigtem Ehrgeiz, jedenfalls der erhöhten beruflichen Chance auf Wiederwahl zum Bürgermeister durchaus eine materielle Besserstellung beimessen[662].

Geht man demnach im Fall C von einem objektiv messbaren Vorteil für B aus, so ist damit allerdings noch nicht gesagt, dass dieser Vorteil auch Gegenstand ihrer Übereinkunft war, d.h., dass die Vertragspartner B und M in ihre Verständigung nicht nur eine Zweckbestimmung für die Sponsorengelder aufgenommen, sondern auch die Chancenerhöhung einer Wiederwahl von M im Amt des Bürgermeisters ausdrücklich miteinbezogen oder zumindest einkalkuliert haben. Die Verneinung einer solchen möglicherweise nur stillschweigenden Verständigung wird von der Plausibilität des Vorbringens politisch gewahrter

661 Vgl. o. unter Fn. 648.

662 Man denke nur an den Berufspolitiker, der sich mit der Einwerbung von Sponsorengeldern für öffentlichkeitswirksame Projekte Hoffnungen auf zählbaren Wählerstimmenzuwachs macht; ebenso wie hier Kuhlen für den Fall des Parteimitglieds, das sich Hoffnungen auf einen besser dotierten Posten machen kann, NStZ 1988, S.433 (437); zurückhaltender Dauster in NStZ 1999, S.63 (65), der nur in Ausnahmefällen die objektive Messbarkeit der Werthaltigkeit eines Leistungstransfers bezüglich der Erhaltung von Karrierechancen für möglich hält.

Neutralität in Bezug auf die Sponsoringmaßnahme abhängen. Im Fall C stehen mit der Tatsache der engen privaten Freundschaft zwischen den Vertragspartnern und der Verflechtung in beruflicher Hinsicht Sachmerkmale im Raum, die einer Entkräftung des Vorwurfs einer unrechtmäßig zustande gekommenen Sponsoring-Absprache eher entgegenstehen, als dass sie sie stützen.

Im Ergebnis ist festzustellen, dass für M erhebliche strafrechtliche Risiken bestehen, sich dem Vorwurf eigennützigen Verhaltens auszusetzen. Gleiches gilt für B bezüglich einer Vorteilsgewährung nach § 333.

dddd) „Für die Dienstausübung“

Zu den rechtlichen Anforderungen an die Ausgestaltung des Beziehungsverhältnisses zwischen Vorteil und Dienstausübung wird auf die Ausführungen zu Fall A verwiesen[663]. Demnach ist nicht Voraussetzung für die Bejahung dieses Tatbestandsmerkmals ein vom Bewusstsein der Parteien getragenes (synallagmatisches) Gegenleistungsverhältnis, sondern es reicht aus, dass über eine rein kausale Verbindung hinaus die Parteien sich der inneren Verknüpfung der dienstlichen Tätigkeit mit der Vorteilsgewährung im Sinne eines Zusammenhangsverhältnisses bewusst sind[664]. Im Fall C ist Inhalt der Vereinbarung die finanzielle Förderung einer Theaterinszenierung, bei der M in seiner Funktion als Bürgermeister und damit Vorsitzender des Theatervereins vor allem die etatmäßigen Abwicklungsaufgaben obliegen. Für die dienstliche Durchführung dieser Aufgaben und sogar als vertragliche Gegenleistung für die von ihm ebenfalls dienstlich zu veranlassende Werbeaktion auf den Theaterkarten zugunsten des B sind ihm die Fördergelder laut Vereinbarung ausgehändigt worden. Damit ist nicht nur ein Zusammenhangsverhältnis, sondern sogar ein Gegenleistungsverhältnis zwischen der Übergabe der Sponsorengelder und den genannten dienstlichen Tätigkeiten des M begründet worden. M und B sind sich auch dieser Verknüpfung beider Vereinbarungsbestandteile bewusst. Das Tatmerkmal „für die Dienstausübung“ liegt im Fall C somit vor.

eeee) Tatbestandliche Einbruchstelle

Der Sinn und Zweck einer Sponsoring-Absprache liegt in der Unterstützung förderungswürdiger Interessen der Allgemeinheit. Nicht notwendig verbunden damit sind Gegenleistungsverpflichtungen auf Seiten des Empfängers von Sponsoringleistungen, der sie ihrem bestimmungsgemäßen Zweck zuführen soll und der dazu – sofern er Amtsträger ist – dienstlich tätig werden muss. Die Untersuchung der Voraussetzungen des Vorteilsbegriffs und der Unrechtsvereinbarung hat aber gezeigt, dass bereits nach der alten Fassung des § 331 das

663 Oben S. 126 ff.

664 In diesem Sinne auch Schönke/Schröder/Cramer, § 331 Rn. 29.

Strafbarkeitsrisiko auf Seiten des Amtsträgers nicht unerheblich ist. Nach neuem Recht genügt jetzt sogar ein Drittvorteil, der im Fall C zur Frage eines Vorteils aus Vertrag zugunsten des Theatervereins geführt hat. Dabei ist völlig offen, mit welchem strafrechtlichen Ergebnis die Rspr. dem beim Sponsoring regelmäßig nicht kompensierten Vorteil auf Nehmerseite im Einzelfall begegnen wird. Der BGH müsste bei konsequenter Anwendung seiner bisherigen Rspr. die Annahme eines Vorteils aus dem Abschluss eines Sponsoring-Vertrages oder zumindest aus dem unausgewogenen Inhalt des Vertrages in Betracht ziehen. Ein solches Ergebnis würde aber der Akzeptanz des Instituts des Sponsorings in Politik und Verwaltung entgegenstehen. Zudem besteht beim Sponsoring die hohe Wahrscheinlichkeit, dass das Tatmerkmal der Unrechtsvereinbarung – jedenfalls nach der neuen Fassung des § 331 – bejaht werden muss. Soweit Sponsoring-Absprachen nach der alten Fassung des § 331 den Nachweis einer auf eine bestimmte, konkretisierbare Diensthandlung gerichteten Unrechtsübereinkunft erforderten, war dem verfassungsrechtlichen Bestimmtheitsgebot hinreichend Rechnung getragen. Nach neuem Recht genügt nach der hier vertretenen Interpretation des Wortlauts des § 331 ein Beziehungszusammenhang zwischen dienstlicher Tätigkeit und Vorteil, der nicht die Qualität eines Gegenleistungsverhältnisses aufweisen muss.

Sponsoring unterliegt damit nach der aktuellen Gesetzesfassung des § 331 einem erheblichen Strafbarkeitsrisiko. Der gesellschaftspolitische, verwaltungsökonomische und strafgesetzgeberische Interessenkonflikt zwischen der Akzeptanz dieses Instituts auf der einen Seite und der strafrechtlichen Sanktionierung auf der anderen Seite sollte mit einer ausdrücklichen Klärung dieser Frage in die eine oder andere Richtung einer gesetzgeberischen Lösung zugeführt werden.

bbb) Ergebnis

Nach den Gesamtumständen besteht ein hinreichender Anfangsverdacht für strafrechtliche Ermittlungen im Hinblick auf eine Vorteilsannahme nach § 331. Einen Prüfansatz könnte nach der Rspr. die Annahme eines Vorteils für Dritte aus dem Vertragsabschluss bzw. eines eigenen Vorteils des M aus der faktischen Verfügungsmöglichkeit über die Sponsorengelder oder zumindest die Bejahung eines immateriellen Vorteils des M bilden. Einer näheren strafprozessualen Begutachtung bedürfte die Unrechtsvereinbarung, die einen im Bewusstsein der Parteien abgebildeten Beziehungszusammenhang zwischen dienstlicher Tätigkeit und Vorteil aufweisen müsste.

dd) Konsequenzen aus den Fallergebnissen?

Bei der Gegenüberstellung der Fallschilderungen A, B und C zu den strafrechtlichen Verbotsnormen der §§ 331, 333 weichen die Ergebnisse einer

Prüfung der strafrechtlichen Sanktionsbedürftigkeit deutlich ab von den Ergebnissen einer strafrechtlichen Subsumtion. Während die Strafwürdigkeit in beinahe allen Fallvarianten in Zweifel steht, unterliegen diese Fälle konträr hierzu einem beachtlichen Strafbarkeitsrisiko. Aus dieser Erkenntnis heraus hat die Medizinprodukteindustrie zur Selbstkontrolle und zur Verhinderung eines Korruptionsverdachts des Unternehmens oder seiner Mitarbeiter den Kodex „Medizinprodukte“ erstellt[665]. Mit diesem Kodex soll „durch geeignete Selbstkontrollmechanismen staatlichen (Über-)Reaktionen“ zuvorgekommen werden[666]. Wie in den Fällen A und B aufgezeigt, nährt sich ein strafrechtlicher Verdacht bei der Drittmittelforschung „aus tatsächlich bestehenden oder auch nur vermeintlichen Beziehungen zwischen Unterstützungsleistungen und dem Produktabsatz von Medizinprodukteunternehmen“[667].

Mit ähnlichen Präventionsabsichten ist für den Bereich des Instituts des Sponsorings im Jahr 1998 eine Richtlinie der Bundesregierung erstellt worden[668].

Neben derartigen, außerstrafrechtliche Präventionsmaßnahmen[669] ergänzenden Regelungsmechanismen stellt sich vorrangig aber die Frage, ob nicht das Strafrecht selbst zur Eingrenzung tatbestandlicher Überdehnungen interne Korrektive bereitstellen muss. Eine Auseinandersetzung mit den in der Wissenschaft diskutierten Ansätzen ist daher an dieser Stelle erforderlich.

---

665 Dieners, JZ 1998, S. 181 (183).

666 Der Kodex soll deutlich machen, welche Aktivitäten in der komplexen Zusammenarbeit zwischen der medizinischen Industrie mit den Krankenhäusern und Ärzten erlaubt sind, ohne sich in der strafrechtlichen Grauzone bereits einem Korruptionsverdacht auszusetzen, Dieners, JZ 1998, S. 181 (183).

667 Dieners, JZ 1998, S.181 (184); zu den 3 Prinzipien Trennungs-, Transparenz- und Dokumentationsprinzip des Kodex s. S. 184/185.

668 BAnz. S. 9665; vgl. den Zweck der die Nr. 18 der Richtlinie ergänzenden Empfehlung des BMI, jeden Anschein fremder Einflussnahme auf die Integrität und die wettbewerbsrechtliche Neutralität des Staates anhand der Vorgabe von Verhaltensregeln vermeiden zu wollen.

669 Dazu zählen auf Seiten der Verwaltung behördeninterne Kontrollinstrumente wie Innenrevision und Verstärkung der Dienst- und Fachaufsicht sowie dienstrechtliche Maßnahmen wie Personalrotation und die Einführung des Vier-Augen-Prinzips, vgl. umfassend Kerner/Rixen, GA 1996, S. 355 (367 ff.) und Dölling, Gutachten C, C 44 ff.

Zweiter Abschnitt: Die strafrechtlichen Korrektive zur Eingrenzung der Strafbarkeit der Vorteilsannahme

Überwiegend haben die Autoren oder Kommentatoren, die sich vertieft mit der Neufassung der Korruptionsdelikte auseinandergesetzt haben, Versuche der Eingrenzung eines zu weit gefassten Tatbestandes der Vorteilsannahme[670] unternommen[671]. Auf die dogmatischen Ansätze wird im Nachfolgenden eingegangen. Übereinstimmung besteht jedenfalls in der Notwendigkeit normeingrenzender Mechanismen, um diejenigen nicht strafwürdigen Fälle wieder aus dem Tatbestand zu eliminieren, die durch die Erweiterung der Tatbestände durch das KorrBekG einen Normverstoß begründen. Für den Betrachter wirkt dies wie Flickschusterei an einem zu groß gewordenen Schuh, in den zwar jeder Fuß passt, der aber für den, der ihn tragen soll, noch zurechtgeschnitten werden muss[672].

I. Bereits nach altem Recht vorhandene Instrumentarien

1. Institut der Sozialadäquanz

Nach diesem seit langem bei den Bestechungsdelikten anerkannten Regulativ sollen geringfügige Zuwendungen dann nicht unter die Bestechungstatbestände fallen, wenn sie den allgemein anerkannten Regeln des sozialen Verkehrs und damit dem Gedanken der sozialen Adäquanz entsprechen[673]. Letztlich können über dieses Institut der Sozialadäquanz nur Bagatellzuwendungen[674] aus dem Tatbestand herausgefiltert werden, wie z.B. das legendäre Neujahrsgeschenk an den Postboten. Keine Hilfe ist von diesem in seinem Anwendungsbereich sehr begrenzten Regulativ in Fällen höherer Zuwendungsbeträge zu erwarten[675], da ein Strafbarkeitsausschluss ohne gesetzliche Fixierung nicht beliebig weit normbegrenzende Wirkung entfalten kann[676]. In den Bereichen der finanziellen Förderung gesellschaftspolitisch förderungswürdiger Themenkreise wie z.B.

---

670 Entsprechendes gilt seit dem KorrBekG für die Vorteilsgewährung.

671 Vgl. u. S. 155 ff., unter II. und III.

672 Treffend auch Schönke/Schröder/Cramer, § 331 Rn. 53a, der kritisiert, dass sich die „heutige Gesetzgebung bei Fassung einer Norm vorwiegend, gelegentlich sogar ausschließlich, an einer einzigen Fallkonstellation orientiert und dabei übersieht, daß die auf den Fall konzipierte, aber abstrakt formulierte Regelung auch eindeutig nicht strafwürdige Fälle ... erfaßt".

673 Vgl. BGHSt 33, S. 336 (339) und 39, S. 45 (47 f.); Rudolphi, SK, § 331 Rn. 23; Tröndle/Fischer, § 331 Rn. 20.

674 Vgl. die Fälle bei Geerds (Fn. 42), S. 73 ff.

675 Korte, NStZ 1997, S. 513 (515); Lüderssen, JZ 1997, S. 112 (116); Dölling, Gutachten C, C 70 f.; Schönke/Schröder/Cramer, § 331 Rn. 53.

676 Ähnlich Schönke/Schröder/Cramer, § 331 Rn. 53.

Kultur, Sport und Ökologie und der finanziellen Unterstützung von Forschungsvorhaben hilft das Institut der Sozialadäquanz nicht weiter, da die gültigen Maßstäbe des Gewohnheitsrechts hier versagen. Sicherlich wäre denkbar, den gegenwärtig gewohnheitsrechtlich gesteckten Rahmen über geringwertige Zuwendungen aus Höflichkeit und Konvention hinaus durch Aufnahme einer Sozialadäquanz-Klausel in das Gesetz auszudehnen. Die Schwierigkeiten einer hinreichenden Konkretisierung der Verhaltensweisen, die dann als sozial adäquat zu qualifizieren wären, wären aber beträchtlich. Eine solche Lösung erscheint daher nicht praktikabel.

2. Institut der Genehmigung nach § 331 Abs. 3

Mit den Genehmigungsregelungen des § 331 Abs. 3 und korrespondierend des § 333 Abs. 3 hat der Gesetzgeber versucht, bestimmte tatbestandsmäßige Verhaltensweisen von der Strafbarkeit auszuschließen. Das Institut der Genehmigung ist in seiner Wechselwirkung zu beamtenrechtlichen Bestimmungen wie auch in der Frage der Rechtsnatur ebenso kompliziert wie umstritten[677], so dass am Ende mehr Zweifel über seinen Anwendungsbereich bestehen bleiben, als dass eine in ihren rechtlichen Auswirkungen verständliche und eindeutige Handhabung gewährleistet erschiene[678].

Lüderssen bezweifelt zudem zu Recht, ob das Erlaubtsein des Zusammenwirkens zwischen Wirtschaft und Verwaltung von einer behördlichen Ermessensentscheidung abhängig gemacht und nicht besser von vornherein mit Allgemeinverbindlichkeit entschieden werden sollte[679]. Tatsächlich sind im Be-

---

677 Nach Schönke/Schröder/Cramer, § 331 Rn. 43/44 ist § 331 Abs. 3 mit den beamtenrechtlichen Vorschriften über die Verpflichtung, eine Genehmigung zur Geschenkannahme einzuholen (für den Bund vgl. § 70 BBG), nicht in Einklang zu bringen, so dass Abs. 3 nach strafrechtlichen Kriterien auszulegen sei; in diese Richtung auch Rudolphi, SK, § 331 Rn. 35 f.; zur Frage der Rechtsnatur der Genehmigung nach Abs. 3 vertritt die h.M. die Auffassung, dass bei der vorherigen Genehmigung immer ein Rechtfertigungsgrund und bei der nachträglichen Genehmigung je nach Fallgestaltung entweder ein Rechtfertigungsgrund oder ein Strafaufhebungsgrund vorliege, vgl. Schönke/Schröder/Cramer, § 331 Rn. 46-50; Lackner/Kühl, § 331 Rn. 16; Jescheck, LK, § 331 Rn. 16; Tröndle/Fischer, § 331 Rn. 31; Dölling Gutachten C, C 71; der Gesetzgeber hatte diese Frage offen gelassen, BT-Drs. 7/550, S. 272, anders noch im E 1962, BT-Drs. IV/650, S. 655.

678 Vgl. nur die zahlreichen Einzelfragen bei Schönke/Schröder/Cramer, § 331 Rn. 42-51; im Detail s. auch Hardtung (Fn. 265), S. 109-156 für die vorherige Genehmigung und S. 157-229 für die nachträgliche Genehmigung; bei Auslagerung staatlicher Aufgaben stellen sich verfahrensrechtliche Fragen zur Genehmigung, wenn beim Täter kein öffentlich-rechtliches Amtsverhältnis besteht, Jutzi NStZ 1991, S. 105 (106 ff.).

679 Lüderssen, JZ 1997, S. 112 (119); Lüderssen hält diese „obrigkeitlich orientierte Technik der Tatbestandsbildung", d.h. die Begrenzung der Anwendbarkeit eines weit gefassten Tatbestandes durch Genehmigungsvorbehalte für nicht mehr zeitgemäß.

reich der Drittmittelforschung wie auch beim Sponsoring Konfliktkonstellationen vorstellbar, in denen sich die zuständige Genehmigungsbehörde nicht vollständig von jeder Parteilichkeit und Interessenbeeinflusstheit freisprechen könnte. Wer im weiteren Sinne als übergeordnete Behörde auf der Seite des Empfängers erwünschter Sponsoring- oder Forschungsgelder steht, müsste sich in den Genehmigungsverfahren besonders restriktiv verhalten, um nicht dem Anschein einer Interessenkollision mit dem dann fragwürdigen Einfluss auf die Fehlerfreiheit der Ermessensausübung ausgesetzt zu sein.

In § 331 Abs. 3 ist zudem nur der Rahmen vorgegeben, unter welchen Voraussetzungen die Vorteilsannahme nicht strafbar ist, unter welchen Voraussetzungen sie genehmigungsfähig ist, entscheidet sich nach der Rechtsordnung[680]. Wenn aber bei der Förderung von Forschung und Lehre Finanzierungshilfen zu diesem Zweck ausdrücklich unter dem Schutz der Verfassung stehen (Art. 5 Abs. 3 Satz 1 GG), spricht einiges für einen daraus abzuleitenden allgemeinen Erlaubnistatbestand, der nicht durch einen Genehmigungsvorbehalt außer Kraft gesetzt werden kann[681]. In dieselbe Richtung weist auch Zieschang, der darauf hinweist, dass nach § 25 Abs. 3 HRG ein Forschungsvorhaben nur anzuzeigen ist, dann aber nicht von einer Genehmigung abhängig gemacht werden darf[682]. In dieser Widersprüchlichkeit offenbart sich die fehlende Harmonisierung eines generalisierenden Vorbehalts mit den in Einzelfällen bereits von der Rechtsordnung entschiedenen Erlaubnisfällen. Für die Institute der Drittmittelforschung und des Sponsoring, bei denen die Rechtsgemeinschaft von der grundsätzlichen Zulässigkeit ausgeht, hilft § 331 Abs. 3 für die Frage einer tatbestandsinternen Begrenzung somit kaum weiter, zumal die Tatbestandsmäßigkeit nach h.M. nicht in Wegfall geraten würde, sondern allenfalls die Rechtswidrigkeit.

II. Auf dem 61. DJT vorgeschlagene Alternative der „Eignung“ des Vorteils

Eine der auf dem 61. DJT vorgeschlagenen Alternativen zur Lockerung der Unrechtsvereinbarung sah vor, an die Eignung des Vorteils, den Amtsträger bei der lauteren Wahrnehmung seiner dienstlichen Aufgaben zu beeinflussen, anzuknüpfen[683]. Der Vorschlag basiert auf Beiträgen von Schlicht, Lüderssen, König und Volk[684], die in der Zielrichtung einer tatbestandlich ausgewiesenen Begrenzung des Vorteilsbegriffs einig sind. Während König bei der tatbestand-

---

680 Tröndle/Fischer, § 331 Rn. 31.

681 Ebenso Dauster NStZ 1999, S. 63 (68).

682 Zieschang, WissR 1999, S. 111 (115).

683 Der Vorschlag wurde mit 45:60:10 Stimmen abgelehnt, Vh. 61. DJT, Bd. II/2, Beschlüsse, L 189.

684 Nachweise s. o. unter den Fn. 446 und 451.

lichen Restriktion vor allem eine materielle Wertgrenze als Abgrenzungskriterium im Auge hat[685], vertreten Lüderssen und Volk weitergehende Ansätze.

1. Auffassung von Lüderssen

Lüderssen, der auf den Begriff der „Unangemessenheit" des Vorteils abstellt, will mit dieser generalklauselartigen tatbestandlichen Fixierung einmal den Rahmen vorgeben, das deutlich höhere Strafbarkeitsrisiko bei unlauteren Handlungen im öffentlichen Dienst im Vergleich zu entsprechenden Handlungen in der Privatwirtschaft der dortigen Beschränkung der Strafbarkeit auf „unlautere" Verhaltensweisen anzugleichen[686]. Hier wie dort gehe es in den Tatbeständen darum, „für die Gemeinschaft schädliche Unlauterkeiten in Austauschverhältnissen zu verändern". In Analogie zum Begriff „unlauter" bei der sogenannten Angestelltenbestechung nach § 299 sei die Formulierung „unangemessener Vorteil" bei der Vorteilsannahme des Amtsträgers zu bewerten[687]. Lüderssen verfolgt ein zweites Anliegen, indem er mit der Begriffsauswahl eine dogmatische Grundlage schaffen will, auf der Regularien für eine adäquate Zusammenarbeit zwischen Industrie und öffentlichen Institutionen in Korrespondenz zu vorhandenen Kodizes[688] entwickelt werden können[689].

2. Auffassung von Volk

Volk schlägt eine Einschränkung des Vorteilsbegriffs auf „unangemessene" oder „rechtswidrige" Vorteile für den Fall vor, dass der Gesetzgeber auf das Tatbestandsmerkmal der Unrechtsvereinbarung ganz verzichten sollte[690]. Tragender Gedanke der Überlegungen von Volk ist sein Verständnis des Korrup-

---

685 König, JR 1997, S. 397 (399); in diese Richtung gehende Vorschläge des 61. DJT wurden ebenfalls abgelehnt, so die Beschränkung auf „nicht nur geringfügige Vorteile" und der Vorschlag einer Festschreibung auf bestimmte Höchstbeträge, Vh. 61. DJT, Bd. II/2, Beschlüsse, L 190; zur Kritik an dem Begriff der „Eignung" siehe Dölling, Vh. 61. DJT, Bd. II/2, L 181, der auf die Unschärfe des Begriffs und die bei Übernahme in dic Gesetzesformulierung neu auftretenden ungeklärten Abgrenzungsfragen hinweist.

686 Lüderssen, JZ 1997, S. 112 (117).

687 Lüderssen, JZ 1997, S. 112 (117).

688 Der Kodex „Medizinprodukte", NJW 1997, Heft 24, S. XX ff., hat zwar nicht den Charakter einer Rechtsnorm, dient aber als Grundsatzregelung für die beigetretenen Organisationen der Transparenz und Dokumentation und soll vermitteln, was in der Zusammenarbeit zwischen Ärzteschaft, Krankenhäusern und Industrie erlaubt ist und was nicht; im Einzelnen siehe Dieners, JZ 1998, S. 181 (183 f.).

689 Lüderssen, JZ 1997, S. 112 (117/120).

690 Dies ist aber nicht geschehen, vgl. o. u. Fn. 431-436 und 447-450; Volk, Referat zum 61. DJT, Vh. Bd. II/1, L 35 (L 52).

tionsbegriffs, der den Tausch von Vorteilen unter Regelverstoß beinhalte[691]. Dieser Regelverstoß müsse im Tatbestand zum Ausdruck kommen, entweder beim Vorteilsbegriff oder beim Austauschverhältnis[692]. Volk befürchtete bei der nicht Gesetz gewordenen Entwurfsfassung eines neuen § 331, der den Drittvorteil einbezog und jeden Zusammenhang mit dem Amt genügen lassen wollte, eine Pönalisierung jedes Amtsträgers, „der ein Geschäft für den Staat macht und damit nur tut, was er soll"[693]. Volk entwickelt Beispiele des Sponsoring und der Drittmittelforschung, um nachzuweisen, dass nach dem oben genannten Entwurf wirtschaftlich vernünftiges Verhalten des Amtsträgers bestraft würde, ohne einen Regelverstoß ausmachen zu können[694]. Dabei weist er auf den fragmentarischen Charakter des Strafrechts hin, wonach „Strafrecht dort zur Bekämpfung der Korruption nicht beitragen kann, wo die moralische Übereinkunft über ihre Verwerflichkeit fehlt"[695]. Ähnlich wie Lüderssen empfiehlt Volk in diesem Zusammenhang eine Angleichung der unterschiedlich hohen Strafbarkeitsrisiken zwischen Korruption im öffentlichen Dienst und Korruption in der Wirtschaft[696].

3. Eigene Auffassung

Die von Volk zum Ausdruck gebrachte Befürchtung einer uferlosen Ausweitung des Tatbestandes der Vorteilsannahme ohne erkennbaren Regelverstoß ist auch nach der Gesetz gewordenen Neufassung des § 331 durchaus berechtigt wie die Untersuchungen im ersten Abschnitt ergeben haben. Bei der Analyse einzelner Fälle wurde deutlich, dass die typischen Grundmuster des Sponsoring und der Drittmittelforschung kaum Anzeichen für gemeinschädliches Verhalten aufweisen, dessen Bekämpfung allein Aufgabe des Strafrechts ist. Wenn die Rechtsgemeinschaft einerseits ökonomisch sinnvolle Unterstützungsleistungen der Industrie zugunsten defizitär ausgestatteter Staatshaushalte befürwortet und andererseits mehr betriebswirtschaftlich ausgerichtetes Denken in den Amtsstuben zum Nutzen des Steuerzahlers erwartet, dann fehlt es in der Rechtswirklichkeit ohne Zweifel an einem moralischen oder sozialen Unwerturteil bezüglich der Zusammenarbeit zwischen Industrie und öffentlicher Verwaltung. Dies gilt dort uneingeschränkt, wo diese Zusammenarbeit von der Rechtsordnung gebilligt wird und die vorgegebenen Verhaltensstandards eingehalten werden.

---

691 Volk, Vh. Bd. II/1, L 35 (L43/51).
692 Volk, Vh. Bd. II/1, L 35 (L 43/52).
693 Volk, Vh. Bd. II/1, L 35 (L 43).
694 Der Angestellte der Privatklinik bliebe dagegen unbestraft, Volk, Vh. Bd. II/1, L 35 (L 42/43).
695 Volk, Vh. Bd. II/1, L 35 (L 50).
696 Volk, Vh. Bd. II/1, L 35 (L 44 f).

Die von Lüderssen und Volk gewählte dogmatische Konstruktion über eine Restriktion des Vorteilsbegriffs kann letztendlich nicht zufrieden stellen, weil mit ihr neue Auslegungsprobleme in den Tatbestand getragen würden[697]. Diese reichen von der Frage einer materiellen Wertgrenze, ab der die Eignung zur Beeinflussung Dritter im Einzelfall zu verneinen wäre, bis zu der Frage, ob nach dem Eignungsbegriff eine abstrakte oder konkrete Sichtweise vorzunehmen wäre. Auch der Begriff des „unangemessenen Vorteils" führt aus dieser Problematik nicht heraus. Um dem berechtigten Anliegen der Herauslösung von Austauschbeziehungen aus der Strafbarkeit nachzukommen, die von der Rechtsordnung für zulässig oder sogar für erwünscht bewertet werden, sollte der Blick weniger auf den materiellen Wert einer Zuwendung als auf die dem Leistungstransfer zugrunde liegenden rechtlichen Maßstäbe gelenkt werden[698].

III. Eingrenzungsversuche auf der Grundlage des geltenden Rechts

1. Der Ansatz von Zieschang

Für die Fälle der Drittmittelforschung untersucht Zieschang die Frage, ob nicht § 25 HRG generell als Rechtfertigungsgrund herangezogen werden kann[699]. Die Absätze 1 bis 4 des § 25 HRG[700] lauten:

> (1) Die in der Forschung tätigen Hochschulmitglieder sind berechtigt, im Rahmen ihrer dienstlichen Aufgaben auch solche Forschungsvorhaben durchzuführen, die nicht aus den der Hochschule zur Verfügung stehenden Haushaltsmitteln, sondern aus Mitteln Dritter finanziert werden; ihre Verpflichtung zur Erfüllung der übrigen Dienstaufgaben bleibt unberührt. Die Durchführung von Vorhaben nach Satz 1 ist Teil der Hochschulforschung.
> (2) Ein Hochschulmitglied ist berechtigt, ein Forschungsvorhaben nach Absatz 1 in der Hochschule durchzuführen, wenn die Erfüllung anderer Aufgaben der Hochschule sowie die Rechte und Pflichten anderer Personen dadurch nicht beeinträchtigt werden und entstehende Folgelasten angemessen berücksichtigt sind; die Forschungsergebnisse sollen in der Regel in absehbarer Zeit veröffentlicht werden.
> (3) Ein Forschungsvorhaben nach Absatz 1 ist anzuzeigen. Die Durchführung eines solchen Vorhabens darf nicht von einer Genehmigung abhängig gemacht werden. Die Inanspruchnahme von Personal, Sachmitteln und Einrichtungen der Hochschule darf nur untersagt oder durch

---

697 Das deutet Lüderssen denn auch an, JZ 1997, S. 112 (117); so auch König, JR 1997, S. 397 (399).

698 Dazu s. u. S. 162 ff.

699 Zieschang, WissR 1999, S. 111 (116).

700 In der Fassung der Bekanntmachung vom 9. April 1987, BGBl. I S. 1170 (1177).

Auflagen beschränkt werden, soweit die Voraussetzungen des Absatzes 2 dies erfordern.

(4) Die Mittel für Forschungsvorhaben, die in der Hochschule durchgeführt werden, sollen von der Hochschule verwaltet werden. Die Mittel sind für den vom Geldgeber bestimmten Zweck zu verwenden und nach dessen Bedingungen zu bewirtschaften, soweit gesetzliche Bestimmungen nicht entgegenstehen. Treffen die Bedingungen keine Regelung, so gelten ergänzend die Bestimmungen des Landes. Auf Antrag des Hochschulmitglieds, das das Vorhaben durchführt, soll von der Verwaltung der Mittel durch die Hochschule abgesehen werden, sofern dies mit den Bedingungen des Geldgebers vereinbar ist; Satz 3 gilt in diesem Falle nicht.

In den Absätzen 1 und 2 wird von einer Berechtigung der in der Forschung tätigen Hochschulmitglieder im Hinblick auf ihre dienstlichen Aufgaben gesprochen, aus Drittmitteln finanzierte Forschungsvorhaben durchzuführen. Das Merkmal der Berechtigung gibt aber nur Auskunft über die Zulässigkeit, in der Eigenschaft als Hochschulmitglied im Rahmen der dienstlichen Aufgaben auch in der Forschung selbständig tätig werden zu dürfen[701]. Zu Recht verneint Zieschang daher bei § 25 HRG einen weitergehenden, die Rechtswidrigkeit strafrechtlicher Tatbestände ausschließenden Effekt. Die Richtigkeit dieser Ansicht wird durch § 25 Abs. 4 Satz 2 HRG bestätigt, der die Zweckbindung des Geldgebers bei der Mittelverwendung mit der Einschränkung versieht, dass gesetzliche Bestimmungen nicht entgegenstehen dürfen[702]. Zieschang spricht sich daher im Ergebnis gegen die „gewagte Konstruktion" aus, § 25 HRG als Rechtfertigungsgrund anzuerkennen. Darin ist ihm von der Gesetzestechnik her zuzustimmen, da § 25 HRG die Rahmenbedingungen und Zulässigkeitsvoraussetzungen für durch Drittmittel finanzierte Forschungsvorhaben an Hochschulen festlegt und nicht der Systematik von Rechtfertigungsgründen folgt. Dem Grundgedanken nach enthält § 25 HRG auch keine rechtfertigende, sondern eine rechtsbegründende Intention. Mit der Einhaltung bestimmter in § 25 HRG normierter Regeln soll die von staatlicher Seite erwünschte Forschungsförderung in ihrer wissenschaftlichen Unabhängigkeit gewährleistet werden. § 25 HRG bringt zum Ausdruck, dass eine Forschungsfinanzierung unter diesen Voraussetzungen eine von der Rechtsordnung anerkannte Form der Forschungsförderung darstellt. In diesem Sinne kommt der Regelung im Hinblick auf § 331 tatbestandsausschließende, nicht rechtfertigende Wirkung zu[703].

---

701 Zieschang, WissR 1999, S. 111 (116).

702 Hierunter fallen auch die §§ 331 ff.

703 Ähnlich Ratzel MedR 1998, S. 98 (99).

2. Der Ansatz von Cramer

Um die nicht strafwürdigen Lebenssachverhalte[704] dem Geltungsbereich der §§ 331, 333 zu entziehen, geht Cramer von einem übergesetzlichen Rechtfertigungsgrund aus, der dann heranzuziehen sei, wenn „überwiegende Interessen einer Vorteilsgewährung an Dritte der Strafbarkeit nach §§ 331, 333 entgegenstehen“[705]. Die Beurteilung, ob überwiegende Interessen bestehen, müsse durch Rückgriff auf die Verfassung und die Gesetze erfolgen. Für das Institut des Sponsorings entwickelt Cramer aus dem Steuerrecht den Grundgedanken, „daß Zuwendungen, die zur Verwirklichung von staatlichen, kulturellen oder karitativen usw. Zwecken bestimmt sind und daher abgesetzt werden können, nicht als rechtswidrige Vorteile in Betracht zu ziehen sind“[706]. Für das Institut der Drittmittelforschung folgert er die Straflosigkeit unmittelbar aus dem Schutz der Verfassung (Art. 5 Abs. 3 GG)[707]. Die Herleitung eines strafrechtsbegrenzenden Rechtfertigungsgrundes aus der übergeordneten Rechtsordnung erscheint plausibel, kann aber auf der Grundlage des von Cramer verfolgten dogmatischen Anknüpfungspunktes in der Gestalt eines „übergesetzlichen Notstandes“[708] nicht überzeugen. Dies wird bei Auflösung des von Cramer angeführten Falls des nach Strafprozessrecht rechtmäßig handelnden Staatsanwalts deutlich. Dessen als tatbestandsmäßig gewürdigtes Verhalten erst über eine notstandsähnliche Rechtfertigung dem Strafbarkeitsrahmen des § 331 zu entziehen, würde die eigentliche Problematik eines zu weit gefassten Tatbestands übergehen. Die dogmatische Anknüpfungsstelle muss daher bereits im Tatbestand der §§ 331, 333 gesucht werden und nicht erst bei der Frage der Rechtswidrigkeit.

3. Der Ansatz von Dauster

Dauster versucht für den Bereich der Forschungsförderung, den Weg aus der Strafbarkeit über eine teleologische Reduktion des Vorteilsbegriffs zu ebnen[709]. Den ersten Schritt vollzieht er durch eine Gegenüberstellung der Sphären der Eigennützigkeit einerseits und einer Staats- oder Forschungssphärennützigkeit

---

704 Cramer greift auf den von Volk im Referat zum 61. DJT, Vh. Bd. II/1 L 42, gebildeten Fall zurück, in dem ein Staatsanwalt für eine Einstellung nach § 153a StPO (= Dienstausübung) eine Geldbuße an einen gemeinnützigen Verein (= einen Dritten) fordert, Schönke/Schröder/Cramer, § 331 Rn. 53 b.

705 Schönke/SchröderCramer, § 331 Rn. 53 b.

706 Schönke/Schröder/Cramer, § 331 Rn. 53 b; Cramer zieht diesen Umkehrschluss aus § 4 Abs. 5 Nr. 10 EStG, nach dem Zuwendungen, die eine Bestrafung ermöglichen, prinzipiell nicht als Betriebsausgaben berücksichtigt werden können, umgekehrt Aufwendungen dann abzugsfähig seien, wenn sie rechtlich nicht zu beanstanden seien.

707 Schönke/Schröder/Cramer, § 331 Rn. 53 c.

708 Schönke/Schröder/Cramer, § 331 Rn. 53 b.

709 Dauster, NStZ 1999, S. 63 (66f.).

andererseits sowie einer Zuordnung des Transfers von Leistungen Privater in diese Sphären. Dabei sollen nur objektiv messbare und wirtschaftlich geldwerte Besserstellungen Berücksichtigung finden[710]. Aus dem Vorteilsbegriff will er sodann den in den Bereich der Staatsnützigkeit fallenden Leistungstransfer ausscheiden. Um diese tatbestandliche Restriktion zu legitimieren, verweist er in einem zweiten Schritt auf die objektive Rechtsordnung, die einen normativen Wertungswiderspruch voraussetze[711]. Bei der durch Art. 5 Absätze 1 und 2 GG geschützten Forschungsförderung durch Dritte liege dieser Widerspruch zur Intention des § 331 darin, dass die Verfassung auch das Recht gewährleiste, nicht nur auf die staatlich limitierte Finanzierung, sondern ebenso auf die wissenschaftliche Zusammenarbeit mit der Industrie zurückzugreifen. Dabei umfasse Wissenschaftsfreiheit auch das Recht, Empfänger von der Verbesserung der Lehr- und Forschungssituation dienender Leistungen zu sein[712]. Derartige Leistungen seien mithin keine Vorteile i.S.d. § 331. Den letzten Schritt zur Annahme einer generellen Erlaubnis von Leistungstransfers Privater an universitäre Forschungsträger zur Förderung von Forschung und Lehre vollzieht Dauster, indem er einen im Zusammenhang mit derartigen Leistungstransfers stehenden, beim Amtsträger möglicherweise eingetretenen Eigennutz grundsätzlich verneint. Entweder seien die auf der Drittfinanzierung beruhenden Besserstellungen im Rahmen der Forschungstätigkeit vom Schutz der Verfassung mitumfasst oder es sei bezüglich des durch die Forschungsbeteiligung gestiegenen persönlichen Renommees des Amtsträgers kein objektiv bewertbarer Vorteil zu erkennen[713].

4. Der Ansatz des BGH

Der BGH spricht sich für den Bereich der Drittmittelforschung in einer neueren Entscheidung[714] dafür aus[715], den Tatbestand des § 331 Abs. 1 mit „Blick auf die hochschulrechtlich verankerte Dienstaufgabe eines Hochschullehrers zur Einwerbung von Drittmitteln einschränkend" auszulegen, um Wertungswidersprüche zwischen Strafrecht und Hochschulrecht zu vermeiden[716]. Nach Auffassung des BGH kann der systematische Einklang zwischen hochschulrechtlicher Aufgabenstellung und der Strafvorschrift über die Vorteilsannahme jedenfalls dann über eine Einschränkung des Anwendungsbereichs der Strafvorschrift hergestellt werden, wenn „es sich bei den einzuwerbenden Dritt-

---

710 Dauster, NStZ 1999, S. 63 (66).
711 Dauster, NStZ 1999, S. 63 (67).
712 Dauster, NStZ 1999, S. 63 (67).
713 Dauster, NStZ 1999, S. 63 (67).
714 BGH NJW 2002, S. 2801 ff.
715 Die Entscheidung erging zwar noch zum Tatbestand der Vorteilsannahme in der Fassung vor der Änderung durch das KorrBekG, ihr kommt aber auch auf der Grundlage der Neufassung des § 331 grundsätzliche Bedeutung zu.
716 BGH NJW 2002, S. 2801 (2803).

mitteln nicht nur der Sache nach um Fördermittel für Forschung und Lehre handelt, sondern ... diese auch dem im Drittmittelrecht vorgeschriebenen Verfahren unterworfen werden."[717] Mit Hinweis auf das Hochschulrecht von Baden Württemberg[718], nach dem die Annahme der Fördermittel angezeigt und genehmigt werden muss, sieht der BGH in denjenigen Fällen, in denen dieses Verfahren eingehalten wird, das geschützte Rechtsgut des § 331 für „nicht in dem vom Gesetzgeber vorausgesetzten Maße strafrechtlich schutzbedürftig" an[719]. Der BGH bezweckt mit dieser tatbstandlichen Lösung, den „Wertungsgleichklang" in diesen Fällen der Annahme von Drittmitteln zur Forschungsfinanzierung zwischen hochschulrechtlichen Erlaubnis-Regelungen und der strafrechtlichen Verbotsnorm des § 331 wieder herzustellen[720].

5. Eigene Auffassung

a) Ausgangspunkt Rechtsgut

Bei der Beurteilung der Strafwürdigkeit und Strafbedürftigkeit infrage stehender Verhaltensweisen im Hinblick auf das Schutzgut der §§ 331 ff. sollte nach der hier vertretenen Auffassung[721] nicht ein isoliert betrachteter Vertrauensschutz eine Reaktion des Strafrechts rechtfertigen können, sondern es sollte mit einem den Gefährdungsbereich konkretisierenden Verständnis vom Schutzzweck dieser Normen argumentiert werden. Korrespondierend mit dem Willen des Gesetzgebers, die Gefährlichkeit abstrakter Gefährdungshandlungen bereits im Vorfeld korruptiver Praktiken strafrechtlich zu sanktionieren[722], sollte der Gefährdungsbezugspunkt objektiviert werden, d.h., es ist auf die Funktionsfähigkeit des Staates abzustellen und damit auf den Schutz vor Beeinträchtigung der sich an rechtsstaatlichen und gemeinwohlorientierten Grundsätzen auszurichtenden Amtshandlungen. Der Vertrauensschutzgedanke wird damit nicht überflüssig. Einerseits ist er mittelbar betroffen und verletzt, wenn der primäre Schutzzweck der Funktionsfähigkeit der Verwaltung beeinträchtigt wird, und dient somit im Gegenzug als Indikator für derartige Funktionsstörungen. Zum anderen kann er dort, wo zwar die Funktionsfähigkeit des Staates nicht in Gefahr gerät, aber dennoch ein Maß an Misstrauen in der Rechtsgemeinschaft verifizierbar ist, den Hinweis auf die bestehende Verpflichtung liefern, im Rahmen von Austauschverhältnissen zwischen Staat und Privaten die erforderliche Transparenz und Dokumentation zu gewährleisten. Andererseits

---

717 BGH NJW 2002, S. 2801 (2804).

718 §§ 8 Abs. 2, 119 Abs. 2, Abs. 3 Nr. 5 Universitätsgesetz des Landes Baden Württemberg i.d.F. vom 30.10.1987.

719 BGH NJW 2002, S. 2801 (2803).

720 BGH NJW 2002, S. 2801 (2805).

721 S. o. S. 53 ff.

722 Vgl. BT-Drs. 7/550, S. 269 f.

seits sollten aus einem vermuteten Vertrauensdefizit keine strafbarkeitsbegründenden Rechtskriterien abgeleitet werden, da fehlendes Vertrauen auf falscher Tatsachengrundlage oder auf fehlerhafter Bewertung von Geschehenszusammenhängen beruhen könnte und damit keine verlässliche Entscheidungsgrundlage liefern kann.

Für die Institute des Sponsorings und der Drittmittelforschung ist im Rahmen von Schutzzweckerwägungen nicht danach zu fragen, ob das Vertrauen der Allgemeinheit bei Transferleistungen zwischen öffentlicher Verwaltung und Privaten nachhaltig durch den Verdacht gegenseitiger Abhängigkeiten beeinträchtigt ist, sondern es ist zu begutachten, ob aus dem Wechselseitigkeitsprinzip der Zusammenarbeit zwischen Staat und Wirtschaft einschließlich der ihr zugrunde liegenden Motivbildung Funktionsbeeinträchtigungen auf Staatsseite zu befürchten sind.

b) Rechtsgut korrespondiert mit der objektiven Rechtsordnung

Die von Cramer und Dauster ins Feld geführten verfassungsrechtlichen und gesetzlichen Vorgaben, aus denen sie normative Wertungswidersprüche zum Wirkbereich der Strafvorschrift des § 331 herleiten, sind zunächst in Einklang mit dem Rechtsgutsbegriff des § 331 zu bringen. Dies bedeutet, dass die Förderinstrumente des Sponsorings und der Drittmittelforschung in der von der Rechtsordnung und der Rechtsgemeinschaft für zulässig und legitim erachteten Form und Ausgestaltung keine Gefährdung des Staates in seiner funktionalen Aufgabenstellung hervorrufen dürfen. Diese Folgerung dürfte jedenfalls für die Grundformen des Sponsorings (= Zuwendung für z.B. kulturelle Gemeinwohlzwecke) und der Drittmittelforschung (= Forschungsgelder für die zu erbringende Forschungsleistung) in den ihnen außerstrafrechtlich zugeschriebenen Zulässigkeitsgrenzen als erfüllt anzusehen sein. Die private Förderung gesellschaftspolitisch erwünschter oder gemeinwohlorientierter Zwecke begründet für sich allein keine Gefährdung der Funktionsfähigkeit des Staates. Dies dürfte auch dann noch gelten, wenn im Rahmen ihrer Zusammenarbeit Wirtschaft und Verwaltung für beide Seiten ökonomisch sinnvolle und rechtlich zulässige Vertragsverhältnisse über die Abnahme erforschter Medizinprodukte abschließen. Gegenteiliges könnte nur angenommen werden, wenn aus dieser Zusammenarbeit eine objektiv messbare und geldwerte Besserstellung des Amtsträgers selbst folgen würde. Hierbei ist allerdings, wie Dauster mit Recht erwähnt[723], zu bedenken, dass die durch Art. 5 Abs. 3 GG garantierte Wissenschaftsfreiheit nicht das Recht auf freie und eigenständige Einwerbung, Empfangnahme und Verwendung der Zuwendungen Dritter zu Forschungszwecken gewährleisten

---

723 Dauster, NStZ 1999, S. 63 (67).

kann, ohne die daraus sich ergebenden Nebenfolgen, die für den einzelnen Amtsträger vorteilhaft wirken, mit einzubeziehen[724].

c) Begrenzung des tatbestandlichen Geltungsbereichs

Wird demnach das Rechtsgut der Bestechungsdelikte durch die von der Rechtsordnung legitimierten Institute des Sponsorings und der Drittmittelforschung in ihrer konkreten Durchführung regelmäßig nicht beeinträchtigt, ist der von Dauster aufgeworfenen Frage nach der Auflösung eines bestehenden normativen Wertungswiderspruchs nachzugehen. Der von Dauster vorgetragene Vorschlag einer Reduktion des Vorteilsbegriffs ist ein diskutabler Weg, der aber in seiner Herleitung das Wagnis enthält, aus der objektiven Rechtsordnung einen Rechtsanspruch auf die betreffende Leistungserbringung des Privaten herleiten zu müssen. Bei der grundgesetzlich geschützten Wissenschaftsfreiheit mag dies im Hinblick auf forschungsnützige Transferleistungen noch darstellbar sein, bei Sponsorenleistungen zu gemeinnützigen kulturellen Zwecken dürfte diese Rechtskonstruktion schon schwieriger zu begründen sein. Dauster argumentiert denn auch ausschließlich für den Bereich privater Spenden zur Förderung von Forschung und Lehre. Die weite Tatbestandsfassung des § 331 muss aber für eine Vielzahl denkbarer Lebenssachverhalte einschränkend interpretiert werden, um auch Wertungswidersprüche bei anderen Konkurrenzverhältnissen wie zwischen Strafprozessrecht und Strafrecht[725] auflösen zu können. Zudem dienen Restriktionsversuche ohne gesetzliche Fixierung nicht der Rechtsklarheit und damit der Rechtssicherheit. Daher kann auch die vom BGH vorgenommene tatbestandseinschränkende Auslegung des § 331 für bestimmte Fälle der Drittmittelforschung[726] nicht überzeugen.

Aus diesem Grund sollte die Tatbestandsfassung der §§ 331, 333 für alle denkbaren Fälle eines Regelungskonflikts zwischen Erlaubnisnorm und strafrechtlicher Verbotsnorm um eine die Rangfolge klarstellende Aussage ergänzt werden.

§ 331 Absatz 1 könnte lauten:

„Ein Amtsträger oder ein für den öffentlichen Dienst besonders Verpflichteter, der <u>ohne Billigung durch die Rechtsordnung</u> für die Dienstausübung einen

---

[724] Zu diesen Nebenwirkungen zählen die dem Amtsträger durch Drittförderung zugute kommende allgemeine Verbesserung der Forschungssituation ebenso wie eine verbesserte Labor-Ausstattung oder das durch die Forschungstätigkeit gestiegene Renommee und seine verbesserten Berufschancen.

[725] Man denke nur an den o. u. Fn. 704 geschilderten Fall des Staatsanwalts.

[726] S. o. S. 161 f.

Vorteil für sich oder einen Dritten fordert, sich versprechen lässt oder annimmt, wird ..."

§ 333 Absatz 1 könnte lauten:

„Wer einem Amtsträger, einem für den öffentlichen Dienst besonders Verpflichteten oder einem Soldaten der Bundeswehr ohne Billigung durch die Rechtsordnung einen Vorteil für diesen oder einen Dritten anbietet, verspricht oder gewährt, wird ..."

Mit dieser tatbestandsbegrenzenden Formulierung wäre erreicht, dass alle von der Rechtsordnung gebilligten oder sogar befürworteten Austauschverhältnisse einschließlich der sozialadäquaten Transferleistungen bereits aus dem Tatbestand der §§ 331, 333 ausgeschieden werden könnten, ohne für diese Fälle noch Genehmigungsregeln vorhalten oder auf Rechtswidrigkeitsebene auf Rechtsinstitute wie den übergesetzlichen Rechtfertigungsgrund zurückgreifen zu müssen. In einer ausführenden Richtlinie der Bundesregierung könnte ergänzend festgelegt werden, in welchen Fällen und ggf. bis zu welcher Wertgrenze Zuwendungen als gebilligt betrachtet werden dürfen[727]. Eine eingrenzende Interpretation des Vorteilsbegriffs auf unangemessene, rechtswidrige, ungebührliche oder unlautere Vorteile wäre dann nicht erforderlich. Der Vorzug dieser Lösung besteht in der Vermeidung normativer Wertungswidersprüche dort, wo die Rechtsordnung bereits Festlegungen wie bei Art. 5 Abs. 3 GG getroffen hat und in den übrigen Fällen in der gesetzgeberischen Möglichkeit, durch ausführende Rechtsvorschriften exakt festzulegen, in welchen Zuwendungsbereichen unter welchen Voraussetzungen ein Austauschverhältnis ausdrücklich für zulässig erachtet wird.

Der Gesetzgeber sollte daher eine Ergänzung des Tatbestands der §§ 331, 333 in der vorgeschlagenen Form erwägen.

IV. Ergebnis Teil B

Die strafrechtliche Begutachtung unterschiedlicher Fallgestaltungen hat gezeigt, dass nach der Neufassung der §§ 331, 333 die Verneinung der Strafwürdigkeit nicht zwangsläufig auch die Verneinung der Frage nach der Tatbestandsmäßigkeit nach sich zieht. Im Gegenteil hat die Untersuchung offen gelegt, dass von der Rechtsordnung sogar ausdrücklich befürwortete Verhaltensweisen, wie die privat finanzierte Forschungsförderung, in den Einzugsbereich

---

727 Vgl. den diesbezüglich nicht sehr mutigen Entwurf des BMI einer umfassenden Neuregelung durch eine „Allgemeine Verwaltungsvorschrift zum Verbot der Annahme von Belohnungen oder Geschenken in der Bundesverwaltung", die das Rundschreiben des BMI vom 25.1.1962 (GMBl. 1962, S. 120) ersetzen soll.

des Strafgesetzes gelangt sind. Die bestehenden Möglichkeiten, ohne eine Gesetzesänderung den tatbestandlichen Wirkbereich auf strafbedürftige Fälle zurückzudrängen, sind wie dargestellt begrenzt und überzeugen aus rechtlichen oder tatsächlichen Gründen nicht. Der hier vorgeschlagene Lösungsweg führt zu einer tatbestandsinternen Klarstellung, die der Gesetzgeber außerhalb des Strafrechts zum Anlass nehmen kann, mit korrespondierenden Rechtsvorschriften, wie z.B. dem § 25 HRG, den Tatbestandsbegriff der „Billigung durch die Rechtsordnung" auszufüllen.

Teil C : Das öffentliche Dienstrecht als rechtliche Alternative zum Strafrecht?

Im Vorfeld des 61. DJT und auf dem Juristentag selbst war Gegenstand der Diskussion über die Reichweite strafrechtlicher Tatbestände auf dem Gebiet der Korruptionsbekämpfung u.a. die Frage nach möglichen Alternativen zu einer Ausweitung des Strafrechts. Das Ergebnis der Falluntersuchungen im Teil B dieser Arbeit bestätigt die Berechtigung dieser Fragestellung, denn die tatbestandliche Erfassung eindeutig nicht strafwürdiger Fälle unterhöhlt den ultima ratio-Gedanken[728], das Strafrecht nur als letztes geeignetes Mittel und letztmöglichen Weg der Pönalisierung sozialschädlichen Verhaltens einzusetzen[729]. Prittwitz ist der Vorfrage nach den auf normativen und/oder empirischen Erwägungen beruhenden Argumenten für oder gegen eine Begrenzung des Strafrechts nachgegangen[730]. Im Ergebnis haben die empirischen Gründe nicht für ein willkürlich und fragmentarisch, sondern für ein eng begrenztes, „an der Gewichtigkeit und Bedrohlichkeit der Taten und ihrer Vorwerfbarkeit an die Täter" orientiertes Strafrecht überzeugt[731]. Prittwitz stellt die ultima ratio als „das entscheidende Strafrechtsbegrenzungspostulat" heraus[732].

Das von Prittwitz u.a. angeführte Argument der begrenzten Ressourcenbereitstellung für Strafrechtsschutz[733] muss im Lichte der hier untersuchten Fälle der Drittmittelforschung und des Sponsorings bekräftigt werden. Die weit gefassten Strafnormen der §§ 331, 333 führen einerseits zu bedeutsamen Mehrkosten für die Strafverfolgungsbehörden, die Ermittlungen nach dem Legalitätsprinzip unabhängig von der Frage der Strafwürdigkeit durchzuführen haben. Dies gilt auch für die Gerichtsbarkeit, die einmal mit der Sache befasst, die hier unter-

---

728 BVerfGE 39, S. 1 (47): „Die Strafnorm stellt gewissermaßen die ‚ultima ratio' im Instrumentarium des Gesetzgebers dar".

729 Strafrecht ist danach nur bei schwersten Verletzungen als das äußerste Mittel legitim, Prittwitz, Der fragmentarische Charakter des Strafrechts, S. 145 (152).

730 Prittwitz (Fn. 729), S. 145 (153 ff.).

731 Prittwitz (Fn. 729), S. 145 (165); als empirische Gründe nennt Prittwitz einmal die von der Gesellschaft begrenzt zur Verfügung gestellten Ressourcen an Sach- und Personalmitteln im Strafverfolgungsbereich, die zur Erhaltung der Effektivität des Rechtsgüterschutzes im Ganzen auf die wichtigen Strafverfolgungsziele im Sinne eines subsidiären Strafrechts beschränkt werden müssten. Zum anderen verweist er auf die durch Erfahrungssätze durchaus nachvollziehbare Alltagstheorie der Abnutzung des Strafrechts bei inflationärem Einsatz und der parallel dann einsetzenden Verdrängung anderer Konfliktlösungsmechanismen.

732 Prittwitz (Fn. 729), S. 145 (165/166): Strafrecht sei „kein anerkanntes Instrumentarium des Staates, sondern der – manchmal vielleicht notwendige – Offenbarungseid, daß irgendetwas passieren muß und der Gesellschaft nichts anderes einfällt, eine Art Notwehr, wenn Staat und Gesellschaft sich nicht anders zu helfen wissen".

733 S. o. unter Fn. 731.

suchten Fälle dann erst über eine restriktive Auslegung des Tatbestandes oder über Rechtfertigungskonstruktionen aus dem Strafbarkeitsbereich ausscheiden könnte. Andererseits entstehen zusätzliche, hohe Kosten auch auf Verwaltungsseite aufgrund der gesteigerten Anforderungen an verwaltungsinterne Regelungswerke, die zur Abgrenzung des legalen Verhaltens von nicht legalem Verhalten erstellt werden müssen. Detaillierte Drittmittelregelungen und Transparenz-Richtlinien für Sponsoringvereinbarungen sind unabdingbare kostenintensive Maßnahmen[734], die allein dazu dienen, extensiv gesetzte strafrechtliche Risiken verwaltungsseitig zu begrenzen. Diese Maßnahmen erhöhen die Bürokratiekosten nicht unerheblich, da Personal für die Erstellung, Anwendung und Überwachung der Regelungen dauerhaft bereitgestellt werden muss. Dabei geht es nicht nur um Kosten für Präventivmaßnahmen im Vorfeld korruptiver Verhaltensweisen, sondern um beträchtliche Zusatzkosten, die der verwaltungsseitigen Absicherung des Dienstherrn vor dem Vorwurf dienen, Verhaltensstandards in der Dienststelle nicht in ausreichendem Maße eingeführt und überwacht zu haben. Da auch der Staat sein Geld nur einmal ausgeben kann, wird das staatliche Haushaltsdefizit durch die genannten Zusatzkosten im Verwaltungshaushalt noch vergrößert mit der möglichen Konsequenz eines unterfinanzierten Forschungshaushalts, was wiederum ursächlich dafür sein könnte, auf Finanzierungszusagen Dritter wie beim Sponsoring und der Drittmittelförderung angewiesen zu sein.

Diese Zusatzkosten verursachenden Maßnahmen reduzieren im Ergebnis auch den Finanzmittelansatz für strafrechtlichen Rechtsgüterschutz in Form vorbeugender Maßnahmen zur Korruptionsbekämpfung im engeren Sinn. In der Rechtswirklichkeit führen solche Kostenspiralen dann nicht selten auch zu einer Absenkung der der allgemeinen Strafverfolgung zugewiesenen Mittelansätze. Die herausgehobene Bedeutung der Ressourcenverantwortung sollte im Gesetzgebungsprozess spätestens bei der Gesetzesvollzugskostenabschätzung durch eine aussagefähige Bezifferung der zu erwartenden Zusatzkosten zum Ausdruck kommen. Im Entwurf der Bundesregierung zum KorrBekG heißt es zum Vollzugsaufwand wenig aussagekräftig nur: „Die Regelungen im Abschnitt ‚Strafrecht' werden Bund und Gemeinden nicht mit Mehrkosten belasten. In welchem Umfang bei den Ländern durch die intensive Verfolgung und Ahndung von Korruptionsstraftaten zusätzliche Kosten durch einen möglichen höheren Aufwand bei der Strafjustiz entstehen, kann nicht hinreichend sicher bestimmt werden"[735].

Das Gebot der Prioritätensetzung beim Einsatz begrenzter finanzieller Ressourcen wird durch den aus dem Rechtsstaatsprinzip verfassungsrechtlich abge-

---

[734] Die zum Teil auch der Wirtschaft entstehen z.B. durch Erstellung von firmeneigenen Verhaltenskodizes.

[735] BT-Drs. 13/6424, S. 2.

sicherten Grundsatz der Verhältnismäßigkeit der Mittel-Zweck-Relation[736] verstärkt. Nach diesem Prinzip wäre der Geltungsbereich des Strafrechts dort zu begrenzen, wo der gesetzgeberische Abwägungsprozess der konkret verfolgten Zwecke – hier die wirkungsintensive Bekämpfung rechtsschutzgefährdender Verhaltensweisen im weiten Vorfeld eigentlichen Bestechungsunrechts – rechtliche Alternativen zur Erreichung dieser Zwecke aufzeigt. Bereitstehende rechtliche Alternativen verdienen den Vorzug, wenn sie unter Schonung des Ressourcenverbrauchs in gleicher Weise effektiv die Erreichung des Primärziels gewährleisten. Der Maßstab einer solchen Abwägung unter mehreren rechtlichen Alternativen sollte sich an der Gewichtigkeit des sozialschädlichen Bedrohungspotenzials ausrichten, das von dem für sanktionsbedürftig erkannten Verhalten ausgeht.

Unter dieser Prämisse ergeben sich ernsthafte Zweifel an der Richtigkeit der vom Gesetzgeber getroffenen Entscheidung, den Geltungsbereich des Strafrechts bei der Vorteilsannahme gemäß § 331 auszudehnen und nicht auf das dienstrechtliche Disziplinarrecht mit seinem sanktionsgleichen Instrumentarium als rechtliche Alternative zum Strafrecht zurückzugreifen.

In der Strafrechtswissenschaft wird die Ansicht vertreten, die Annahme bzw. das Gewähren von Vorteilen für Dritte sei grundsätzlich nur im Rahmen der §§ 332, 334 strafwürdiges Unrecht, weil dort die Entgeltlichkeit von pflichtwidrigen Amtshandlungen als das eigentliche Kernunrecht korruptiver Verhaltensweisen infrage stehe[737]. Hieran schließt die Frage an, ob sich der Gesetzgeber mit der Ausdehnung der Tatbestände der §§ 331, 333 bei gleichzeitig bestehender rechtlicher Alternative unter ultima ratio-Erwägungen außerhalb der Befugnis zur strafrechtlichen Reaktion bewegt.

Im Nachfolgenden sollen die Meinungen zu dieser Frage dargestellt werden, um anschließend zu begutachten, ob das Disziplinarrecht im Einwirkungsbereich strafrechtlich relevanter Handlungsweisen tatsächlich eine rechtliche Alternative zum Strafrecht abbilden kann.

---

736 Prittwitz sieht unter Hinweis auf das Abtreibungsurteil des BVerfG von 1975, BVerfGE 39, S. 1 (47), in dem Verhältnismäßigkeitsprinzip ein „formales Prinzip" zur Begrenzung des Strafrechts, das nur die Angemessenheit des eingesetzten Mittels regele, aber einen korrespondierenden Zweckbezug schon voraussetze, (Fn. 729) S. 145 (158).

737 Schönke/Schröder/Cramer, § 331 Rn. 53 b.

I. Meinungen im Schrifttum

1. E. Schmidt

E. Schmidt, der in seiner Monographie die Entwicklung der Rspr. bei den Bestechungsdelikten unter dem RStGB von 1871 dargestellt hat, ist nicht müde geworden, vor der Gefahr einer maßlosen Ausdehnung des Strafrechts zu warnen. In Bezug auf rechtliche Alternativen hat er sich wie folgt geäußert: „Es ist ganz sicher Aufgabe der Justiz, der Korruption entgegenzuwirken. Aber die Gefahr, hierbei die strafrechtliche Gerechtigkeit zu verfehlen, ist heute sehr viel größer als ehedem ... Es ist sicher, daß auch außerhalb des strafrechtlichen Unrechtsbereichs sich bedenkliche Mißbräuche und rechtswidrige Verhaltensweisen einstellen können, von denen aus sich leicht die Tür zu strafrechtlich erheblicher Korruption öffnen kann. Das darf für die Strafgerichte kein Anlaß sein, die Tatbestandsbegriffe mit Hilfe ‚weiter Auslegung' zu überdehnen, so daß die tatbestandlichen Grenzen verwischt werden und die vom Gesetzgeber getrennten Deliktstypen ineinander übergehen. Ein Bedürfnis dazu besteht um so weniger, als dem Beamten gegenüber das Dienststrafrecht[738] mit seinen weitgespannten Ahndungsmöglichkeiten gegen jede Art von Verfehlung zur Verfügung steht und, wachsam und energisch gehandhabt, mittels Abschreckung und Unschädlichmachung zur Erhaltung der Reinheit der Amtsführung und des Ansehens des Staates eingesetzt werden und sehr viel leisten kann"[739]. Mit seinem Plädoyer für einen verstärkten alternativen Einsatz des Disziplinarrechts steht E. Schmidt heute nicht allein.

2. Wagner

Wagner hat auf dem 61. DJT 1996 in Karlsruhe auf der Grundlage der Gesetzesfassung der §§ 331 ff. vor Inkrafttreten des KorrBekG von 1997 die Meinung vertreten, dass bei anzunehmendem gleichgelagerten Rechtsgüterschutz das Strafrecht begründen müsse, „worin das besondere Unrecht, das strafrechtlich zu verfolgen ist, gegenüber dem Disziplinarunrecht besteht"[740]. Wagner verweist zunächst auf die Intention des Gesetzgebers, der bei der ursprünglichen Abfassung der Bestechungsdelikte den Unterschied zwischen disziplinarem und kriminellem Unrecht einmal in der Verknüpfung von Vorteil

---

[738] E. Schmidt nimmt mit diesem Begriff Bezug auf die mit dem Gesetz zur Änderung und Ergänzung des Dienststrafrechts vom 26.11.1952 erlassene Bundesdisziplinarordnung (BDO), die in ihrer Strukturierung und ihren Begrifflichkeiten noch einen sehr engen Bezug zum Strafrecht aufwies; dies änderte sich erst mit dem Gesetz zur Neuordnung des Bundesdisziplinarrechts vom 20.7.1967, BGBl. I S. 725, durch das Begriffe wie „Disziplinarstrafe" in „Disziplinarmaßnahme" und „Beschuldigter" in „Beamter" abgeändert und nicht mehr im Terminus des Strafrechts formuliert wurden.

[739] E. Schmidt (Fn. 61), S. 129 f.

[740] Wagner, Vh. Bd. II/2, L 118.

und Diensthandlung und zum anderen in der Eigennützigkeit des Amtsträgers gesehen habe. Nachdem nun schon diese Verknüpfung durch die Einbeziehung mittelbarer Vorteile und einer Aufweichung der Konkretisierung der Diensthandlung inzwischen weiter als vom Gesetzgeber vormals gewertet gelockert worden sei, stelle sich die Frage, warum diesen Unterschiedsmerkmalen plötzlich keine Geltung mehr zukommen sollte. Dies sei deshalb von Bedeutung, weil Rechtsgüterschutz durch das Disziplinarrecht im Hinblick auf die Lauterkeit des öffentlichen Dienstes bei nicht genehmigter Entgegennahme von Vorteilen gewährleistet sei. Lücken im Rechtsschutz gebe es daher nicht[741].

3. Hamm

Hamm bekräftigt diese Ansicht von Wagner auf dem 61. DJT[742] mit der Begründung, das Rechtsgut der beamtenrechtlichen Vorschrift des Geschenkannahmeverbots des § 70 BBG bestehe in der Vermeidung eines bösen Anscheins der Beeinflussbarkeit, während das Rechtsgut des Strafrechts zur Aufgabe habe, Amtshandlungen und dienstliche Entscheidungen von sachwidrigen Einflüssen freizuhalten. Hamm plädiert daher für eine Beibehaltung der Unrechtsvereinbarung in der vom Gesetzgeber im EGStGB von 1974 bestimmten Ausprägung.

4. Hettinger

Hettinger, der den Entwurf eines KorrBekG des Bundesrats vom 3.11.1995[743] kritisch begutachtet, vertritt die Auffassung, dass das Recht des öffentlichen Dienstes schon immer das sanktioniere, was künftig nach dem Entwurf des Bundesrats mit Strafe belegt werden solle, wenn auch primär aus Gründen der innerbetrieblichen „Hygiene“[744]. Zumindest die am schwersten wiegende Disziplinarmaßnahme der Entfernung aus dem Dienst sei eine präventiv wirkende, äußerst bedrohliche Rechtsfolge für den Amtsträger, über deren abschreckende Wirkung man kaum spekulieren müsse. Aus der anhand von vorhandenen Statistiken und empirischen Belegen kaum eindeutig verifizierbaren Vermutung eines Vollzugsdefizits bezüglich der im Disziplinarrecht bereit gestellten Instrumente könne zwar Nachbesserungsbedarf interpretiert werden, dies rechtfertige eine Ausdehnung der Strafzone aber nicht. Nur die Hereinnahme des Elements der Unrechtsvereinbarung als entscheidendem Abgrenzungsmerkmal zwischen Straftat und bloßem Dienstvergehen habe überhaupt die Hochstufung der disziplinarwidrigen Geschenkannahme zur Straftat als abstraktes Vorfeld-

---

741 Wagner, Vh. Bd. II/2, L 118/119.
742 Hamm, Vh. Bd. II/2, L 139 (L140).
743 BR-Drs. 298/95.
744 Hettinger, NJW 1996, S. 2263 (2271).

gefährlichkeitsdelikt legitimieren können[745]. Für eine abgeschwächte Unrechtsvereinbarung – auch in der von Dölling vorgeschlagenen vermittelnden Form – bestehe angesichts der dienstrechtlichen Möglichkeiten keine Notwendigkeit[746].

5. Möhrenschlager

Möhrenschlager, der mit Hinweis auf die Subsidiarität des Strafrechts die Bedenken einer strafrechtlichen Lösung von Wagner grundsätzlich teilt, spricht der disziplinarrechtlichen Lösung aber insoweit die Brauchbarkeit ab, als sie den Vorteilsgeber nicht zu erfassen vermag[747]. Die Konsequenz der Anwendung des Disziplinarrechts beim Amtsträger und des Strafrechts beim Zuwendenden teilt Möhrenschlager ersichtlich nicht. Es erscheint aber fragwürdig, ob man der disziplinarrechtlichen Lösung allein aus systematischen Erwägungen die grundsätzliche Eignung absprechen sollte. Dem ultima ratio-Gedanken gebührt der Vorrang vor gesetzestechnischen Konstruktionsfragen, zumal der von Möhrenschlager angeführte Gedanke bei § 333 die Konsequenz zivilrechtlicher Alternativregelungen begründen könnte.

6. Dölling

Dölling argumentiert bei der Frage der alternativen Heranziehung des Disziplinarrechts im Bereich der Bestechungsdelikte gegen die disziplinarrechtliche Lösung, da sich mit dem Korruptionsstrafrecht „Wirkungen der positiven und negativen Generalprävention“ erzielen ließen und zudem spezialpräventive Zwecke verfolgt werden könnten[748]. Das Disziplinarrecht reiche zur Erfüllung dieser Aufgaben nicht aus. Im Übrigen stünden in den betroffenen Fällen öffentliche Angelegenheiten in Rede, auf die das öffentliche Strafrecht reagieren müsse[749]. Zusätzlich greift Dölling ein verfahrensrechtliches Argument auf, indem er dafür votiert, dass die Ermittlungen in der Sache nicht von der in der Angelegenheit involvierten Verwaltung selbst geführt werden, sondern von der Justiz als unabhängiger Stelle[750].

---

745 Hettinger, NJW 1996, S. 2263 (2272).

746 Hettinger, NJW 1996, S. 2263 (2272 unter Fn. 120).

747 Möhrenschlager, Vh. Bd. II/2, L 130 (L 131).

748 Dölling, Gutachten C, C 43.

749 Dölling, Vh. Bd. II/2, L 121 (L 122); ähnlich Jähnke, 61. DJT, Vh. Bd. II/2, L 135, der auf die unterschiedliche Zielrichtung der beiden Rechtskreise abstellt; danach reagiere das Disziplinarrecht im Innenverhältnis zum Dienstherren unter dem Aspekt der Eignung des Beamten, während das Strafrecht im Außenverhältnis den Zweck verfolge, die verletzte Rechtsordnung wieder herzustellen bzw. das Bewusstsein der Allgemeinheit von der Unverbrüchlichkeit der Rechtsordnung i.S. einer positiven Generalprävention zu sichern.

750 Dölling, Vh. Bd. II/2, L 121 (L 122); in die gleiche Richtung tendiert Lemhöfer, 61. DJT Vh. Bd. II/2, L 137 (L 138), der die Wirkkraft des Disziplinarrechts und des

7. Zwischenergebnis

Die Meinungen in der Wissenschaft reichen von einer uneingeschränkten Befürwortung der disziplinarrechtlichen Lösung bis zu deren überzeugten Ablehnung. Bei den Befürwortern kann unterstellt werden, dass sie über die alte Fassung des § 331 hinaus keine weitere Grenzverschiebung zu Ungunsten des Disziplinarrechts vorgenommen hätten. Als Anhänger einer disziplinarrechtlichen Lösung können sie geltend machen, dass bereits mit dem EGStGB von 1974 der kriminalpolitischen Forderung nach einer nachhaltigen Korruptionsbekämpfung bis in den Bereich originären Disziplinarunrechts nachgegeben wurde. Dies wird durch die Begründung des Gesetzes belegt, die von „der zum kriminellen Unrecht erhobenen Disziplinarwidrigkeit der Vorteilsannahme" spricht.[751] Dass der Gesetzgeber mit der Neufassung der Bestechungsdelikte durch das KorrBekG von 1997 zumindest auch prozessualen Beweisschwierigkeiten begegnen wollte, die sich auf dem Rechtszustand des EGStGB ergaben, kann kaum ernsthaft bestritten werden. Mit der Lockerung des Kernelements der Unrechtsvereinbarung kumulativ mit der Hereinnahme der Drittvorteile in die §§ 331, 333 hat er eine Verfestigung der Kriminalisierung originär disziplinaren Unrechts bewirkt. Den Gesichtspunkt der Subsidiarität des Strafrechts hat er erkennbar nicht in die Abwägung mit einbezogen.

Die Bevorzugung der strafrechtlichen Lösung vor der rechtlichen Alternative einer disziplinarrechtlichen Regelung kann unter dem ultima ratio-Postulat aber nur dann gerechtfertigt werden, wenn die disziplinarrechtliche Lösung aufgrund einer der folgenden Ausschlusskriterien als unhaltbar verworfen werden müsste:

- Die Durchsetzung des öffentlich-rechtlichen Strafanspruchs wird in unzulässiger Weise eingeschränkt (II.)
- Die materielle beamtenrechtliche Pflichtennorm gewährleistet keinen ausreichenden Rechtsgüterschutz (III.)
- Die verfügbaren Disziplinarmaßnahmen sind im Vergleich zum strafrechtlichen Instrumentarium nicht ausreichend (IV.)
- Das Disziplinarverfahrensrecht genügt nicht den strengen strafprozessualen Ansprüchen an die Verfolgung entsprechender Pflichtverstöße und der Vollzug des bestehenden repressiven Maßnahmenpotenzials des Disziplinarrechts ist nicht hinreichend gesichert (V.).

Disziplinarvorgesetzten als zu bescheiden ansieht und im Verhältnis zum Justizapparat mit den Möglichkeiten eines „guten Dorfpolizisten alter Art" vergleicht.

751 Vgl. BT-Drs. 7/550, S. 270.

II. Öffentlich-rechtlicher Strafanspruch

Das Bestrafungsrecht des Staates rekrutiert sich aus dem Sinn und Zweck der staatlichen Strafe, die „nicht die Aufgabe hat, Schuldausgleich um ihrer selbst willen zu üben, sondern nur gerechtfertigt ist, wenn sie sich zugleich als notwendiges Mittel zur Erfüllung der präventiven Schutzaufgabe des Strafrechts erweist“[752].

1. Strafzwecke

Da das StGB keine eindeutige Auskunft darüber erteilt, welche Strafzwecke mit welcher Bedeutung und in welchem Verhältnis zueinander bestehen, hat der BGH anhand des in den §§ 47 Abs. 1 und 56 Abs. 3 genannten Begriffs „Verteidigung der Rechtsordnung“ auf der Grundlage des 1. StrRG[753] die verschiedenen Strafzwecke bewertet[754]. Eine bedeutsame Aussage hat der BGH zum qualitativen Verhältnis zwischen General- und Spezialprävention getroffen: „Die Tatsache, daß das Gesetz den Strafzweck der Generalprävention im Gegensatz zur mehrfachen Erwähnung des Gedankens der sozialen Anpassung (...§§ 46 I 2, 47 I, 56 I StGB) nicht ausdrücklich nennt, läßt für die Bemessung der Strafe eine bedeutsame Schwerpunktverlagerung auf den spezialpräventiven Gesichtspunkt im weitesten Sinne erkennen“[755].

Zur Generalprävention, die sich im Begriff der „Verteidigung der Rechtsordnung“ (vgl. §§ 47 Abs. 1, 56 Abs. 3 und 59 Abs. 1 Nr. 3) widerspiegelt, teilt der BGH zu diesem Teilaspekt der Aufgabe der staatlichen Strafe mit, dass „das Recht gegenüber dem vom Täter begangenen Unrecht durchzusetzen, die Unverbrüchlichkeit der Rechtsordnung damit vor der Rechtsgemeinschaft zu erweisen und zugleich künftigen ähnlichen Rechtsverletzungen potentieller Täter vorzubeugen“ sei „(spezielle Generalprävention)“[756].

---

752 BGHSt 24, S. 40 (42) zum 1. Strafrechtsreformgesetz von 1969.

753 BGBl. I (1969), S. 645.

754 Überholt ist demnach die isolierte Betrachtung einzelner Strafzwecke, wie sie bei einem reinen Sühne- oder Vergeltungsstrafrecht, einer Strafe nur als Mittel zur Abschreckung der Allgemeinheit oder einer rein täterbezogenen Zweckstrafe vorläge, vgl. BGHSt 24, S. 40 (42 ff.).

755 BGHSt 24, S. 40 (42); der BGH fährt zum spezialpräventiven Aspekt fort: „Bei diesem Grundsatz der ‚Individualisierung‘ geht es nicht allein um die gezielte Einwirkung auf einen schon entsozialisierten Täter, die Verurteilung und sinnvoller Vollzug erreichen sollen (Resozialisierung), sondern auch um die Vermeidung unbeabsichtigter Nebenwirkungen von Verurteilung und Vollzug, etwa der Gefahr, daß die Strafe einen bisher sozial ausreichend eingepaßten Täter aus der sozialen Ordnung herausreißt. Die Strafvollstreckung soll sich nicht in einem sinnlosen Absitzen erschöpfen, sondern Behandlung im Vollzug sein“.

756 BGHSt 24, S. 40 (44); hinzu tritt weiter das subjektive Element der Erhaltung der Rechtstreue der Bevölkerung (45).

Zu diesen general- und spezialpräventiven Gesichtspunkten tritt das Schuldprinzip hinzu, dem in § 46 Abs. 1 Satz 1 bei der Zumessung der Strafe Rechnung getragen wird.

Den Aussagen des BGH lässt sich entnehmen, dass staatlicher Strafe einmal eine präventive Schutzaufgabe zukommt und dass ihr zweckgerichtet und in Vorrangstellung zu generalpräventiven Zumessungserwägungen spezialpräventive Zielsetzungen zugrunde liegen. Damit bekennt sich der BGH zu den Befürwortern der vorherrschenden Vereinigungstheorie, die die verschiedenen Strafzwecke allerdings in unterschiedlicher Gewichtung miteinander verknüpft[757].

Mit Blickrichtung auf den ultima ratio-Ansatz, der das Strafrecht quasi als Notwehrinstrument für die Verteidigung der Rechtsordnung der Gemeinschaft begreift, wenn sich die Gesellschaft nicht mehr anders zu helfen vermag, vermittelt das Strafrecht bei der Durchsetzung des Schutzes der Allgemeinheit durch Strafandrohung zunächst einen repressiven Charakter, der durch seinen abschreckenden Effekt für die Zukunft zugleich allgemeiner generalpräventiver Natur ist. Mit der gesetzlich angedrohten Strafe für zu kriminellem Unrecht erhobenen Verhalten ist der am Schuldmaßprinzip orientierte Ausgleich der Rechtsverletzung vorzunehmen, der durch seine öffentliche Missbilligung auf jene einwirkt, die Gefahr laufen, ähnliche Taten zu begehen. Hinzu tritt im Rahmen spezialpräventiver Strafzwecke die Überlegung, den Täter als Individuum auf den Pfad der Tugend zurückzubringen und ihm dabei nicht nur repressiv die Achtung vor dem Recht abzuverlangen, sondern ihm bei der Bewältigung von Sozialisationsproblemen zu helfen. Daher muss staatliche Strafe einen zukunftsgerichteten positiven spezialpräventiven Zweck der Hilfe bei der Einbindung in die Rechtsgemeinschaft verfolgen (vgl. § 46 Abs. 1 Satz 2).

Die Ausgangsfrage nach einer unzulässigen Verkürzung des öffentlichen Strafanspruchs für den Fall der Bevorzugung der disziplinarrechtlichen Lösung setzt ein Eingehen auf die Zwecke des Disziplinarrechts und die Prüfung voraus, ob es Gemeinsamkeiten und/oder Unterschiede gibt, die den Rückgriff auf das Strafrecht zwingend erscheinen lassen.

---

757 Vgl. nur Tröndle/Fischer, § 46 Rn. 3, der das Schuld-Sühne-Prinzip hervorhebt; Roxin JuS 1966, S. 377 (384 f.), der wesentlich auf die präventiven Strafzwecke unter Zurückdrängung des Schuldprinzips abhebt; Horstkotte JZ 1970, S. 122 (123), der den spezialpräventiven Ansatz favorisiert.

2. Zwecke des Disziplinarrechts

a) Meinung des Bundesdisziplinaranwalts

Der Bundesdisziplinaranwalt äußert sich in seinen Bemerkungen zur Aufgabe des Disziplinarrechts in bemerkenswerter Weise zur Problematik der Vereinbarkeit politischer Modernisierungsziele mit dem rechtsstaatlichen Auftrag der öffentlichen Verwaltung[758]. Dort heißt es: „Die moderne Verwaltung soll im Ergebnis mehr leisten und weniger kosten. Zweifellos brauchen wir eine solche leistungsstarke und kostengünstige öffentliche Verwaltung, die bürgernah, effektiv und effizient unter Einsatz modernster Informationstechnik handelt. Es darf jedoch nicht übersehen werden, dass dabei der rechtsstaatliche Auftrag der öffentlichen Verwaltung (Art. 20 Abs. 3 GG) unverändert fortbesteht ... Die rechtsstaatliche Verwaltung ist ohne Normendisziplin, Präzision und Kontinuität nicht denkbar. Nach den Modernisierungskonzepten werden andererseits in steigendem Maße Elastizität, zweckorientiertes Durchsetzungsvermögen, schöpferische Gestaltungskraft und Wirtschaftlichkeit notwendig. Es erfordert naturgemäß besondere Anstrengungen aller Beteiligten, diesen unterschiedlichen Anforderungen nachzukommen"[759]. Der Bundesdisziplinaranwalt vertritt dabei die Auffassung, dass das Disziplinarrecht auch unter diesen veränderten Rahmenbedingungen noch zeitgemäß und als Steuerungsinstrument zur Sicherung einer funktionsfähigen, gesetzestreuen Verwaltung zwingend erforderlich ist[760].

b) Urteil des BVerwG vom 30.8.2000

Der Bundesdisziplinaranwalt wird in seiner Auffassung durch das BVerwG bestätigt, das zwar eine einschränkende Modifizierung der disziplinaren Verfolgung außerdienstlichen Fehlverhaltens vorgenommen hat[761], an der Aufgabe

---

758 S. Jahresbericht des Bundesdisziplinaranwalts 2000 zur Aufgabe des Disziplinarrechts, zum Berufsbild der Beamten (dazu BVerwG 1 D 37.99) und zur Disziplinarpraxis in den Bundesverwaltungen; ähnlich der Jahresbericht des Bundesdisziplinaranwalts für das Jahr 2001, S. 3.

759 S. 3 des Jahresberichts 2000.

760 S. 3 f. des Jahresberichts 2000; vgl. auch S. 3 des Jahresberichts 2001, dort heißt es: „Gelingt der für den Erhalt der Integrität notwendige dauerhafte Prozess der ‚Selbstreinigung' der öffentlichen Verwaltung nicht, sind z.B. Misstrauen in den Behörden und gegen die Behörden sowie ihre Ineffizienz die Folge. Damit würde das Gegenteil dessen eintreten, was mit der Verwaltungsmodernisierung erreicht werden soll".

761 BVerwG, ZBR 2001, S. 39; das Gericht interpretiert § 77 Abs. 1 Satz 2 BBG i.V.m. § 54 Satz 3 BBG dahingehend einschränkend, als es nur noch dann eine Pflichtverletzung des Beamten im außerdienstlichen Bereich annimmt, wenn durch das Verhalten des Beamten das „Vertrauen in Bezug auf sein konkretes Amt oder das Ansehen des Berufsbeamtentums beeinträchtigt sind"; vgl. ferner die Urteile des BVerwG zu außerdienstlichen Verfehlungen in NJW 2001, S. 3565 und in Dok.Ber. 2001, S. 329.

des Berufsbeamtentums und damit des Disziplinarrechts[762], eine unparteiische, funktionsfähige, verfassungs- und gesetzestreue Verwaltung zu sichern, aber ohne Einschränkung festhält[763]. In die gleiche Richtung tendieren ältere Entscheidungen des BVerfG, in denen dokumentiert ist, dass die Disziplinarmaßnahmen der Aufrechterhaltung des geordneten Dienstbetriebs dienen und nicht Gegenstand eines moralischen Unwerturteils sind[764].

c) Stellungnahme

Ähnlich wie beim Strafrecht auf den Sinn und Zweck der staatlichen Strafe abzustellen ist, verkörpert die „Disziplinarstrafe" die nach außen gerichtete Zielrichtung des Disziplinarrechts.

aa) Gesetzlich dokumentierter Reinerhaltungszweck

Das Beamtenverhältnis ist gemäß § 3 Abs. 1 Satz 2 BRRG auf Lebenszeit ausgerichtet. Die zwangsweise Auflösung dieses Lebenszeitverhältnisses bildet die Ausnahme und unterliegt deshalb strengen Voraussetzungen. Nach § 48 BBG endet das Beamtenverhältnis mit der Rechtskraft eines Strafurteils, in dem der Beamte wegen einer Vorsatztat zu einer Freiheitsstrafe von mindestens einem Jahr verurteilt wurde[765]. Diesen gesetzlich normierten Fällen liegt der Gedanke der Untragbarkeit zugrunde, einen Beamten bei derart schweren strafrechtlichen Verstößen im Beamtenverhältnis zu belassen. Als Korrelat zum Lebenszeitprinzip besteht ein legitimes staatliches Interesse, sich in diesen Fällen vom Beamten wieder trennen zu können.

Die unfreiwillige Beendigung des Beamtenverhältnisses tritt im Übrigen auch durch die Verhängung der schwersten Disziplinarmaßnahme mit der Entfernung aus dem Beamtenverhältnis ein (§§ 5 Abs. 1, 10 BDG)[766]. Für diese Fälle,

---

762 Das dem Beamtenrecht zuzuordnen ist, vgl. BVerwGE 83, S. 1 (4).

763 BVerwG, ZBR 2001, S. 39 (41).

764 BVerfGE 21, S. 378 (384) und BVerfGE 28, S. 264 (278); ebenso jetzt das BVerwG in ZBR 2001, S. 39 (41) wo es heißt: „Die Wahrung des ‚Ansehens des Berufsbeamtentums' dient als disziplinarrechtliche Kategorie der Erhaltung der Grundlagen eines allgemeinen Vertrauens in eine rechtsstaatliche gesetzestreue Verwaltung. Sie bezieht sich nicht auf das gesellschaftliche Ansehen des Beamten, indem dieser in die erzieherische Rolle eines Vorbilds für die Gesellschaft gedrängt und an bestimmten Moral- und Anstandsregeln gemessen wird".

765 Dies gilt auch bei Verurteilung wegen eines vorsätzlichen Staatsschutzdelikts zu einer Freiheitsstrafe von mindestens sechs Monaten, § 48 Abs. 1 Nr. 2 BBG.

766 Das BDG vom 9. Juli 2001 (BGBl. I, S. 1510) ist zum 1.1.2002 in Kraft getreten und löst die BDO ab; zu den wesentlichen Gesetzesänderungen im Einzelnen s. u. S. 193 unter 4.; da die Regelungen des neuen BDG nicht unerheblich von den Regelungen der einzelnen Bundesländer abweichen, ist die Untersuchung auf die Rechtssituation im Bundesbereich beschränkt.

in denen das Verhältnis zum Dienstherrn derart schwerwiegend beeinträchtigt und vertrauensgestört ist, dass nur seine Auflösung in Betracht kommen kann, gilt ebenfalls der Gedanke der Untragbarkeit, wobei eine Prognoseentscheidung zur Persönlichkeit des Beamten im Hinblick auf sein künftiges Verhalten mit einzubeziehen ist[767].

Ein musterhaftes Beispiel liefert die BVerwG-Entscheidung vom 9. Februar 1999[768], in der der Senat zunächst noch einmal feststellt, dass die Entfernung des Beamten aus dem Dienst[769] bei Bestechlichkeit oder auch nur bei Annahme von Geschenken oder Belohnungen in Bezug auf das Amt regelmäßig zu erfolgen habe, wenn „dieser die ihm als Äquivalent des angebotenen, geforderten oder gewährten Vorteils angesonnene pflichtwidrige Amtshandlung tatsächlich vorgenommen oder wenn er bares Geld angenommen hat". Die Hemmschwelle in dieser Form zu überwinden, deute auf ein „hohes Maß an Pflichtvergessenheit und Rücksichtslosigkeit gegenüber den Interessen der Allgemeinheit"[770]. Der Senat bejaht im Anschluss diese Voraussetzungen für eine Entfernung des Beamten aus dem Dienst und sieht dennoch von dieser Höchstmaßnahme ab, „weil das Vertrauen der Bahn zu dem Beamten als noch nicht restlos zerstört anzusehen" sei und die besonderen persönlichkeitsbezogenen Umstände des Einzelfalls zu berücksichtigen seien[771].

bb) Generalpräventiver Zweck und Vergeltungsgedanke

Es ist kaum zu bestreiten, dass zumindest von der schwersten Disziplinarmaßnahme, der Entfernung aus dem Beamtenverhältnis (§ 10 BDG), aber wohl auch von der zweitschwersten Maßnahme der Zurückstufung, d.h. der Versetzung in ein Amt derselben Laufbahn mit geringerem Endgrundgehalt (§ 9 BDG), ein auf die Gesamtheit der Beamtenschaft wirkender allgemeiner Abschreckungseffekt ausgeht. Dem Disziplinarrecht kommt daher als Regelungseinheit ein generalpräventiver Zweck durch die Androhung der für den einzel-

---

767 Täterbezogene in die Zukunft gerichtete Milderungsgründe, die dem Gedanken der Untragbarkeit entgegenstehen könnten, hat die Rechtsprechung des BVerwG herausgearbeitet; dazu zählen „die unverschuldete, unausweichliche wirtschaftliche Notlage", vgl. BVerwGE 33, S. 3 (5 ff.), „die psychische Ausnahmesituation", BVerwGE 76, S. 145, „die einmalige persönlichkeitsfremde Gelegenheitstat", BVerwG DÖD 1979, S. 129, und seit 1988 auch „die Wiedergutmachung des Schadens bzw. Offenbarung vor Tatentdeckung", BVerwG DÖD 1988, S. 215; zu den Milderungsgründen s. auch Claussen/Janzen BDO, Einl. D 4 b ff.

768 Az.: 1 D 1/98.

769 So noch der Terminus in der inzwischen vom BDG abgelösten BDO.

770 Ständige Rspr. des BVerwG, s. auch BVerwGE 93, S. 294 (295 f.).

771 Mit entgegengesetztem Ergebnis der Abwägung eines Einzelfalls, nämlich der Entfernung aus dem Beamtenverhältnis vgl. BVerwG vom 14. Oktober 1998, Az.: 1 D 109/97.

nen Beamten höchst empfindlichen Sanktionen in seiner Aufgabe zu, das Funktionieren der inneren staatlichen Ordnung sicherzustellen. Fraglich ist nur, ob auch mit den einzelnen Disziplinarmaßnahmen generalpräventive Zwecke verfolgt werden. Dies wird in der Rspr. und Literatur zum Teil bejaht[772]. Offensichtlich sind die generalpräventiven Zwecke jedenfalls bei den beiden schwersten Disziplinarmaßnahmen, bei denen die maßnahmenbedingte Außenwirkung eine innerbetriebliche Geheimhaltung kaum zulässt und damit die warnende und abschreckende Funktion der Einzelmaßnahme in ihrer öffentlichen Missbilligung der Wahrnehmung der Beamtenschaft unterliegt.

Demgegenüber werden die Disziplinarmaßnahmen des Verweises (§ 6 BDG), der Geldbuße (§ 7 BDG) und der Kürzung der Dienstbezüge (§ 8 BDG) als verwaltungsinterne Personalvorgänge vertraulich bearbeitet[773], ohne dass sie der öffentlichen Wahrnehmung unterliegen. Hier wird somit nicht publik, welcher Beamte gemaßregelt wird, so dass man der einzelnen Disziplinarmaßnahme eine generalpräventive Zweckorientierung nur in eingeschränktem Umfang zuschreiben kann.

Der Vergeltungsgedanke sollte im Disziplinarrecht nach allgemeiner Auffassung keine Rolle spielen[774], könnte der einzelnen Disziplinarmaßnahme aber insoweit anhaften, als sie sich in ihrer Abstufung und Auswahlentscheidung zu sehr an der Art und Schwere der Dienstpflichtverletzung orientiert und damit eine am Fehlverhalten ausgerichtete Sühne beinhaltet[775].

cc) Erziehungszweck

In erster Linie sehen Rspr. und Schrifttum den tieferen Sinn und Zweck der Disziplinarmaßnahme in der Erziehungsfunktion[776]. Mit dem Mittel der erzieherischen Einwirkung soll dem einzelnen Beamten für die Zukunft vor allem die Beachtung der sogenannten Wohlverhaltenspflicht aus § 54 Satz 3 BBG vor Augen geführt werden, sein Verhalten innerhalb und außerhalb des Dienstes dem Achtungs- und Vertrauensanspruch anzupassen, den sein Beruf erfordert.

---

772 BVerwGE 46, S. 64 (67) und 63, S. 42 (56); ferner BVerwG in NJW 1992, S. 587 (588) und in ZBR 1992, S. 159; Claussen/Janzen BDO, Einl. D1b; Weiß GKÖD Bd. II, J 033, Rn. 12.

773 Vgl. § 33 Abs. 1 BDG, wonach diese drei Maßnahmen in die Disziplinarbefugnis des Dienstherrn fallen; anders die Fälle der Zurückstufung und Entfernung aus dem Beamtenverhältnis bzw. Aberkennung des Ruhegehalts, in denen ein Klageverfahren vor dem Verwaltungsgericht zu erheben ist, vgl. § 34 Abs. 1 BDG.

774 BVerwGE 76, S. 43 (45); Claussen/Janzen BDO, Einl. A, Rn. 4.

775 Vgl. Weiß GKÖD, Bd. II, J 033, Rn. 19, der den Vergeltungsgedanken als noch nicht aus dem Disziplinarrecht verbannt ansieht.

776 Vgl. Weiß GKÖD, Bd. II, J 033, Rn. 11 und 14; Claussen/Janzen BDO, Einl. A, Rn. 4; BVerfGE 28, S. 264 (278); zuvor schon BVerfGE 21, S. 378 (384).

Nur so kann die Aufrechterhaltung eines ordnungsgemäßen Dienstbetriebes und damit die Funktionsfähigkeit der Verwaltung insgesamt sichergestellt werden. Der in der Disziplinarmaßnahme zum Ausdruck kommende Pflichtenappell soll auf die Persönlichkeit des Beamten einwirken, sich künftig pflichtgemäß zu verhalten. Der Erziehungsgedanke hat somit eine spezialpräventive Ausrichtung, wenngleich er nicht mit der strafrechtlichen Intention der Resozialisierung vermengt werden darf. Ihm liegt vielmehr die Absicht der Besserung des Beamten im Hinblick auf die dienstbezogene Zielsetzung zugrunde[777].

3. Vergleich der Strafzwecke mit den Zwecken des Disziplinarrechts

Sowohl die Kriminalstrafe wie auch einzelne Disziplinarmaßnahmen verfolgen generalpräventive Zwecke, indem sie der Begehung von Straftaten bzw. beamtenrechtlichen Pflichtverstößen generell entgegenwirken und den Einzelnen von der Begehung ähnlicher Rechtsverstöße abhalten sollen. Diese Übereinstimmung, die zwar bestätigt, dass auch das Disziplinarrecht durchaus die Aufgabe der nach außen abschreckend wirkenden Dokumentation der Unverbrüchlichkeit der Rechtsordnung übernehmen kann, sollte in ihrer Bedeutung für die Straf- bzw. Maßnahmenbemessung aber nicht überbewertet werden, da die Wirkungen generalpräventiver Zwecke empirisch schwer zu belegen und daher höchst umstritten sind[778]. Der Blick ist daher auf eine andere Gemeinsamkeit von Strafe und Disziplinarmaßnahme zu lenken.

In spezialpräventiver Hinsicht ergibt ein Vergleich beider Zielsetzungen Gemeinsamkeiten in der Einwirkung auf den Täter bzw. Beamten, ihm die Erforderlichkeit der Überwindung sozialer Anpassungsschwierigkeiten, die sich in der Tatbegehung bzw. Pflichtverletzung widerspiegeln, vor Augen zu führen, ihm Besserung abzuverlangen und ihm dabei zu helfen[779]. Der Teilaspekt spezialpräventiver Strafzwecke, den Täter dort auszuschalten, wo weder Abschreckung hilft noch Besserungsfähigkeit besteht (Sicherungsprinzip), kommt auch im Disziplinarrecht bei der Maßnahme der Entfernung aus dem Beamtenverhältnis zur Geltung. Auch der Sanktionscharakter der abgestuft einsetzbaren Mittel ist in beiden Rechtskreisen vergleichbar[780]. Wenn demnach das Straf-

---

777 Anders Els, Die disziplinarrechtliche Ahndung von Dienstvergehen, der die Anwendung des Erziehungsgedankens im Disziplinarrecht als verfassungswidrige Zielsetzung zurückweist und die Disziplinarmaßnahme nur als ein „formalisiertes Instrument des Tadels" auffasst, S. 58-61; seine angeführten Argumente überzeugen aber nicht, da der persönlichkeitsbezogene Besserungsaspekt auch heute noch in der Verwaltung Gültigkeit beanspruchen kann; wie hier Lambrecht, Strafrecht und Disziplinarrecht, S. 46.

778 Vgl. zu den Einwänden Maurach/Gössel/Zipf, Strafrecht Allg. Teil II, S. 585 f.

779 So auch im Ergebnis Lambrecht (Fn. 777), S. 47 f.

780 Lambrecht (Fn. 777), S. 47, die auf eine bemerkenswerte Entscheidung des Bundesverwaltungsgerichts von 1969 verweist, wo es heißt: „Disziplinarrecht ist seinem

recht sich mit der Anerkennung des Resozialisierungsprinzips hingewendet hat zu einem täterbezogenen Maßnahmerecht, dann lässt sich darin eine weitgehende Angleichung zur disziplinarrechtlichen Grundphilosophie des Erziehungs- und Besserungsgedankens erkennen. Reagiert somit Strafrecht und Disziplinarrecht in weitreichender Übereinstimmung ihrer Zweckausrichtungen wesensgleich[781], so fällt die Antwort auf die Ausgangsfrage eindeutig aus. Unter ultima ratio-Überlegungen kann der Anspruch auf Einsatz strafrechtlicher Maßnahmen nicht in rechtsstaatlich bedenklicher Weise beeinträchtigt sein, wenn ein außerstrafrechtliches Disziplinierungsinstrument mit den einer Kriminalstrafe vergleichbaren Intentionen verfügbar ist. Im Besonderen gilt dies für den hier infrage stehenden Grenzbereich zwischen disziplinar- und strafwürdigem Unrecht.

Die vom Gesetzgeber bereits 1974 mit dem EGStGB vorgenommene Verschiebung der „Grenzmarke" zugunsten des Strafrechts folgt denn auch mehr kriminalpolitischen Erwägungen als einer unter strafrechtlichen Subsidiaritätsgesichtspunkten nachvollziehbar begründeten Abwägung zwischen zwei bestehenden rechtlichen Alternativen[782].

Unter Berücksichtigung der für das Verhältnismäßigkeitsprinzip wesentlichen Merkmale[783] gerät hier schon der Aspekt der Erforderlichkeit der Kriminalstrafe in Zweifel. Einmal sind die Wirkungen von Strafe und Disziplinarmaßnahme bei der Geldstrafe einerseits und der Geldbuße bzw. der Gehalts-

---

Wesen nach vergeltungsfreies Maßnahmerecht, dem sich das Strafrecht mit zunehmender Betonung der Resozialisierung erst zu nähern beginnt. Von den korrespondierenden Zwecken des Disziplinarrechts, der Reinerhaltung des Berufsbeamtentums von ungeeigneten Beamten und der Erziehung noch geeigneter Beamter, ist nur die Erziehungsfunktion der strafrechtlichen Resozialisierung vergleichbar", BVerwG Az.: II D 32.69.

781 Lambrecht (Fn. 777), S. 50.

782 Bestätigt wird dies durch Formulierungen in der Gesetzesbegründung zum EGStGB, wenn es dort zur Strafrahmenerhöhung heißt: „Hierdurch wird der auf Grund von Erfahrungen in den letzten Jahren erhobenen kriminalpolitischen Forderung Rechnung getragen, das Gesetz möge der Korruption nachhaltiger als bisher entgegentreten", BT-Drs. 7/550, S. 271; zum KorrBekG heißt es in der Beschlussempfehlung des Rechtsausschusses zur Straftatbestandserweiterung der Vorteilsannahme: „Aus dem Bereich der Strafverfolgungspraxis und der Strafrechtswissenschaft wird eine Lockerung des Merkmals der ‚Unrechtsvereinbarung' insbesondere in Fällen hoher Zuwendungen, die keinen Diensthandlungen zugerechnet werden können, gefordert. Um die strafwürdigen und strafbedürftigen Fälle zu erfassen, bei denen die Annahme oder Gewährung eines Vorteils als Gegenleistung ‚für eine Diensthandlung' nicht nachgewiesen werden kann, wird ... künftig bereits das ... Annehmen von Vorteilen ‚für die Dienstausübung' unter Strafe gestellt", BT-Drs. 13/8079, S. 15.

783 Dazu vgl. Lambrecht (Fn. 777), S. 51 ff., die der Frage der Verhältnismäßigkeit im Rahmen der grundsätzlichen Problematik der Doppelbestrafung bei gleichzeitiger Anwendung von Strafrecht und Disziplinarrecht nachgeht.

kürzung andererseits im Hinblick auf die Verschlechterung der Vermögenssituation des Betroffenen und seiner Familie vergleichbar[784]. Zum anderen ähneln sich wie ausgeführt die Zielrichtungen beider Sanktionssysteme in general- wie spezialpräventiver Hinsicht, wobei die disziplinarrechtliche Sanktion der Entfernung aus dem Beamtenverhältnis sogar als die für die wirtschaftliche Existenz des Beamten bedrohlichste Rechtsfolge erscheint. Dieser Betrachtung wird immer wieder das arg strapazierte Argument der Strafwürdigkeit des einschlägigen Tatverhaltens entgegengehalten. Ohne eine differenzierte Betrachtung und Auseinandersetzung mit den Regelungszwecken beider Sanktionssysteme vorzunehmen, stützt sich die kriminalpolitische Diskussion in einem Anflug von Hilflosigkeit zur Begründung der Inanspruchnahme eines in seinen Grenzen nicht mehr klar umrissenen Straftatbestandes auf die Schwierigkeiten beim Nachweis einzelner Tatmerkmale wie der Unrechtsvereinbarung[785]. Einen Eingriff des Strafrechts vermögen diese Bekundungen unter Verhältnismäßigkeitsgesichtspunkten kaum zu rechtfertigen.

4. Ergebnis

Ein Vergleich der strafrechtlichen mit den disziplinarrechtlichen Zwecken führt zu dem Ergebnis, dass eine strafrechtliche Reaktion nicht allein aufgrund ihrer Zweckausrichtung vorrangig geboten erscheint, wenn nicht andere Wesensunterschiede wie ein unterschiedlicher Rechtsgüterschutz hinzutreten. Eine unzulässige Beschränkung der Durchsetzung des öffentlich-rechtlichen Strafanspruchs wäre mit dem Verzicht auf die strafrechtliche Lösung jedenfalls nicht zu befürchten.

III. Unterschiedlicher Rechtsgüterschutz?

Die Erforderlichkeit einer strafrechtlichen Reaktion könnte aber durch einen unterschiedlich ausgeformten Rechtsgüterschutz begründet sein.

---

784 Richtig daher die Kritik von Lambrecht (Fn. 777), S. 50, an der Entscheidung des BVerfG, BVerfGE 21, 391 (407), das noch eine Unterschiedlichkeit darin erkennt, dass der Beamte von der Disziplinarmaßnahme nur in seinen Rechten aus dem Wehrverhältnis und damit bezüglich seiner Dienstbezüge, nicht aber bezüglich seines sonstigen Vermögens betroffen werde. Es dürfte aber letztlich egal sein, aus welchem Vermögens-„Topf" das Geld entnommen wird und damit die Vermögensschmälerung insgesamt bewirkt. Vielfach wird das Vermögen eines Beamten auch nur aus angesparten Dienstbezügeanteilen bestehen mit der Folge der werthaltigen Identität von Dienstbezügen und Vermögen.

785 S. unter Fn. 782.

1. Wirkbereich

An dieser Stelle könnte man einwenden, dass ein qualitativer Unterschied zwischen Disziplinarrecht und Strafrecht in der gegensätzlichen Wirkfunktion liege, der Maßregelung der nach innen ins Dienstverhältnis einwirkenden Verletzung der beamtenrechtlichen Pflichten im Disziplinarrecht und der Sanktionierung der nach außen tretenden Erschütterung der Integrität des Staates und seiner Einrichtungen im Strafrecht. Daraus wäre zu entnehmen, dass das Strafrecht die schwerer wiegenden Pflichtverletzungen als Straftaten zu verfolgen hätte, während dem Disziplinarrecht nur die Aufgabe der Umsetzung der Rechtsfolgen im Hinblick auf dienstrechtliche Erfordernisse wie z.B. die der Reinhaltung des Berufsbeamtentums dienende Maßnahme der Entlassung aus dem Beamtenverhältnis zukäme. Das Disziplinarrecht würde als Mittel der Ergänzung des Strafrechts in den durch die Straftat ausgelösten Nebenfolgen für das Dienstverhältnis bestehen und damit eine untergeordnete Funktion einnehmen[786].

Bei genauer Betrachtung lässt sich diese Schlussfolgerung aber keineswegs generalisierend ziehen. Zwar übt das Disziplinarrecht im Hinblick auf die Bindungswirkung von strafrichterlichen Urteilen[787] eine nachgeordnete Funktion der Disziplinierung aus. So einmal in Fällen, in denen eine zusätzliche erzieherische Einwirkung zwecks Pflichtenmahnung erforderlich ist[788], und zum anderen in Fällen, in denen trotz strafrichterlichem Freispruch im abgeurteilten Sachverhalt ein Dienstvergehen liegt[789]. Andererseits implizieren diese Fälle eines „disziplinaren Überhangs“ die weiterreichende Wirkung des Disziplinarrechts gegenüber dem Strafrecht gerade im Hinblick auf den für das künftige Verhalten bedeutsamen erzieherischen Effekt. Auch dürfte es für den Beamten im Einzelfall wesentlich unangenehmer sein, in ein behördeninternes Disziplinarverfahren verwickelt zu werden und sich vom Dienstherrn zur Verantwortung ziehen lassen zu müssen mit der zu erwartenden nachteiligen Folge für die

---

786 Lambrecht prüft daher konsequent die Frage der Abschaffung des Disziplinarrechts unter dem Aspekt der Vermeidung von Doppelbestrafungen, kommt aber zu dem Ergebnis, dass eine Wechselbeziehung beider Rechtskreise bestehe und daher ein Verzicht auf das Disziplinarrecht nicht in Betracht zu ziehen sei, sondern umgekehrt müsse das Strafrecht die möglicherweise „größere vorbeugende Erziehungswirkung“ der Disziplinarmaßnahme anerkennen, (Fn. 777) S. 122 ff.; Lambrecht geht daher noch einen Schritt weiter und formuliert die Frage nach der Abschaffung der Strafe für Beamte unter Beschränkung auf eine disziplinarische Einwirkung, geht dieser Fragestellung aber dann doch nicht vertieft nach, so dass ihr in dieser Allgemeinheit kaum Ernsthaftigkeit zukommen kann.

787 Vgl. §§ 14, 21 Abs. 2, 22 Abs. 1, 23 Abs. 1 und 57 Abs. 1 BDG.

788 § 14 Abs. 1 BDG.

789 § 14 Abs. 2 BDG.

berufliche Entwicklung[790]. Allein auf die formale Überordnung des Strafrechts abzustellen, wäre daher verfehlt.

2. Schutzzweck des Disziplinarrechts

Vom Schutzzweckgedanken ausgehend ist im Disziplinarrecht die ältere Auffassung überwunden[791], die aus der besonderen Treueverpflichtung des Beamten zum Staat und seiner Pflichtenstellung über die allgemeinen Strafgesetze hinausreichende, mit der Disziplinarmaßnahme zu verteidigende Wertelemente wie Ehre, Sitte und Moral folgerte. Heute vorherrschend ist die Meinung, das Disziplinarrecht habe eine letztlich die Funktionsfähigkeit der Verwaltung sichernde Aufgabe der Aufrechterhaltung der Ordnung und Integrität des Berufsbeamtentums und seines Dienstbetriebes[792]. Es habe daher die Funktion, die sachgemäße Aufgabenerledigung innerhalb der Verwaltung zu überwachen[793]. Die Hinwendung der Rspr. und Lehre zu einem vom Funktionalitätsprinzip beherrschten Schutzzweckgedanken ist unverkennbar. Diese an der Rechtswirklichkeit orientierte Betrachtung stellt konkretisierend auf messbare und für den einzelnen Beamten nachvollziehbare Anforderungen ab, anhand derer innerhalb der Aufbau- und Ablauforganisation eines Dienstbetriebes einschließlich der mit ihr zusammenhängenden Pflichtenbindungen die Gesetzmäßigkeit des Verwaltungshandeln zu gewährleisten ist. Das Disziplinarrecht schützt somit allgemein die inneren und äußeren Funktionsbedingungen staatlicher Verwaltung und lehnt sich daher eng an den Rechtsgüterschutz der Bestechungsdelikte an[794].

3. Schutzzweck des § 70 BBG

Bei dienstrechtlichen Verstößen stellt sich im Disziplinarrecht immer die Frage, ob dienstliche Belange berührt wurden und daher die Dienstbezogenheit der Verfehlung bejaht werden kann[795]. Diese für eine disziplinare Ahndung maßgebliche Dienstbezogenheit wird in § 70 BBG durch die Formulierung „in

---

790 Lambrecht weist zu Recht auf die Gefahr des Bekanntwerdens des disziplinaren Vorwurfs im Kollegenkreis hin, auf die dann mögliche Beeinträchtigung der auch heute noch subjektiv empfundenen Berufsehre und auf das Risiko des Wegfalls der Existenzgrundlage bei Maßnahmen wie der Entfernung aus dem Beamtenverhältnis , (Fn. 777) S. 124.

791 Vgl. BVerfGE 28, S. 264 (278) und Urteil des BVerwG vom 30.8.2000 in ZBR 2001, S.39 (41); für die ältere Auffassung vgl. BDHE Bd. 1, S. 55 (60).

792 BVerwGE 46, S. 64 (67) und 83, S. 1 (5); Claussen/Janzen, BDO, Einl. A Rn. 2 und 4.

793 Köhler/Ratz, BDO, Einf. II 2., S. 79.

794 So auch Lambrecht für die Amtsdelikte insgesamt, (Fn. 777) S. 137.

795 Vgl. Weiß, GKÖD Bd. II, J 033, Rn. 1.

bezug auf sein Amt"[796] hergestellt. Nach § 70 Satz 1 BBG in der Fassung des Art. 10 des KorrBekG vom 13. August 1997[797] darf der Beamte – auch nach Beendigung des Beamtenverhältnisses – keine Belohnungen und Geschenke[798] in Bezug auf sein Amt[799] annehmen. Eine Ausnahme gilt bei Zustimmung der obersten Dienstbehörde (§ 70 Satz 2 BBG)[800]. Materielle Änderungen sind mit der Neufassung nicht verbunden, sie dient nur der Klarstellung des Regel-Ausnahme-Verhältnisses[801].

Zum Rechtsschutzziel des § 70 BBG enthält die Entscheidung des BVerwG vom 20.1.2000 bedeutsame Aussagen. So schütze die Vorschrift die Integrität der öffentlichen Verwaltung in der Weise konstitutiv für die vollziehende Gewalt, als sie nach den hergebrachten Grundsätzen des Berufsbeamtentums die Rechtsstaatlichkeit des öffentlichen Dienstes gewährleiste[802]. Mit einer Aufzählung beamtenrechtlicher Pflichten, wie die unparteiliche und gerechte Amtsführung (§ 52 Abs. 1 Satz 2 BBG) sowie die uneigennützige Verwaltung des Amtes (§ 54 Satz 2 BBG), bekräftigt das Gericht die Zielrichtung des von § 70 BBG ausgehenden Rechtsgüterschutzes. Dieser besteht in der Vermeidung jeden Anscheins der Beeinflussbarkeit des Beamten in seiner amtlichen Tätigkeit, um das „unverzichtbare Vertrauen in die Integrität des öffentlichen Dienstes" sicherzustellen.

---

796 Die gleiche Formulierung besteht in der Rahmenvorschrift des § 43 BRRG für die Länder.

797 BGBl. I, S. 2038 (2041).

798 Belohnungen und Geschenke sind alle nach Abzug etwaiger außerdienstlicher Gegenleistungen des Beamten verbleibenden wirtschaftlichen Vorteile, die dem Beamten von anderer Seite als vom Dienstherrn unmittelbar oder mittelbar gewährt werden, wobei es beim Geschenk auf das Motiv oder das Ziel der Zuwendung nicht ankommt, st. Rspr., BVerwGE 73, S. 71 (73); 100, S. 172 (175) und Urteil vom 20.1.2000, Dok.Ber. B 2000, S. 173 (174/175).

799 Der Zusammenhang zwischen Amtsführung und Vorteilszuwendung besteht schon dann, „wenn die dienstliche Tätigkeit für die Gewährung des Vorteils maßgebend ist, ohne daß es auf einen Kausalzusammenhang zwischen der Annahme des Vorteils und einer bestimmten Diensthandlung ankommt", st. Rspr., zuletzt BVerwG vom 20.1.2000, Dok.Ber. B 2000, S. 173 (175); der entscheidende Unterschied zur Vorteilsannahme nach § 331 besteht in der hier nicht geforderten Unrechtsvereinbarung; das vom Beamten ausgeübte Amt muss vielmehr nur eine wesentliche Bedingung, wenn auch nicht die alles entscheidende Voraussetzung für die Gewährung des Vorteils sein, also nach der Gebervorstellung zumindest mitkausal für die Zuwendung sein.

800 Ob diese erteilt werden kann, steht im pflichtgemäßen Ermessen der zuständigen Behörde, BVerwGE 100, S. 172 (177 f.), die nur im Ausnahmefall – wie jetzt die Hervorhebung in Satz 2 des § 70 BBG deutlich macht – die Zustimmung erteilen darf, BVerwG vom 20.1.2000, Dok.Ber. B 2000, S. 173 (176).

801 Vgl. Begründung zu Art. 2 Nr. 3 (Dienstrecht) des Entwurfs eines KorrBekG, BT-Drs. 13/5584, S. 10.

802 BVerwG, Dok.Ber. B 2000, S. 173 (174).

Man könnte schnell geneigt sein, die Schutzzwecke des § 331 und des § 70 BBG gleichzusetzen[803], würde dann aber einen Teilaspekt des Rechtsgüterschutzes von § 70 BBG übergehen, der bei § 331 nicht mitbetroffen ist. Es geht um den Vorfeldbereich begründeter Verdachtsmomente eines eigennützigen Verhaltens, der schon durch den Genuss von Vorteilen betreten wird, die der Beamte wegen seiner Amtsstellung nicht entgegennehmen darf. Ein Anscheinsverdacht der Parteilichkeit ist hier nicht gänzlich auszuschließen, und gerade dies will § 70 BBG vermeiden. Der Beamte soll von Anfang an jedem möglichen Interessenkonflikt aus dem Weg gehen, in den er durch Entgegennahme von Vorteilen geraten könnte. Das sogenannte „Anfüttern" würde hier also schon genügen, um diesen Konflikt zwischen Genuss von Vergünstigungen und Amtsstellung auszulösen. Das BVerwG weist daher auf den gegenüber den §§ 331, 332 weitergehenden Schutzbereich des § 70 BBG ausdrücklich hin[804]. Dem BVerwG ist zuzustimmen, allerdings mit der Ausnahme, dass der vom Gericht erwähnte Vertrauensgedanke nicht zum tragenden Gesichtspunkt der Schutzzweckerwägungen erklärt wird. Bei § 70 BBG sollte dieser in seinen konkreten Auswirkungen eher konturenlose Rechtsschutzaspekt des Vertrauens in Übereinstimmung zu den schon bei § 331 geäußerten Bedenken[805] allenfalls ergänzend herangezogen werden.

Im Ergebnis ist in objektivierender Betrachtung primär auf den Schutzzweck eines auf sachliche, unparteiische und uneigennützige Dienstverrichtung angewiesenen öffentlichen Dienstes abzustellen, der nach objektiven Wertmaßstäben und den Grundsätzen der Gesetzmäßigkeit staatlichen Handelns seine ihm obliegenden Aufgaben erfüllt. Damit wird die Funktionsfähigkeit der Verwaltung insgesamt vor der Einflussnahme Dritter geschützt.

4. Ergebnis

Die Ausgangsfrage muss an dieser Stelle weiter offen gehalten werden, da sich der strafrechtliche Rechtsgüterschutz bei § 331 nicht wesentlich vom Schutzzweck des beamtenrechtlichen Verbots des § 70 BBG unterscheidet. Der Schutzzweck des § 70 BBG reicht sogar weiter und kann daher nicht als Argument fehlenden Rechtsschutzes für die Bevorzugung der strafrechtlichen Lösung herangezogen werden.

---

803 So wohl Hettinger, NJW 1996, S. 2263 (2270) unter Berufung auf BVerwG in NVwZ-RR 1994, S. 681.

804 BVerwG, Dok.Ber. B 2000, S. 173 (174).

805 S. o. S. 53 ff.

IV. Sind die verfügbaren Disziplinarmaßnahmen als Sanktionsmittel im Vergleich zu den strafrechtlichen Sanktionen ausreichend?

Die Beantwortung dieser Frage setzt einen Blick auf die in § 5 BDG enumerativ aufgelisteten Maßnahmen voraus.

1. Verweis und Geldbuße

Der Verweis als schriftlicher Tadel eines bestimmten Verhaltens des Beamten (§ 6 BDG) und die Geldbuße, die bis zur Höhe der monatlichen Dienst- oder Anwärterbezüge des Beamten auferlegt werden kann (§ 7 BDG), stellen in der Stufenfolge der Schwere der Disziplinarmaßnahmen den unteren Bereich dar, was auch dadurch zum Ausdruck kommt, dass die Verhängung dieser Maßnahmen einer Beförderung grundsätzlich nicht entgegenstehen. Dies ergibt sich aus dem Umkehrschluss der §§ 8 Abs. 4 und 9 Abs. 3 BDG, die für die schwerer wiegenden Maßnahmen der Kürzung der Dienstbezüge und der Zurückstufung Beförderungsverbote vorsehen. Das System der Abstufung der Disziplinarmaßnahmen wird bestätigt bei der Regelung der Kompetenzen zum Erlass einer Disziplinarverfügung. In § 33 Abs. 1 BDG ist zunächst festgelegt, dass im Rahmen des behördlichen Disziplinarverfahrens und daher ohne Erhebung einer Disziplinarklage[806] die Maßnahmen des Verweises, der Geldbuße und der Kürzung der Dienstbezüge bzw. des Ruhegehalts durch Disziplinarverfügung auszusprechen sind. § 33 Abs. 2 BDG regelt dann die Befugnis für die Verhängung der beiden niedrigsten Maßnahmen. Diese darf jeder Dienstvorgesetzte gegen die ihm unterstellten Beamten verhängen. Diese an dem Schweregrad der einzelnen Sanktion orientierte Systematik der Aufteilung der Disziplinarbefugnisse auf die Hierarchie der einzelnen Dienstvorgesetzten bekräftigt die abgestufte unterschiedliche Eingriffsgewichtung der einzelnen Maßnahmen. Der höhere Differenzierungsgrad bei den Disziplinarmaßnahmen gegenüber den strafrechtlichen Sanktionen ermöglicht zudem eine angemessene Reaktion auf die beamtenrechtliche Pflichtverletzung.

2. Kürzung der Dienstbezüge

Inhalt dieser Maßnahme nach § 8 Abs. 1 BDG ist die bruchteilsmäßige Verminderung der monatlichen Dienstbezüge des Beamten um höchstens ein Fünftel auf längstens drei Jahre. Der Gesetzgeber hat hier gegenüber dem alten Recht aus Gründen der beschleunigten Durchführung der Disziplinarverfahren die Neuerung eingeführt, dass nun der Dienstherr – und nicht mehr ausschließ-

---

[806] Diese ist bei den Maßnahmen der Zurückstufung und der Entfernung aus dem Beamtenverhältnis bzw. der Aberkennung des Ruhegehalts erforderlich, § 34 BDG.

lich die Gerichte – zur Verhängung dieser Maßnahme befugt sind[807]. In der Beschränkung der Dienstbezügekürzung auf längstens drei Jahre soll in der Wirkung dieser Maßnahme der Abstand zur nächst höheren Sanktion der Zurückstufung gewahrt werden[808]. Während der Zeitdauer der Kürzung darf der Beamte grundsätzlich nicht befördert werden (§ 8 Abs. 4 BDG). Diese Disziplinarmaßnahme im mittleren Bereich von Dienstpflichtverletzungen beinhaltet somit schon erhebliches „Sanktionspotenzial", das über die Wirkungen einer Geldstrafe hinausreicht, weil eine zeitlich verzögerte Beförderung eine weitere finanzielle Einbuße für den Beamten bedeutet.

3. Zurückstufung

Die in § 9 BDG geregelte zweitschwerste Disziplinarmaßnahme der Versetzung des Beamten in ein Amt derselben Laufbahn mit geringerem Endgrundgehalt (Zurückstufung) enthält neben dieser Hauptfolge weitere, für den Beamten einschneidende Disziplinierungselemente wie die fünfjährige Beförderungssperre (Abs. 3) sowie den Verlust von Ehrenämtern und Nebentätigkeiten (Abs. 1).

4. Entfernung aus dem Beamtenverhältnis

Mit dieser schwersten Disziplinarmaßnahme[809] tritt die Beendigung des Beamtenverhältnisses ein mit der Folge, dass kein neues Beamtenverhältnis begründet werden kann (§ 10 Absätze 1 und 6 BDG). Die Sekundärfolgen sind der Verlust des Anspruchs auf Dienstbezüge und Versorgung sowie das Verbot der Führung der Amtsbezeichnung und des im Zusammenhang mit dem Amt verliehenen Titels (§ 10 Abs. 1 BDG). Das einzig Tröstliche, was dem „entlassenen" Beamten zugesprochen werden kann, um ihm den Übergang in einen anderen Beruf zu erleichtern, ist die Zahlung eines Unterhaltsbeitrages für die Dauer von sechs Monaten in Höhe von 50 Prozent der Dienstbezüge (§ 10 Abs. 3 BDG). Aber auch diesen Beitrag erhält der Beamte nur, wenn er der Zahlung würdig und bedürftig ist. Im Ergebnis wird dem Beamten die gesamte berufliche und wirtschaftliche Existenzgrundlage entzogen, was unzweifelhaft die Bedrohungswirkung einer auch hohen Geldstrafe übersteigt. Andererseits endet das Beamtenverhältnis nach § 48 BBG bei einem wegen vorsätzlicher Tat auf mindestens ein Jahr Freiheitsstrafe lautenden Strafurteil parallel zur staatlichen Strafe automatisch. Da in diesen Fällen strafrechtliche und disziplinarrechtliche Sanktion immer nebeneinander stehen, ist eine vergleichende Bewertung dieser beiden schwersten Sanktionen nur unterhalb der Jahresgrenze sinn-

---

807 Begründung des Gesetzentwurfs zur Neuordnung des Bundesdisziplinarrechts (BDiszNOG), BT-Drs. 14/4659, S. 43 zu § 32 BDG.

808 Begründung Entwurf BDiszNOG, BT-Drs. 14/4659, S. 35 zu § 8 BDG.

809 Bei Ruhestandsbeamten erfolgt Aberkennung des Ruhegehalts, § 12 BDG.

voll. Hier wird man ernsthaft nicht bestreiten, dass die nach § 56 Abs. 1 in aller Regel zur Bewährung auszusetzende Freiheitsstrafe bis zu einem Jahr einen Beamten nicht in der Nachhaltigkeit treffen würde wie dies bei einem Verlustgehen der gesamten Existenzgrundlage der Fall wäre.

5. Ergebnis

Die in der Stufenfolge schwerer wiegenden Disziplinarmaßnahmen stehen in der Bedrohungswirkung und in ihren tatsächlichen Folgen den strafrechtlichen Sanktionen keinesfalls nach. Die Notwendigkeit des Einsatzes der strafrechtlichen Lösung ist daher nicht aufgrund fehlender Wirksamkeit des disziplinarrechtlichen Sanktionsinstrumentariums indiziert.

V. Verfahrensrechtliche Unterschiede des neuen BDG im Vergleich zum Strafverfahrensrecht; Vollzugsproblematik

Für die Ausgangsfrage könnte entscheidend sein, dass die strengen strafprozessualen Anforderungen an die Verfolgung materieller Rechtsverstöße im Disziplinarverfahrensrecht keine hinreichende Entsprechung finden.

1. Legalitätsprinzip

Im Unterschied zum Strafprozessrecht[810] gilt im Disziplinarrecht das Legalitätsprinzip nur im Hinblick auf die Einleitung des Verfahrens bei Vorliegen „zureichender tatsächlicher Anhaltspunkte" (§ 17 Abs. 1 BDG), nicht aber für die Rechtsfolgenseite bei der Maßregelung[811]. Der Dienstvorgesetzte ist demnach zur Aufklärung eines hinreichend konkreten Verdachts eines Dienstvergehens innerhalb der Förmlichkeiten des Disziplinarverfahrensrechts verpflichtet[812]. Es besteht somit ein Verfolgungsgebot ab einem über bloße Vermutungen hinausgehenden Konkretisierungsgrad der Verdachtsmomente. Unterhalb dieser Schwelle können sogenannte Verwaltungsermittlungen zur weiteren Aufklärung bestehender Gerüchte oder anonymer Hinweise durchgeführt werden, um die Entscheidung über die Einleitung des Disziplinarverfahrens anhand konkretisierter Anhaltspunkte treffen zu können[813].

Dieses Verfolgungsgebot ist deshalb von besonderer Bedeutung, weil im Disziplinarrecht die Dienstpflichtverletzungen nicht in klar umrissenen Dienstvergehenstatbeständen definiert sind. Zwar ist eine gewisse Typisierung von be-

---

810 Vgl. § 152 Abs. 2 StPO: danach besteht im Strafverfahren Verfolgungs- und Anklagezwang, Kleinknecht, Kommentar zur StPO, § 152 Rn. 2.

811 Zum dort geltenden Opportunitätsprinzip s. u. Nr. 2.

812 Vgl. Begründung des Entwurfs des BDiszNOG, BT-Drs. 14/4659, S. 39 zu § 17 BDG.

813 BT-Drs. 14/4659, S. 39 zu § 17 BDG.

stimmten Vergehensbereichen – wie z.B. dienstliche Verstöße im Zusammenhang mit Alkoholgenuss – durch Richterrecht erfolgt. Grundsätzlich sind die beamtenrechtlichen Pflichten – mit wenigen Ausnahmen wie beim Geschenkannahmeverbot des § 70 BBG – nur generalklauselartig und nicht konkretisierend ausformuliert[814]. In Grenzfällen ist die inhaltliche Festlegung des beamtenrechtlichen Pflichtenkreises daher nicht immer einfach. Sie setzt genaue Kenntnis der durch die Rspr. näher konkretisierten Pflichtenklauseln voraus. Im Einzelfall hängt dann die Einleitung eines Disziplinarverfahrens von dieser Vorkenntnis und der richtigen Einschätzung ab, ob die erkundeten Tatsachen einen Pflichtverstoß begründen können.

Eng mit der Verpflichtung zur Aufklärung des infrage stehenden Sachverhalts verknüpft ist das an bestimmte Zeitabläufe gebundene Maßnahmeverbot des § 15 BDG[815]. Eine Verjährung im strafrechtlichen Sinn tritt bei entsprechendem Zeitablauf für die Maßnahmen des Verweises (§ 15 Abs. 1 BDG), der Geldbuße und der Kürzung der Dienstbezüge (§ 15 Abs. 2 BDG) sowie der Zurückstufung (§ 15 Abs. 3 BDG) aber nicht ein, d.h., es liegt nur ein relatives Verfahrenshindernis vor, das wegfällt, wenn nach dem Grundsatz der Einheit des Dienstvergehens später eine weitere Pflichtverletzung zu dem bis dahin überprüften und wegen Zeitablaufs nicht mehr zu ahndenden Sachverhalt hinzukommt[816]. Insoweit besteht im Disziplinarrecht im Unterschied zum endgültigen Verfahrenshindernis der Verjährung im Strafrecht kein an bestimmte Zeitabläufe gebundenes absolutes Verfolgungshindernis.

2. Opportunitätsprinzip

Dem Ermittlungszwang auf der Feststellungsseite steht das Opportunitätsprinzip auf der Rechtsfolgenseite gegenüber (§ 13 Abs. 1 BDG)[817]. Dieses besagt, dass die Entscheidung, ob ein Beamter wegen eines Dienstvergehens disziplinar gemaßregelt werden soll und welche Maßnahme erfolgen soll, nach pflichtgemäßem Ermessen zu treffen ist[818]. Dabei können unter Berücksichti-

---

814 Vgl. die Umschreibung der Pflichten in den §§ 52 ff. BBG, insbesondere in § 54 BBG, aus deren Verletzung sich dann ein Dienstvergehen nach § 77 BBG ergeben kann.

815 Im alten Recht der BDO war dieser Bereich als Verfolgungsverbot konzipiert, vgl. § 4 BDO; die Neufassung als Maßnahmeverbot hängt damit zusammen, dass nach neuem Recht keine Unklarheit mehr darüber bestehen kann, dass zunächst das Disziplinarverfahren eingeleitet werden darf, um dann im Rahmen des Verfahrens über einen möglichen Zeitablauf und das dadurch begründete Maßnahmeverbot zu befinden, Begründung Entwurf BDiszNOG, BT-Drs. 14/4659, S. 38 zu § 15 BDG.

816 Entwurf BDiszNOG, BT-Drs. 14/4659, S. 38 zu § 15 BDG.

817 Bislang in § 3 BDO enthalten.

818 Entwurf BDiszNOG, BT-Drs. 14/4659, S. 37 zu § 13 BDG; kein Ermessensspielraum besteht allerdings bei der schwersten Disziplinarmaßnahme der Entfernung aus dem Beamtenverhältnis, vgl. § 13 Abs. 2 BDG; auch im gerichtlichen Verfahren gilt der

gung der in § 13 Abs. 1 BDG genannten Kriterien in Einzelfällen voneinander abweichende Disziplinarmaßnahmen selbst dann festgesetzt werden, wenn der objektive Tatbestand gleichgelagert war[819]. Die Frage nach der Erforderlichkeit einer Disziplinarmaßnahme und ggf. nach deren Höhe richtet sich wesentlich nach den Gesamtumständen einschließlich dem Persönlichkeitsbild des Beamten und einer darauf beruhenden Prognoseentscheidung[820]. Das öffentliche Verfolgungsinteresse tritt vor allem bei der Frage, ob überhaupt eine disziplinare Reaktion erforderlich ist, in den Hintergrund[821]. Andererseits wird durch die vorgelagerte Verpflichtung zur näheren Aufklärung des Sachverhalts verhindert, dass die behördeninterne Aufklärungsarbeit gegen Kollegen nur nachlässig vorgenommen wird.

Das im Vergleich zum Strafrecht eingeschränkt geltende Legalitätsprinzip im Disziplinarrecht führt aber in seinen tatsächlichen Auswirkungen nicht zu einer bedeutsamen Abweichung von der Strenge des Strafprozessrechts, da für die schwerer wiegenden Disziplinarmaßnahmen der Zurückstufung und der Entfernung aus dem Beamtenverhältnis die Entscheidungskompetenz dem Gericht obliegt und damit gesichert ist, dass schwere Dienstverfehlungen nicht von der Dienstbehörde bzw. dem Dienstvorgesetzten sanktioniert werden (vgl. §§ 33 Abs. 1, 34 Abs.1 BDG)[822].

Ein Verstoß gegen das Verbot der Geschenkannahme nach § 70 BBG, der regelmäßig zugleich das Gebot uneigennützigen Verhaltens nach § 54 Satz 2 BBG und das Gebot achtungs- und vertrauensgerechten Verhaltens nach § 54 Satz 3 BBG verletzt, wiegt sehr schwer und wird in der überwiegenden Zahl der Fälle eine der beiden schwersten Disziplinarmaßnahmen erfordern[823]. In diesen Fällen ist daher grundsätzlich die Maßnahmen-Entscheidung durch ein Gericht gewährleistet.

Opportunitätsgrundsatz, vgl. § 60 Abs. 3 BDG, wonach bei einer Klage gegen eine Disziplinarverfügung das (Verwaltungs-)Gericht auch die Zweckmäßigkeit der angefochtenen Entscheidung zu prüfen und damit eine – abweichend von § 114 VwGO – eigene Ermessensentscheidung zu treffen hat.

819 In diesem Sinne Gansen BDG, § 13 Rn. 2 und 7; ebenso für § 3 BDO Köhler/Ratz, BDO, § 3 Rn. 7.

820 Vgl. zu den einzelnen Kriterien des § 13 Abs. 1 Sätze 2-4 Gansen BDG, § 13 Rn. 7-20.

821 Wobei es sich in diesem Zusammenhang immer nur um minder gewichtige Dienstverfehlungen im Sinne von Bagatellverstößen handeln kann; bei Bagatellfällen kann aber auch die Staatsanwaltschaft teilweise auch ohne Zustimmung des zuständigen Gerichts von der Verfolgung absehen, wenn neben einer nur geringen Schuld des Täters kein öffentliches Verfolgungsinteresse anzunehmen ist, § 153 Abs. 1 Sätze 1und 2 StPO.

822 Voraussetzung ist allerdings, dass der Dienstherr Disziplinarklage erhebt.

823 Vgl. das Urteil des BVerwG vom 26.9.2000, 1 D 66/99, in dem das Gericht die Maßnahme der Zurückstufung für angemessen hält; siehe auch die Rechtsprechungs-Übersicht bei Gansen BDG, § 13 Rn. 36 und 37.

3. Beschleunigungsgrundsatz

Soweit nach dem Legalitätsprinzip ein Disziplinarverfahren einzuleiten ist, rückt der erstmals im Bundesdisziplinarrecht gesetzlich normierte Beschleunigungsgrundsatz ins Blickfeld, der über die gesamte Durchführung des Disziplinarverfahrens zu beachten ist (§ 4 BDG). Der Zweck dieser Vorschrift besteht darin, dem auch in weiteren Vorschriften enthaltenen Beschleunigungsgebot[824] nicht nur in Teilbereichen des Verfahrens, sondern über den gesamten Ablauf hinweg als „objektives Disziplinarrecht" Geltung zu verschaffen[825].

Eine wichtige Bestätigung des Beschleunigungsgebots liegt in der mit dem BDiszNOG neu eingeführten Möglichkeit der Konzentration der Disziplinarverfahren durch Ausscheidung einzelner, für die zu erwartende Disziplinarmaßnahme nicht ins Gewicht fallender Handlungen (§ 19 Abs. 2 BDG). In Anlehnung an das alte Recht (§ 66 BDO), aber mit weiter reichenden Konsequenzen hat der Gesetzgeber für den Fall der Verletzung des Beschleunigungsgrundsatzes[826] ein gerichtliches Fristsetzungsverfahren vorgesehen, in dem die vom Gericht bestimmte Frist bei Nichteinhaltung die zwingende Folge der gerichtlichen Einstellung des Disziplinarverfahrens nach sich zieht (§ 62 Absätze 1 und 3 BDG). Der Dienstherr muss sich also beeilen, will er nicht die Disziplinierungsmöglichkeit im Einzelfall verlieren.

Dem Beschleunigungsgebot kommt damit in der Praxis künftig erhebliches Gewicht zu, da nach Einleitung eines Disziplinarverfahrens dessen behördeninterne Verschleppung kaum mehr möglich ist. Dem häufig vorgetragenen Vorwurf mangelnder Effektivität von Disziplinarverfahren und zu langer Verfahrensdauer wird mit diesem aus dem Rechtsstaatsprinzip des Artikel 20 Abs. 3 GG[827] hergeleiteten Grundgebot des Disziplinarrechts ein erhebliches Stück der Boden entzogen.

---

824 Vgl. z. B. für die Nachtragsdisziplinarklage in § 53 BDG den Unterschied zum bisherigen § 67 BDO, der darin liegt, dass jetzt der Fortgang und Abschluss eines anhängigen Disziplinarverfahrens nicht mehr durch eine vorgesehene nachträgliche Einbeziehung neuer Handlungen übermäßig verzögert wird. So ist jetzt anders als noch in § 67 Abs. 3 BDO in § 53 Abs. 3 BDG eine Kann-Vorschrift enthalten, nach der das Gericht bei drohender erheblicher Verzögerung des Disziplinarverfahrens von einer Aussetzung des Verfahrens absehen darf.

825 Vgl. Begründung im Entwurf des BDiszNOG, BT-Drs. 14/4659, S. 35 zu § 4 BDG; ferner Gansen BDG, § 4 Rn. 2.

826 Nach § 62 Abs. 1 BDG gilt eine sechsmonatige Frist, nach der das Disziplinarverfahren abgeschlossen sein muss.

827 Aus diesem Prinzip erwächst auch eine Fürsorgeverpflichtung gegenüber dem Beamten, gegen ihn laufende belastende Verfahren zügig zum Abschluss zu bringen, Gansen BDG, § 4 Rn. 3.

Andererseits könnte von Skeptikern eingewendet werden, der Dienstherr könne sich künftig durch provozierten Fristablauf unangenehmer Disziplinarverfahren auf diese feine Art entledigen. Mit Blick auf die Rechtswirklichkeit wird die Verwirklichung dieser Befürchtung jedenfalls dann zu verhindern sein, wenn eine ausreichende behördeninterne Stellenausstattung für die im Disziplinarverfahren wahrzunehmenden Aufgaben erfolgt[828] und die Personalauswahl mit der Zielsetzung einer langfristig aufzubauenden Fachkompetenz vorgenommen wird. Begründete Zweifel bezüglich der Bereitstellung der genannten Ressourcen könnten allerdings aufgrund der spärlich verfügbaren staatlichen Mittel aufkommen. Es bietet sich daher eine Bestandsaufnahme nach einer Verweildauer von ein bis zwei Jahren an.

Für die Entscheidungsfindung in der Ausgangsfrage ist mit dem Ressourcenargument ein wesentliches Element angesprochen. Die staatliche Ressourcenbereitstellung wird über das Gelingen des Vorhabens des Gesetzgebers, ein straffes behördliches Disziplinarverfahren nicht nur gesetzlich zu verankern, sondern auch im Gesetzesvollzug bestätigt zu finden, wesentlich mitentscheiden. Sicherlich besteht auch bei den Staatsanwaltschaften das Problem enger werdender finanzieller Verteilungsspielräume. Die daraus entstehenden Restriktionen im innerbehördlichen Vollzug fallen aber unterschiedlich aus. Während man im Bereich der Strafverfolgung die Konzentrationsmöglichkeiten der Strafprozessordnung verstärkt einsetzen kann, besteht im Bereich der Verwaltungsbehörden die Wahrscheinlichkeit einer Bündelung der verfügbaren Personal- und Sachmittel bei den originären Verwaltungsaufgaben unter Vernachlässigung der behördeninternen „Hygiene", d.h., der gegen Kollegen zu führenden unliebsamen Ermittlungsverfahren.

Bevor den voranstehenden Überlegungen vertieft nachgegangen wird, ist zunächst ein Blick auf die Neugestaltung des Disziplinarverfahrensrechts erforderlich.

4. Neugestaltung des Bundesdisziplinarrechts

Mit dem Inkrafttreten des BDG zum 1.1.2002 sind zahlreiche Änderungen im Rahmen einer grundlegenden Reform der bis dahin geltenden BDO eingeführt worden, die die Anforderungen an ein effizientes und modernes Disziplinarrecht erfüllen sollen[829].

---

828 Die Notwendigkeit einer angemessenen Ressourcenausstattung ergibt sich mittelbar aus dem Beschleunigungsgebot, Gansen BDG, § 4 Rn. 2.

829 Zur Kritik an dem neuen BDG siehe Müller-Eising, NJW 2001, S. 3587 ff.; Lemhöfer, Recht im Amt 2002, S. 53 (54/55); Weiß, Die Personalvertretung 2002, S. 2 ff. insbesondere S. 13.

a) Bezug zur Strafprozessordnung

Das Disziplinarrecht hat sich von seiner bisherigen verfahrensrechtlichen Bindung an das Strafprozessrecht[830] gelöst und lehnt sich jetzt an das Verwaltungsverfahrensrecht (VwVfG) und das Verwaltungsprozessrecht (VwGO) an (§ 3 BDG). Von dieser Grundregel bestehen aber noch Ausnahmen, soweit Einzelvorschriften auf die StPO verweisen[831].

Als Begründung für diesen „Kurswechsel“ führt der Gesetzgeber an, die Anbindung des Disziplinarrechts an die Strafprozessordnung sei nicht mehr zeitgemäß und ein Überbleibsel des früher in naher Verwandtschaft zum Strafrecht stehenden Dienststrafrechts. Eine erhebliche Effizienzsteigerung sei bei Heranziehung der der Materie des Disziplinarrechts näher stehenden Verwaltungsverfahrensregelungen zu erwarten, weil die Anwendung vieler strafverfahrensrechtlicher Vorschriften in der Praxis Schwierigkeiten bereitet hätte[832]. Mit „Schwierigkeiten“ umschreibt der Gesetzgeber die im Rahmen der Durchführung des förmlichen Disziplinarverfahrens anfallende Aufklärungstätigkeit des von der Einleitungsbehörde bestellten unabhängigen Untersuchungsführers[833]. Die in Disziplinarermittlungen häufig ungeübte Person des Untersuchungsführers konnte dem Anspruch an die beschleunigte Durchführung des Verfahrens vielfach nicht gerecht werden, weil sie sich im Umgang mit den strengen strafprozessualen Beweisregeln als unerfahren bewies.

Mit der Loslösung des Disziplinarrechts vom Strafprozessrecht eng verknüpft ist die vollständige Umgestaltung des behördlichen und gerichtlichen Verfahrens.

b) Verfahrenssystematik

aa) Einheitliches Verwaltungsverfahren

Mit einem einheitlichen behördlichem Ermittlungsverfahren wird auf die bisherige Unterscheidung in ein nichtförmliches Vorermittlungs- (§ 26 BDO) und

---

830 Vgl. § 25 BDO.

831 Vgl. §§ 25 und 58 Abs. 3 BDG für die Beweisaufnahme durch Zeugen und Sachverständige und § 28 BDG für die Form und den Inhalt des Protokolls.

832 Begründung Entwurf BDiszNOG, BT-Drs. 14/4659, S. 33 und S. 34/35.

833 Vgl. § 56 i.V.m. § 33 BDO; auf die Institution des Untersuchungsführers wird nach neuem Recht verzichtet, weil die bislang geltende Mittelbarkeit der gerichtlichen Beweisaufnahme, d.h. die Erhebung der Beweise bereits im Stadium der Untersuchung durch den Untersuchungsführer (vgl. § 57 Abs. 1 BDO), unter rechtsstaatlichen Erwägungen bedenklich erschien und daher die Beweiserhebung unmittelbar durch das Gericht entsprechend den Bestimmungen der VwGO durchgeführt werden soll, Begründung Entwurf BDiszNOG, BT-Drs. 14/4659, S. 49 zu § 58 BDG.

ein förmliches Untersuchungsverfahren (§ 33 BDO) verzichtet. Der Grund für diese Neukonzeption ist leicht nachvollziehbar. Nach dem bisherigen Ablauf der Verfahren trat nicht selten eine nicht unerhebliche Verzögerung durch doppelten Ermittlungsaufwand ein, der durch die verfahrensmäßige Gestaltung des Nacheinander von durchzuführenden Vorermittlungen und – soweit erforderlich – nachfolgender Durchführung eines förmlichen Untersuchungsverfahrens nicht zu vermeiden war. Nunmehr ist auf der Grundlage der einmalig durchzuführenden Ermittlungen zu entscheiden, ob das Verfahren einzustellen ist (§ 32 BDG), eine Disziplinarverfügung nach § 33 BDG zu erlassen oder eine Disziplinarklage (§ 34 BDG) zu erheben ist[834].

bb) Zuständigkeit der Verwaltungsgerichtsbarkeit

In § 45 Abs. 1 Satz 1 BDG ist in Abweichung vom alten Recht[835] geregelt, dass die Verwaltungsgerichtsbarkeit die Aufgaben der Disziplinargerichtsbarkeit wahrzunehmen habe[836]. Der Gesetzgeber begründet die Zuständigkeitsverlagerung zunächst mit der Herstellung eines gerichtsverfassungsrechtlichen Normalzustandes durch Etablierung des normalen Drei-Instanzen-Zuges, der dem Rechtsschutzbedürfnis des Beamten wie des Dienstherrn jetzt genauso nachkomme wie dies in anderen beamtenrechtlichen Streitfällen wie z.B. bei Versetzungen schon bisher der Fall sei[837].

In der Praxis wird sich erst noch erweisen müssen, ob das ausdrücklich zum Verfahrensgrundsatz erhobene Beschleunigungsgebot damit tatsächlich Wirkung entfaltet. Denn die Notwendigkeit der Durchführung eines Widerspruchsverfahrens vor Erhebung der Klage durch den Beamten (§ 41 Abs. 1 Satz 1 BDG)[838] wie auch die Einschaltung einer weiteren Gerichtsinstanz rufen Zweifel an der Schlüssigkeit der gesetzgeberischen Intention hervor. Berücksichtigt man die bekanntermaßen lange durchschnittliche Verfahrensdauer vor den Verwaltungsgerichten und setzt diese in Relation zu den durchschnittlich

834 Will der Beamte klageweise gegen eine Disziplinarverfügung vorgehen, muss grundsätzlich ein Widerspruchsverfahren nach den Bestimmungen der §§ 68 ff. VwGO durchgeführt werden, § 41 Abs. 1 Satz 1 BDG.

835 Danach war das gesondert eingerichtete Bundesdisziplinargericht mit Sitz in Frankfurt am Main für die erstinstanzlichen Disziplinarangelegenheiten zuständig, §§ 42 ff. BDO und § 67 BDO, und das Bundesverwaltungsgericht für die Berufungsfälle, §§ 55 und 80 BDO. Im Unterschied zu allen übrigen Revisions-Senaten war der Disziplinarsenat beim BVerwG demnach nur Berufungsinstanz.

836 Dies begründet eine Erweiterung des Instanzenzugs von zwei auf drei Instanzen, nämlich die Zuständigkeit der Verwaltungsgerichte in erster Instanz, der Oberverwaltungsgerichte in zweiter Instanz und die Zuständigkeit des Bundesverwaltungsgerichts in der Revisionsinstanz.

837 Begründung Entwurf BDiszNOG, BT-Drs. 14/4659, S. 46 zu § 44 BDG.

838 Ein Widerspruchsverfahren findet nach § 41 Abs. 1 Satz 2 BDG nicht statt, wenn die angefochtene Entscheidung durch die oberste Dienstbehörde erlassen worden ist.

nur drei Monate dauernden Bearbeitungszeiten vor dem Bundesdisziplinargericht[839] erhärten sich die Zweifel an der Durchsetzbarkeit der gesetzgeberischen Ziele.

Zur weiteren Begründung führt der Gesetzgeber an, mit seiner Entscheidung der Mehrzahl der Bundesländer nur nachzufolgen, die die Sondergerichtsbarkeit bereits aufgelöst und die Aufgaben mit Erfolg den Gerichten der Verwaltungsgerichtsbarkeit zugeordnet hätten[840]. Außerdem sei der atypische Einsatz des BVerwG als Tatsacheninstanz zurückzuführen auf die eigentlich zugedachte Rolle als Revisionsgericht. Damit werde auch die institutionelle Voraussetzung geschaffen, den Ländern den Zugang zum BVerwG als Revisionsinstanz über § 187 VwGO zu ermöglichen und somit erstmals eine einheitliche Revisionsrechtsprechung für Bundes- und Landesbeamten aufbauen zu können[841].

Auch hier tun sich Zweifel hinsichtlich der Erwartungshaltung des Gesetzgebers bezüglich einer einheitlichen Revisionsrechtsprechung auf. Die weitgehend fehlende Kodifizierung des materiellen Disziplinarrechts gerade auch bei der Frage der Bemessung der Disziplinarmaßnahme spricht eher gegen eine häufig zu erwartende Zulassung der Revision[842]. Andererseits besteht die Befürchtung einer Zersplitterung der bislang gewährleisteten Einheitlichkeit der Disziplinarrechtsprechung auf Bundesebene durch voneinander abweichende Entscheidungen der Verwaltungs- und Oberverwaltungsgerichte der einzelnen Bundesländer[843]. Dies gilt umso mehr als Bundesverwaltungen mit Standorten ihrer Dienststellen in mehreren Bundesländern damit rechnen müssen, in vergleichbar gelagerten Sachverhalten voneinander abweichende Urteile der jeweiligen Landesverwaltungsgerichtsbarkeit zu erwirken. Das BVerwG als reine Revisionsinstanz wird dieser Entwicklung in der Mehrzahl der in den Tatsacheninstanzen abschließend beurteilten Fällen kaum nennenswert entgegenwirken können[844].

---

839 So die Angabe der Richterin am Bundesdisziplinargericht Müller-Eising, NJW 2001, S. 3587 (3588).

840 Begründung Entwurf BDiszNOG, BT-Drs. 14/4659, S. 46 zu § 44 BDG.

841 Begründung Entwurf BDiszNOG, BT-Drs. 14/4659, S. 46/47 zu § 44 BDG.

842 Müller-Eising, NJW 2001, S. 3587 (3590), die in diesem Zusammenhang auf die im Disziplinarrecht eher selten bestehenden Revisionszulassungsgründe des § 132 Abs. 2 VwGO verweist.

843 Weiß befürchtet „Präjudizlöcher“, wenn das BVerwG als Revisionsgericht qualitativ nur noch mit wenigen Fällen befasst sein wird, Die Personalvertretung 2002, S. 2 (11).

844 Vgl. Weiß, Die Personalvertretung 2002, S. 2 (11).

c) Abschaffung der Institution des Bundesdisziplinaranwalts

Die Abschaffung der Institution des Bundesdisziplinaranwalts, die 1952[845] als selbständige Stelle und frei von Einflüssen der die disziplinare Entscheidung treffenden Verwaltungsdienststelle mit dem Ziel gegründet worden ist, die einheitliche Anwendung des Disziplinarrechts zu gewährleisten, gilt als ein Kernelement der Neuordnung des Disziplinarrechts. Die verfahrensrechtliche Bedeutung des Wegfalls der Institution des Bundesdisziplinaranwalts wird vom Gesetzgeber nicht allzu hoch eingeschätzt. So seien einerseits die im förmlichen Disziplinarverfahren angefallenen Aufgaben nach dessen Abschaffung als Teilaufgabe für den Bundesdisziplinaranwalt ebenfalls weggefallen und andererseits könne die für die Behörden wichtige Beratungsfunktion des Bundesdisziplinaranwalts ebenso durch eine zentrale „Service-Stelle" wahrgenommen werden[846]. Die Nichteinhaltung des Legalitätsprinzips sei nicht zu befürchten, da die Dienstvorgesetzten erwartungsgemäß ihrer Verantwortung gerecht würden[847].

Auch bei dieser Maßnahme muss sich der Gesetzgeber vorhalten lassen, dass gerade die das Legalitätsprinzip absichernde Funktion des Bundesdisziplinaranwalts vornehmlich bei verwaltungsinternen Korruptionsvorfällen die nötige Neutralität und Nachhaltigkeit bei der Aufklärung entsprechender Vorkommnisse sicherstellen konnte[848]. Die Beratungsaufgabe einer „Service-Stelle"[849] gerät da von ihrer Bedeutung eher in den Hintergrund.

d) Bedeutsame Einzelvorschriften im Hinblick auf die Korruptionsbekämpfung

aa) § 14 BDG

§ 14 Abs.1 Nr.1 BDG betrifft die Frage, welche Disziplinarmaßnahmen neben einer Strafe, Geldbuße oder jetzt auch ausdrücklich einer Einstellung nach

---

845 Mit dem Gesetz zur Änderung und Ergänzung des Dienststrafrechts vom 28.11.1952, BGBl. I S. 749.

846 Begründung Entwurf BDiszNOG, BT-Drs. 14/4659, S. 34.

847 BT-Drs. 14/4659, S. 34; nach altem Recht konnte der Bundesdisziplinaranwalt die Einleitung eines förmlichen Verfahrens bei bestimmten schweren Dienstpflichtverletzungen und entsprechender Maßnahmenandrohung erzwingen, § 39 BDO.

848 Müller-Eising, NJW 2001, S. 3587 (3588); Lemhöfer verweist denn auch auf das Bestreben in Bund, Ländern und Gemeinden, zur Bekämpfung der Korruption unabhängige Stellen gegenüber der allgemeinen Verwaltung neu einzurichten, Recht im Amt 2002, S. 53 (54).

849 Aufschluss über die Bedeutung und Effektivität dieser Beratungsstelle wird deren personelle Ausstattung und Qualität der Fachberatung in der Zukunft liefern.

§ 153 a StPO[850] bei Sachverhaltsidentität nicht mehr verhängt werden dürfen. Eine Verschärfung gegenüber dem bisherigen Recht hat der Gesetzgeber für die mittleren Disziplinarmaßnahmen vorgenommen, bei denen das Doppelahndungsverbot nicht gilt. So verzichtet der Wortlaut des § 14 Abs. 1 Nr. 2 BDG auf das bisherige Erfordernis der Notwendigkeit der Verhängung einer zusätzlichen Disziplinarmaßnahme zur „Wahrung des Ansehens des Beamtentums"[851] und fordert für die ausnahmsweise Bejahung einer disziplinaren Ahndung neben einer Strafe, Geldbuße oder Ordnungsmaßnahme nur noch das Vorliegen eines zusätzlichen Erziehungsbedürfnisses[852]. Mit dieser gesetzgeberischen Korrektur wird die Möglichkeit der Verhängung einer zusätzlichen Disziplinarmaßnahme neben einer strafrichterlichen Verurteilung erleichtert. Ergänzt wird die Regelung des § 14 Abs. 1 BDG durch dessen Abs. 2, der eine disziplinare Ahndung wegen derselben Tatsachen nach einem rechtskräftigen strafrichterlichen Freispruch nur bei einem disziplinaren Überhang zulässt, der die Pflichtverletzungen eines Beamten umfasst, die von der Geschehensseite für den Vorwurf einer Straftat nicht ausreichen[853]. Hierzu zählen Fälle wie der Verstoß gegen das Geschenkannahmeverbot des § 70 BBG bei gleichzeitigem Freispruch von dem Vorwurf der Vorteilsannahme nach § 331 mangels Vorliegens der erforderlichen Unrechtsvereinbarung.

bb) § 80 BDG

Der erst mit dem KorrBekG vom 13. August 1997 in die BDO eingestellte § 11a[854] sah vor, dass das kooperative Verhalten eines Beamten, der sein Wissen über eine Korruptionsstraftat offenbart, im Disziplinarverfahren zu seinen Gunsten, d.h. durch die Zahlung einer Unterhaltsleistung ab dem 65. Lebensjahr, berücksichtigt werden kann. Diese jetzt auch in § 80 BDG aufgenommene Regelung soll dem Zweck dienen, im Interesse einer effektiven Korruptionsbekämpfung und einer wirkungsvollen Selbstreinigung des öffentlichen Dienstes Anreize für die Mithilfe bei der Aufklärung oder Verhinderung von Korruptionsstraftaten gerade für diejenigen Beamten zu schaffen, deren Entfernung aus dem Dienst unausweichlich erscheint[855]. Es liegt kein Zahlenmaterial darü-

---

850 Die Einbeziehung des § 153a StPO in das Doppelahndungsverbot des bisherigen § 14 BDO war umstritten: das BVerwG hatte die Möglichkeit einer Analogie verworfen, BVerwG, Dok.Ber. B 1991, S. 95 (96 ff.), das Bundesdisziplinargericht diese Möglichkeit dagegen bejaht, vgl. in DÖD 1988, S. 217 f.

851 So noch § 14 BDO.

852 Der Gesetzgeber sah keinen Grund, auf eine individuelle erzieherische Einwirkung auf den Beamten zu verzichten, nur weil der Schutz des insoweit abstrakten Ansehens des Beamtentums dies nicht erfordere, BT-Drs. 14/4659, S. 38 zu § 14 BDG.

853 Vgl. für die entsprechende Vorschrift des § 17 Abs. 5 BDO Köhler/Ratz, § 17 BDO Rn. 17.

854 Sog. „Kleine Kronzeugenregelung", BGBl. I (1997), S. 2038 (2041).

855 BR-Drs. 553/96, S. 22/23.

ber vor, wie häufig von dieser Regelung Gebrauch gemacht wurde. Da im Jahr 2001 auf Bundesebene aber nur in 9 Fällen Disziplinarmaßnahmen wegen Bestechlichkeit, Vorteilsannahme oder verbotener Geschenkannahme getroffen wurden[856], dürfte die „Kleine Kronzeugenregelung" wenn überhaupt nur in sehr wenigen Einzelfällen zur Anwendung gekommen sein.

cc) Wegfall des § 28 Abs. 2 BDO

Mit dem am 1. Juli 1997 in Kraft getretenen Gesetz zur Reform des öffentlichen Dienstrechts[857] wurde § 28 Abs. 2 BDO eingeführt. Nach dieser Vorschrift bestand die Verpflichtung, bei jedem nicht ausgeräumten Verdacht eines Verstoßes gegen das Verbot der Annahme von Belohnungen und Geschenken ein förmliches Disziplinarverfahren einzuleiten. Dem Dienstvorgesetzten war in diesen Fällen im Rahmen seines ihm bei der Entscheidung über eine Disziplinarmaßnahme eingeräumten Ermessens[858] die Möglichkeit genommen, das Verfahren einzustellen oder durch den Erlass einer Disziplinarverfügung zu beenden.

Die von dieser Vorschrift ausgehende Präventivwirkung bestand darin, in allen Fällen einer zumindest mit Restzweifeln belegten Sachverhaltsaufklärung ein förmliches Untersuchungsverfahren mit seinen gegenüber dem Vorermittlungsverfahren strengeren prozessualen Voraussetzungen durchzuführen. Mit der Schaffung eines einheitlichen behördlichen Ermittlungsverfahrens nach dem BDG war die Vorschrift des § 28 Abs. 2 BDO nicht mehr systemgerecht und musste daher gestrichen werden. Der Wegfall dieser präventiv wirkenden Regelung ist im Zusammenhang mit dem Wegfall der Institution des Bundesdisziplinaranwalts besonders bedeutsam, da damit auch dessen Überwachungs- und Leitungsfunktion[859] im förmlichen Disziplinarverfahren ausfällt und jetzt keine unabhängige Kontrollinstanz mehr die behördlichen Ermessensentscheidungen hinterfragt[860].

856 S. Jahresbericht 2001 des Bundesdisziplinaranwalts, S. 9/10; für die Vorjahre ergibt sich folgendes Zahlenmaterial: 2000 waren es 7 Fälle, 1999 17 Fälle, 1998 5 Fälle, 1997 12 Fälle und 1996 18 Fälle, in denen ein förmliches Disziplinarverfahren wegen dieser Delikte durchgeführt wurde. Die Zahl der Fälle, in denen auf die höchste Disziplinarmaßnahme erkannt wurde, dürfte aber niedriger sein.

857 BGBl. I S. 322 (340).

858 Jetzt § 13 Abs. 1 BDG, vorher § 3 BDO.

859 Vgl. § 39 BDO.

860 Der Bundesdisziplinaranwalt wurde grundsätzlich über alle Ermittlungen und Untersuchungen in den einzelnen Behörden unterrichtet, um eine einheitliche Ausübung der Disziplinargewalt sichern zu können, vgl. § 37 BDO.

dd) § 27 BDG

Mit der Begründung einer effektiven Korruptionsbekämpfung wurde auf Vorschlag des Bundesrats[861] eine Vorschrift in das BDG aufgenommen, die die Möglichkeit einer richterlichen Anordnung der Beschlagnahme oder Durchsuchung innerhalb des Ermittlungsverfahrens der Verwaltung vorsieht. Voraussetzung dieser Anordnung nach § 27 Abs. 1 BDG ist, dass der Beamte des ihm zur Last gelegten Dienstvergehens dringend verdächtig ist und die Maßnahme zu der Bedeutung der Sache und der zu erwartenden Disziplinarmaßnahme nicht außer Verhältnis steht. Die Staatsanwaltschaft ist in diesen Fällen schwerwiegender Dienstvergehen – wozu auch ein Verstoß gegen § 70 BBG zählt – im Wege der Amtshilfe in Anspruch zu nehmen (§ 27 Abs. 2 BDG).

5. Stellungnahme

Nach den Motiven des Bundesgesetzgebers soll die Neuordnung des Bundesdisziplinarrechts neben strukturellen Verbesserungen vor allem der Verfahrensbeschleunigung und einer inhaltlichen Effizienzsteigerung dienen[862]. Gegen solche Absichten wäre kaum etwas einzuwenden, wäre ihre Umsetzung durch das neue BDG gewährleistet. Dann wäre im Rahmen einer ultima ratio-Abwägung den Gegnern einer disziplinarrechtlichen Lösung zumindest das Argument eines Vollzugsdefizits entzogen, Disziplinarverfahren würden viel zu lange dauern, im schlimmsten Fall sogar regelrecht „verschleppt". Indes bestehen erhebliche Zweifel an der Umsetzbarkeit der vom Gesetzgeber verfolgten Ziele.

Positiv zu erwähnen ist zwar zunächst die zu erwartende Verfahrensbeschleunigung durch die Schaffung eines einheitlichen Verwaltungsermittlungsverfahrens unter Verzicht auf das bisherige Nebeneinander von Vorermittlungs- und Untersuchungsverfahren[863]. Dieser mögliche Beschleunigungseffekt wird aber nicht nur in den Fällen aufgezehrt, in denen zusätzlicher Verwaltungsaufwand aufgrund der nach neuem Recht durchzuführenden Widerspruchsverfahren gemäß §§ 40 ff. BDG entsteht. Hauptsächlich ursächlich ist die Übertragung der gerichtlichen Zuständigkeit für Disziplinarsachen von Bundesbeamten auf die allgemeine Verwaltungsgerichtsbarkeit. Mit der damit verbun-

---

861 S. die Stellungnahme des Bundesrats zum Entwurf des BDiszNOG, BT-Drs. 14/4659, S. 60 und die Gegenäußerung der Bundesregierung, S. 64.

862 Begründung Entwurf BDiszNOG., BT-Drs. 14/4659, S. 33/34.

863 Dieses Nebeneinander hat häufig dazu geführt, dass zunächst bei den Vorermittlungen der Sachverhalt mit der Zielrichtung einer Disziplinarverfügung aufgeklärt wurde, um anschließend aufgrund der gewonnenen Erkenntnisse die Einleitung eines förmlichen Untersuchungsverfahrens zu prüfen. In diesem Verfahren musste dann erneut der Sachverhalt unter strengeren strafprozessualen Bedingungen aufgeklärt werden.

denen Erweiterung des Instanzenzuges von zwei auf drei Instanzen[864] und der im Vergleich zum Bundesdisziplinargericht erfahrungsgemäß überlangen Verfahrensdauer vor den Verwaltungsgerichten[865] verkehrt sich das Ziel einer Verfahrensbeschleunigung in sein Gegenteil.

Ein weiterer, die Verfahrensbeschleunigung hemmender Effekt könnte durch die Einführung der gerichtsunmittelbaren Beweiserhebung nach § 58 Abs. 1 BDG eintreten[866]. Diese beinhaltet eine Verlagerung der bislang bereits im förmlichen Verwaltungsuntersuchungsverfahren vorgenommenen Beweiserhebung in das gerichtliche Verfahren[867]. Der inhaltliche und zeitliche Aufwand, der dadurch entsteht, dass die im Ermittlungsverfahren bereits erworbene Sachkenntnis nicht unmittelbar in einer verwaltungsseitig durchzuführende Beweisaufnahme genutzt werden kann, sondern für die gerichtliche Beweisaufnahme umfangreich erneut über die Klageschrift dargelegt werden muss, dürfte nicht unerheblich sein.

Es ist daher zu vermuten, dass die angestrebte Verfahrensverkürzung nicht erreicht werden kann, sondern umgekehrt eher verfahrensbedingte Verzögerungen eintreten werden. Mit dem Argument einer künftigen Verfahrensbeschleunigung kann der Vorzug einer disziplinarrechtlichen vor der strafrechtlichen Lösung daher nicht begründet werden.

Das Disziplinarrecht stellt sich als rechtliche Alternative zum Strafrecht aber auch mit der verfahrensrechtlichen Loslösung vom Strafprozessrecht infrage.

Im Disziplinarverfahren geht es ähnlich wie im Strafverfahren beim Verdacht einer Straftat darum, den Nachweis einer Dienstpflichtverletzung zu erbringen, die Schwere der Verfehlung und der individuellen Schuld zu bewerten und das Maß der erforderlichen disziplinaren Einwirkung zu bemessen[868]. Demgegenüber geht es in den Verfahren vor den Verwaltungsgerichten nicht um die

---

[864] Die Anzahl der verfahrensbedingt beteiligten Berufsrichter erhöht sich nach dem BDG für den Instanzenzug deutlich, vgl. Müller-Eising, NJW 2001, S. 3587 (3590).

[865] Bei den Landesbeamten, deren Disziplinarstreitsachen vor den Verwaltungsgerichten ausgetragen werden, ist die Situation schon jetzt unter rechtsstaatlichen Erwägungen bedenklich, wenn die gerichtlichen Verfahren sich über Jahre hinziehen, vgl. dazu Quambusch, Die Personalvertretung 1999, S. 453 ff.

[866] Ebenso Weiß, Die Personalvertretung 2002, S. 2 (10).

[867] Vgl. für das alte Recht §§ 56 ff. BDO; danach war eine Beweiserhebung vor Gericht nur fakultativ vorgesehen, §§ 68, 71 Abs. 1 BDO.

[868] Zu Recht Müller-Eising, NJW 2001, S. 3587 (3588), die die inhaltliche Verwandtschaft des Disziplinarverfahrens mit dem Strafrecht damit begründet, dass es hier um die „Beurteilung eines menschlichen Fehlverhaltens“ gehe und nicht „um einen Verwaltungsvorgang“; kritisch auch Weiß, der einen Wesensbruch zu dem keinen Schuldvorwurf im berufsmoralischen Sinne kennenden allgemeinen Streitverfahren aus dem Beamtenverhältnis feststellt, Die Personalvertretung 2002, S. 2 (4).

Schuld oder Unschuld des Betroffenen, sondern um die Überprüfung der Rechtmäßigkeit eines Verwaltungsakts und damit um einen vom Schuldspruch eines Strafgerichts oder der Festsetzung einer Disziplinarmaßnahme sich unterscheidenden Parteienprozess. Widersprüchlich zum Ziel der Loslösung vom Strafprozessrecht ist auch, dass die VwGO zwar kein Ermittlungsverfahren wie die StPO kennt, dieses aber dennoch nach dem neuen BDG (§ 21) verwaltungsseitig durchzuführen ist[869].

Der Wortgehalt des § 21 Abs. 1 BDG entspricht denn auch in Abweichung zu den Grundsätzen im Verwaltungsverfahren dem des § 160 Abs. 2 StPO, wonach nicht nur die belastenden, sondern auch die entlastenden Umstände zu ermitteln sind.

Die Klage des Dienstherrn im Disziplinarverfahren (§ 52 BDG) ist mit der Anklageschrift der StPO vergleichbar, müsste demzufolge im gerichtlichen Verfahren auch einen Freispruch ermöglichen. Die VwGO wiederum kennt nur die Klageabweisung, was dem Interesse des betroffenen Beamten, im Falle der Unschuld auch freigesprochen zu werden, elementar zuwiderläuft. Der im Strafprozess wie im Disziplinarverfahren geltende Grundsatz „in dubio pro reo" ist dem Verwaltungsgerichtsverfahren fremd, in dem sich die Beteiligten – Dienstherr und beschuldigter Beamte – gleichberechtigt gegenüberstehen[870]. Der bis zur Verurteilung geltenden Unschuldsvermutung kann das Verwaltungsverfahrensrecht in einem kontradiktorischen Verfahren kaum hinreichend Rechnung tragen[871].

Die Konsequenzen einer engen Angleichung der Disziplinarverfahren an die Prozessregeln der VwGO münden in eine Verflüchtigung des der Disziplinarmaßnahme bisher anhaftenden Sanktionscharakters. Damit geht ein Bedeutungsverlust des erzieherischen Einwirkungspotenzials der Disziplinarmaßnahme einher. Die vom Dienstherrn behauptete persönliche Verfehlung des Beamten wird vor Gericht in der Form einer streitigen Tatsache verhandelt und damit als persönlicher Schuldvorwurf gleichsam „neutralisiert".

Die Beurteilung der Ausgangsfrage, ob das öffentliche Dienstrecht und mit ihm das Disziplinarrecht im Berührungsbereich strafbarer Vorteilsannahme eine rechtliche Alternative zum Strafrecht abbilden kann, hängt wesentlich von der

---

869 Querverweise auf die StPO waren daher nicht zu vermeiden, vgl. o. unter Fn. 831.

870 Die Rechtsposition des Beamten dürfte sich im verwaltungsgerichtlichen Parteiprozess daher verschlechtern, wenn dort nicht in entsprechender Weise wie bisher vor dem Disziplinargericht elementare Schutzvorschriften wie die des § 244 StPO zum Beweisantragsrecht Berücksichtigung finden.

871 In diesem Sinn auch Müller-Eising, NJW 2001, S. 3587 (3588); Weiß, Die Personalvertretung 2002, S.2 (4).

bisher im Disziplinarrecht gewährleisteten Einhaltung des Legalitätsprinzips bei der Verfolgung von dienstrechtlichen Verfehlungen ab. Die Sicherstellung dieses Prinzips erscheint auf der Grundlage des neuen BDG aber sehr zweifelhaft. Für diese Zweifel sprechen mehrere Gründe.

Zum einen ist mit der Abschaffung der Institution des Bundesdisziplinaranwalts eine neutrale Einrichtung aufgelöst worden, die unabhängig, frei von Weisungen und ohne internen Druck, gegen einen Kollegen ermitteln zu müssen, ihren Auftrag erfüllen konnte. Dieser bestand in der Sicherung der einheitlichen Ausübung der Disziplinargewalt und in der Wahrnehmung des Interesses des öffentlichen Dienstes und der Allgemeinheit (§ 37 BDO). Mit der Auflösung der Institution ist der Sinngehalt des § 37 BDO aber nicht hinfällig geworden. Die Überzeugung des Gesetzgebers, eine ohne Überwachung minder ernsthafte Beachtung des Legalitätsprinzips durch die Dienstbehörden sei nicht zu befürchten[872], kann in dieser Allgemeinheit nicht geteilt werden.

Bei einer weiter zunehmenden, unter dem Einsparungspostulat stehenden spürbaren Verschlankung des Staates und seiner Verwaltungseinrichtungen werden die Personal- und Sachmittelressourcen zunehmend begrenzt sein. Jeder Dienstherr wird die vorhandenen Personalressourcen primär den originären Fachaufgaben seiner Behörde zuführen, um den von der Politik eingeforderten Nachweis des Effizienzgewinns erbringen zu können. Nur soweit Finanzmittel verbleiben, wird er sie zur Ausübung seiner kaum Wirtschaftlichkeitseffekte auslösenden Disziplinargewalt einsetzen. Im Unterschied zum alten Recht nehmen dabei seine Aufgaben sogar noch zu[873]. Ohne den Einsatz einer die Einhaltung des Legalitätsprinzips einfordernden neutralen Stelle wird der Druck auf die Dienstvorgesetzten zur konsequenten Umsetzung ihrer Disziplinargewalt abnehmen. An den künftig zu erhebenden Fallzahlen wird sehr schnell sichtbar werden, ob die Dienstvorgesetzten ihrer disziplinaren Verantwortung in dem geforderten Umfang noch nachkommen.

Die obersten Dienstbehörden haben in ihrem und dem ihnen nachgeordneten Behördenbereich die Verfolgung von Dienstpflichtverletzungen nach § 17 Abs.1 Satz 2 BDG sicherzustellen. Die Leitung der Ressorts ist mit politischen und fachlichen Aufgaben aber voll ausgelastet. Es kommt daher nur eine Delegation der Wahrnehmung der mit der Disziplinargewalt verbundenen Aufgaben auf eigene Mitarbeiter in Betracht. Diesem Personenkreis obliegt, wenn auch

---

872 Begründung Entwurf BDiszNOG, BT-Drs. 14/4659, S. 34.

873 Nach dem BDG zählen zu den zusätzlichen Aufgaben u.a. die Erstellung der Klageschrift, Führen von Rechtsstreitigkeiten, ggf. die Durchführung eines Widerspruchsverfahrens, die bundesweite Auswertung der Entscheidungen der Verwaltungsgerichte der Länder und die Einlegung von Rechtsmitteln.

nicht formal-juristisch[874], so doch faktisch die Entscheidung, gegen in Verdacht geratene Kollegen Ermittlungen anzustellen. Wer die Rechtswirklichkeit nicht aus den Augen verliert erkennt, welcher enormen innerbetrieblichen Anstrengung es bedarf, auch ggf. gegen Spitzenbeamte des eigenen Verwaltungsbereichs bei Verdacht dienstrechtlicher Verstöße diesen konsequent nachzugehen. Nach bisherigem Recht konnte die starke Position des Bundesdisziplinaranwalts als Kontrollorgan, sein Antragsrecht nach § 39 BDO sowie die Erstellung der Anschuldigungsschrift durch ihn als externer Stelle gewährleisten, die Disziplinargewalt auch gegen höhere Beamte und Vorgesetzte durchzusetzen. Künftig ist nicht auszuschließen, dass in Einzelfällen Ermittlungen unterbleiben oder verzögert erfolgen und eine behördeninterne, falsch verstandene Solidarität gegenüber Kollegen tatkräftigem Einschreiten entgegensteht. Auch das Interesse des Dienstherrn weist in diese Richtung, denn er wird seine Behörde nach außen korrekt und frei von Vorwürfen korruptiver Machenschaften präsentieren wollen. Die naturgemäß behördenintern als unangenehm empfundene Auseinandersetzung mit disziplinarrelevanten Vorgängen setzt zudem großes verfahrensrechtliches Wissen und persönliches Handlungsgeschick voraus, das künftig ohne die Möglichkeit der Einschaltung des Bundesdisziplinaranwalts den eingesetzten Ermittlungsbeamten noch mehr Kompetenz abverlangen wird.

Die vorgenannte Einschätzung wird noch durch einen anderen Gesichtspunkt bestätigt. Nach neuem Recht wurde die Disziplinarbefugnis des Dienstherrn auf die Maßregelung von Dienstpflichtverletzungen im mittelschweren Bereich ausgeweitet. Neben Verweis und Geldbuße kann er nun auch eine Kürzung der Dienstbezüge oder des Ruhegehalts durch Disziplinarverfügung aussprechen (§ 33 Abs. 1 BDG). Der Gesetzgeber verfolgt mit dieser Befugniserweiterung das Ziel einer Beschleunigung des Disziplinarverfahrens[875]. Er hat aber vorerst nur erreicht, dass nach dieser Regelung mittelschwere Dienstpflichtverletzungen nicht mehr einer gerichtlichen Entscheidung vorbehalten sind, sondern der Ermessensentscheidung des Dienstherrn nach § 13 BDG unterliegen. Mit gutem Grund sah die bisherige Rechtslage davon ab, dem Dienstherrn diese Kompetenz zu solchen in die Rechte des betroffenen Beamten besonders stark eingreifenden Maßnahmen wie der Kürzung der Dienstbezüge zu erteilen. Weder das Nähe- und Abhängigkeitsverhältnis zwischen Dienstherr und Mitarbeitern und innerhalb der Kollegenschaft noch der dem Dienstherrn eingeräumte verfahrensrechtliche Ermessensspielraum bei der Bemessung der Disziplinarmaßnahme bilden eine geeignete Grundlage für eine derartige Kompetenzerweiterung. Die Objektivität des Zustandekommens der Disziplinierung – egal ob es sich um einen Mitarbeiter der unteren Dienstränge oder einen höheren Beamten mit Vorgesetzteneigenschaft handelt – erscheint nicht mehr garantiert. Beim

---

874 Für die förmliche Einleitung eines Disziplinarverfahrens ist immer der Dienstvorgesetzte zuständig, § 17 Abs. 1 Satz 1 BDG.

875 Begründung Entwurf BDiszNOG, BT-Drs. 14/4659, S. 43 zu § 32 BDG..

höheren Beamten könnte man eher geneigt sein, zwecks Vermeidung einer disziplinar-gerichtlichen Überprüfung der behördlichen Entscheidung und damit öffentlichen Aufsehens, die Disziplinarmaßnahme entsprechend „mild" ausfallen zu lassen. Denn es ist nicht zu erwarten, dass die betroffenen Beamten eine Kürzung der Dienstbezüge klaglos hinnehmen würden. Es muss daher bezweifelt werden, dass die Verwirklichung des gesetzgeberischen Anspruchs einer gleichmäßigen Durchsetzung der Disziplinargewalt, für die bislang die neutrale durchsetzungsfähige Institution des Bundesdisziplinaranwalts Sorge getragen hat, für die Zukunft gesichert ist.

VI. Ergebnis Teil C

Die Ausgangsfrage der rechtlichen Alternative des öffentlichen Dienstrechts gegenüber dem Strafrecht muss insbesondere vor dem Hintergrund der Neuordnung des Bundesdisziplinarrechts verneint werden.

Das nach dem neuen BDG durchzuführende verwaltungsinterne Ermittlungsverfahren genügt den strengen strafprozessualen Ansprüchen durch seine weitgehende Loslösung vom Strafprozessrecht nicht mehr. Mit der Angleichung des Disziplinarrechts an das Verwaltungsprozessrecht wurde die Umgestaltung des Disziplinarverfahrens in ein Verwaltungsstreitverfahren vollzogen, in dem die Parteien um die Rechtmäßigkeit einer Verwaltungsmaßnahme streiten. Damit verliert nicht nur der Sanktionscharakter der Disziplinarmaßnahme erheblich an Bedeutung, sondern auch die ehemals nach strafrechtlichen Prinzipien ermittelte Disziplinarmaßnahme als strafrechtsgleiche Reaktion auf dienstbezogenes menschliches Fehlverhalten.

Zudem besteht das Risiko eines disziplinarrechtlichen Vollzugsdefizits in zweifacher Hinsicht. Einmal im Hinblick auf eine haushalterische Beschränkung der Personal- und Sachmittelressourcen, die zu einem verwaltungsinternen Verdrängungswettbewerb führen könnte, bei dem Aufgaben- und Zuständigkeitsbereiche ohne nennenswerten Wirtschaftlichkeitsfaktor eher vernachlässigt werden. Zum anderen fehlt nach der Abschaffung der Institution des Bundesdisziplinaranwalts eine neutrale Stelle mit Überwachungsfunktion, die die einheitliche Handhabung der Disziplinargewalt gerade auch gegen höhere Beamte mit Vorgesetztenfunktion sicherstellen könnte. Unter diesen Rahmenbedingungen überwiegen insgesamt die Zweifel, dass das vorhandene repressive Maßnahmenpotenzial des Disziplinarrechts in der rechtlich geforderten Weise ohne Einschränkung eingesetzt wird.

Die disziplinarrechtliche Lösung kann daher nicht als rechtliche Alternative gegenüber der strafrechtlichen Lösung in Erwägung gezogen werden.

VII. Zusammenfassung der Ergebnisse aus Teil A, B und C

Die Untersuchung der subjektiven Tatumstände in der Rechtsentwicklung vom RStGB von 1871 über das EGStGB von 1974 bis zum KorrBekG von 1997 hat ergeben, dass seit den Entscheidungen RGSt 74, 251 und 77, 75 eine sukzessive Ausdehnung der Strafbarkeitsgrenzen bei den Bestechungsdelikten vollzogen wurde. Der Gesetzgeber hat die Entwicklung der Rspr. nachgezeichnet und in das StGB eingefügt. Mehrfach ist dabei eine Vorverlegung der Strafbarkeit in das Gefährdungsvorfeld des eigentlichen Unrechtsbereichs an verschiedenen tatbestandlichen Einbruchstellen erfolgt. Mit dem EGStGB sind die Absätze 3 der §§ 332, 334 in das StGB eingefügt worden, die vor allem die Unklarheiten zur Frage der Vollendung der Tat beim Ermessensbeamten beseitigen sollten. Hier sind aber neue Zweifelsfragen im Hinblick auf subjektive Vorbehalte und Fehlvorstellungen bei den Tatverdächtigen entstanden.

Beim Abbau der subjektiven Anforderungen bei der sog. Unrechtsvereinbarung hat sich der BGH ebenso wie zuvor schon das RG beteiligt. Nachdem der Gesetzgeber mit dem EGStGB die Vorteilsannahme als zu kriminellem Unrecht erhobene Disziplinarwidrigkeit neu gefasst hatte, hat er mit der Neukonzeption der §§ 331 ff. durch das KorrBekG eine weitere Lockerung dieser Anforderungen an die Unrechtsvereinbarung vorgenommen. Die Begründungen des Gesetzgebers für diese Straftatbestandserweiterungen beinhalten im Wesentlichen kriminalpolitische Überlegungen, die vorhandene prozessuale Nachweisschwierigkeiten belegen. Insgesamt offenbart die Rechtsentwicklung bei den Bestechungsdelikten die eigentliche Schwäche dieser Tatbestände, nämlich die Beweisproblematik bei den subjektiven Tatumständen.

Auf der anderen Seite hat der Gesetzgeber mit der Angleichung des Strafrechts bei der internationalen Korruptionsbekämpfung mit dem EUBestG und dem IntBestG nur die geforderten Mindeststandards gesetzt, indem er den Anwendungsbereich dieser Gesetze auf künftige, pflichtwidrige Diensthandlungen beschränkt hat. Dass der Gesetzgeber aus eigener rechtspolitischer Überzeugung auf eine umfassende, rechtmäßige Diensthandlungen einschließende internationale Bekämpfung der Korruption verzichtet hat, dokumentiert für den Anwendungsbereich der beiden Gesetze seine sehr zurückhaltende Positionierung im Rahmen strafrechtlicher Sanktionierung vorteilsbehafteter pflichtgemäßer Diensthandlungen.

Diese Zurückhaltung des Gesetzgebers bei der Bekämpfung der internationalen Bestechungskriminalität könnte – gewollt oder ungewollt – den richtigen Weg für die Zukunft weisen. Denn nach den Ergebnissen der Falluntersuchungen in Teil B der Arbeit erfasst die Bekämpfung der Korruption im nationalen Bereich inzwischen mit den weit gefassten Strafnormen der Vorteilsannahme und Vorteilsgewährung auch eindeutig nicht strafwürdige Lebenssachverhalte, die daher aus dem Strafbarkeitsbereich wieder herausgelöst werden müssen.

Die Prüfung der rechtlichen Möglichkeiten zur Eingrenzung der §§ 331, 333 auf strafwürdige und strafbedürftige Fälle hat Folgendes ergeben:

- Beim Rechtsgut der Bestechungsdelikte sollte zwecks Vermeidung einer Überreaktion des Strafrechts kein isoliert betrachteter Vertrauensschutz zur Begründung strafbaren Verhaltens herangezogen werden, sondern der tragende Rechtsgutsgedanke sollte auf die Funktionsfähigkeit des Staates und seiner Einrichtungen abstellen und damit auf den Schutz vor Beeinträchtigung der sich an rechtsstaatlichen und gemeinwohlorientierten Grundsätzen auszurichtenden, sachgemäßen Aufgabenerledigung der Bediensteten

- Mit diesem Rechtsgutsverständnis müssen alle denkbaren Fälle eines Regelungskonflikts zwischen Erlaubnisnorm (Folge: fehlende Strafwürdigkeit) und strafrechtlicher Verbotsnorm durch eine tatbestandsbegrenzende Ergänzung der §§ 331, 333 gelöst werden. Dazu wird ein Formulierungsvorschlag unterbreitet, der die Aufnahme des Zusatzes „ohne Billigung durch die Rechtsordnung" in die Tatbestände der §§ 331, 333 enthält.[876]

Die in Teil C der Arbeit unter dem ultima ratio-Gedanken geprüfte Frage, ob das öffentliche Dienstrecht/Disziplinarrecht eine rechtliche Alternative gegenüber der durch das KorrBekG vorgenommenen Ausweitung des strafrechtlichen Sanktionsbereichs der §§ 331, 333 darstellen kann, muss verneint werden. Mit dem zum 1.1.2002 in Kraft getretenen BDG genügen die nach diesem Gesetz durchzuführenden verwaltungsinternen Ermittlungsverfahren nach der weitgehenden Loslösung vom Strafprozessrecht nicht mehr den strengen strafprozessualen Ansprüchen. Mit der Umgestaltung des Disziplinarverfahrens in ein Verwaltungsstreitverfahren verliert die Disziplinarmaßnahme ihren Sanktionscharakter i.S. einer strafrechtsgleichen Reaktion auf dienstbezogenes, menschliches Fehlverhalten. Mit der gleichzeitigen Abschaffung der Institution des Bundesdisziplinaranwalts ist zudem die verwaltungsseitig bestehende neutrale Stelle entfallen, die in ihrer Überwachungsfunktion den Vollzug der einheitlichen Handhabung der Disziplinargewalt sicherstellen konnte.

---

876 S. o. S. 164 f.

Anhang 1

Auszug aus dem RStGB vom 15.5.1871, RGBl. I, S. 127 (191/192)

Verbrechen und Vergehen im Amte.

§. 331.
Ein Beamter, welcher für eine in sein Amt einschlagende, an sich nicht pflichtwidrige Handlung Geschenke oder andere Vortheile annimmt, fordert oder sich versprechen läßt, wird mit Geldstrafe bis zu Einhundert Thalern oder mit Gefängniß bis zu sechs Monaten bestraft.

§. 332.
Ein Beamter, welcher für eine Handlung, die eine Verletzung einer Amts- oder Dienstpflicht enthält, Geschenke oder andere Vortheile annimmt, fordert oder sich versprechen läßt, wird wegen Bestechung mit Zuchthaus bis zu fünf Jahren bestraft.

Sind mildernde Umstände vorhanden, so tritt Gefängnißstrafe ein.

§. 333.
Wer einem Beamten oder einem Mitgliede der bewaffneten Macht Geschenke oder andere Vortheile anbietet, verspricht oder gewährt, um ihn zu einer Handlung, die eine Verletzung einer Amts- oder Dienstpflicht enthält, zu bestimmen, wird wegen Bestechung mit Gefängniß bestraft; auch kann auf Verlust der bürgerlichen Ehrenrechte erkannt werden.

Sind mildernde Umstände vorhanden, so kann auf Geldstrafe bis zu fünfhundert Thalern erkannt werden.

§. 334.
Ein Richter, Schiedsrichter, Geschworener oder Schöffe, welcher Geschenke oder andere Vortheile fordert, annimmt oder sich versprechen läßt, um eine Rechtssache, deren Leitung oder Entscheidung ihm obliegt, zu Gunsten oder zum Nachtheile eines Betheiligten zu leiten oder zu entscheiden, wird mit Zuchthaus bestraft.

Derjenige, welcher einem Richter, Schiedsrichter, Geschworenen oder Schöffen zu dem vorbezeichneten Zwecke Geschenke oder andere Vortheile anbietet, verspricht oder gewährt, wird mit Zuchthaus bestraft. Sind mildernde Umstände vorhanden, so tritt Gefängnißstrafe ein.

Anhang 2

Auszug aus dem Strafgesetzbuch in der Fassung des am 1.1.1975 in Kraft getretenen EGStGB vom 2.3.1974, BGBl. I, S. 469 (496)

§ 331. Vorteilsannahme. (1) Ein Amtsträger oder ein für den öffentlichen Dienst besonders Verpflichteter, der einen Vorteil als Gegenleistung dafür fordert, sich versprechen läßt oder annimmt, daß er eine Diensthandlung vorgenommen hat oder künftig vornehme, wird mit Freiheitsstrafe bis zu zwei Jahren oder mit Geldstrafe bestraft.

(2) Ein Richter oder Schiedsrichter, der einen Vorteil als Gegenleistung dafür fordert, sich versprechen läßt oder annimmt, daß er eine richterliche Handlung vorgenommen hat oder künftig vornehme, wird mit Freiheitsstrafe bis zu drei Jahren oder mit Geldstrafe bestraft. Der Versuch ist strafbar.

(3) Die Tat ist nicht nach Absatz 1 strafbar, wenn der Täter einen nicht von ihm geforderten Vorteil sich versprechen läßt oder annimmt und die zuständige Behörde im Rahmen ihrer Befugnisse entweder die Annahme vorher genehmigt hat oder der Täter unverzüglich bei ihr Anzeige erstattet und sie die Annahme genehmigt.

§ 332. Bestechlichkeit. (1) Ein Amtsträger oder ein für den öffentlichen Dienst besonders Verpflichteter, der einen Vorteil als Gegenleistung dafür fordert, sich versprechen läßt oder annimmt, daß er eine Diensthandlung vorgenommen hat oder künftig vornehme und dadurch seine Dienstpflichten verletzt hat oder verletzen würde, wird mit Freiheitsstrafe von sechs Monaten bis zu fünf Jahren, in minder schweren Fällen mit Freiheitsstrafe bis zu drei Jahren oder mit Geldstrafe bestraft. Der Versuch ist strafbar.

(2) Ein Richter oder Schiedsrichter, der einen Vorteil als Gegenleistung dafür fordert, sich versprechen läßt oder annimmt, daß er eine richterliche Handlung vorgenommen hat oder künftig vornehme und dadurch seine richterlichen Pflichten verletzt hat oder verletzen würde, wird mit Freiheitsstrafe von einem Jahr bis zu zehn Jahren, in minder schweren Fällen mit Freiheitsstrafe von sechs Monaten bis zu fünf Jahren bestraft.

(3) Falls der Täter den Vorteil als Gegenleistung für eine künftige Handlung fordert, sich versprechen läßt oder annimmt, so sind die Absätze 1 und 2 schon dann anzuwenden, wenn er sich dem anderen gegenüber bereit gezeigt hat,

1. bei der Handlung seine Pflichten zu verletzen oder,

2. soweit die Handlung in seinem Ermessen steht, sich bei Ausübung des Ermessens durch den Vorteil beeinflussen zu lassen.

§ 333. Vorteilsgewährung. (1) Wer einem Amtsträger, einem für den öffentlichen Dienst besonders Verpflichteten oder einem Soldaten der Bundeswehr als Gegenleistung dafür, daß er eine in seinem Ermessen stehende Diensthandlung künftig vornehme, einen Vorteil anbietet, verspricht oder gewährt, wird mit Freiheitsstrafe bis zu zwei Jahren oder mit Geldstrafe bestraft.

(2) Wer einem Richter oder Schiedsrichter als Gegenleistung dafür, daß er eine richterliche Handlung künftig vornehme, einen Vorteil anbietet, verspricht oder gewährt, wird mit Freiheitsstrafe bis zu drei Jahren oder mit Geldstrafe bestraft.

(3) Die Tat ist nicht nach Absatz 1 strafbar, wenn die zuständige Behörde im Rahmen ihrer Befugnisse entweder die Annahme des Vorteils durch den Empfänger vorher genehmigt hat oder sie auf unverzügliche Anzeige des Empfängers genehmigt.

§ 334. Bestechung. (1) Wer einem Amtsträger, einem für den öffentlichen Dienst besonders Verpflichteten oder einem Soldaten der Bundeswehr einen Vorteil als Gegenleistung dafür anbietet, verspricht oder gewährt, daß er eine Diensthandlung vorgenommen hat oder künftig vornehme und dadurch seine Dienstpflichten verletzt hat oder verletzen würde, wird mit Freiheitsstrafe von drei Monaten bis zu fünf Jahren, in minder schweren Fällen mit Freiheitsstrafe bis zu zwei Jahren oder mit Geldstrafe bestraft.

(2) Wer einem Richter oder Schiedsrichter einen Vorteil als Gegenleistung dafür anbietet, verspricht oder gewährt, daß er eine richterliche Handlung

1. vorgenommen und dadurch seine richterlichen Pflichten verletzt hat oder

2. künftig vornehme und dadurch seine richterlichen Pflichten verletzen würde,

wird in den Fällen der Nummer 1 mit Freiheitsstrafe von drei Monaten bis zu fünf Jahren, in den Fällen der Nummer 2 mit Freiheitsstrafe von sechs Monaten bis zu fünf Jahren bestraft. Der Versuch ist strafbar.

(3) Falls der Täter den Vorteil als Gegenleistung für eine künftige Handlung anbietet, verspricht oder gewährt, so sind die Absätze 1 und 2 schon dann anzuwenden, wenn er den anderen zu bestimmen versucht, daß dieser

1. bei der Handlung seine Pflichten verletzt oder,

2. soweit die Handlung in seinem Ermessen steht, sich bei der Ausübung des Ermessens durch den Vorteil beeinflussen läßt.

Anhang 3

Auszug aus dem Strafgesetzbuch in der Fassung des am 20.8.1997 in Kraft getretenen Artikel 1 des KorrBekG vom 13.8.1997, BGBl. I, S. 2038 (2039)

§ 331. **Vorteilsannahme.** (1) Ein Amtsträger oder ein für den öffentlichen Dienst besonders Verpflichteter, der für die Dienstausübung einen Vorteil für sich oder einen Dritten fordert, sich versprechen läßt oder annimmt, wird mit Freiheitsstrafe bis zu drei Jahren oder mit Geldstrafe bestraft.

(2) Ein Richter oder Schiedsrichter, der einen Vorteil für sich oder einen Dritten als Gegenleistung dafür fordert, sich versprechen läßt oder annimmt, daß er eine richterliche Handlung vorgenommen hat oder künftig vornehme, wird mit Freiheitsstrafe bis zu fünf Jahren oder mit Geldstrafe bestraft. Der Versuch ist strafbar.

(3) Die Tat ist nicht nach Absatz 1 strafbar, wenn der Täter einen nicht von ihm geforderten Vorteil sich versprechen läßt oder annimmt und die zuständige Behörde im Rahmen ihrer Befugnisse entweder die Annahme vorher genehmigt hat oder der Täter unverzüglich bei ihr Anzeige erstattet und sie die Annahme genehmigt.

§ 332. **Bestechlichkeit.** (1) Ein Amtsträger oder ein für den öffentlichen Dienst besonders Verpflichteter, der einen Vorteil für sich oder einen Dritten als Gegenleistung dafür fordert, sich versprechen läßt oder annimmt, daß er eine Diensthandlung vorgenommen hat oder künftig vornehme und dadurch seine Dienstpflichten verletzt hat oder verletzen würde, wird mit Freiheitsstrafe von sechs Monaten bis zu fünf Jahren bestraft. In minder schweren Fällen ist die Strafe Freiheitsstrafe bis zu drei Jahren oder Geldstrafe. Der Versuch ist strafbar.

(2) Ein Richter oder Schiedsrichter, der einen Vorteil für sich oder einen Dritten als Gegenleistung dafür fordert, sich versprechen läßt oder annimmt, daß er eine richterliche Handlung vorgenommen hat oder künftig vornehme und dadurch seine richterlichen Pflichten verletzt hat oder verletzen würde, wird mit Freiheitsstrafe von einem Jahr bis zu zehn Jahren bestraft. In minder schweren Fällen ist die Strafe Freiheitsstrafe von sechs Monaten bis zu fünf Jahren.

(3) Falls der Täter den Vorteil als Gegenleistung für eine künftige Handlung fordert, sich versprechen läßt oder annimmt, so sind die Absätze 1 und 2 schon dann anzuwenden, wenn er sich dem anderen gegenüber bereit gezeigt hat,

1. bei der Handlung seine Pflichten zu verletzen oder,

2. soweit die Handlung in seinem Ermessen steht, sich bei Ausübung des Ermessens durch den Vorteil beeinflussen zu lassen.

§ 333. Vorteilsgewährung. (1) Wer einem Amtsträger, einem für den öffentlichen Dienst besonders Verpflichteten oder einem Soldaten der Bundeswehr für die Dienstausübung einen Vorteil für diesen oder einen Dritten anbietet, verspricht oder gewährt, wird mit Freiheitsstrafe bis zu drei Jahren oder mit Geldstrafe bestraft.

(2) Wer einem Richter oder Schiedsrichter einen Vorteil für diesen oder einen Dritten als Gegenleistung dafür anbietet, verspricht oder gewährt, daß er eine richterliche Handlung vorgenommen hat oder künftig vornehme, wird mit Freiheitsstrafe bis zu fünf Jahren oder mit Geldstrafe bestraft.

(3) Die Tat ist nicht nach Absatz 1 strafbar, wenn die zuständige Behörde im Rahmen ihrer Befugnisse entweder die Annahme des Vorteils durch den Empfänger vorher genehmigt hat oder sie auf unverzügliche Anzeige des Empfängers genehmigt.

§ 334. Bestechung. (1) Wer einem Amtsträger, einem für den öffentlichen Dienst besonders Verpflichteten oder einem Soldaten der Bundeswehr einen Vorteil für diesen oder einen Dritten als Gegenleistung dafür anbietet, verspricht oder gewährt, daß er eine Diensthandlung vorgenommen hat oder künftig vornehme und dadurch seine Dienstpflichten verletzt hat oder verletzen würde, wird mit Freiheitsstrafe von drei Monaten bis zu fünf Jahren bestraft. In minder schweren Fällen ist die Strafe Freiheitsstrafe bis zu zwei Jahren oder Geldstrafe.

(2) Wer einem Richter oder Schiedsrichter einen Vorteil für diesen oder einen Dritten als Gegenleistung dafür anbietet, verspricht oder gewährt, daß er eine richterliche Handlung

1. vorgenommen und dadurch seine richterlichen Pflichten verletzt hat oder

2. künftig vornehme und dadurch seine richterlichen Pflichten verletzen würde,

wird in den Fällen der Nummer 1 mit Freiheitsstrafe von drei Monaten bis zu fünf Jahren, in den Fällen der Nummer 2 mit Freiheitsstrafe von sechs Monaten bis zu fünf Jahren bestraft. Der Versuch ist strafbar.

(3) Falls der Täter den Vorteil als Gegenleistung für eine künftige Handlung anbietet, verspricht oder gewährt, so sind die Absätze 1 und 2 schon dann anzuwenden, wenn er den anderen zu bestimmen versucht, daß dieser

1. bei der Handlung seine Pflichten verletzt oder,

2. soweit die Handlung in seinem Ermessen steht, sich bei der Ausübung des Ermessens durch den Vorteil beeinflussen läßt.

§ 335. Besonders schwere Fälle der Bestechlichkeit und Bestechung.
(1) In besonders schweren Fällen wird

1. eine Tat nach

   a) § 332 Abs. 1 Satz 1, auch in Verbindung mit Abs. 3,
   und
   b) § 334 Abs. 1 Satz 1 und Abs. 2, jeweils auch in Verbindung mit Abs. 3,

   mit Freiheitsstrafe von einem Jahr bis zu zehn Jahren
   und

2. eine Tat nach § 332 Abs. 2, auch in Verbindung mit Abs. 3, mit Freiheitsstrafe nicht unter zwei Jahren

bestraft.

(2) Ein besonders schwerer Fall im Sinne des Absatzes 1 liegt in der Regel vor, wenn

1. die Tat sich auf einen Vorteil großen Ausmaßes bezieht,

2. der Täter fortgesetzt Vorteile annimmt, die er als Gegenleistung dafür gefordert hat, daß er eine Diensthandlung künftig vornehme, oder

3. der Täter gewerbsmäßig oder als Mitglied einer Bande handelt, die sich zur fortgesetzten Begehung solcher Taten verbunden hat.

Literaturverzeichnis

Achenbach, Hans, Historische und dogmatische Grundlagen der strafrechtssystematischen Schuldlehre, Abhandlungen zur rechtswissenschaftlichen Grundlagenforschung, Bd. 12, Berlin 1974.

Bauchrowitz, Wolfgang, Der immaterielle Vorteilsbegriff der Bestechungstatbestände im StGB, Dissertation, Europäische Hochschulschriften, Reihe II, Bd. 724, Frankfurt am Main, Bern, New York, Paris 1988.

Baumann, Jürgen, Zur Problematik der Bestechungstatbestände, Tübingen 1961.

Baumann, Jürgen, Zur Problematik der Bestechungstatbestände, BB 1961, 1057 ff.

Berresheim, Gunther, Die Korruption aus der Sicht des Verteidigers, Düsseldorf 1960

Binding, Karl, Lehrbuch des gemeinen deutschen Strafrechts, Besonderer Teil Bd. II2, Leipzig 1905 (Aalen 1969).

Blei, Hermann, Strafrecht II Besonderer Teil, 12. Aufl., München 1983.

Bockelmann, Paul, Strafrecht – Besonderer Teil I, ZStW 72 (1960), 251 ff.

Bruhn, Manfred, *Mehlinger* Rudolf, Rechtliche Gestaltung des Sponsoring, Bd. I, Vertragsrecht, Steuerrecht, Medienrecht, Wettbewerbsrecht, 2. Aufl., München 1995.

Bundesdisziplinaranwalt, Jahresbericht 2001 zur Disziplinarpraxis in den Bundesverwaltungen, Frankfurt am Main 2002.

Bundesdisziplinaranwalt, Jahresbericht 2000 zur Aufgabe des Disziplinarrechts, zum Berufsbild des Beamten (BVerwG 1 D 37.99) und zur Disziplinarpraxis in den Bundesverwaltungen, Frankfurt am Main 2001.

Claussen, Hans Rudolf, Korruption im öffentlichen Dienst, mit einem Beitrag von Herbig, Gottfried, Köln, Berlin, Bonn, München 1995.

Claussen, Hans Rudolf, *Janzen*, Werner, Bundesdisziplinarordnung unter Berücksichtigung des materiellen Disziplinarrechts, Handkommentar, 8. Aufl., Köln, Berlin, Bonn, München 1996.

Dauster, Manfred, Private Spenden zur Förderung von Forschung und Lehre: Teleologische Entschärfung des strafrechtlichen Vorteilsbegriffs nach § 331 StGB und Rechtfertigungsfragen, NStZ 1999, 63 ff.

Dieners, Peter, Selbstkontrolle der Wirtschaft zur Verhinderung von Korruption, JZ 1998, 181 ff.

Dölling, Dieter, Betrug und Bestechlichkeit durch Entgeltannahme für eine vorgetäuschte Dienstpflichtverletzung? – BGH, NJW 1980, 2203, JuS 1981, 570 ff.

Dölling, Dieter, Empfehlen sich Änderungen des Straf- und Strafprozeßrechts, um der Gefahr von Korruption in Staat, Wirtschaft und Gesellschaft wirksam zu begegnen? Gutachten C zum 61. Deutschen Juristentag Karlsruhe 1996, München 1996.

Dölling, Dieter, Die Neuregelung der Strafvorschriften gegen Korruption, ZStW 112 (2000), 335 ff.

Els, Stefan, Die disziplinarrechtliche Ahndung von Dienstvergehen, Unter besonderer Berücksichtigung von Alkoholverstößen, Dissertation, Europäische Hochschulschriften, Reihe II Bd. 1252, Frankfurt am Main, Berlin, Bern, New York, Paris , Wien 1992.

Eser, Albin, *Überhofen* Michael, *Huber* Barbara, Korruptionsbekämpfung durch Strafrecht, Ein rechtsvergleichendes Gutachten zu den Bestechungsdelikten im Auftrag des Bayerischen Staatsministeriums der Justiz, Beiträge und Materialien aus dem Max-Planck-Institut für ausländisches und internationales Strafrecht Freiburg, Bd. S 61, Freiburg im Breisgau 1997

Bearbeiter: Barth, Holger (Frankreich), Benseler, Justus (USA), Cornils, Karin (Schweden), Hein, Susanne (Italien), Hoffmann, Markus (Spanien), Huber, Barbara (England und Wales), Hünerfeld, Peter (Belgien), Lammich, Siegfried (Rußland), Lenz, Karl-Friedrich (Japan), Papacharalambous, Charis (Griechenland), Richter, Thomas (Volksrepublik China), Überhofen, Michael (Östereich), Tellenbach, Silvia (Türkei), van de Reyt, Ingrid W. D. M. (Niederlande), Weigend, Ewa (Polen).

Fätkinhäuer, Hans-Jürgen, Korruption in Deutschland – Die Strafdrohung/Strafrechtspflege, der kriminalist 1995, 285 ff.

Feuerbach, Paul Johann Anselm, Themis oder Beiträge zur Gesetzgebung, Landshut 1812.

Fuhrmann, Hans, Berechtigung der Rechtsprechung des Reichsgerichts und des Bundesgerichtshofs zu § 332 StGB über den Ermessensbeamten, ZStW 72 (1960), 534 ff.

Fürst, Walther, Gesamtkommentar Öffentliches Dienstrecht (GKÖD), Bearbeiter: Weiß, Hans-Dietrich, Bd. II (Disziplinarrecht des Bundes und der Länder), Einführung J012 ff., Berlin 1974.

Gansen, Franz Werner, Disziplinarrecht in Bund und Ländern, Kommentar, Heidelberg 2002.

Gänßle, Peter, Das Antikorruptionsstrafrecht – Balsam aus der Tube der symbolischen Gesetzgebung? –, NStZ 1999, 543 ff.

Geerds, Friedrich, Über den Unrechtsgehalt der Bestechungsdelikte und seine Konsequenzen für Rechtsprechung und Gesetzgebung, Tübingen 1961.

Geerds, Friedrich, Zur Frage der Unrechtsvereinbarung bei Zuwendung eines geringwertigen Geschenks an einen Justizvollzugsbeamten durch einen Gefangenen, Urteil des BGH v. 19.11.1992 – 4 StR 456/92 (BGHSt. 36, 45; richtig:39,45), JR 1993, 211 ff.

Geerds, Friedrich, Anmerkung zu dem Beschluss des OLG Zweibrücken vom 15.12.1981 – 1 Ss 3/81 –, JR 1982, 384 ff.

Geppert, Klaus, Jura Repetitorium: Strafrecht, Amtsdelikte (§ 331 ff. StGB), Jura 1981, 42 ff.

Göben, Jens, Die Auswirkungen des Gesetzes zur Bekämpfung der Korruption auf die Forschungstätigkeit von Hochschulangehörigen, MedR 1999, 345 ff.

Graupe, Johannes, Die Systematik und das Rechtsgut der Bestechungsdelikte, Dissertation, München 1988.

Gribl, Kurt, Der Vorteilsbegriff bei den Bestechungsdelikten, Dissertation, Augburger Rechtsstudien, Bd. 16, Heidelberg 1993.

Hailbronner, Kay und *Geis*, Max-Emanuel, Kommentar zum Hochschulrahmengesetz, 28. Lieferung, Heidelberg 2002.

Hardtung, Bernhard, Erlaubte Vorteilsannahme – §§ 331 StGB, 70 BBG, 10 BAT –, Zugleich ein Beitrag zur Einheit der Rechtsordnung und zur „Rückwirkung" behördlicher Genehmigungen im Strafrecht, Strafrechtliche Abhandlungen, Neue Folge, Bd. 89, Berlin 1994.

Hassemer, Winfried, Symbolisches Strafrecht und Rechtsgüterschutz, NStZ 1989, 553 ff.

Henkel, Heinrich, Die Bestechlichkeit von Ermessensbeamten, JZ 1960, 507 ff.

Henkel, Heinrich, Die Selbstbestimmung des Menschen als rechtsphilosophisches Problem, in: Festschrift für Karl Larenz zum 70. Geburtstag, München 1973.

Hettinger, Michael, Das Strafrecht als Büttel? Fragmentarische Bemerkungen zum Entwurf eines Korruptionsbekämpfungsgesetzes des Bundesrates vom 3.11.1995, NJW 1996, 2263 ff.

Hirsch, Hans Joachim, Literaturbericht, ZStW 88 (1976), 772 ff.

Hofmeister, Karl, Die Bestechung im geltenden Strafrecht und im Vorentwurf mit Berücksichtigung des österreichischen Vorentwurfs, Dissertation, Borna-Leipzig 1911.

Horstkotte, Hartmuth, Die Vorschriften des Ersten Gesetzes zur Reform des Strafrechts über die Strafzumessung (§§ 13-16, 60 StGB), JZ 1970, 122 ff.

Jaques, Henning, Die Bestechungstatbestände unter besonderer Berücksichtigung des Verhältnisses der §§ 331 ff. StGB zu § 12 UWG, Dissertation, Europäische Hochschulschriften, Reihe II, Bd. 2020, Frankfurt am Main, Berlin, Bern, New York, Paris, Wien 1996.

Jutzi, Siegfried, Genehmigung der Vorteilsannahme bei nicht in einem öffentlich-rechtlichen Amtsverhältnis stehenden Amtsträgern, NStZ 1991, 105 ff.

Kaufmann, Arthur, Das Schuldprinzip, Heidelberg 1961.

Kaufmann, Arthur, Anmerkung zum Urteil des BGH v. 20.1.1959 (1 StR 518/58), JZ 1959, 375 ff.

Kerner, Hans-Jürgen, *Rixen*, Stephan, Ist Korruption ein Strafrechtsproblem? - Zur Tauglichkeit strafgesetzlicher Vorschriften gegen die Korruption - ,GA 1996, 355 ff.

Killias, Martin, Korruption: Vive La Repression! – Oder was sonst?, in: Festschrift für Hans Joachim Schneider, Berlin, New York 1998, S. 239-254.

Kirschbaum, Schmitz, Grenzen der Bestechungstatbestände, GA 1960, 321 ff.

Kleinknecht, Theodor, *Meyer-Goßner*, Lutz, Strafprozeßordnung, Kommentar, 44. Aufl., München 1999.

Klug, Ulrich, Psychologische Vereinfachungen und strafrechtliche Folgerungen bei der Auslegung der Bestechungstatbestände, JZ 1960, 724 ff.

Köhler, Heinz, *Ratz*, Günter, Bundesdisziplinarordnung und materielles Disziplinarrecht, Kommentar für die Praxis, 2. Aufl., Köln 1994.

König, Peter, Neues Strafrecht gegen die Korruption, JR 1997, 397 ff.

Korte, Matthias, Kampfansage an die Korruption, NJW 1997, 2556 ff.

Korte, Matthias, Bekämpfung der Korruption und Schutz des freien Wettbewerbs mit den Mitteln des Strafrechts, NStZ 1997, 513 ff.

Korte, Matthias, Der Einsatz des Strafrechts zur Bekämpfung der internationalen Korruption, wistra 1999, 81 ff.

Krönig, Georg, Kleine Beiträge, Die Bestechungstatbestände, NJW 1960, 2083.

Kuhlen, Lothar, Zu den Tathandlungen bei Vorteilsannahme und Bestechlichkeit – Zugleich eine Besprechung von BGH-4 StR 554/87-, NStZ 1988, 433 ff.

Kuhlen, Lothar, Nomos Kommentar zum Strafgesetzbuch, §§ 331 ff., 11. Lfg. 2001.

Lackner, Karl, *Kühl*, Kristian, Strafgesetzbuch mit Erläuterungen, 24. Aufl., München 2001.

Lambrecht, Ute, Strafrecht und Disziplinarrecht, Abhängigkeiten und Überschneidungen, Dissertation, Schriften zum Strafrecht und Strafprozeßrecht, Bd. 27, Frankfurt am Main, Berlin, Bern, New York, Paris, Wien 1997.

Leipziger Kommentar, StGB, Bearbeiter: Jescheck, Hans-Heinrich (Einleitung), 11. Aufl., Berlin, New York 1992.

Leipziger Kommentar, StGB, Bearbeiter: Jescheck, Hans-Heinrich (§§ 331-335a),11. Aufl., Berlin, New York 1997.

Lemhöfer, Bernt, Das neue Disziplinarrecht des Bundes: Licht und Schatten, Gewinn an Systematik und Straffung – aber Abbau von Integritätsschutz, offene Fragen im Einzelnen, Recht im Amt 2002, 53 ff.

Letzgus, Klaus, Der Begriff der Diensthandlung und des Vorteils bei der Bestechlichkeit sowie die Konkurrenz zwischen Bestechlichkeit und "strafbarer" Diensthandlung, Anmerkung zum Urteil des BGH vom 28.10.1986 - 5 StR 244/86- (NStZ 1987, 326), NStZ 1987, 309 ff.

Loos, Fritz, Zum "Rechtsgut" der Bestechungsdelikte, in: Festschrift für Hans Welzel zum 70. Geburtstag, Berlin, New York 1974.

Lüderssen, Klaus, Antikorruptions-Gesetze und Drittmittelforschung, JZ 1997, 112 ff.

Lüderssen, Klaus, Die Zusammenarbeit von Medizinprodukte-Industrie, Krankenhäusern und Ärzten – strafbare Kollusion oder sinnvolle Kooperation?, Stuttgart 1998.

Lüderssen, Klaus, Sollen Submissionsabsprachen zu strafrechtlichem Unrecht werden?, BB 1961, Beilage 11 zu Heft 25, 1ff.

Maiwald, Manfred, Die Amtsdelikte, JuS 1977, 353 ff.

Maiwald, Manfred, Anmerkung zu dem Urteil des BGH vom 26.10.1993 - 4 StR 347/93 -, NStZ 1994, 489 f.

Maurach, Reinhart, *Gössel*, Karl Heinz, *Zipf*, Heinz, Strafrecht Allgemeiner Teil Teilband 2, Lehrbuch, 7. Aufl., Heidelberg 1989.

Merges, Hans Dieter, Die Strafausschließungsgründe der Bestechungsdelikte, Dissertation, Tübingen 1995.

Miller, Manfred, Korruption, Kontrolle und Konzepte zum Abbau von Misständen in Politik und Verwaltung, Die Verwaltung 1990, 227 ff.

Möhrenschlager, Manfred, Strafrechtliche Vorhaben zur Bekämpfung der Korruption auf nationaler und internationaler Ebene, JZ 1996, 822 ff.

Möllering, Jürgen, Prävention oder Strafe – Eine kritische Würdigung aktueller Gesetzentwürfe zur Bekämpfung der Korruption, WPR 1997, 933 ff.

Mommsen, Theodor, Römisches Strafrecht, Darmstadt 1955.

Müller-Eising, Claudia, Paradigmenwechsel im deutschen Disziplinarrecht, NJW 2001, 3587 ff.

Otto, Harro, Grundkurs Strafrecht, Allgemeine Strafrechtslehre, 6. Aufl., Berlin, New York 2000.

Pelke, Bernhard, Die strafrechtliche Bedeutung der Merkmale „Übel" und „Vorteil", Zur Abgrenzung der Nötigungsdelikte von den Bestechungsdelikten und dem Wucher, Dissertation, Rechtswissenschaftliche Forschung und Entwicklung, Bd. 263, München 1990.

Pelz, Christian, Die Bekämpfung der Korruption im Auslandsgeschäft, StraFo 2000, 300 ff.

Pfeiffer, Gerd, Von der Freiheit der klinischen Forschung zum strafrechtlichen Unrecht?, NJW 1997, 782 ff.

Pieth, Mark, Internationale Harmonisierung von Strafrecht als Antwort auf transnationale Wirtschaftskriminalität, ZStW 109 (1997), 756 ff.

Prittwitz, Cornelius, Der Mitbeschuldigte im Strafprozeß, Dissertation, Frankfurt am Main 1984.

Prittwitz, Cornelius, Der fragmentarische Charakter des Strafrechts, in: Herausforderungen an das Recht: alte Antworten auf neue Fragen?, Rostocker Antrittsvorlesungen 1993-1997, Rostocker Rechtswissenschaftliche Abhandlungen, Bd. 1, Berlin 1997, 145 ff.

Ransiek, Andreas, Strafrecht und Korruption, Zum Gutachten C für den 61. DJT, StV 1996, 446 ff.

Ratzel, Rudolf, Arzt und (Pharma-)Industrie, Ein Überblick unter Berücksichtigung des neuen Berufsrechts, MedR 1998, 98 ff.

Ricks, Sven, Ökonomische Analyse der Wirtschaftskriminalität unter besonderer Berücksichtigung der Korruption und Bestechung, Dissertation, Akademische Abhandlungen zu den Wirtschaftswissenschaften, Berlin 1995.

Roxin, Claus, Zur Abgrenzung von bedingtem Vorsatz und bewußter Fahrlässigkeit, JuS 1964, 53 ff.

Roxin, Claus, Sinn und Grenzen staatlicher Strafe, JuS 1966, 377 ff.

Schaller, Hans, Neue Vorschriften zur Korruptionsbekämpfung, Recht im Amt 1998, 9ff.

Schaupensteiner, Wolfgang, Bekämpfung von Korruptionsdelinquenz, Vom Unwesen des Bestechens und Bestochenwerdens, Kriminalistik 1994, 514 ff.

Schaupensteiner, Wolfgang, Das Korruptionsbekämpfungsgesetz, Eine scharfe Waffe gegen ein verbreitetes Übel?, Kriminalistik 1996, 237 ff.

Schaupensteiner, Wolfgang, Korruption in Deutschland, Ursachen, Erscheinungsformen, Bekämpfungsstrategien, der kriminalist 1996, 7 ff.

Schmidhäuser, Eberhard, Strafrecht Allgemeiner Teil, 2. Aufl., Tübingen 1984.

Schmidt, Eberhard, Die Bestechungstatbestände in der höchstrichterlichen Rechtsprechung von 1879 bis 1959, München und Berlin 1960.

Schmidt, Eberhard, Kleine Beiträge, Die Grenze zwischen schwerer und leichter passiver Bestechung eines Ermessensbeamten, NJW 1960, 802 ff.

Schmidt-Leichner, Die Bestechungstatbestände in der höchstrichterlichen Rechtsprechung von 1879 - 1959, Zugleich Besprechung der gleichnamigen Monographie von Eberhard Schmidt, NJW 1960, 846 ff.

Schmitt, Rudolf, Die Bestechungstatbestände im Entwurf 1960 (Übersicht und Kritik), ZStW 73 (1961), 414 ff.

Schönherr, Roland, Vorteilsgewährung und Bestechung als Wirtschaftsstraftaten, Eine Untersuchung über die Zuweisung dieser Delikte zur Wirtschaftskriminalität durch die Staatsanwaltschaften, Kriminologische Forschungsberichte aus dem Max-Planck-Institut für ausländisches und internationales Strafrecht, Bd. 23, Freiburg 1985.

Schönke, Adolf, *Schröder* Horst, Strafgesetzbuch, Kommentar, Bearbeiter: Cramer, Peter (§§ 331 ff.), Eser, Albin (§§ 1 ff.), 26. Aufl., München 2001
und
Cramer, Peter, (§§ 331 ff.), 25. Aufl., München 1997.

Schröder, Horst, Das Rechtsgut der Bestechungsdelikte und die Bestechlichkeit des Ermessensbeamten, GA 1961, 289 ff.

Schwieger, Dirk, Der Vorteilsbegriff in den Bestechungsdelikten des StGB, Dissertation, Schriften zum Strafrecht und Strafprozeßrecht, Bd. 25, Frankfurt am Main, Berlin, Bern, New York, Paris, Wien 1995.

Stein, Albert, Der Streit um die Grenzen der Bestechungstatbestände, NJW 1961, 433 ff.

Stock, Ulrich, Entwicklung und Wesen der Amtsverbrechen, Leipziger rechtswissenschaftliche Studien, Heft 67, Leipzig 1932.

Systematischer Kommentar zum Strafgesetzbuch, Bd. 2, Besonderer Teil (§§ 80 – 358), Bearbeiter: Rudolphi, Hans-Joachim, 4. Aufl., 1991.

Tröndle, Herbert, *Fischer*, Thomas, Strafgesetzbuch und Nebengesetze, 49. Aufl., München 1999.

Überhofen, Michael, Korruption und Bestechungsdelikte im staatlichen Bereich: Ein Rechtsvergleich und Reformüberlegungen zum deutschen Recht, Max-Planck-Institut für ausländisches und internationales Strafrecht, Freiburg im Breisgau 1999.

Vahle, Jürgen, Der Kampf gegen die Korruption - ein Überblick über die jüngsten gesetzgeberischen Aktivitäten auf Bundesebene, Verwaltungsrundschau 1998, 325 ff.

Vahlenkamp, Werner, *Knauß*, Ina, Korruption - hinnehmen oder handeln? Ergebnisse eines Forschungsprojektes, BKA - Forschungsreihe, Bd. 34, Wiesbaden 1995.

Verhandlungen des einundsechzigsten Deutschen Juristentages Karlsruhe 1996, Herausgegeben von der Ständigen Deputation des Deutschen Juristentages Bd. II, Beiträge von: Dölling, Dieter (Bd. II/ 2, L 121 f., L 180 ff.), Eser, Albin (Bd. II/ 2, 72 ff.), Hamm, Rainer (Bd. II/ 2, L 139 ff.), Jähnke, Burkhard (Bd. II/ 2, L 135 f.), Lemhöfer, Bernt (Bd. II/ 2, L 137 ff.), Möhrenschlager, Manfred (Bd. II/ 2, L 130 ff.), Schaefer, Hans Christoph (Bd. II/1, L 9 ff.), Schaupensteiner, Wolfgang (Bd. II/ 2, L 110 ff.), Schlicht, Peter (Bd. II/2, L 116 ff.), Volk, Klaus (Bd. II/1, L 35 ff.), Wagner, Heinz (Bd. II/2, L 118 f.), München 1996.

Wagner, Heinz, Amtsverbrechen, Strafrechtliche Abhandlungen, Neue Folge, Bd. 24, Berlin 1975.

Weigend, Thomas, Bewältigung von Beweisschwierigkeiten durch Ausdehnung des materiellen Strafrechts? in: Festschrift für Otto Triffterer zum 65. Geburtstag, Wien 1996, 695 ff.

Weiß, Hans-Dietrich, Aktuelles aus dem Disziplinarrecht: Das neue Bundesdisziplinarneuordnungsgesetz (BDiszNOG) 2001, Die Personalvertretung 2002, 2 ff.

Wintrich, Hermann, Neufassung der Bestechungstatbestände im Strafgesetzbuch 1975, Neue Polizei 1976, 82 ff.

Wolters, Gereon, Die Änderungen des StGB durch das Gesetz zur Bekämpfung der Korruption, JuS 1998, 1100 ff.

Zieschang, Frank, Das EU-Bestechungsgesetz und das Gesetz zur Bekämpfung internationaler Bestechung, NJW 1999, 105 ff.

Zieschang, Frank, Die Auswirkungen des Gesetzes zur Bekämpfung der Korruption auf den Forschungsbereich, WissR 1999, 111 ff.

MIX
Papier | Fördert gute Waldnutzung
FSC® C083411

Kolibri 360 GmbH
Ferdinand-Jühlke-Straße 7
99095 Erfurt, Deutschland
produktsicherheit@kolibri360.de

Druck:
CPI Druckdienstleistungen GmbH
im Auftrag der
Kolibri 360 GmbH
Ferdinand-Jühlke-Str. 7
99095 Erfurt